SPACES OF GLOBALIZATION

D1198768

A GUILFORD SERIES

Perspectives on Economic Change

Editors

MERIC S. GERTLER
University of Toronto

PETER DICKEN
University of Manchester

**Spaces of Globalization:
Reasserting the Power of the Local**
KEVIN R. COX, *Editor*

**The Golden Age Illusion:
Rethinking Postwar Capitalism**
MICHAEL J. WEBBER and DAVID L. RIGBY

**Work-*Place:*
The Social Regulation of Labor Markets**
JAMIE PECK

**Restructuring for Innovation:
The Remaking of the U.S. Semiconductor Industry**
DAVID P. ANGEL

**Trading Industries, Trading Regions:
International Trade, American Industry,
and Regional Economic Development**
HELZI NOPONEN, JULIE GRAHAM, and ANN R. MARKUSEN, *Editors*

SPACES OF GLOBALIZATION
Reasserting the Power of the Local

Edited by

KEVIN R. COX

THE GUILFORD PRESS
New York   London

© 1997 The Guilford Press
A Division of Guilford Publications, Inc.
72 Spring Street, New York, NY 10012

Printed in the United States of America

This book is printed on acid-free paper.

Last digit is print number: 9 8 7 6 5 4 3 2 1

Library of Congress Cataloging-in-Publication Data

Spaces of globalization : reasserting the power of the local/edited
by Kevin R. Cox.
      p.   cm. — (Perspectives on economic change)
   Includes bibliographical references and index.
   ISBN 1-57230-196-1. — ISBN 1-57230-199-6 (pbk.)
   1. International economic relations.   2. Industrial location.
3. International business enterprises.   4. International division of
labor.   I. Cox, Kevin R.   II. Series.
HF1359.S69   1997
337—dc21   96-30010
                                                         CIP

Contents

Contributors

Gordon L. Clark, PhD, School of Geography, University of Oxford, Oxford, United Kingdom

Kevin R. Cox, PhD, Department of Geography, The Ohio State University, Columbus, Ohio, United States

Meric S. Gertler, PhD, Department of Geography, University of Toronto, Toronto, Ontario, Canada

Andrew Herod, PhD, Department of Geography, University of Georgia, Athens, Georgia, United States

Murray Low, PhD, Department of Geography, The University of Reading, Reading, United Kingdom

Andrew Mair, PhD, Department of Management and Business Studies, Birkbeck College, University of London, London, United Kingdom

Ton Notermans, PhD, Department of Political Science, University of Tromsoe, Tromsoe, Norway

Kevin O'Connor, PhD, Department of Geography, Monash University, Melbourne, Australia

Michael Storper, PhD, School of Public Policy and Social Research, University of California—Los Angeles, Los Angeles, California, United States

Erik Swyngedouw, PhD, School of Geography, University of Oxford, Oxford, United Kingdom

SPACES OF GLOBALIZATION

Introduction

GLOBALIZATION AND ITS POLITICS IN QUESTION

Kevin R. Cox

CONTEXT

Arguments about the globalization of economic relations have become commonplace, part of the everyday diet of social science and public affairs alike. Typically they are backed up by reference to a wide variety of empirical tendencies. These include the growth of multinational and transnational corporations, the expansion of trade and foreign investment, the New International Division of Labor, the enhanced mobility of money capital across international boundaries, intensified international competition with the rise of the Newly Industrializing Countries (NICs), and the globalization of markets for consumer goods.

Less common but not to be excluded are analogous arguments at subnational scales. Improvements in transportation and communications and the deskilling of work processes are widely heralded as laying the conditions for the displacement of production to Third World peripheries. But similar processes are resulting in the growth of peripheries in North America and Western Europe: for example, the American Sun Belt and small towns everywhere. Left behind by these displacements are the hollowed out cores and rust belts of the First World.

Alongside these "global shifts," and in many ways related to them, are yet other changes. In the First World there are the so-called new industrial spaces of Silicon Valley, the Third Italy, Baden-Württemberg, and Orange County. And the emergence of new firm spatial divisions of labor and the telecommunications revolution have provided the basis for the rise of the so-called "world cities."

The old is challenged by the new, old industrial cores are eclipsed by new peripheries, centers of mass production are displaced by new industrial districts employing more flexible forms of work process, and the spatial organi-

zation of the global economy undergoes dramatic changes. In short, new economic geographies are in the making: economic geographies that are global
in their reach, changes that produce competition on a global scale and that reflect new conditions of production. Such are the arguments that have become
pervasive, even hegemonic.

In addition it is widely believed that these new economic geographies are
associated with the emergence of new *political* geographies. The intensification
of competition between firms in different places, the rapidity of many of the
shifts in production that have occurred as well as in associated flows of goods,
services, and money, and the implications of these shifts for macroeconomic
policy and for the politics of local economic development, have provided the
material for arguments that, depending on the politics of those articulating
them, range from the pessimistic to the enthusiastic.

Variously described as a new hypermobility of capital or as a scale disso-
nance between the organization of the political and the economic, there are
new pressures being brought to bear upon agencies of the state and upon labor. Capital can move, can create new forms of organization at scales where it
is beyond the reach of state agencies and nationally organized forms of worker representation. The dependence of the state for its own revenue on private
investment in a particular territorial space, and the relative immobility of
workers, it is claimed, places them with respect to capital in a new and disad-
vantageous bargaining situation. In the First World the signs of this are virtually everywhere: worker givebacks, the intensified competition of central and
local branches of the state for new investment, the retreat of the welfare state,
the falling membership of the labor unions, and the sidelining of democratic
institutions as states position themselves for the hard political decisions that
have to be taken in a period of retrenchment and intensified competition.

For more conservative observers these are welcome changes, subjecting
workers and states to a new discipline, eliminating waste, reducing the power
of the state, and so opening up new vistas of individual freedom and opportunity as states respond to the new competition with rounds of privatization and
deregulation. The more dominant interpretation, however, has pointed to the
adverse implications of these transformations for democracy, for the nation-
state, and for equality. Democracy is emasculated if political equality can be
made meaningless by economic inequality in the way implied by the hypermobility of capital. The equality of opportunity underpinned by state expenditure, the safety net implied by unemployment compensation and minimum
wages, the achievement of health and safety in the workplace and of cleaner
air and water are all rendered moot by the competition for footloose investment. The power of the state to make a difference retreats. Full employment
is no longer a realistic goal and has to be displaced, for fear of short-term capital flight, by concerns for price stability.

Whether catastrophist or triumphalist in tone, claims of this nature have become pervasive in the social science literature. Perhaps not coincidentally, the hegemony of globalization has become a popular motif in the media. Yet there are now signs of a critical reaction to these arguments. An early step in this direction was a paper by Gordon:

> . . . I would argue that we have *not* witnessed movement toward an increasingly "open" international economy, with productive capital buzzing around the globe, but that we have moved rapidly toward an increasingly "closed" economy for productive investment, with production and investment decisions increasingly dependent upon a range of institutional policies and activities and a pattern of differentiation and specialization among the countries in the LDCs [less developed countries]. The international economy, by the standards of traditional neoclassical and Marxian models of competition, has witnessed *declining* rather than *increasing* mobility of productive capital. (1988, p. 63)

Gordon's approach was empirical. A major goal of his paper was to confront the claims of the globalization school with the evidence. What this showed was that while there had indeed been changes in economic geographies, they were much more complex than might be imagined from the generalizations of publicists and overheated academic imaginations.

It makes a big difference for First World economies, for instance, if the new global relations are largely confined to their relations with each other or if those connections are being displaced by ones with Third World countries. Important questions are the degree to which First World imports are shifting from First World in the direction of Third World origins, and the degree to which First World investment is increasingly oriented away from the First to the Third World. Gordon (1988) expressed extreme skepticism on both these scores. In a survey of the available evidence, he found that in 1983 the developed market economies imported a smaller proportion of their total imports from the non-oil-exporting LDCs than they had in 1959, and that even though the import penetration by the NICs had increased since 1966, it had barely regained the level enjoyed in 1959 (p. 48). With regard to investment, Gordon likewise states: ". . . it is difficult to sustain the conclusion that investment capital is racing away from the advanced economies, draining off our shores at an accelerating pace" (p. 50).[1]

Moreover, the changes that have occurred can usefully be placed in a longer term historical perspective. There *has* been a progressive internationalization of money and capital markets since the 1970s. But international financial penetration of the United Kingdom and other economies was greater between 1905 and 1914 than between 1982 and 1986, a fact which Notermans picks up on in Chapter 8 of this book. The same applies to trade as a percentage of Gross National Product (GNP). And while there *has* been a progressive development of internationalized corporations, as Hirst and Thompson affirm, there are few truly transnational corporations that are relatively foot-loose in all their operations:

> The real question to ask of MNCs [multinational corporations] is not why they are always threatening to up and leave a country if things seem to go bad for them there, but why the vast majority of them fail to leave and continue to stay put in their home base and major centers of investment? MNCs are very reluctant to uproot themselves because they get entrenched in specific national markets, and with local suppliers and dealers. (1992, p. 368)

The work of Gordon and, more recently, that of Hirst and Thompson blow fresh air into a literature that has been subject to overgeneralization and hype. Indeed, Hirst and Thompson's (1996) recent book fortifies the evidence adduced by Gordon, as well as arguments made in their earlier papers. They precisely document the way in which, in some respects, the current international economy is less open than it was before 1914. They show how the foreign direct investment and trade supposedly resulting in changes in global economic geography to the benefit of the Third World are, in fact, highly concentrated among First World countries.[2]

Yet critique calls not just for a careful examination of the evidence. There are also conceptual needs. Just how is the more complex picture painted by people like Gordon and Hirst and Thompson to be understood? What are its conditions of existence? And given those conditions could we reasonably expect any other geographies than the sorts we actually see and which resist the overgeneralization and astigmatism that has become all too common in the globalization literature? One of the aims of this collection has been precisely to move the argument on to this level.

A critical wedge already exists, therefore, but a case can be made for widening it. Geographers might seem to be well positioned to contribute to this. The central idea of globalization, the idea of a global–local relation, puts space on the agenda. Likewise, their traditional interest in areal differentiation should, in theory at least, make geographers more sensitive to the variety of empirical outcomes observable in new economic and political geographies. This is not to say that geographers too have not joined in the general chorus of globalization claims and concomitant genuflections. There have been plenty of instances of succumbing to the flattery of recognition by other social scientists: a recognition, that is, not so much of their work as of the significance of their central object of interest. Even so, there is a *critical* human geography, and the contemporary globalization literature seems a worthwhile focus for it. This is not to say that all the contributors to this volume are professional geographers, but only one does not have substantial amounts of geography in his background.

To the extent that there are major claims in this book, one would have to be that any assessment of the globalization debate has to take into account not just the deterritorializing forces, the emergence of a world of enhanced locational substitutability, but also the territorializing: those conditions, those social relations that result in enduring commitments to particular places, which can in turn be a source of competitive advantage and so serve to reinforce those commitments. This is a major theme in the Chapters by Storper, Gertler, Mair, and myself.

But if deterritorializing–territorializing is a dualism that has generally not been picked up in the globalization literature, there are others that could usefully be subject to criticism. Perhaps the most obvious is the global–local dualism itself. That scale in contemporary economic and political geography can be so reduced is clearly problematic. Swyngedouw (Chapter 6) not only makes the point, but also uses it as a point of departure for a discussion of the construction of geographic scale. He shows how scale is the outcome of struggle as contending classes create new arenas of action that provide them with a leverage that opposing forces will find difficult to match. This theme is also picked up on by Herod (Chapter 7) who describes recent attempts by organized labor in the United States to organize workers elsewhere around the world, to coordinate respective activities across international boundaries, and so to enhance their own leverage vis à vis those capitals that, according to some, have become "hypermobile." The same theme of the construction of geographic scales, albeit shorn of the emphasis on conflict, is also apparent in the Chapter by Clark and O'Connor (Chapter 4), and they too eschew the simple global–local polarity.

Other Chapters in this collection illustrate the point that the global–local distinction translates in concrete terms into a wide variety of different expressions. Notermans's (Chapter 8) concern with macroeconomic policy and its relation to international financial transactions prioritizes the nation-state as "the local," but Gertler's chapter (Chapter 2) on the adoption of machine tools in different countries also highlights the significance of national regulatory institutions. Storper's (Chapter 1) concepts of territorialization and deterritorialization, on the other hand, clearly have an abstract quality that allows their applicability to diverse concrete scales and, indeed, to their construction.

THE CHAPTERS

I have organized the Chapters into two broad groups. The first includes those chapters whose principal focus of concern is the economics of globalization: these are the chapters by Storper, Gertler, Mair, and Clark and O'Connor. The second group builds on ideas of the economics of globalization but focuses more on its politics; the contributors here are Swyngedouw, Herod, Notermans, Low, and myself.

Michael Storper (Chapter 1) starts out by setting the scene for much of the debate that has taken place around the idea of an increasing globalization of economic geographies. As he indicates, a good deal of the force behind these arguments is the fact of recently greatly increased flows of products, services, information, capital, and people across regional and national lines. But, as he wishes to emphasize, this does not necessarily mean that contemporary economies are losing their status as places, becoming parts of a mere space of flows, with the result that agencies of the state, local, or national governments, are losing their powers to regulate and to redistribute. Much rides on the degree to which economic development is still territorialized. To the extent that it is then, it is possible that national governments and workers still have some bargaining power and ability to give form to the development process. Storper's chapter consists of an examination of the idea of territorialized economic development and how it relates to more deterritorialized forms.

Territorialized economic development refers to development that is dependent on resources that are territorially specific or place-dependent: resources, that is, which enjoy properties of locational nonsubstitutability. The globalization debate foregrounds flows that, through their more globalized character, seem to indicate a deterritorialization of economic activity. But the examination of production and the conditions of production is a necessary complement if one is to be in a position to draw the sorts of distributional conclusions associated with much of the literature. Rather, the increasing globalization of markets is often a condition for the territorialization of production activities around place-specific production potentials that provide some insulation from the forces of global competition.

This is not to say that some production is *not* being deterritorialized. But the situation is a complex one about which it is difficult to generalize. One can find, even in the same sector, high levels of globalization in production systems combining *both* the deterritorialization and territorialization of activity. So in some of their activities firms may be able to deterritorialize, while in other aspects of their input chain resources for which substitutes are difficult to find elsewhere continue to be important.

On the other hand, the mere existence of territorialization does not mean that local or national states can exercise strong regulatory control over the economic development process. Territorialization is a necessary but not a sufficient condition for a strong state role, because territorialization itself may involve hierarchies that are in turn inserted into larger contexts. Firms with highly elaborated interterritorial divisions of labor may make decisions with respect to the location of various activities, or may move highly skilled technical personnel around—decisions that, while rational from their standpoint as firms, eliminate intraterritorial spillovers important for other firms in particular places.

Gertler (Chapter 2) provides a good example of precisely the sorts of territorializing effects that Storper is talking about. His focus is advanced industrial machinery and its place-specific utility: an important focus if one is concerned with evaluating claims about the hypermobility of capital. What he finds is that the effective use of that machinery is, in territorial terms, highly specific. This is due to the relation between machine users and machine producers. He draws on an empirical investigation of difficulties experienced by Canadian users of advanced industrial machinery in employing the products of German machine tool firms. To some extent the difficulties are ones of spatial separation: problems in installation and after-sales service that could be obviated by face-to-face interaction in the field, but not by a simple telephone call.

But a major problem is one of differences in worker aptitudes, workplace norms, and attitudes about the worker–technology relation. These differences in turn have as their condition differences in national regulatory structures. Advanced industrial machinery tends to be produced in a particular national context and—in this instance—the German context is not the Canadian one. So when the machinery is exported, it may be to a situation in which there is a poor fit between machinery and user. In other words, technology is socially constructed. As Gertler affirms: "The chief failures in technology implementation stem from the fact that users are trying to utilize these advanced machines and systems without due regard for the social relations surrounding their use" (Chapter 2, p. 58).

The degree to which national boundaries remain significant is also the focus of Andrew Mair (Chapter 3) though from a different angle. His concern is the degree to which multinational corporations are becoming truly global: the degree, that is, to which Massey's (1984, Chap. 3) clone structures are being replaced by firm divisions of labor that accord more with her parts–process model; and the extent to which truly international versions of a product are displacing national versions in particular markets. In other words, to what degree is corporate strategy truly global rather than working through a sum of national parts?

Mair's approach is to examine this issue in terms of the experience of one multinational corporation, Honda. Honda's practice is explored along numerous dimensions of corporate globalization–localization strategies: products, research and development (R&D), production, parts sourcing, production methods, employees, and so on. What he finds are patterns that are much more complicated than either of the ideal types around which the debate about the global corporation has tended to congeal. There is some localization of R&D, as in product design appropriate to particular local road conditions, but basic research and product technology have been retained in Japan. There is some localization of production with respect to particular markets, but some production is also for markets elsewhere, depending in part on the global output of particular models. Disaggregation of the different dimensions themselves also helps in understanding parts sourcing strategies: in the United States and in general, the more sophisticated parts, like the electronic, are brought in from Japan. And while hard technology and organization have been globalized, local incentive structures are molded significantly by on-site managerial staffs with the local cultural environment in mind.

There is, in brief, a pattern of what Mair calls "strategic localization," rather than the melting away of national boundaries foreseen by the more vigorous of advocates of a new globalized economic geography. National-specific practice, as underlined by Gertler, remains significant. Some aspects of production have been globalized and others are less so, the complexity of the case echoing Storper's arguments about the balance between the territorializing and the deterritorializing. But in evaluating the question, the disaggregation of categories like "R&D" or "parts sourcing" is clearly important.

Storper, Gertler, and Mair all take as their point of reference the production of "hard" commodities, and this has certainly been a major focus of argument about the globalization of economic geographies. But alongside this have been interventions, as well as theses, that draw on the related geography of finance: not just the flows that have tended to receive most attention but also the production of the financial products themselves. An influential book in the literature on globalization has been O'Brien's (1992) aptly titled *Global Financial Integration: The End of Geography*. O'Brien's argument relies heavily on the idea that recent developments in telecommunications have brought about an integration of financial markets around the world. The uniform availability of information both between and within markets means that no one place is any better than another as a market for financial products. Geography no longer matters since it is a matter of indifference to the producers and traders where they locate: either in one place or in a multitude of places. In their chapter (Chapter 4), Clark and O'Connor seek to counter this line of argument.

Their rebuttal rests on the assumption of variability in the informational content of different financial products. There is, they argue, a "geography of information that is embedded in the provision of specific financial products," (p. 90). Key elements in this geography include the locally specific information networks of producers and their locally specific monitoring of the financial and investment performance of firms. In addition, markets are not just, as per O'Brien (1992), locations of trading but are centers of information collection and the formal exchange of specialized knowledge. This is a geography of information, in other words, that is, depending on the product in question, impervious to the sorts of leveling forces emphasized by O'Brien.

There are some products that come close to O'Brien's (1992) ideal. These are what Clark and O'Connor (Chapter 4) call "transparent" products: products whose properties are so well known or observable that investment houses can trade in them merely on the basis of price trends. One result of this transparency is a relatively low risk-adjusted rate of return. There are, however, other products that, in accordance with different degrees of "transparency," Clark and O'Connor term "translucent" and "opaque" and that offer the possibility of higher returns. A "translucent" product is exemplified by a balanced equity product that reflects the expertise regarding target firms of the firm putting it together. Knowledge of firm performance—both of the firms designing these products and the firms they are investing in—is highly differentiated over space and time, so the institutions buying them trade in those about which they have more information. Not surprisingly, there is a clustering of the designers of the funds, the investors, and the firms whose stocks comprise the balanced equity product. In accordance with the national organization of trading in firm securities, this creates a space for financial product markets with a strongly national emphasis.

Opaque products, on the other hand, are ones for which the information on which they are based is the exclusive property of the firm designing them. The logic on the basis of which they are constructed is private information, as is the knowledge of the particular firms in which they are investing. This means that much rides on the investor's estimation of the reputability of the firm designing and selling the product and the reputability of the firms in which they are investing. Often this means that local knowledge is very important in assessing these products. Limited partnerships investing in local real estate would be one example.

The geography of information embedded in different financial products therefore provides one crucial condition for a spatially hierarchical structure for the financial products industry. There are, in other words, spaces for global, national, and local markets; hardly the single point or multitude of markets foreseen by O'Brien's (1992) "end of geography."

These four chapters all highlight, albeit in critical fashion, arguments about the globalization of capital through, for example, elongated commodity chains, new hierarchical and internationalized forms of firm governance, and trade in financial products. It is, however, the conjunction of this supposed mobility of capital, its ability to engage in rounds of spatial substitution, with the immobility of labor and states that forms the basis for quite central arguments in the politics of globalization. It is this conjunction that is addressed in my own chapter (Chapter 5).

Through its mobility or potential mobility, capital, it is asserted, has been able to achieve an enhanced bargaining power with respect to states and workers. Rollbacks of the welfare state, worker givebacks, the retreat of labor unions, the marginalization of corporatism, and the enhanced salience of "business climate" in the politics of economic development are just so many concrete expressions of this new context. What I argue, however, is that these contrasting spatialities oversimplify a much more complex ensemble of forces.

In the first place, they oversimplify in terms of the concrete forms of "the global" and "the local." It matters a great deal whether we are talking about the colonization of peripheries in the First or Third World, just as it matters whether the mobility of capital is in the direction of Third World sites or is more confined to First World countries than much of the literature might have us believe.

As far as the mobility of capital is concerned, the conditions believed to be necessary for the enhanced locational substitutability implied by globalization arguments—the deskilling of labor processes, improvements in transportation and communication, and the vertical integration of labor processes within firms—have been seriously overgeneralized. In this regard Storper's arguments about the territorialization of economic activity are an important starting point, and I put some concrete flesh on his more abstract statements. In particular, the globalization literature underestimates the character of capitalist development as a social learning process. This is facilitated by processes of spatial convergence, whether within- or between-plant, which are difficult to replicate or reconstitute elsewhere. The underpinning of these social relations through appropriate forms of governance or regulatory mechanisms further serves to embed the firms involved. Accordingly, I reiterate Storper's point that this creates a bargaining space for labor, though I emphasize that, depending on circumstances of time and place, workers may not be the ones to gain from this process and some workers may gain at the expense of others.

But just as capital is not nearly as mobile as many arguments would have us believe, neither is labor as *im*mobile. At the most abstract level, and given the production relations of capital—Marx's "double freedom" of labor power—it would be surprising if it were otherwise. Some workers are more mobile than others: the young or those whose moves are sponsored by the employer-to-be, and more generally those less tied down by family or by home ownership. But mobility does occur, at least intra-nationally, in such a way as to make tendencies toward the equilibration of interregional labor markets not a figment of the imagination.

Allusions to the global and the local imply a particular stance on the question of geographic scale. Swyngedouw (Chapter 6) makes the issue of scale the central object of his critique. His focus is that reification of scale that he sees expressed in so much of the contemporary globalization literature. That scale is reduced to the polarized, seemingly absolute, categories of the global and the local rather than being seen in relational terms is something that is picked up by other contributors to this collection. As Swyngedouw emphasizes, scales do not interact: rather, it is firms, workers, and local governments that act, within and between arenas that can be defined in scale terms. Instead of being considered finished, self-sufficient objects, scales should be understood as socially constructed through processes of struggle: relative scale is a condition for the successful prosecution of struggle. Rather than conceptualizing changes in economic geographies in terms of an interaction of the global and the local, Swyngedouw urges in contrast a focus on the politics of scale: on scaled spaces as arenas of conflict and compromise, domination and marginalization, transformation and stabilization.

He exemplifies this program of conceptual reconstruction through an interpretation of the politics of regulation: the scales of Fordism and the construction of those new scales through which Fordism was undone. Fordist regulation depended on the spatial integrity of capitalisms organized primarily at the scale of the nation-state. It was the undoing of that spatial integrity through the internationalization of exchange and competition that was in turn the condition for the deliquescence of Fordism. The subsequent politics of scale has resulted in a rescaling of regulatory practices that Swyngedouw refers to as "glocalization": a contested reconstruction of scales that are more global than the national on the one hand and more local on the other. So, and to exemplify, the interventionism of the state in the economy is rescaled, either downward to the level of the city or the region, as in the efflorescence of various local economic development initiatives, or upward to various new institutional structures like the European Community (EC), the North American Free Trade Agreement (NAFTA), the Group of Seven (G-7) and so forth.

For the most part the politics of globalization is silent on the role of labor and the difference that labor can make. It is common to subsume labor under some globalizing logic that is orchestrated by capital and of which labor is a passive victim: logics of relocation to global peripheries, of deindustrialization and reindustrialization under the conditions of drastically stripped-out welfare states, and so on. In his chapter (Chapter 7) Herod seeks to counter that image and show how, in fact, labor, through its representative organizations, has been, to some degree at least, instrumental in the construction of more globalized economic relations; and, furthermore, depending on conditions, how it has also fought, through its own international organizations and linkages, to counter the detrimental effects of capital's globalized structures.

His arguments draw primarily upon the experience of the U.S. labor movement and the way in which its foreign policies, the precise spatial fixes for labor that it tried to instantiate, have reflected the changing relation of the United States to the global economy. Particularly striking is how, for most of this century, the U.S. labor movement has been active in creating conditions conducive to the expansion of U.S. corporations overseas. The global activities of U.S. corporations were seen as expanding the market for U.S. goods abroad and so fortifying their home base and hence the demand for labor there. Herod quotes Samuel Gompers: "'The nation which dominates the markets of the world will surely control its destiny. To make of the United States a vast workshop [for the world] is our manifest destiny and our duty. . .'" (p. 171). And the way to do that was to spread, through programs of technical aid, through the formation of regional labor organizations, and through the destruction of more radical organizations, often with the financial backing of the U.S. government, U.S. labor's version of unionism: economistic, anticommunist, and collaborationist.

But the material conditions that made this strategy of class alliance an appropriate one are fast fading. A New International Division of Labor and the NICs, pose a challenge that is quite different from that of an American capitalism whose overseas links were primarily for purposes of exporting the product of American workers or importing raw materials not available in the United States. There have accordingly been some moves by U.S. unions to counter the power of globally organized corporations: to coordinate wage bargaining across the different country-specific work forces of a particular MNC; to organize the unorganized masses of the Third World, and so forth. To some degree this is clearly self-serving: a way of reducing the comparative advantage that supposedly Third World locations presently enjoy with respect to labor costs and benefits. Accordingly, we should not be surprised if transnational organizing is only a qualified success, but we would be in error not to recognize that it does have successes to be qualified.

Most of the chapters in this volume take as their implicit backdrop arguments about changes in the geography of production and trade. But as I discussed earlier in this introduction, the internationalization of financial transactions, the creation of global markets in bonds and other forms of securities, has also provided an important point of reference for arguments about the declining regulatory power of the state, the emasculation of macroeconomic policy, and the contemporary emphasis on policies of what Albo (1994) has called "competitive austerity." It is this internationalization of financial transactions and its supposed relation to social democracy that forms the object of concern for Ton Notermans's chapter (Chapter 8).

A common line of argument appeals to a—supposedly unparalleled—surge in international financial transactions over the last few years. This activity has seriously limited the macroeconomic powers of states. Wealth holders use their power to shift their investments in financial instruments to other countries in order, in effect, to exercise a new control over the macroeconomic objectives of states. Maintaining the value of the currency against speculative shifts of capital overseas has become a major concern of states, and this conflicts with policies aimed at reflating the economy—policies of monetary or fiscal stimulation, for example—so as to alleviate the unemployment that has become so prevalent in the advanced industrial economies in the late 20th century.

While noting that there is nothing new about this, since a similar constellation of globalized financial markets and restrictive national policies was characteristic of the 1920s, Notermans's main emphasis is to offer an alternative explanation, foregrounding the significance of maintaining price stability for policies of full employment and economic growth. Growth in a market economy can occur without succumbing to inflationary pressures, but it is difficult to accomplish. The introduction of policies designed to bring inflation under control, like increased unemployment, can be unpopular. Consequently, there is a search for an external anchor to which a restrictive macroeconomic policy can be subordinated. This external anchor has been fulfilled by regimes of convertible currencies: first by the Gold Standard and more recently by direct convertibility. It certainly *looks* as if it is the level of international transactions that is causally determinant rather than the desire to rein in inflationary pressures that have their origin within countries. But the globalization of financial transactions is by no means a necessary condition for the discipline wealth holders exercise over macroeconomic policy. This is because they can retreat, and historically have retreated, into debt or speculative real assets like property or precious metals.

The final chapter (Chapter 9) in the collection is by Murray Low, and the reason it is left till last is that it is different. It is different in the way it points beyond the terms of the globalization debate: terms that in some essential ways are internalized by the other contributors to this volume—in other words, not just by those being criticized but by the critics as well. Low's immediate concern is what he calls "the politics of place," a politics that he sees expressed in, and indeed dominating, the current debate about the politics of globalization. This politics of place is a particular way of viewing politics in spatial terms. As such it contrasts with alternative ways which could provide an avenue out of the constricted terms of the globalization debate.

Specifically, the politics of place is an *areal* view. Politics is seen as a set of areal phenomena. Political spaces are bounded, as in the case of electoral constituencies or the territorially defined jurisdictions of states and their different branches. This areal view incorporates the idea of a series of spatial correspondences between political, economic, and cultural spaces, which makes democracy possible. It is the contemporary spatial noncorrespondence of the political and the economic brought about by globalization that underlies much of the gloom about the future of democracy. For the most part, solutions to this dilemma are seen to lie in the direction of reestablishing a politics of place at a scale that will internalize the new economic spaces, an approach that finds an echo in Swyngedouw's argument. It is an approach, in other words, that is taken for granted. And it is one that Low seeks to destabilize.

For in contrast to areal definitions of the spatial form of politics there are also more networked forms. There are a variety of transnational social movements like Greenpeace. Low is also keen to show how the networks of relations that underpin democratic politics as we know it are unconstrained by areal forms. The financial support for political parties may come from multinational corporations. In their voting decisions individuals represent interests that in many cases cannot be confined to a particular constituency or nation-state; the votes of emigrés are obvious cases in point, though contemporary

approaches to voting behavior tend to marginalize this sort of effect and reinforce the dominance of an areal view.

Although Low draws back from scenarios for a future for democracy, he
is both skeptical of those proposed along the lines of expanded areal state
forms and unwilling to see the answer purely in terms of a more networked
view of politics. Democracy in its areal form was never anything to be uncritical of, even before the strains provoked by globalization, suggesting that larger territorial spaces are unlikely to improve matters. Rather, he believes that
democracy necessarily involves both areal and networked forms of space: the
areal cannot contain the networks through which people engage in a democratic form of life, and any serious proposal for new geographies of democracy has to take that into account.

SOCIETY AND SPACE

Finally, I want to make a summary comment that should probably appear at
the end of the book, but might usefully be borne in mind from the start. It
concerns one of the original intents of this volume, an intent that, given the
nature of the contributions, has been difficult to achieve, though there is
much that is pertinent, if implicit. For one of the several ideas I had when
thinking of putting together this volume looked beyond the literatures that are
its critical focus. This was the idea of exploring the implications of these debates for broader questions of the relation between society and space: more
specifically, the degree to which a critical confrontation with the various ideas
extant in the globalization literature would allow a reevaluation of the role of
space and the difference that space makes in understanding society.

Most of those writing on globalization and providing interpretations of
its effects from a more radical standpoint would readily argue that it is difficult
to understand the globalizing thrust of the world economy apart from the
class conflicts endemic in capitalist development. The productivity crisis of
the 1970s, the collapse of the class compromise that was Fordism, the flight of
hot money in search of safe havens, even the continual search of capitalist
firms for cheaper labor, however overgeneralized that perception might be,
are commonly called on in attempts to understand the new economic and political geographies of the last couple of decades. Moreover, through the colonization of peripheries, both national and international, capital has been able
to discipline workers, push back the welfare state, and reestablish the conditions for profitability that were threatened in the mid-1970s.

That there was a crisis of accumulation seems clear, and the continuing
flirtation with deflation suggests that it is far from over. Glyn (1995) has provided an excellent survey of the distributional conflicts that emerged in the
1970s in the advanced capitalist countries and the subsequent disciplining of

labor by unemployment. But he is far from convinced that that unemployment can be laid at the door of globalization:

> It is a central argument of this paper that increased international integration, whilst a convenient scapegoat, does not constitute the fundamental block to full-employment policies. Openness to trade, and thus the real costs of maintaining external payments balance, has increased only modestly. Openness to international financial flows has added to the speed at which, and the drama with which, financial markets bring retribution on governments whose policies are not 'credible.' This credibility is calibrated by indicators such as government deficits, wage pressure, strikes, profitability, and inflation. But maintaining such credibility only rules out the expansion of employment if there are no means other than unemployment for regulating conflicting claims over distribution and control. Viable policies for expanding employment entail costs which must be explicitly counted and willingly shouldered by the mass of wage and salary earners. (1995, p. 55)

We will return to Glyn's arguments regarding alternatives. But my immediate concern is to argue that globalization, whether through its intended effects for those capitals engaging in it or its unintended effects for capital in general, is by no means the only strategy available in the search to reestablish conditions for accumulation. Deterritorialization, yes, but, as Storper, Gertler, and Mair argue, territorialization can also provide, depending on circumstances, the way back to competitiveness. As far as financial flows are concerned, and as Notermans makes clear, there is no necessary relation between their internationalization and macroeconomic policy.

The classical social theorists have been chastised for their aspatiality. But often this can provide a useful corrective to the point at which Sayer's (1985) strictures regarding the contingency of geographies seem thoroughly well taken. Marx's emphasis on restoring capitalist discipline through technological change and the creation of the industrial reserve army, while oversimplified, can provide a valuable corrective. As Jenkins (1987, p. 78) has asserted, "To focus on industrial relocation of production as the major threat to workers in the advanced capitalist countries . . . serves to divert attention from often more important threats such as automation, [and] reorganization of labor processes. . . ."

But if globalization theses are flawed, if they are vastly overgeneralized, as a form of discourse they do have their value for capital. As Piven has suggested:

> The key fact of our historical moment is said to be the globalization of national economies which, together with 'post-Fordist' domestic restructuring, has had shattering consequences for the economic well-being of the working class, and especially for the power of the working class. I don't think this

explanation is entirely wrong but it is deployed so sweepingly as to be misleading. And right or wrong, the explanation itself has become a political
force, helping to create the institutional realities it purportedly merely describes. (1995, p. 108)

She adds later on in the same paper: "Put another way, capital is pyramiding
the leverage gained by expanded exit opportunities, or perhaps the leverage
gained merely by the spectre of expanded exit opportunities, in a series of vigorous political campaigns" (p. 110).

From the standpoint of the political options, even within the limits of a
reformist program, it is clear that subordination to the global marketplace, to
the new spatial fetishism of the commodity represented by globalization arguments, is not the only option. There have been a number of advocates of new,
national cross-class alliances as a vehicle for reestablishing growth but without
the threat of inflation. Prices and incomes policies have always been the alternative to unemployment as a means of maintaining price stability, though, as
Notermans emphasizes in his chapter, they are difficult to defend in a context
of overheated labor markets. The condition for avoiding this constraint is a
continual upgrading of productivity. Not surprisingly, the new proposals have
at their center visions of systems of governance of the capital–labor relation
that would create the conditions for such an upgrading.

Hirst and Thompson (1992) are among these advocates. According to
them, the state must construct a distributional coalition that wins the acceptance of key economic actors and the organized interests representing them
for a sustainable distribution of national income and expenditure that pro-
motes competitive manufacturing performance. To make this possible, the
state must orchestrate social consensus: this requires the sort of collaborative
political culture that is not available everywhere.[3] Cox (1987) has made similar proposals in the form of what he calls "state capitalism." Like Hirst and
Thompson, he sees this strategy as, on the whole, limited to late industrializing countries like France and Germany with strong traditions of "close coordination between state and private capital in pursuit of common goals" (Cox,
1987, pp. 292–294).

This is not to endorse such policies. Rather, it is merely to indicate that
globalization does not entrain some single, unidirectional, sociospatial logic.
All strategies, individual or collective, are necessarily spatial, since all social
activity mobilizes the useful properties of space relations in some way. The
globalization of production represents one such strategy of the individual
firm for coping with the challenges of the working class, but not the only one.
Wealth holders anxious about changing currency values can move into foreign currencies, but greater regulation of international financial transactions
would not stem the flight from holding the national money. At the same time,
the outcomes of these different strategies create the conditions to which others

must react, either through their own deterritorializations or through further rounds of territorialization.

New economic geographies are a fact, though it would be better if we had an improved sense of their dimensions, something toward which Gordon and Hirst and Thompson have made useful contributions. Likewise, the sorts of effects that can make one pessimistic about the future of working-class power and about democracy do occur. But the contemporary conjuncture is much more complicated and varied than this, and, given the nature of people, societies, and space, necessarily so.

Another way of viewing the question of globalization, and complementary to a standpoint rooted in the relations between society and space, is that of the relation between space and place. As Storper underlines in the first chapter in this book, globalization needs to be viewed against a background of the territorializing: place-specific conditions of production that are either unavailable or difficult to reconstitute elsewhere. The standard approach to globalization emphasizes the expanding horizons of locational substitutability now available to capitals. But for many firms this option can be exaggerated. Moreover, place-specific conditions are often the source of their continuing competitive advantage. These conditions, set in the context of more global circulations of value, generate their own political geographies, as Harvey (1985) made brilliantly clear, a politics involving the sorts of cross-class alliances foregrounded by Herod in this volume. This analysis also casts a very different light on the gloomy distributional prognostications of the standard arguments.

Thus, in at least two respects the claims seemingly made for space stand in need of qualification. "Space," in the form of sets of locational opportunities and constraints, needs to be viewed, just as much as "place" does, in the context of the social structures by virtue of which agents are both empowered and constrained. At the same time, the changes set in motion by new rounds of deskilling, monetarism, and changes in transportation and in the spatial divisions of labor of firms are also enacted with respect to agents, not just workers but also capitals, which are necessarily and sometimes by choice embedded in particular places. Both in more metaphorical senses, therefore, and in literal senses, "space" needs to be put in its "place." It has been the aim of the contributors to this volume to do precisely that.

NOTES

1. This idea is echoed by Hirst and Thompson:

Within the contemporary international economy the important relationships remain those between the more developed economies, the members of the Organization of Economic Cooperation and Development (OECD). Indeed these economies have increased in their relative importance over recent years in terms of their share of world trade and investment. In 1989 over 80% of world trade was conducted between the OECD economies and this rose to 85% if the ex-Eastern European and Soviet economies were included. The Group of Five (G5) main economies accounted for 75% of foreign direct investment. Thus for all practical intents and purposes it is the advanced industrial economies that constitute the membership of the "global" economy, if that entity can be said to exist. The LDCs, and even the NICs, still constitute a very small part of the international economy, however regrettable or disappointing that may be. (1992, p. 366)

2. Another useful critical piece is McIntyre (1991).

3. "The political process and the interest group culture in societies like the UK and the USA does not favor rapid adaptation in a more co-operative direction, rather it emphasizes competition and the dumping of social costs on those who are both least organized or influential and least able to bear them" (Hirst & Thompson, 1992, p. 375).

REFERENCES

Albo, G. (1994). "Competitive austerity" and the impasse of capitalist employment policy. In R. Miliband & L. Panitch (Eds.), *Between globalism and nationalism* (pp. 144–170). London: Merlin Press.

Cox, R. (1987). *Production, power and world order.* New York: Columbia University Press.

Glyn, A. (1995). Social democracy and full employment. *New Left Review, 211,* 33–55.

Gordon, D. (1988). The global economy: New edifice or crumbling foundations? *New Left Review, 168,* 24–65.

Harvey, D. (1985). The geopolitics of capitalism. In D. Gregory & J. Urry (Eds.), *Social relations and spatial structures* (pp. 128–163). London: Macmillan.

Hirst, P., & Thompson, G. (1992). The problem of "globalization": International economic relations, national economic management and the formation of trading blocs. *Economy and Society, 21,* 357–396.

Hirst, P., & Thompson, G. (1996). *Globalization in question.* Cambridge, UK: Polity Press.

Jenkins, R. (1987). *Transnational corporations and uneven development: The internationalization of capital and the Third World.* London: Methuen.

Massey, D. (1984). *Spatial divisions of labour.* London: Macmillan.

McIntyre, R. (1991). The political economy and class analytics of international capital flows: US industrial capital in the 1970s and 80s. *Capital and Class, 43,* 179–202.

O'Brien, R. (1992). *Global financial integration: The end of geography.* London: Royal Institute of International Affairs.

Piven, F. F. (1995). Is it global economics or neo-lassez-faire? *New Left Review, 213,* 107–115.

Sayer, A. (1985). The difference that space makes. In D. Gregory & J. Urry (Eds.), *Social relations and spatial structures* (pp. 49–66). London: Macmillan.

CHAPTER 1

Territories, Flows, and Hierarchies in the Global Economy

Michael Storper

GLOBALIZATION AND THE INSTITUTIONS OF ECONOMIC DEVELOPMENT

In recent years, the flows of goods, services, information, capital, and people across national and regional lines have increased greatly, giving rise to the notion that modern economic activity is somehow becoming "globalized." Do these phenomena mean that contemporary economies are becoming place-less, mere flows of resources via corporate hierarchies, which are themselves not rooted in national or regional territories and therefore not subject to territorially based state institutions? This view is the underlying message of many contemporary analyses (Castells, 1989). Though many commentators assign territorially based institutions, especially nation-states, a continuing role in the global economy, the balance of power is thought to be tipping in favor of globalized organizations, networks, practices, and flows. Hence, the locus of control over important dimensions of the economic development process— both in the narrow sense of formal decision making and resource deployment and in the larger sense of influences to which we must respond—is passing from territorialized institutions such as states to deterritorialized institutions such as intrafirm international corporate hierarchies or international markets that know no bounds (Gilpin, 1975; Ohmae, 1990; Reich, 1990). The perfection of hierarchies and markets, as management systems and transactional structures, is said to be gaining on territorial barriers, specificities, and frictions (Julius, 1990; Ostry, 1990; Veltz, 1993).

There is another view, of course, and it comes from the rich literature on different ways that organizations and markets are shaped by political and business institutions. The "Japanese model" and J-firm, the "German model," and the like, are different ways that advanced capitalist activity can be organized (Albert, 1992). There is a competition between such territorially based institutionally organized production systems for world market share in many sectors.

These two views correspond, in many ways, to the two main disciplinary discourses that deal with globalization—economics and political science. Much of the former implies that economic development is becoming deterritorialized, while there is a strong body of research in the latter that indicates continued territorial specificity in development patterns owing to the institutions alluded to previously. Political economists and political scientists have begun to consider the effects of global capitalism on the margin of maneuver left to nation-states (Carnoy, 1993), but curiously have devoted less attention to scrutinizing how globalized capitalism really is. As a result, the theoretical meaning and practical impact of economic globalization remain obscure.

In this chapter I propose to sketch out what a confrontation between the territorialization of economic development and the emergence of global hierarchies and flows would look like. The reason for this confrontation is the hypothesis that the ability of territorially bounded states and other institutions to bargain with hierarchical global business organizations, and to shape the development process in general, should rise with the territorialization of economic activity. Territorialization thus becomes the analytical key to the debate about the politics and economics of globalization.

Defining Territorialization in Economic Terms

Territorialized economic development may be defined as something quite different from mere location or localization of economic activity. It consists, for our purposes, in economic activity which is dependent on resources that are territorially specific. These "resources" can range from asset specificities available only from a certain place or, more importantly, assets that are available only in the context of certain inter-organizational or firm-market relationships that necessarily involve geographical proximity, or where relations of proximity are markedly more efficient than other ways of generating these asset specificities. Geographically proximate relations constitute valuable asset specificities if they are necessary to the generation of spillover effects–positive externalities–in an economic activity system. So territorialization is often tied to specific interdependencies in economic life. Proximity would also be a basis of valuable specific assets insofar as these latter are necessary to the efficient functioning of the firm under normal circumstances, where the firm cannot replace them, either by internalizing functions or by carrying out its external relations in a way that does not involve proximity in them. The assets to which we refer can be hard—labor, technology—or soft—information, conventions of interaction, relation-specific skills. We shall develop this notion of relationally specific assets further as we go along (Asanuma, 1989).

An activity is fully territorialized when its economic viability is rooted in assets (including practices and relations) that are not available in many other places and that cannot easily or rapidly be created or imitated in places that lack them. Locational substitutability is not possible, and feasible locations are small in number, making locational "markets" highly imperfect. This definition of territorialization thus does not cover all cases of agglomeration or localization or urbanization, but a distinctive subset of those cases.

Let us now set these definitions into motion.

A REVIEW OF MAINSTREAM ARGUMENTS ABOUT GLOBALIZATION AND WHAT THEY OMIT

As noted, huge research efforts have been devoted to the behavior of firms in a global economy, to consequences for markets, and to the ways that institutions shape markets and firms. There are major lacunae in these efforts because they do not pose the question of territorialization clearly.

Who Is Us?: Markets versus Hierarchies

In the United States, the recent debate over the national economy in a global economy, made famous because it was carried out by two scholars who are now high-ranking members of the Clinton administration, illustrates this conceptual lacuna well. On one side, it was argued that development-inducing investment will flow to those areas that possess appropriate factors of production, which, in the global economy, means high-quality labor ("symbolic analysts"), infrastructure, and so on (Reich, 1990). The argument, then, was implicitly about the importance and mobility of foreign direct investment, and that ownership of assets—the nationality of firms—is unimportant. The role of regions and nations is to develop appropriate factor supplies so as to attract this highly mobile investment. But the argument said nothing about whether those factors are territorialized or not, in the sense defined here. As such, it can be interpreted either as an endorsement of globalization as placelessness or of globalization as the attraction of capital to territorialized economic formations. There is simply nothing in the argument that gets at the issue.

On the other side of the debate, it was claimed that ownership—the nationality of firms—is important (Tyson, 1991). It is necessary for political reasons to have firms that produce all technologies essential to national security, and even major multinational firms concentrate their core technology-producing activities in their home territories. Even without security concerns, the existence of technological spillovers means that for an economy to carry out certain innovation and development processes, it must possess a complement of other capacities. Both these claims are probably quite sound, in and of themselves; but they do not say much of anything about globalization. On one hand, the argument does not show why even major multinationals continue to concentrate their principal technology-based activities at home and therefore why the factor/market-attraction argument is not valid (see also Amendola, Guerrieri, & Padoan, 1992; Carnoy, 1993; OECD, 1991; Papconstantinou, 1993; Patel & Pavitt, 1989, 1991). As a result, it could still be claimed that investment is becoming increasingly mobile and that the observed rootedness of major multinationals in their home economies is a transitory, not necessary, condition. On the other hand, while it correctly suggests interdependence-through-spillover as key to many of the most important forms of innovation, it does not say why such spillovers should be localized within a national economy, except for security reasons. There is no economic reasoning about the territorialization of such spillovers, in other words. So the debate over "who is us?" tells us little about who we really are in a global economy.

Commodity Trade

The growth of commodity trade figures prominently in claims that the economy is globalizing. Rising intra-industry trade is said to be evidence of globalization as firms create a global functional division of labor.[1] One possibility is that intra-industry trade is accompanied by the advent of global oligopolistic supply structures for many commodities and for knowledge inputs (Ernst, 1990; OECD, 1991, p. 361ff.).[2] The big firms who dominate these supply chains benefit from entry barriers due to scale and the firm-specific assets they deploy on a global scale. This argument, however, says nothing about the problem of territorialization per se. Global supply structures, even highly oligopolistic ones, could reflect (1) an internalized supply structure of assets, in which case it could be considered deterritorialized (Dicken, 1988); or (2) an attempt by firms to optimize access to factors of production in order to produce the inputs to their global supply structures in the sense described by Robert Reich (1990), another form of deterritorialization, in the sense that regions and nations must simply make themselves attractive to mobile investments; or (3) also an attempt by firms to optimize access to territorialized factors of production (which meet the criteria of our definition). The point is that without a conceptual apparatus specific to the problem, the existing evidence can be made to reveal little about it. Note that the oft-cited rise in foreign direct investment, which is the vehicle of rising intra-industry and intrafirm trade, suffers from the same conceptual void (cf. Julius, 1990; Ostry, 1990). It suggests a rise in activity by major world firms, and the development of a finely grained world division of labor, but little about the meaning of globalization-as-deterritorialization.

The Global Business Hierarchy

As noted, much attention has been devoted to the apparent rise of global business hierarchies, the organizations that manage global supply structures. From theorizing about the "multinational," "transnational" or even "multidomestic" firm in the 1960s and 1970s, concern has shifted to organizations that manage global production and investment systems in "real time," involving simultaneous manipulation and optimization of manufactured inputs, capital, information, and marketing (Ballance, 1987; Dicken, 1988; Glickman & Woodward, 1989; OECD, 1991; Ohmae, 1990).

There was considerable optimism about the possibility of such organizations in the late 1970s and early 1980s. Ford Motor Company announced its intention to build a "world car"; General Motors (GM) invested tens of billions of dollars in telecommunications and other infrastructure intended to permit not only worldwide supply and market coordination, but also worldwide concurrent engineering (i.e., innovation and knowledge production). Some analysts label the outcome of development of such systems the global "hypermobility" of capital, as firms search for ever better deals from presumably substitutable locations.

The importance of such an approach is the notion of a production system spread across the world, involving intrafirm trade in inputs, between locations lacking specificities (Frobel, Heinrichs, & Kreye, 1980; Hymer, 1976). Were such a model to become dominant, we would expect intermediate products to account for a very high share of world trade; but this is not the case, as can be seen in Table 1.1. We would also expect international sourcing to be very important, and it is in some industries; the problem is that we cannot know whether such sourcing emanates from substitutable locations or territorialized locations. Further, we would expect that finished product trade, which is high in some industries, would be the result of such locationally substitutable sourcing in intermediates, and not the result of territorialized sourcing, knowledge production, and assets. The statistics shed no light on these issues.

Anecdotally, the results of attempts to build worldwide, locationally substitutable, sourcing systems have been mixed, in that the coordination of such an organization has proven to be much more problematic than was initially envisioned. Ford and GM have substantially cut back their earlier ambitions in favor of highly regionalized operations (Morales, 1994). Still, the management literature suggests that it is the ultimate ideal of many firms in both manufacturing and advanced services (Caves, 1982; Dicken, 1988; Ohmae, 1990; Vernon & Spar, 1989). It would seem that the possibility is limited to a set of special cases, however: certain kinds of assembly and fabrication activities carried out at high scale, involving low levels of firm- or industry-specific human and physical capital, and therefore highly substitutable locations for

TABLE 1.1. Pattern of Globalization of the Surveyed Industries

Industries included in the survey	Trade				Direct investment				Cooperative agreements		
	Finished prods. (%sales)	Interm. prods. (%sales)	Intl. sourcing (%tot.ste)	Intrafirm (%trade)	Flows (%gfcf)	AFFs sales (%sales)	M&As (%ops)	Equity parts (%ops)	Devel. purpose (%agrs)	Prod. purpose (%agrs)	Market purpose (%agrs)
Pharmaceuticals	10	8	10–30	70	50–70	40–50	52	48	38–68	13–29	19–41
Computers	26	14	20–60	50–80	30–40	50–60	43	57	50–70	15–28	17–32
Semiconductors	20	n.a.	10–40	70	15–25	20–25	39	61	n.a.	n.a.	n.a.
Motor vehicles	21	13	25–35	50–80	15–25	10–20	33	67	24–48	39–66	9–20
Consumer electronics	55	30	10–40	30–50	20–35	20–30	39	61	24–40	35–62	12–33
Nonferrous metals	21	21[a]	30–50	30	20–35	15–25	45	55	n.a.	n.a.	n.a.
Steel	27	35–45[b]	15–25	5–10	5–10	15–25	72	28	n.a.	n.a.	n.a.
Clothing	25–30	25–30[c]	10–40	5–10	15–20	5–15	n.a.	n.a.	(limited)		

Note. Data from OECD, Industry Division compilation (1993). Elaborated from data sources used for the sector case studies. Please note that gfcf = gross fixed capital formation; ops = overseas partners; agrs = agreements; AFFs = all foreign firms; M&As = mergers and acquisitions; and tot.ste = total subcontracting and exports.

[a]Unwrought aluminum.
[b]Iron ore, coking coal, scrap.
[c]Textiles.

global sourcing. But these operations certainly do not add up to hypermobility-as-deterritorialization of contemporary capitalism as a whole. Indeed, they likely constitute a relatively modest share of the economic process today, by any measure (Carnoy, 1993).

The same is true for discussions of global business hierarchies in the generation of knowledge and technological innovation. It appears that many forms of innovation require investments so great that even the biggest firms, to earn a decent return, attempt to monopolize returns on global markets (Dunning & Norman, 1985; Krugman, 1990). Once such knowledge is developed, it often becomes a global state-of-the-art in product or process. It rests on temporarily non-rival and excludable firm-specific assets which firms use as the basis for earning temporary superprofits (Grossman & Helpman, 1991). The character of these assets encourages firms to internalize them. But does this mean deterritorialization? Not necessarily. The production of firm-specific assets might occur only via use of complementary territorialized resources, that is, the mobilization of territory-specific resources in the firm's core location that permit it to invade world markets by virtue of technological superiority; it could then be made firm-specific via intellectual property rights, and thereby serve as the basis of a global, monopolistic supply structure, deterritorialized from the areas that receive it (Dosi, Pavitt, & Soete, 1990; Patel & Pavitt, 1991). This interpretation is consistent with the fact that intrafirm trade accounts for a high proportion of foreign direct investment in high-technology industries (Table 1.1).

Things are not unambiguous even in these cases, however, for the very same set of risks pushes firms to enter into risk- and cost-sharing strategic alliances with other major firms; some such alliances come about because firms want to tap into other firms' expertise in order to avoid the concomitant risk of technological lock-in (by making the wrong, very expensive, firm-specific asset choices) (Mytelka, 1992; OECD, 1991). Where does such expertise come from? Perhaps from those firms' deterritorialized, fully internalized capabilities, but just as likely from the territorial contexts in which they are inserted. Clearly, the deployment of advanced technology and knowledge, especially if it is firm-specific and where access is subject to significant legal or economic barriers to entry, means major developmental power in today's world, and the global business organization seeks such power of deployment. There are major effects on receiving economies. But the search for this power, again, says little about territorialization or deterritorialization of technology and knowledge generation in the world economy, and much more about corporate supply of such knowledge and technology once developed.

Indeed, in place of the model of the international firm as vertically integrated worldwide business hierarchy, much recent reflection about the organization of global business has turned on the notion of the firm as the central node in a variety of global linkages, ranging from ownership to alliance, and including cross-investment, technology and production partnerships, and research and development (R&D) collaborations (Mowery, 1988; Mytelka, 1992). This may well be a new kind of "nexus" business organization, whose impacts on economic development processes we have barely begun to glimpse; but such a model of the global firm does not so much imply deterritorialization of the economic process as a recasting of the role of territories in complex, intraorganizationally and inter-organizationally linked global business flows.

Foreign Direct Investment

I have left the most obvious category of globalization for consideration until now because, as can be readily seen, it is a chaotic conception. Foreign direct investment is a catchall category that refers to the volume of international investment in subsidiary operations of firms. It leads to intra-industry, interindustry and intrafirm trade, but, then again, it may reduce commodity trade when it leads to installation of locally serving final output capacity in major markets, so-called "regional" or "Triad" locational patterns. So foreign direct investment may be a vehicle for or substitute for trade. It may reflect firm strategies to control foreign markets via intrafirm trade, but then again it may reflect the need to tap into intermediate inputs produced by firms, through alliances and local trade. It may reflect global supply oligopolies in goods, intellectual property, or technology, but, then again, it may reflect needs to be in contact with territorially rooted foreign contexts of goods or technology development. The statistic reveals little about the territoriality of economic dynamics.

Another argument, which underlies much of the claim that the global economy is deterritorializing in favor of global business organizations, has to do with corporate power. It has been correctly observed that the biggest global firms are getting bigger: there is ongoing concentration of capital. It has also been remarked that there is a certain centralization of capital, in that the shares of the largest 100 or 500 corporations in global output are greater than they were 20 years ago (OECD, 1991). These large organizations, so it goes, are increasingly powerful across territorial boundaries. Their deployment of investments can shape markets, determine which technologies get developed, and, above all, exercise influence on national and regional governments (Harrison, 1994).

Power, in this sense, probably does have impacts on territorialization as we have defined it. But we need to examine precisely how. One of the paradoxes of globalization, in the sense of interpenetration of markets by companies from different nations, is that many market structures in many industries have actually become less concentrated over the past 30 years; there are more competitors in them than when such markets were composed of national or regional firms, though at a world level the first 10 or 20 companies control high proportions of output in many industries, especially technology-intensive ones (OECD, 1991). Global firms, while constituting a small club, especially in industries with very high barriers to entry, are therefore locked into competitive battle; they do not rule their world markets in any straightforward sense, as any major automobile, computer, clothing, or chemical company will readily attest.

Still, their power to shift vast quantities of capital, technology, or human capital across territorial borders, into different product markets, into R&D programs, is considerable. These firms can obviously shape the development of markets by shaping supply structures through their decisions. And they can bargain with territorially rooted states in so doing. But the image of nations and regions as Davids facing the global Goliaths cannot be straightforwardly assumed by the mere existence of global firms, for the latter are subject to all the complexities of territorialization described in preceding paragraphs. Merely being bigger does not give them command-and-control and pricing power in the sense that Berle and Means (1933) thought of it, nor does it confer locational substitutability.

The Poverty of Categories

The traditional categories in which the globalization debate has been framed—foreign direct investment, commodity trade, the global business hierarchy, the global supply structure of commodities, knowledge, and technology—seem instinctively to indicate the steady deterritorialization of economic power. But upon closer observation, these conceptual categories are inadequate to the job of shedding light on the question of territorialization and deterritorialization. It is, indeed, quite curious that a fundamentally geographical process labeled with a geographical term—"globalization"—is analyzed as a set of resource flows largely without considering their interactions with the territoriality of economic development.

REFRAMING THE QUESTION: TERRITORIES AND FLOWS

In order to see what the terms territorialized and deterritorialized might mean with respect to the global economy, we can imagine two polar opposite cases, a fully deterritorialized "economy of flows and substitutions" and a fully territorialized "economy of interdependencies and specificities." In constructing these images, we will combine reasoning about organizations (firms), assets, markets, and places.

A Pure Flow-Substitution Economy

Imagine the extreme case of a fully realized global supply oligopoly. Resources would flow between parts of a firm, between places, without having any particular dependence on any particular place. Such assets—whether goods or information—would be producible in so many different places as to constitute a true (almost) perfect "market" in locations for their production. It matters little whether they are actually produced at many locations; one could imagine the extreme case of global supply from a single place (due to scale economies, for example), but where that place has no specificities that render it immune to substitution by another place.

This sort of economy could be the result of two possible developmental processes. On one hand, activities that are well developed in a wide variety of places make necessary productive resources available in near ubiquity, but have historically been separated by transport barriers or differentiated tastes. Improvements in transportation, standardization of tastes, or increases in the possible scale of production open up this wide variety of locations to global business organizations, who then profit from a huge potential locational choice and ubiquitous markets, but they are bound by no locational specificities or local interdependencies. On the other hand, such organizations perfect production processes that eliminate the need for locationally scarce specific assets: technological change via product standardization and routinization of production processes does the job.

In both cases, a pure flow form of globalization becomes possible. It matters little whether the flows are via markets or hierarchies: global firms could purchase locally and sell through global commodity trade, for example. It matters little whether the flows concern intermediate or finished products. Those considerations, well analyzed through industrial organization theory, are simply different forms that the global flows of resources and optimization of factor use and capacity may take. The essential condition for a pure flow economy is that locations offer factors of production that could potentially be substituted by a large number of other locations. One can even imagine the extreme case where the only international flows of resources are financial and intellectual, but where, in the presence of few scale economies, a global firm administers many local production systems as opposed to a few that serve broad territories; in this case, the possibility of switching from local to centralized systems would be critical to enforce the condition of substitutability, in concert with the absence of locally specific assets.

This case of nonspecific, locationally substitutable and perfectly elastic factor supplies is probably not found in pure form anywhere. But in some sectors, notably certain manufacturing industries and consumer services, these conditions are increasingly close to reality. Low-wage, low-skill, low sunk-cost manufacturing processes; certain highly standardized consumer durable manufacturing (where sunk costs are higher, but modular and widely available equipment is used); and certain consumer services where centralized production can be combined with local delivery come to mind.

One could imagine a pure market version of this globalization process, where numerous local economies, characterized by relatively small firms, competed with each other on global markets. Purchasers, armed with perfect information and highly developed and very flexible marketing networks, could switch from one locality's product to another almost instantaneously. Hierarchy is not necessary, then, to the flow economy's definition, in contrast to the image of oligopoly = globalization often implied in the literature. In reality, however, this ability to switch tends to be associated with scale in marketing and an ability to coordinate supplies from different, substitutable sources.

The potential political consequences of flow economies are what bother many of the critics of globalization (e.g., Harrison, 1994). Instead of seeing such flows as the means to resource optimization at a world scale, their point of departure is that economic progress has always depended on political economics, where everything ranging from the distribution of income between labor and capital to the correction of a wide variety of market failures is carried out by territorially rooted institutions such as nation-states. The advent of deterritorialized flow economies would seem to reduce the margin of maneuver of such nation-states dramatically, in favor of that of the private sector and thereby to open up a number of unfavorable consequences in both distributional and efficiency terms (Frobel et al., 1980; Glickman & Woodward, 1989; Harrison, 1994; Hymer, 1976).

A Pure Territorial Economy of Interdependencies and Specificities

A fully territorialized economic activity would satisfy conditions quite opposite to those just described. The essential condition of territorialization is that the activity be dependent on resources with specificities that are strongly territorialized and where the supply of these resources is subject to important inelasticities. The traditional case of scarce natural resources is a pure example but little relevant to most productive activity, where "resources" are mostly produced inputs such as labor and technology. We know that for many labor and technology inputs, there are no functional substitutes at any price, but even though such labor and technology are highly product-specific (heterogeneous is the accepted term), in many cases they are nonetheless widely available or easily produced, at rather different prices. In this case, territorialization is not in evidence. Where they are not widely available at any price, however, that is, where scarcities or inelasticities are in evidence, then not only localization but territorialization exist due to the geographically limited conditions of their production.

It is really with respect to special meanings of the terms "labor" and "technology" that territorialization becomes most relevant in today's economy. Certain kinds of labor qualities are different from mere skills. There are many contexts where nonroutine judgments are made and where the success of the judgment depends on how a condition of uncertainty that involves other people is interpreted, or where noncodified traditions and ways of doing things are essential to the job. The former corresponds to demands for creativity or convention, the latter to learned custom. In all these cases, labor qualities are produced in what may be called a relation-specific fashion: they are produced and are exercised via insertion into a system of relations, whether it be interpersonal or bounded by specific, not-fully-codifiable rules of the game (Asanuma, 1989). These skills are not only specific in nature but subject to important supply inelasticities in the medium-run (Amin & Thrift, 1993; Lecoq, 1993).

Analogous observations may be made about technology, if what we mean by this is not merely hardware, but know-how, especially know-how that involves an outwardly moving and unknown scientific frontier (as in high technology) or an uncertain movement around such dynamics as product differentiation (for many low-technology or fashion-dependent industries and services). It is likely to involve asset specificities and supply inelasticities (Dosi et al., 1990; Rallet, 1993).

This probably understates the extent of relation- and place-specific assets in production. Many production systems, as has been amply demonstrated in recent years, turn on an intricate web of external interfirm transactions or internal, intrafirm transactions. In some cases, there are—at one moment or another—various sorts of standard economizing reasons for such transactions to be carried out across limited geographical distances: in these cases, territorialization is the result of necessary *relations of proximity* in the production system, which limit the number of sites at which production can be carried out (Rallet, 1993). Over time, however, such cost barriers tend to be eroded due to transport improvements or to change in the nature of the transactions themselves, which lead to higher scale, greater certainty, and lower costs of covering distance.

But cost barriers are not the only reasons for the existence of relations of proximity in production systems. Many such relationships—buyer–supplier interfirm relations, or R&D–producer relations, or firm–labor market relations—come to be structured in ways that are highly specific to a given, initially geographically bounded, transactional context (usually regions or nation-states). Over time, they become more and more specific as unwritten rules of the game (conventions), formal institutions, and customary forms of knowledge are built up and become indispensable to admission to the producers' community and to efficient interpretation of how to reciprocate via transactions with other agents under conditions of uncertainty. In other words, regional or national production systems become nexuses of interdependencies between organizations and persons which involve relational asset specificities (Amin & Thrift, 1993; Storper & Salais, 1997; Saxenian, 1994; Storper, 1995). These interdependencies must, of course, be efficient in some sense (e.g., a factor in cost minimization or innovation–improvement).

Territorialization is thus not equivalent to geographical proximity or agglomeration, although such agglomeration may be at some times cause and at others effect territorialization: it is an effect when scarcities and specificities of key resources such as labor and technology draw producers to a place, and when nonsubstitutabilities keep them there; it is a cause when the transactional structure of production draws producers into an agglomeration, and then key dimensions of the production system become relation-specific and key to its ongoing efficiencies.

There are very few industries where pure territorialization, in the sense of a unique possible efficient location for the totality of the industry's output, exists; in this case, there would be a localized global supply monopoly. But the condition of territorialization, in the sense of a few possible locations for significant parts of the industry's output, can be found quite frequently. Certain very high quality goods, those that involve technological innovation or ongoing rapid differentiation, or highly specialized services come to mind as examples. There are two very different versions of this territorialization. One concerns activities that serve such localized tastes that the localized supply structure corresponds to a unique localized demand structure. The more interesting case, of course, is that where the localized supply structure satisfies a national or global demand, and where there is therefore the possibility of entry by competitors in other places. This is likely to show up as a case of commodity trade exports, whether intra- or interindustry. It is analytically indifferent to ownership (that is, the definition says nothing about whether ownership of territorialized assets must be local). In practice, most such cases of multinational corporations who have core activities in their home country and in a specific region of that country also have national ownership (Patel & Pavitt, 1991; Tyson, 1991), but counterexamples, such as Sony's ownership of Columbia Pictures, are reasonably abundant. Territorialization, therefore, cuts across the standard terms of the globalization debate (such as "who is us?") and exports.

THE DYNAMICS OF GLOBALIZATION

What should be clear from the preceding is that global capitalism is being constructed through interactions between flow economies and territorial economies. Internationalization of capitalism has long been measured simply as a function of the increasing intensities of flows, but little was said about territories. Globalization is said to refer to something qualitatively different, in the sense of an economy or its subsystems that operate globally. That is, globalization should involve not merely international flows of resources, but economic systems that operate as international flow economies, as they have been defined here. If globalization is truly gaining on territorial economic organization, then we should find evidence not merely of increasing international flows of resources, but also of decreasing territorialization.

Some of the possible interactions are represented schematically in Figure 1.1. On the horizontal axis is the degree of territorialization of economic activities, and on the vertical axis the level of international flows associated with these activities. The first case (type 1) comprises those activities that are both highly territorialized and highly internationalized: territorially specific, nonsubstitutable assets are involved, but there are relationships that are not bound by such territorialization. Examples include the high-technology production system where the firm has certain important territorialized activities, but engages in intrafirm trade in intermediate inputs, and intrafirm trade for its worldwide marketing network. Intermediate inputs might be sourced for cost reasons alone (in which case this part of the system is effectively deterritorialized) or because the firm is tapping into territorial contexts of expertise elsewhere. Other examples are the now-famous industrial districts, where local-

Territorialization of Production System

	High	Low
International Flows in Production System — High	**(type 1)** Intrafirm trade with asset specificities Intermediate outputs of FDI Intermediate markets served from territorial cores Industrial districts Interfirm and interindustry trade	**(type 2)** International divisions of labor (e.g., in routinized manufacturing) International markets (e.g., in consumer services) Interfirm and interindustry trade without territorial core
International Flows in Production System — Low	**(type 4)** Locally serving production to specialized tastes with low international competition	**(type 3)** Local commerce in basic services not delivered via big-firm hierarchies

FIGURE 1.1. Territorialization and internationalization.

ized production systems serve world markets. Both interfirm and interindustry trade, within complex social divisions of labor, can involve highly territorialized production for international commodity chains. Foreign direct investment is a means to carry out some of these processes as well.

The second cell (type 2) describes cases of low levels of territorialization and high levels of international flow, and includes territorially dispersed commodity chains where no nonsubstitutable locations are involved (where technological standardization has reached a high level of development, generally) (Frobel et al., 1980; Hymer, 1976). It also includes dispersed production systems oriented to international markets, as in many consumer services. Note that this category would lead to interfirm, intrafirm, and interindustry trade, as well as foreign direct investment.

The third cell (type 3) consists of systems with low territorialization and low levels of international flow, that is, such things as local commerce in basic services that are not provided by far-flung big-firm hierarchies. In this cell we would find the industries of yore, which were localized due to transportation barriers but not truly territorialized; today we might find them there because of very low economies of scale, but less so due to transport barriers.

Finally, in the last cell (type 4), there are highly territorialized systems with few international connections. These are not simply localized due to insurmountable cost barriers to serving other areas from the local production system; they are territorialized because of nonsubstitutable local assets, as in the case of industries producing to specialized regional tastes.[3]

The caricatural version of globalization is based on the notion that advanced capitalism has substituted type 2 production systems for type 3 production systems; and some of this has indeed come about with the progressive reduction of transport barriers, increase in scale of delivery of commodities and services, and changes in trading regimes. Many manufactured goods, including both durables and nondurables, that were formerly produced in isolated regional economies, were first converted to national production systems in the postwar period (most especially in Europe), and then to commodity chains that are now, at least in part, internationalized (Vernon & Spar, 1989).

An even more extreme set of cases is that of type 4 becoming type 2, that is, formerly territorialized and mostly closed production systems now becoming international commodity chains. This is in evidence because as more internationalized, middle-class ways of life and tastes sweep their way across many places, old place-specific tastes disappear and with them the economic reasons for local asset specificity. When needs are redefined, so is demand, which can then be served via other kinds of products, furnished by production systems with assets available at many different locations, and without territorial cores. Crucial to this set of events is *not* changes in transportation, nor even scale, but actual product substitutions—the culture of demand is the key causal mechanism.

Many sophisticated analyses also call attention to a transformation of production systems from type 1 to type 2: this is the movement from "internationalization" of production to its true "globalization." Now it can be seen that the real claim here is not simply that there are high levels of international flow, of whatever sort, involved in the operation of these systems; in and of themselves, they do not transform these production systems into deterritorialized flow economies. The claim is rather that substitutability of locations increases; and territorially specific assets decrease dramatically in their importance to competitive production (Dunning, 1992). There is almost no way to distinguish the two cases or a movement between them using common statistical measures such as foreign investment or the various forms of trade. In manufacturing, such cases might be production systems for goods for which little technological change is occurring, and where scale, capital intensity, and standardization of tastes are very high; this probably corresponds to large parts of the commodity chains of certain consumer durables.

Two other important cases, however, seem to characterize the current era. The first is transformation of type 3 and 4 production systems not to type 2, but to type 1 systems. Formerly highly territorialized but not internationalized systems can become internationalized as they gain the ability to market their products around the world, without losing their locationally specific assets. This requires, as we have noted, development of demand for their products beyond local or regional borders. This is precisely what appears to have happened in the cases of many European industrial districts in the postwar period: the product qualities once prized locally have become desired elsewhere, and the relationally specific assets that exist in producer regions now permit those regions to meet broader demands through downstream internationalization, but not through internationalization of production itself (Becattini, 1987; Bianchi, 1993; Colombo, Mariotti, & Mutinelli, 1991).

Perhaps even more important is the transformation of type 2 production systems into type 1 systems: from highly internationalized but not especially territorialized systems, to ones increasingly territorialized and internationalized. The mass production industries of the postwar period, for example, seemed at one point to be on the road to ever greater standardization and, with it, locational substitutability, but forces such as increased product differentiation, and newly revived product-based technological learning have given a new lease on life to locationally specific relational assets in production.

Indeed, the *principal* trend to which we can call attention today is that in many sectors, there is *simultaneous and ongoing development of the characteristics of both both type 1 and type 2 systems*: the latter as ongoing standardization of tastes and techniques occurs, the former as technological learning, product differentiation, and the separating off of new branches of production, materials, and processes occur, all of which are causes of locational specificity, but also precisely outcomes of the interactive processes permitted by the locationally specific relational assets that underlie territorialization. This form of territorialization is qualitatively quite different from that of type 4 systems, in that it is not developed as the result of "tradition via isolation," but via what might be called the ongoing reinvention of relational assets in the context of high levels of geographical openness in trade and communications.

The formation of this *global context* of trade, investment, and communications and organized networks of human relations in production is perhaps the clearest dimension of globalization. The global economy is being constructed as an increasingly widely spread and accepted "grid" of these sorts of transactions, akin to a new global lingua franca of commerce, investment, and organization, based on historical and secular advances in transportation and communication technologies, and the development and diffusion of modern organizational "science," both of these in the context of the increasingly global political order of trade (cf. Lung & Mair, 1993; Naponen, Graham, & Markusen, 1993). But the paradox is that it is precisely this global grid or language that leads both to type 2 and to type 1 outcomes. In the former case, it breaks down barriers of taste, transport, and scale. In the latter case, it opens up markets to products based on superior forms of "local knowledge"; it consolidates markets and leads to such fantastic product differentiation possibilities that markets refragment and, with them, new specialized and localized divisions of labor reemerge; and it in some ways heats up the competitive process (albeit among giants), creating new premia on technological learning that require the same firms that become new global supply oligopolists to root themselves in locationally specific relational assets. The point is that globalization and territorialization are not just about the the geography of flows and its technological or organizational determinants, but are in some cases dependent on the ways production systems and their products are changed by new patterns of competition unleashed by territorial integration.

To summarize, four principal territorial–organizational dynamics can be isolated from these complex, intersecting forces. In some cases, the opening up of interterritorial relations places previously existing locationally specific assets into a new position of global dominance. In a second set of cases, those assets are devalued via substitution by other products that now penetrate local markets; this is not a straightforward economic process, however; it is culturally intermediated. In a third set of cases, territorial integration permits the fabled attainment of massive economies of scale and organization, devalues locationally specific assets and leads to deterritorialization and widespread market penetration. In a fourth set of cases, territorial integration is met by differentiation and destandardization of at least some crucial elements of the commodity chain, necessitating the reinvention of territory-specific relational assets.

HIERARCHY, REGULATION, AND COMPETITION: INSTITUTIONAL DILEMMAS

State institutions exercise their authority over limited territories. But they do so in fields of forces—whether political or economic—that extend well beyond these borders. At least in matters of economic affairs, for much of the postwar period the economic authority of nation-states and the substantive power to back it up was considerable within the national territory. Globalization of economic processes seems to have weakened that substantive power, if not the formal authority. The global business organizations that control certain important international resource flows seem, in many cases, to be deterritorialized, and thus not directly dependent on processes that states, whether regional or national, can effectively regulate.

Yet, as we have seen, the mere existence of large-scale international flows does not lead directly to a conclusion that a productive activity is deterritorialized. Likewise, we can now see that the mere existence of territorialization does not mean that local or national states can exercise strong regulatory control over the economic development process (Carnoy, 1993; Dunning, 1992). Territorialization is a necessary, but not a sufficient, condition for a strong state role, because territorialization itself may involve hierarchies that are in turn inserted into larger contexts. We now want to sketch out some of the complex interactions between territorial economies and flow economies, and the ways they may mix hierarchical, market and network forms of governance of production systems. Territorially based state institutions are now forced to confront these sorts of interactions in undertaking economic development strategies.

Figure 1.2 shows different ways of governing production systems, in the context of different levels of territorialization and international flows. Forms of governance where authority is largely internalized within large business organizations are labeled "hierarchies," while those that are carried out via high levels of external relations of large numbers of agents, where no single or small number of agents is dominant, are labeled "networks and markets." These represent two fundamentally different nexuses of decision-making power, centralized and decentralized, whose existence is widely recognized in the literature. The point is not that power only exists in the presence of hierarchy, but that the nature of possible interactions between state institutions and the private sector will depend both on the degree of territorialization of the latter, and on its mix of hierarchies, networks, and markets. What follows is just a suggestion of some of these configurations.

It can be seen from the top half of the Figure 1.2 that for productive activities with high levels of international flow, there is evidence of both territorialization and deterritorialization: high levels of flow do not necessarily imply

	Territorialization of Production System			
	High		Low	
International Flows in Production System	Hierarchies	Networks/Markets	Hierarchies	Networks/Markets
Low — Networks/Markets	Intrafirm trade, where firm has territorial core	Territorial core systems (especially if high tech industries)	Global supply oligopolists with world division of labor (manufacturing and services)	Isolated captive suppliers to global oligopolists
Low — Hierarchies	Global supply, oligopolists, strategic alliances	Industrial districts	Global supply oligopolists with few intermediates	Isolated specialist suppliers or contractors
High — Networks/Markets	Local champion firm(s) with little internationalization		Global supply oligopolists via franchising and brand name strategies	
High — Hierarchies		Locally serving production to specialized tastes		Local commerce in basic services

FIGURE 1.2. Hierarchies, territories, and flows.

deterritorialization. Moreover, there is a great diversity of institutional arrangements that govern both the primary dynamic of the production system—that is, investment and technology or knowledge dynamics—and their international flows. For example, many global high technology firms manage extensive intrafirm supply chains, but at the same time are inserted into one or multiple territorialized production systems where network or market relations are dominant. Their power is more absolute with respect to their international flows than it is with respect to the other firms in their industry's territorial core. In certain other industries, global supply oligopolists are highly territorialized and interact locally via hierarchical relations, but then must compete on international markets with other such oligopolists, or they may enter into strategic alliances for marketing or for certain input supplies. The paradox is that while such oligopolists may exercise considerable power over those local suppliers and partners, to the extent that they depend on locationally specific relational assets, the state in those places may have considerable potential bargaining power with them.

Industrial districts are frequently characterized by strongly territorialized network relations in the core region, and by networked markets internationally: the institutional construction of international market networks is critical to them. We know from experience that states can play strong roles in supporting the competitiveness of such districts (Bianchi, 1993).

The classical image of globalization is, of course, the global supply oligopolist which has a low level of territorialization and a high degree of hierarchical control over its inputs and markets on a worldwide basis (Hymer, 1976). This can be found as a tendency in certain manufacturing industries and certain consumer service sectors. Isolated captive suppliers to these global oligopolists also have little territorialization and are subject to the strong hierarchy of these firms in their sales relations (semiconductor assemblers in Asia or clothing firms in developing countries are examples). Global supply oligopolists with few intermediate inputs and little territorialization are likely to have little intrafirm trade and foreign direct investment, and instead are likely to internationalize through global sales via markets (Dunning & Norman, 1985). Isolated specialized suppliers or contractors, on the other hand, will interact internationally via networks or markets, as they do with any local suppliers, the terms of their interactions being set by the degree and nature of substitutability of their products by the purchasing firm.

At the bottom half of Figure 1.2 may be found cases of low levels of international flows, and various combinations of both their territorialization and governance. Local champion firms, for example, who dominate a market, will tend to govern their territorialized production systems in a hierarchical way and have little internationalization, whereas other forms of localized production, for localized and specialized tastes, will probably correspond to the nonhierarchical system of traditional local firms. They may export some of their excess output, but this will likely be a small proportion of the total. Global supply oligopolists may not always have high levels of international flow— oligopoly can be attained through control of intellectual and intangible assets, such as knowledge and brand names, but carried out through franchising; hence, low flows but hierarchically governed.

These are just a few of the many possible examples of complex configurations of institutions with respect to territoriality and flows in production systems. Small firms can enjoy relatively great market, network, or even hierarchical power, sometimes territorially and other times globally, while big firms can be subject to the forces of other big firms or markets they do not control, whether in their territorialized or their global interactions.

Policy Problems

Many dilemmas of aligning the governance of production systems with efficient and desirable patterns of territorialization and flow present themselves in the contemporary world economy; these are problems faced not only by territorially bound state institutions, but also by the private sector.

The most obvious set of problems concerns the cases on the right-hand side of Figure 1.2. Where territorialization is low or declining, that is, where locational substitution becomes more and more possible, there is often a "race to the bottom" for territorially defined states, a competitive bidding war for economic activity that transfers increasing amounts of benefit from the public to the private sector. In the United States, this has been the history of postwar routinized manufacturing, encouraged not only by federalism but by the passage of the Taft–Hartley Act in the late 1940s, which enabled states to make a big institutional concession to employers by making unionization locally more difficult. More recently, such bidding has become a frenetic activity of states and localities. There is evidence that similar trends are developing within the European Union, and we can certainly see them on broader international scales within North America and Southeast Asia. Moreover, this dynamic is no longer limited to manufacturing. Corporate headquarters learned that they could demand concessions for remaining in New York, for example, in the 1970s, and since then have generalized these demands. Hollywood film productions now expect to be wooed to locations in order to shoot films there. Corporations involved in relatively routine administration, such as in the consumer service or retailing sectors, now also regularly demand concessions or threaten to move.

The demands of firms are usually less naked when territorialization of activity is strongly in evidence, precisely because they have less locational substitutability, at least in the short run. Nonetheless, the fact that certain kinds of productive activity are territorialized does not mean that they are wedded permanently to one single territory. Global companies do not just scan the globe for single locations; some interact with multiple territorial economies. To some extent, these territorial economies cannot be substituted by these firms, since the latter are inserted into them in order to tap into the technological or knowledge specificities of such territorial systems. The firm thus has a division of labor that involves multiple territories, which are functionally specialized. For the moment global technology firms remain mostly attached to territorialized resources in their nations of origin (Dosi et al., 1990). But one could imagine that for inputs that are not on the cutting edge of technological knowledge, such firms could over time develop parallel territories, in the same way that mass production firms in the 1970s developed parallel assembly or fabrication plants. Developmental states in Southeast Asia, for example, have had some successes in helping their firms to build up territory-specific relational assets, and these assets are now enjoyed by firms from elsewhere. The paradox here is that states participate in a kind of *competitive* endogenous development, which creates new forms of capital mobility even in the territorialized parts of the contemporary economy. Much more needs to be theorized and investigated about these dynamics.

A second concern is that when major hierarchical global business organizations interact with different territorial economies, there may be little harmony between the rules by which such firms intend to relate to these environments and the relational assets already built up in those places. Problems of this nature, however, only become apparent over time, and when they do, multinational firms may not have the commitment required to work them out. And they are problems that are not generally technical, but relational in nature and thus slow to resolve. We might think here of subcontracting policies established by such firms, which are designed to economize for them, but at the medium-term price of the region's subcontracting tissue as a whole (Dunning, 1992).

A third concern has to do with territorialized developmental spillovers. Territorial economies exist as such in part because there are knowledge or technology spillovers between activities, and the overall developmental trajectory of a territorial economy is strongly influenced by such spillovers. But firms whose primary loyalties lie outside a particular territorial economy— firms with a highly elaborate interterritorial division of labor—may inadvertently make decisions that undercut development of such spillovers, precisely by territorially dividing what might better (from the territory's and technology's standpoint) be kept in proximity (Markusen, 1994). This is not a problem unique to "foreign" firms, but to all multilocational, multiterritorial firms.

A corollary is that when territorialized technological spillovers exist, there is an efficiency rationale for targeted technology policies, even from the standpoint of global output. Where such spillovers do not exist or are not territorialized, however, technology policies tend merely to transfer technological performance from one place to another, usually at a high overall cost (Grossman & Helpman, 1991). The problem is to construct such policies where the community of subjects of the policy is not only local but global; many firms operate in many different institutional and conventional contexts. Such policies therefore have to be "translated" for them, and these global business organizations must find ways to reconcile operations in very different contexts.

The management literature has raised many issues with respect to the operation of global supply and marketing systems. They have not conceptualized some of these problems, however, as the need for global business organizations to operate in multiple territorial economies, that is, to interact with specific relational assets in different places. This is clearly a major challenge to firms that require such assets, whether for innovation or for sales, but whose mission is precisely to rationalize the allocation of resources on a global basis.

REMAPPING THE GLOBAL ECONOMY: A RESEARCH AGENDA

Much of what has been laid out in this chapter is just a prelude to a research agenda that would enable us to understand globalization systematically in terms of this tension between territorialization and deterritorialization. We need research that constructs, activity by activity, a new map of the global economy as a consequence of these forces. This map would be not only geographical, but inherently organizational, for the territorialized complexes of activity we are likely to find will be combinations of filières or parts of filières, not whole input–output chains or industries. That is, territorialized systems will not organizationally correspond to commodity chains as a whole. Beyond merely mapping activity systems in these terms, we would need to separate them into two components: those that principally serve the local population system, and those that export to other areas. This was the task identified by export-base regional economics in the Keynesian tradition. Only those activities that are territorialized and oriented toward markets well beyond their boundaries can be considered "strongly" territorialized, in the sense that their geographical pattern is not determined principally by the geographical distribution of demand, but also by the geography of production interdependencies. We would also need to measure the composition of investment in territorialized systems, breaking it into local, national, and international components, in order to see the extent to which investment is endogenous, and to test the hypothesis that high-quality foreign direct investments are attracted overwhelmingly to the territorial cores of recipient industries. Finally, the mapping of the global economy should be carried out over long time periods in order to assess the magnitude and direction in degree and content of territorialization and deterritorialization.

NOTES

1. There are measurement problems having to do with the level of statistical aggregation. If it is not fine enough, it mixes together products that are so different as to belong to different commodity chains.

2. This is not a new idea, either. The earliest use of global supply oligopolies apparently comes from Vernon (1974). Some of the most recent work on this topic has been carried out by C. Sauviat in Paris, at the Institut de Recherches Économiques et Sociales (IRES). See also, most recently, Lafay and Herzog (1989) and Mathis, Mazier, and Rivaud-Danset (1988).

3. The forerunners of many successful world market-serving industrial districts in Italy today were locally serving industrial complexes, with specific assets related to particular local tastes. This comes out in the historical work on Tuscany carried out by Becattini's group (Becattini, 1978) (the Prato histories) and on Emilia-Romagna, by Cappecchi (1990). An overall review of European cases is found in Sabel and Zeitlin (1985). Some of the Italian literature is reviewed in Storper and Salais (1997).

REFERENCES

Albert, M. (1992). *Capitalismes contre capitalismes*. Paris: Seuil.

Amendola, G., Guerrieri, P., & Padoan, P. C. (1992). International patterns of technological accumulation and trade. *Journal of International and Comparative Economics, 1*, 173–197.

Amin, A., & Thrift, N. (1993). Globalization, institutional thickness and local prospects. *Révue d'Économie Régionale et Urbaine, 3*, 405–430.

Asanuma, B. (1989). Manufacturer–supplier relationships in Japan and the concept of relation-specific skill. *Journal of the Japanese and International Economies, 3*, 1–30.

Ballance, R. H. (1987). *International industry and business: Structural change, industrial policy and industry strategies*. London: Allen & Unwin.

Becattini, G. (1978). The development of light industry in Tuscany: An interpretation. *Economic Notes, 7*(2–3), 107–123.

Becattini, G. (1987). *Mercato e forze locali*. Bologna: Il Mulino.

Berle, A., & Means, G. (1933). *The modern corporation and private property*. New York: Macmillan.

Bianchi, P. (1993). The promotion of small-firm clusters and industrial districts: European policy perspectives. *Journal of Industry Studies, 1*(1), 16–29.

Cappecchi, V. (1990). L' industrializzazione a Bologna nel novecento: Dal secondo dopoguerra ad oggi. *Storia Illustrata di Bologna, 9*, 161–180.

Carnoy, M. (1993). Multinationals in a changing world economy: Whither the nation-state? In M. Carnoy, M. Castells, S. Cohen, & F. H. Cardoso (Eds.), *The new global economy in the information age* (pp. 45–96). University Park: Pennsylvania State University Press.

Castells, M. (1989). *The informational city*. Oxford: Blackwell.

Caves, R. (1982). *Multinational enterprise and economic analysis*. Cambridge: Cambridge University Press.

Colombo, M. G., Mariotti, S., & Mutinelli, M. (1991). *The internationalisation of the Italian economy* (Monitor–Fast Dossier Prospective No. 2). Brussels: European Union, DGXIII-H-3.

Dicken, P. (1988). *Global shift: Industrial change in a turbulent world*. London: Chapman.

Dosi, G., Pavitt, K., & Soete, L. (1990). *The economics of technical change and international trade*. London: Harvester.

Dunning, J. (1992). The global economy, domestic governance strategies and transnational corporations: interactions and policy implications. *Transnational Corporations, 1*(3), 7–45.

Dunning, J., & Norman, G. (1985). Intra industry production as a form of international economic involvement: An exploratory analysis. In A. Erdilek (Ed.), *Multination-*

als as mutual invaders: Intra industry foreign direct investment (pp. 9–28). New York: St. Martin's Press.

Ernst, D. (1990). *Global competition, new information technologies and international technology diffusion—implications for industrial latecomers.* Paris: OECD Development Centre.

Frobel, F., Heinrichs, J., & Kreye, O. (1980). *The new international division of labor.* New York: Cambridge University Press.

Gilpin, R. (1975). *US power and the multinational corporation: The political economy of foreign direct investment.* New York: Basic Books.

Glickman, N., & Woodward, D. (1989). *The new competitors: How foreign investors are changing the US economy.* New York: Basic Books.

Grossman, G., & Helpman, E. (1991), *Innovation and growth in the global economy.* Cambridge, MA: MIT Press.

Harrison, B. (1994). *Lean and mean: The resurrection of corporate power in an age of flexibility.* New York: Basic Books.

Hymer, S. (1976). *The international operations of national firms: A study of direct foreign investment.* Cambridge, MA: MIT Press.

Julius, de Anne. (1990). *Global companies and public policy.* London: Pinter.

Krugman, P. (1990). *Rethinking international trade.* Cambridge, MA: MIT Press.

Lafay, G., & Herzog, C. (1989). *Commerce international: La fin des avantages acquis.* Paris: Economica.

Lecoq, B. (1993). Proximité et rationalité économique. *Révue d'Économie Régionale et Urbaine, 3,* 469–487.

Lung, Y., & Mair, A. (1993). Innovation institutionnelle, apprentissage organisationnel, et contrainte de proximités: Les enseignements de la géographie du juste-à-temps. *Révue d'Économie Régionale et Urbaine, 3,* 387–404.

Markusen, A. (1994, 28–29 April). *The intersection of regional and industrial policies: Evidence from four countries.* Paper presented at the World Bank's Annual Conference on Development Economics, Washington, DC.

Mathis, J., Mazier, J., & Rivaud-Danset, D. (1988). *La compétitivité industrielle.* Paris: Dunod.

Morales, R. (1994). *Flexible production: Restructuring of the international automobile industry.* Cambridge: Polity Press.

Mowery, D. (Ed.). (1988). *International collaborative ventures in US manufacturing.* Cambridge: Ballinger.

Mytelka, L. (Ed.). (1992). *Strategic partnerships: States, firms, and international competition.* Rutherford, NJ: Farleigh Dickinson University Press.

Noponen, H., Graham, J., & Markusen, A. R. (Eds.). (1993). *Trading industries, trading regions.* New York: Guilford Press.

OECD (Organization for Economic Cooperation and Development). (1991). *Background report concluding the technology/economy programme.* Paris: OECD (OECD Counsil of Ministers [91]14).

Ohmae, K. (1990). *The borderless world.* London: Collins.

Ostry, S. (1990). *Governments and corporations in a shrinking world: Trade and innovation policies in the United States, Europe and Japan.* New York: Council on Foreign Relations Press.

Papconstantinou, G. (1993 7–9 October). *Globalisation, technology, and employment: Characteristics, trends, and policy issues.* Paper presented at the Conference on Technology, Innovation Policy and Employment, Helsinki. Paris: OECD.

Patel, P., & Pavitt, K. (1989). *Do large firms control the world's technology?* (Discussion Paper). Brighton: Science Policy Research Unit.

Patel, P., & Pavitt, K. (1991). Large firms in the production of the world's technology: An important case of non-globalization. *Journal of International Business Studies, First Quarter*, 1–21.

Rallet, A. (1993). Choix de proximité et processus d'innovation technologique. *Révue d'Économie Régionale et Urbaine, 3*, 365–386.

Reich, R. (1990, January–February). Who is Us? *Harvard Business Review*, pp. 53–64.

Sabel, C., & Zeitlin, J. (1985). Historical alternatives to mass production: Politics, markets, and technology in nineteenth century industrialization. *Past and Present, 108*, 133–176.

Saxenian, A. (1994). *Regional advantage: Culture and competition in Silicon Valley and Route 128*. Cambridge, MA: Harvard University Press.

Storper, M. (1995). The resurgence of regional economies, ten years later: The region as a nexus of untraded interdependencies. *European Urban and Regional Studies, 2*(3), 191–221.

Storper, M., & Salais, R. (1997). *Worlds of production: The action frameworks of the economy*. Cambridge, MA: Harvard University Press.

Tyson, L. (1991, Winter). They are not us. *The American Prospect*, pp. 49–54.

Veltz, P. (1993). *L'économie des villes, entre la montée du global et le retour du local*. Paris: LATTS/CERTES, École Nationale des Ponts et Chaussées.

Vernon, R. (1974). The location of economic activity. In J. Dunning (Ed.), *Economic analysis and the multinational enterprise* (pp. 89–114). London: George Allen & Unwin.

Vernon, R., & Spar, D. L. (1989). *Beyond globalism: Remaking American foreign economic policy*. New York: Free Press.

CHAPTER 2

Between the Global and the Local

THE SPATIAL LIMITS TO PRODUCTIVE CAPITAL

Meric S. Gertler

INTRODUCTION

It has been taken as an article of faith for some time that we live in a global economy. Frequent pronouncements by academics, journalists, and policy analysts alike continue to assert publicly the "fact" of globalization with numbing frequency. Bound up in such pronouncements are the ideas that globalization both is a reality and, as a process, constitutes an inevitable and inexorable development. Accepting this "global vision," governments throughout the industrialized (and industrializing) world have taken steps to get their respective houses "in order" by bringing their economic and social policies "in line" with those of the world's dominant economic forces. In the face of threats, implicit or explicit, from the owners of potentially mobile capital that they will redeploy their investments elsewhere, nation-states and subnational governments have increasingly been induced to ensure that their corporate tax rates are not too high, their social programs too rich, their economic policies too restrictive, or their environmental legislation too punitive.

At the center of this increasingly pervasive line of argumentation is the presumption that capital is indeed highly mobile, although the validity of such claims is rarely investigated. They are most often inspired by observations emanating from the world of global finance, and extrapolated, without a second thought, to cover *all* forms of capital. While it is beyond the scope of this chapter to examine critically the recent discourse on global finance, it is worth noting briefly two important points here. First, the appropriateness of transposing a financial metaphor to the analysis of other forms of capital should, upon a few moments' reflection, strike one as a problematic venture. Second, when one scrutinizes this conception by examining more carefully the empirical realities of contemporary financial markets, one finds that even many of these "received truths" are not fully borne out (see Clark & O'Connor, Chapter 4, this volume; Gertler, in press-a; Helleiner, 1996; and Leyshon & Thrift, 1992; for further discussion of this theme).

My intent in this chapter is to subject to critical scrutiny the prevailing wisdom within economic geography (and the other social sciences) concerning globalization and the mobility of capital, by focusing on the case of "fixed" capital in the form of advanced industrial machinery. In the subsequent sections of this chapter, I briefly review the commonly held views on the subject of globalization and capital mobility. This is followed by an examination of the recent literature on the production and adoption of advanced manufacturing technologies which, among other things, raises serious doubts about the basic premises underlying the globalization thesis. In a subsequent section, I summarize the key findings of my own empirical research, conducted since 1991, on the development, production, and use of advanced manufacturing technologies. This research, based on case studies of Canadian firms, as well as German firms active in Canada, the United States, and elsewhere, indicates that there are indeed significant and enduring obstacles to the free and unproblematic flow of industrial capital between countries, despite the many advances in telecommunications and transportation technologies in the second half of the 20th century. The chapter concludes by considering the implications of this work for our theoretical and empirical understanding of globalization and contemporary capitalist dynamics, as well as for current policy debates. In doing so, I also consider some critical implications for those who subscribe to the common alternative to the globalization thesis—namely, the localization thesis.

FIVE TOUCHSTONES OF GLOBALIZATION

Since the efflorescence of international political economy and radical economic geography beginning in the 1970s (Bluestone & Harrison, 1982; Massey, 1978; Fröbel, Heinrichs, & Kreye, 1980; Massey & Meegan, 1982), the narrative on globalization has typically been based on five closely interrelated assertions. Most basic to this thesis is the argument that capital has become significantly more mobile than in previous times. The motivation for this mobility is as old as capitalism itself—namely, the search for expanded profits, achieved through either the pursuit of higher rates of return on investment available elsewhere, or the spatial expansion of markets (Harvey, 1982). This has produced a greatly expanded spatial range for financial and fixed capital, both within and between individual countries.

Second, innovations in the organizational form of the capitalist firm have facilitated this process of interregionalization and internationalization (Chandler, 1962; Dicken, 1992a; Storper & Walker, 1989). The multiregional firm arose with the innovation of the M-form (multidivisional) organization, whose multilocational structure was based either on a functional specialization (producing a spatial division of labor) or the creation of geographically organized divisions for the pursuit of spatially distinct markets. This same organizational form came to be replicated at an international scale, producing an international division of labor.

Third, this geographical expansion of capital has been enabled and facilitated by the development of space-transcending technologies of transportation and communication. These have served not only to extend the spatial reach of capital, but also to speed up the rate of circulation. Hence, the process of realization of surplus value, achieved through the transformation of capital from its financial (circulating) to its fixed (constant) form and back again, has been dramatically speeded up, particularly in the last quarter of the 20th century (Harvey, 1989). This has produced, according to Harvey, a process of time–space compression or, to put it another way, the annihilation of space through time.

Fourth, the expanding internationalization of production systems, in which multi- and transnational corporations have constructed elaborate divisions of labor, has a paradoxical character to it. On the one hand, this internationalization has been driven by the prior existence of geographical differentiation (Walker, 1978), as capital seeks to exploit local differences in the supply and price of inputs, the quality of the production environment, markets, historically grounded social relations, and politics. On the other hand, the very process of internationalization itself acts as a leveling or homogenizing force. This spatial homogenization is achieved in a number of ways. However, most relevant to the discussion in this chapter is the interregional and international transfer of production technologies. The principal vector in this diffusion process is the multilocational firm, which is seen as bringing its production methods (both "hard" technologies and "soft" forms of work organization) to new locations through the establishment of branch plants. This process ultimately serves to erode the distinctive character of regions and nation-states.

Fifth, and contributing to this process of erosion, is the contention that, with their heightened powers of mobility and expanded spatial reach, global corporations are able to undermine the regulatory purchase of individual regions and nation-states. As noted in the introduction to this chapter, a process of locational blackmail (or "whipsaw" effect) pits one government against another, as nation-states prostrate themselves before these powerful private actors for the sake of attracting much-coveted employment and investment. The result is what has been referred to in common parlance as "the race to the bottom," as nation-states liberalize economic policies and scale back their social welfare effort. Furthermore, the multinational basis of these firms' organization allows them to shelter profits from taxation and continue to pursue socially or environmentally regressive practices in more permissive jurisdictions. Hence, so the argument goes, the nation-state has become "hollowed out" and obsolete as a regulatory force (Jessop, 1993). Taking its place are, alternatively, either supranational institutions such as the European Union, the North American Free Trade Agreement (NAFTA) and the General Agreement on Tariffs and Trade (GATT) or subnational states (Cooke, 1993; Ohmae, 1993).

Having now reviewed the fundamentals of the globalization thesis, I wish to argue that it contains at least two key flaws. First, its characterization of the ease with which production technologies diffuse from one location (or country) to another is simplistic in the extreme. Second, the assertion that the nation-state is no longer functional as a regulatory influence in the economy is, at best, premature and, at worst, ill founded. In the remainder of this chapter, I aim to demonstrate that fixed capital (particularly the more advanced forms of industrial machinery and production systems) is, in fact, much more strongly rooted in place, and considerably less "portable" than has been implied in the literature on globalization. However, in making this case, I rely less on arguments of spatial fixity in the weak sense (that is, stemming from the simple physical immutability and immobility of fixed capital; see Richardson, 1973), and more on the nature of the social context surrounding the development, production, and use of such technologies. Furthermore, in arguing the case that machinery production and use are firmly rooted in place, I do not wish to privilege strictly *local* institutions, culture, and regulatory forces to the exclusion of other scales of influence. Hence, I will also argue that, while such local and regional forces do indeed have a role to play, they assert their influence within an institutional and regulatory space that is still defined and circumscribed largely by the nation-state.

In the following section, I review the recent literature on the production and use of advanced manufacturing technologies, laying the theoretical foundations for the arguments just advanced. In the section following this, I provide some empirical substantiation of these claims, by reviewing the findings of my own recent study of the problems and difficulties arising in the long-distance transfer of advanced process technologies.

MACHINE PRODUCTION AND USE: THE SPATIAL CONSTRUCTION OF CAPITAL

The relationship between machine users and producers has been the subject of theoretical and empirical work, first by economic historians (Rosenberg, 1976, 1982a, 1982b), and more recently by students of industrial organization and technological change (Lundvall, 1985, 1988; Porter, 1990). This literature has suggested that "closeness" between the users and producers of advanced machinery is important for a variety of reasons, laid out briefly as follows.[1]

The argument begins with the general insight that capital goods differ in important ways from the other kinds of inputs purchased by manufacturers. Their function, when combined with labor, is of obvious central importance to the success of a manufacturer's operations. Furthermore, they tend to be long-lived (by definition), and hence the firm will have to rely on such assets for a long period of time. Add to this the consideration that frequently—particularly when the firm is purchasing recently developed, leading-edge technology—a large degree of uncertainty surrounds the future use qualities of these capital goods. Because of these properties, the wise firm will prefer not to purchase advanced capital goods through a simple, discrete, "off-the-shelf" market transaction, but will be more inclined toward engaging in a transaction in which there is extensive interaction and communication with the producer of the machinery—what Lundvall (1988) refers to as an *organized market* transaction.

This mode of purchase is said to offer a number of benefits to prospective machinery users and producers alike, so that complex production equipment is not only more likely to be *adopted* successfully when there is close and frequent interaction between producer and user, but is also likely to be *produced* more successfully as well. This interactive mode of technology acquisition allows users to gather as much information as possible about the properties of the machinery under consideration, and to gauge the reliability and trustworthiness of the producer. Furthermore, it may allow the user to make its technological needs more readily and clearly known to the producer, creating the conditions under which the effective customization of the product to the user's particular application is more likely. To allow customization to occur, however, users must reveal to an outside firm certain proprietary details concerning their products or production processes, and they may be unwilling to do so unless they have been able to build up a sufficient level of trust with machine producers, resulting from a process of close interaction over an extended period of time.

At the same time, this kind of interaction is also important and beneficial for machinery producers. Research on capital goods innovation has demonstrated that prospective users—particularly demanding and technologically sophisticated customers—represent a vital source of creative stimulus for producers, who are more likely to develop important innovations when compelled to meet their customers' needs (Lotz, 1990; Teubal, Yinnon, & Zuscovitch, 1991; von Hippel, 1988). These innovations not only help producers themselves compete more successfully, but also bring obvious benefits to the users who are fortunate enough to enjoy a close relationship with producers, characterized by this process of mutual learning.

Other benefits for users may arise in later stages of the machinery acqui-

sition process. The interactive perspective sees the acquisition process as one
of considerable duration, consisting of three distinct stages. Beyond the benefits arising in the preinstallation phase of design and production just described, the second phase (installation and start-up) is likely to proceed more
smoothly when producer and user enjoy a close relationship, since (1) the producer will more likely be on hand to assist in the installation and break-in of
the new machine or system, providing useful on-site training and assistance,
and (2) the start-up process is likely to be easier (i.e., requiring less adjustment
and adaptive behavior by the user) when the machine or system has been
properly tailored to meet the user's precise specifications. Similarly, the third
phase—of "normal" operation of the new machinery postinstallation—will
also be more successful (i.e., with fewer breakdowns and coming closer to
meeting users' expectations concerning productivity, quality, and functional
capabilities) if a close relationship with the producer facilitates the adjustments and debugging that are bound to be necessary as the experience of regular, full-time operation brings to light inevitable operational problems.

Clearly, these kinds of benefits, and the closeness between users and producers that is said to facilitate the technology acquisition process, are most
likely to be important when the technology involved is expensive, complex,
and rapidly developing. Presumably, when the process technology in question
is less expensive, or represents more mature or familiar technology, an interactive mode of acquisition will be less important. For cheaper, well-established,
or "tried-and-true" technologies, an off-the-shelf mode of purchase should
suffice.

A number of significant implications flow directly from this approach.
First, these arguments suggest that a large measure of the success enjoyed by
manufacturers in the celebrated industrial districts of Europe and Asia may
be attributed to the close and constructive relationship they are able to maintain with nearby producers of innovative machinery. Second, viewed from this
perspective, it should come as no surprise that machinery producers in these
same regions have become highly successful competitors in international markets in recent years. Third, and perhaps most significantly for the present
analysis, this literature implies (although it does not make this point explicitly;
see Gertler, 1993) that many of the problems arising when manufacturers in
the mature industrial regions of the United States, the United Kingdom, or
Canada attempt to implement new, technologically advanced process technologies stem from the fact that the most important sources of innovation and
production of these technologies are themselves now a considerable distance
from would-be users in these countries—notably in countries like Japan, Germany, and Italy.[2] As a result, users in North America might be expected to
have growing difficulties in developing and maintaining a "close" relationship
with advanced machine producers. Forced instead to acquire complex technologies using a mode of acquisition more akin to an off-the-shelf transac-

tion, such users are much more likely to encounter the kinds of problems documented by previous case studies.[3]

Despite the compelling nature of these arguments, certain countervailing forces might conceivably intervene to reduce or qualify the attenuating influence of simple physical distance between user and producer. Three, in particular, might be considered. First, it is possible that, despite a preference for direct, face-to-face interaction, users and producers might be able to communicate quite adequately for many purposes by using modern and increasingly effective telecommunications media (especially the fax machine and telephone). For those functions that cannot be provided over the wire, rapid air transportation of technical personnel (or key parts) might serve as a reasonable compromise when users are far away from their advanced machinery producers. In addition, it should be recognized that many European and Asian producers contract with distributors, sales representatives, and maintenance firms in North America to perform on-site service functions on their behalf. Such intermediaries might be able to compensate for the long distances intervening between North American users and overseas producers.

Second, as noted in the previous section, large, multilocational (including multinational) firms have often been portrayed as highly effective, distance-transcending agents of (intrafirm) technology transfer.[4] According to this view, production regions that might be viewed as peripheral (with respect to the location of leading machinery producers) may nevertheless be characterized by the presence of advanced machinery that is being used effectively by the local branch plant operations of such large, multisite firms. The close organizational ties between such branch plants and their foreign head offices (or sister plants elsewhere) may allow the branch operations to benefit from the considerable expertise and experience that exist within the larger firm. If the parent firm has developed its own advanced process technologies, at its head office or other production or research sites, these are likely to be transferred quite effectively to branch plant users at distant sites. According to this argument, then, what matters more than simple physical distance is what one might call *organizational distance.*[5]

Third, one might consider another interpretation of the difficulties encountered by the users of advanced machinery in "peripheral" locations, one that has more to do with differences in cultures, institutions, and the legacy of past industrial practices than with the problems caused by the intervening distance between users and producers. For example, at the most basic level, Lundvall (1988) argues the importance of a common culture and language shared by users and producers, to facilitate the transmission of highly encoded information concerning users' needs and the capabilities and proper operation of complex and rapidly changing process technologies (see also Storper, 1992). Others point to differences in training cultures and attitudes toward technology as the crucial issues (Gordon, 1989; Stowsky, 1987), implicating the distinct set of practices and attitudes peculiar to Anglo-American firms as the true source of technology implementation problems.

According to this latter view, the typical American, British, or Canadian firm regards technology as something *embodied* entirely within the physical properties and design of machinery and production systems themselves. This stands in sharp contrast to the approach more typical of European and Japanese manufacturers, who not only appreciate the necessity of social interaction for effective machine production and use, but also regard the technological capabilities of a production process as being produced through the interaction between machines and skilled workers who have built up a wealth of knowledge and problem-solving abilities through many years of training and learning by doing.

The consequence of this difference is that Anglo-American users of advanced machinery, who espouse what Block (1990, p. 152) refers to in the macroeconomic context as an "intravenous" model of capital investment, typically expect to be able to extract the full capabilities of such technologies merely by installing them correctly and "flipping the switch."[6] In contrast to their European and Asian counterparts, and in response to the national institutions shaping relations in their labor market, they tend systematically to undervalue the importance of training and to maintain shorter term relations with their workers (instead making extensive use of external labor markets). A further consequence is that an advanced machine designed and built, for example, in Germany will be considerably more difficult to implement successfully in a North American user plant than in a German user plant because the "culture" of industrial practices peculiar to Germany (high skill levels of factory workers, stability of the employment relation, cooperative decision making on the shopfloor, strong emphasis on training) has been incorporated into the design of the German-made machine. According to this view, then, physical distance is really just a proxy for *cultural distance*, where "culture" refers to a set of dominant workplace practices shaped in large part by legislative definitions of employment relations and the nature of the (public and private) industrial training system. Furthermore, as we shall outline in a later section of this chapter, this approach would seem to ascribe continuing importance to nation-states and the economic and social institutions created by them (see Gertler, 1992).[7]

THE PRODUCTION AND CONSUMPTION OF ADVANCED MACHINERY

Over the past several years, I have been pursuing a research project whose findings challenge the blithe notions associated with the globalization thesis about the easy transferability of process technologies and work practices from one country to another. My analysis also highlights the continuing influence of national-level regulation on intrafirm changes and interfirm relations (see Gertler, 1993, 1995a, 1995b, 1996, in press-b). This study began by focusing on a simple question: why have manufacturing firms in Ontario (as well as in other mature industrial regions such as the U.S. Midwest and the British Midlands) apparently had such a dismal experience when they have tried to implement various forms of advanced manufacturing technologies (AMTs)? The technologies in question include the range of different types of computerized, programmable automation for fabrication, testing, and handling. They also include various information technologies to link up different functions within single plants and between buyers and suppliers. Hence, the object of study here has been the very technologies said to be at the heart of the transition to the "new" competition, the "new social economy," or post-Fordist flexible specialization.

As noted earlier, the leading world sites for the development and production of these technologies are to be found in Germany, Japan, Italy, and other European and Asian countries. According to the globalization thesis, the process of international diffusion of such technologies from these sites should be straightforward and unproblematic, enabled as it is by the use of telecommunications technologies, and propelled by the spread of multinational enterprise throughout the adopting regions and nations. However, the experiences documented amongst technology users in four Ontario industries indicate strongly that this has not been the case.[8] In total, over 400 technology implementation experiences were documented through the use of a postal survey. Follow-up interviews were conducted with 30 user firms in the original sample, which was constructed to include user firms of all sizes, and both Canadian and foreign-owned plants (see Gertler, 1995a, for details on sampling). In subsequent phases of the study, some 15 interviews were conducted with machinery producers in one of the major supplier countries (Germany). In addition, a further 22 interviews were conducted with Canadian-based producers as well as sales representatives or distributors for foreign-manufactured advanced machinery and systems.

A brief overview of my findings will bear out the argument I have just made. First, distance from the producer of AMTs does seem to matter to AMT users (Gertler, 1995a): a healthy majority indicated that it was important and preferable to have their major advanced machinery producers located at least within the same country (the same region—within 75 kilometers—was even better), and over three-quarters reported a strong preference that their machinery producers be located in Canada or the United States. Second, going beyond mere preferences, the evidence suggested that Ontario users were significantly more likely to experience difficulty in operating their advanced production systems or machines when the sources of such technologies were farther away—particularly in Europe or Asia. Third, domestically owned user plants, especially small or medium-sized and independently owned operations, appeared to be most profoundly affected by such intervening distances. This resulted in part from their relative inability to marshall in-house resources (such as skilled technical personnel) to help them overcome the negative consequences of spatial separation from suppliers.

For larger user plants, and those belonging to multilocational (including multinational) organizations, the effects of relative isolation from advanced machinery producers, while less extreme *were, nevertheless, still quite significant.* This was so despite the fact that larger plants were more likely to receive more attentive and higher quality service from distant machinery producers than were smaller users (because the former made larger purchases at any one time, were more likely to make further purchases in the future, and were regarded by the producers as prestigious or "showcase" customers). Larger users were also better able to afford the cost of achieving more extensive face-to-face interaction with their (frequently distant) machinery producers *before installation*—that is, during the design and development phase. Smaller user firms often found this practice to be prohibitively expensive and tried to make do with less effective, non-face-to-face forms of contact. Larger users were also better able to pay for *postinstallation* service visits directly from the machinery producer (both planned and unplanned) once the warranty period had passed. Furthermore, they were considerably more likely to receive personal site visits from producers (from *any* location) during both the installation and operation phases of technology acquisition. It is also true that user plants belonging to multilocational organizations were considerably more likely to enjoy some of the benefits of a "close" relationship with a distant producer of their advanced machinery, either because another branch of the same firm had forged a close, collaborative link with the producer, or because another branch of the same firm actually produced the equipment in question. However, despite all these advantages, these larger plants still experienced significant problems in implementation.

The reasons why physical distance between users and producers seemed to matter, as far as the users were concerned, ranged from simple, straightforward issues to much more fundamental problems. In the former category were such considerations as time-zone differences and the difficulties associated with moving personnel, machinery, and parts across international borders. Physical separation also usually meant some degree of cultural difference between user and producer, beginning with attributes such as language. However, even when both user and producer shared the same language, it was apparent that the inherent difficulty of communicating complex technical information and concepts without direct, face-to-face interaction remained a source of continuing problems in the technology implementation process, despite the extensive use of telephone, fax, and modem.

Users frequently attributed more fundamental implementation problems to "cultural" differences between them and their foreign machinery suppliers, but it became clear upon further investigation that these problems should ultimately be understood in a different way. While it is indeed tempting to conclude from these findings that *local* culture, institutions, and processes of regulation might exert the most important determining force in the relationship between AMT users and producers, there is good reason to be as skeptical of such claims as one should be of the globalization thesis. A further discussion of my findings bears out this argument.

Users of advanced technologies produced in northern European countries frequently complained of the "rigidity" or "inflexibility" of their machinery suppliers, who seemed (to users) to be unwilling to take their specific technical requirements seriously. When operational difficulties arose (as they frequently did, even for large, sophisticated users) these foreign producers were seen as being quick to blame the "inferior" technical skills of user-plant managers and shopfloor workers, since European users of similar technologies had, according to the producers, experienced few difficulties. Underlying what was recognized as a "cultural" trait was really a set of differences in approaches to technology, training practices, and degrees of empowerment of shopfloor employees in the workplace. These differences were themselves reproduced and reinforced by divergences in the regulatory frameworks that structured the social and economic context within which machinery production and use each take place.

Hence, to take one common example, the set of industrial norms and practices prevalent in Germany stood in stark contrast to those prevailing in most North American workplaces. In particular, North American industrial workers were generally less extensively educated, received less training on the job, had less say in decisions affecting both the day-to-day plant operations and longer term, more strategic decisions of the firm (including technology adoption decisions), and experienced less employment stability and more interfirm mobility than did their German counterparts. Hence, when these same North American workers were asked to implement a new process technology developed for application in a very different setting (involving highly educated, intensively trained, and relatively empowered workers, enjoying long, stable associations with the same employer), problems of implementation were bound to arise (for further elaboration, see Gertler, 1995b). In this sense, then, the physical distance separating the northern European producer from the North American user is also a proxy for distance in terms of the *labor market norms and workplace practices that vary across nation-states and, to some extent, subnational regulatory jurisdictions.*

This situation turns out to be a problem not just for the users in Ontario, but for at least some of the producers abroad as well (Gertler, 1996). A subsequent phase of the study involving interviews with German producers of AMTs supplying customers in the Ontario sample of users revealed that, at least initially, these German engineering firms were just as oblivious to the existence and source of this problem as were their customers. In particular, they failed to appreciate the extent to which the nationally shaped workplace regulations, norms, and practices prevailing in the plants of their German users (and indeed their own plants) had come to be reflected in the very design and operation of their advanced machinery and machine tools.

When their initial forays into the North American market led them to realize that U.S. and Canadian workers and workplaces were "different" from their own, the German machinery producers were still likely to see the sources of such differences as a matter of "culture" or "mentality." While it is possible that such differences did arise originally from cultural traits, it is clear that such differences are enshrined and reproduced by the national regulatory frameworks prevailing in each country. Confirmation of this argument is found in the fact that the machinery-producing firms selected as cases for the study were located in several different regions of Germany, including Baden–Württemberg, North Rhine–Westphalia, Hesse, and Lower Saxony, with similar difficulties in user–producer relations and implementation experiences arising with firms in each of these regions. Furthermore, interviews with the producers revealed that, while they frequently sold their machinery to customers in many different regions of Germany, the kinds of implementation difficulties that did arise within their domestic users' plants (generally minor in comparison to what was found in Ontario) had little to do with "cultural" differences, and more to do with the logistical difficulties arising when frequent site visits are not quite as easy to sustain.

These findings are strongly consistent with recent scholarship on the continuing significance of national regulatory features in shaping the trajectory of contemporary change in the workplace.[9] Lane (1987, 1988, 1989, 1991), a sociologist, has assembled an impressive body of empirical research on the role played by national institutional characteristics in producing distinctive workplace outcomes in manufacturing and financial service enterprises. Drawing on evidence from detailed firm-level studies in Germany, Britain, and France during the 1980s, she has produced important insights into the particular aspects of industrial organization and national regulation that facilitate or frustrate the implementation of new manufacturing practices, such as policies to promote enhanced labor flexibility. In British plants, these efforts were impeded by the general nature of the prevailing employment relation, characterized by high turnover rates in the labor force, rigid job demarcations, poor communication and little trust between workers and managers, and very little devolution of power to shopfloor workers. The impact of these traits was exacerbated by British management's almost universal focus on cost control as its principal objective (in contrast to German management's primary interest in competing on the basis of quality). The most obvious result of such differences (themselves largely produced—and reproduced—by national systems of labor market and industrial relations regulation) was a consistent tendency by British manufacturers to pursue *numerical* forms of labor flexibility, while German firms were far more effective in capitalizing on the benefits of *functional* flexibility in their workforce.

More recently, Christopherson (1993) has shown how the US macroregulatory framework differs significantly from that of Germany's (or Japan's), and argues that this holds significant consequences for the form of "post-Fordist" production systems now emerging in each of these countries. In particular, she notes how the national regulation of capital markets, industrial relations, and labor markets creates a set of incentives for American firms to privilege short-term considerations over long-term ones and to create instability in employment relations characterized by high rates of employee turnover, leading to serious disincentives for employers to invest in employee training. Furthermore, in a system with highly decentralized wage determination and reliance on external labor markets, firms compete directly (and ultimately, unproductively) with one another over wage rates and skilled labor. Despite some notable differences, the Canadian and British systems of macroregulation in capital markets, labor markets, and labor relations systems are (due to their common heritage) considerably closer to the American situation than to that of Germany or Japan.

Returning again to the study of advanced machinery implementation in Ontario, it was also apparent that the conditions Ontario AMT users face are not very conducive to the formation of collaborative relations with manufacturers of advanced equipment for the purpose of jointly designing customized, advanced process technologies, suggesting that these users are being deprived of the full range of benefits arising from such intensive, cooperative interaction. In particular, two findings stand out (Gertler, in press-b). First, it seems to be very difficult to establish and maintain such a close, collaborative relationship with technology producers that are long distances away. For all the reasons stated earlier, overseas relationships of this sort have proven to be especially difficult to strike up and keep going, and they are less likely to lead to beneficial outcomes for either party. Second, within the Ontario user plants, and in great contrast to the "who is 'us'?" arguments of Reich (1991) or Ohmae's (1993) "borderless world," *foreign-owned firms are far more likely to establish collaborative relations with AMT producers in their home country*, and far less likely to seek out local suppliers for the same technology, even when such local sources exist and can be shown to be internationally competitive. Similarly, Canadian-owned firms are far more likely to engage in collaborative relations with, and to source their customized equipment from, local AMT producers. In short, *the nationality of ownership still matters*!

CONCLUSIONS: THE SPATIAL LIMITS TO
PRODUCTIVE CAPITAL

Three principal conclusions flow from the research described in this chapter. First, this work suggests that there are real and continuing limits to the effectiveness with which capital, in the form of leading-edge machinery and production systems, can move over long distances. Despite advances in the technologies of transportation and communication, long intervening distances between machinery producers and users do apparently make it considerably more difficult for these two parties to achieve and sustain the kind of close relationship necessary to support the effective deployment of such production technologies. Indeed, one might argue that the increasingly complicated nature of computer-controlled production technologies offsets many of the space-transcending benefits of innovations in communication and transportation systems.

Second, notwithstanding the implementation problems arising solely from the logistical difficulties of sustaining a user–producer relationship over long distances when the product being "used" is highly complex in nature, the truly fundamental difficulties arising in this relationship flow less from logistical limitations or physical realities and more from the fact that *technology is socially constructed*. The chief failures in technology implementation stem from the fact that users are trying to utilize these advanced machines and systems without due regard for the social relations surrounding their use. Because the social relations in the typical Ontario (or American, or British) workplace are so different from those prevailing in machinery production sites such as Baden–Württemberg (or North Rhine–Westphalia), the failure by users to acknowledge these differences in social context means that they have ignored many considerations crucial to the successful implementation of newly acquired machinery and equipment. In this sense, the continuing geographical specificity of these social relations imposes significant limits on the "portability" of advanced production technologies from one location to another.

Third, while logistical difficulties are indeed likely to increase with the simple physical distance between user and producer, divergences in social relations are more likely to arise when producer and user are in different nation-states. Furthermore, these divergences (and the resulting implementation problems) are likely to be especially pronounced when the two nation-states have developed along distinct historical paths. Because Canada's predominantly Anglo-American systems of industrial finance, labor market institutions, and labor relations (with their emphasis on decentralized individualism and short-term time horizons) are *so* different from the German system (corporatist, consensus-based, with long time horizons and stable employment relations), major problems are bound to arise when users in Ontario (or, for that matter, British Columbia) implement German-built machinery. By the same token, one should expect far fewer (and less fundamental) problems when the two nation-states involved share a common (in this case, Anglo-American) heritage and regulatory system, despite long intervening distances.[10]

At least for the economic relations studied in this chapter, the principal scale of regulation remains the nation-state, as it is at this level that the major institutions shaping workplace practices (including technology use) persist. While I do not wish to deny the importance of subnational institutions and "culture" in shaping the social character of production systems, it seems that the continuing role of nation-state institutions has been very much underplayed within the recent literature on innovation networks, industrial districts, flexible specialization, and related issues. On the other hand, the relatively recent literature on national systems of innovation (Nelson, 1993) makes the case that the policies of national governments have been (and continue to be) critical in shaping the possibilities for generating new products, processes, and modes of workplace organization, while precluding others.

It seems clear from this discussion that one of the pressing concerns for economic geography, as well as for the related disciplines of political science, economic sociology, and industrial economics, will be to sort out more systematically the relationship between different spatial scales of regulation—in particular, the relative importance of subnational, nation-state, and international institutional forces in regulating economic processes. What is also clear is that explanations based on only a single scale of analysis (whether it be local, national, or global) will likely prove inadequate. There is thus much work still to be done.

ACKNOWLEDGMENTS

I wish to acknowledge gratefully the Social Sciences and Humanities Research Council of Canada for its support of the work discussed in this chapter. I would also like to thank Kevin Cox for his helpful comments on an earlier draft of this chapter. Portions of this chapter originally appeared in Gertler (1995a). Copyright 1995 by Clark University. Adapted by permission.

NOTES

1. The discussion here draws particularly from Lundvall's (1985, 1988) work, since he provides the most systematic treatment of these issues. For a more thorough review of this work, see Gertler (1993). Throughout the balance of this chapter, the term "user" refers to a firm that has acquired and implemented some form of advanced manufacturing technology in its production process. The term "producer" denotes the manufacturer of advanced equipment, machinery, or integrated systems.

2. While the United States has been an important source of advanced manufacturing machinery since the middle of the 19th century, the industry there entered a period of long-term decline starting in the postwar period of the 20th century (Graham, 1993). By 1987, the U.S. industry produced roughly one-third of all machinery shipped by OECD producers, while Japan, Germany, and Italy constituted over one-half between them. In terms of OECD machinery exports, the U.S. industry's share declined steadily through most of the 1970s and 1980s, so that by 1987 it was responsible for less than 15% of total exports by OECD countries. Meanwhile, Germany's share held fairly steady at around 23–25%, and Japan's share rose consistently from under 5% (in 1975) to about 12% (Science Council of Canada, 1992).

3. For an early recognition of the off-the-shelf manner in which most independent Canadian firms are forced to acquire their production technology, as well as some of the inadequacies of this mode of technology acquisition, see Britton and Gilmour (1978, Chap. 6).

4. See the excellent review of this literature provided in Dicken (1992, Chap. 12).

5. Lundvall (1988) offers similar speculations about the possible importance of spatial–organizational structure, but provides no concrete evidence to support or refute his observations.

6. Block (1990) resorts to such terminology to reflect the idea that, in the prevailing Anglo-American approach, the primary determinant of changes in industrial output is simply the *volume* of capital and the flow of investment. Such a view ignores the crucial impact of the *social relations* within which production itself occurs. Block's objective is thus to show how such relations exert considerable influence over the volume and quality of output, productivity, and success with utilizing advanced workplace technologies.

7. Storper (1992) provides a useful discussion of the importance of shared culture within territorial production complexes characterized by what he calls product-based technological learning. He also discusses the concept of user–producer interaction in more general terms, noting its relevance not only to users and producers of capital goods, but also to users and producers of components, materials, information, and final products. However, Storper's conception of "culture" depends far less on state regulatory frameworks than does the approach espoused here, emphasizing instead the traditions, norms, and practices developing from close interaction between spatially clustered economic agents over an extended period of time. For a critical assessment of the treatment of culture in the "new industrial geography," see Gertler (1995b).

8. The sectors are transportation equipment (automotive/aerospace), electrical and electronic products, fabricated metal products, and plastic and rubber products.

9. The classic sources are Maurice, Sellier, and Silvestre (1986); Sorge and Warner (1986); and Streeck (1991). For a recent critical review and synthesis of this literature, see Smith and Meiksins (1995).

10. This observation goes some way toward explaining Canadian manufacturers' traditional and long-standing reliance on, first, British and, then, American production technologies (Innis, 1933). It also suggests that the decline of the U.K. and U.S. machinery industries was as much a problem for the Canadian economy as it was for those two countries.

REFERENCES

Block, F. (1990). *Postindustrial possibilities: A critique of economic discourse.* Berkeley: University of California Press.

Bluestone, B., & Harrison, B. (1982). *The deindustrialization of America.* New York: Basic Books.

Britton, J., & Gilmour, J. (1978). *The weakest link: A technological perspective on Canadian industrial development* (Background Study 43). Ottawa: Science Council of Canada.

Chandler, A. (1962). *Strategy and structure.* Cambridge, MA: MIT Press.

Christopherson, S. (1993). Market rules and territorial outcomes: The case of the United States. *International Journal of Urban and Regional Research, 17,* 274–288.

Cooke, P. (1993). Globalization of economic organization and the emergence of regional interstate partnerships. In C. H. Williams (Ed.), *The political geography of the New World Order* (pp. 46–58). London: Belhaven Press.

Dicken, P. (1992). *Global shift: The internationalization of economic activity* (2nd ed.). New York: Guilford Press.

Fröbel, F., Heinrichs, J., & Kreye, O. (1980). *The new international division of labor.* Cambridge: Cambridge University Press.

Gertler, M. S. (1992). Flexibility revisited: Districts, nation-states, and the forces of production. *Transactions of the Institute of British Geographers, New Series, 17,* 259–78.

Gertler, M. S. (1993). Implementing advanced manufacturing technologies in mature industrial regions: Towards a social model of technology production. *Regional Studies, 27,* 665–80.

Gertler, M. S. (1995a). "Being there": Proximity, organization, and culture in the development and adoption of advanced manufacturing technologies. *Economic Geography, 71,* 1–26.

Gertler, M. S. (1995b, 3–6 January). *Manufacturing culture: The spatial construction of capital.* Paper presented in the special sessions on "Society, Economy, Place" at the annual meeting of the Institute of British Geographers, Newcastle upon Tyne.

Gertler, M. S. (1996). Worlds apart: The changing market geography of the German machinery industry. *Small Business Economics, 8,* 87–106.

Gertler, M. S. (in press-a). Globality and locality: The future of "geography" and the nation-state. In P. Rimmer (Ed.), *Pacific Rim development: Integration and globalization in the Asia–Pacific economy.* Sydney, Australia: Allen and Unwin.

Gertler, M. S. (in press-b). In search of the new social economy: Collaborative relations between users and producers of advanced manufacturing technologies, *Environment and Planning A, 28.*

Gordon, R. (1989, 3–5 September). *Beyond entrepreneurialism and hierarchy: The changing social and spatial organization of innovation.* Paper presented at the Third International Workshop on Innovation, Technological Change and Spatial Impacts, Selwyn College, Cambridge, U.K.

Graham, J. (1993). Firm and state strategy in a multipolar world: The changing geography of machine tool production and trade. In H. Noponen, J. Graham, & A. R. Markusen (Eds.), *Trading industries, trading regions: International trade, American industry, and regional economic development* (pp. 140–174) New York: Guilford Press.

Harvey, D. (1982). *The limits to capital.* Oxford: Blackwell.

Harvey, D. (1989). *The condition of postmodernity.* Oxford: Blackwell.

Helleiner, E. (1996). Post-globalization: Is the financial liberalization trend likely to be reversed? In R. Boyer & D. Drache (Eds.), *States against markets: the limits of globalization* (pp. 193–210). London: Routledge.

Innis, H. (1933). *Problems of staple production in Canada.* Toronto: Ryerson Press.

Jessop, B. (1993). Towards a Schumpeterian workfare state? Preliminary remarks on post-Fordist political economy. *Studies in Political Economy, 40,* 7–39.

Lane, C. (1987). Capitalism or culture? A comparative analysis of the position in the labour process and labour market of lower white-collar workers in the financial services sector of Britain and the Federal Republic of Germany. *Work, Employment and Society, 1,* 57–83.

Lane, C. (1988). Industrial change in Europe: The pursuit of flexible specialization in Britain and West Germany. *Work, Employment and Society, 2,* 141–68.

Lane, C. (1989). *Management and labour in Europe: The industrial enterprise in Germany, Britain and France.* Aldershot, England: Edward Elgar.

Lane, C. (1991). Industrial reorganization in Europe: Patterns of convergence and divergence in Germany, France and Britain. *Work, Employment and Society, 5,* 515–539.

Leyshon, A., & Thrift, N. (1992). Liberalisation and consolidation: The Single European Market and the remaking of European financial capital. *Environment and Planning A, 24,* 49–81.

Lotz, P. (1990, 28 February–2 March). User–producer interaction in the Danish medical equipment industry. In T. M. Khalil & B. Bayraktar (Eds.), *Management of technology II* (Proceedings of the Second International Conference on Management of Technology, pp. 129–39). Norcross, GA: Industrial Engineering and Management Press.

Lundvall, B–A. (1985). *Product innovation and user–producer interaction* (Industrial Development Research Series, Report No. 31). Aalborg, Denmark: Aalborg University Press.

Lundvall, B–A. (1988). Innovation as an interactive process: From user–producer interaction to the national system of innovation. In G. Dosi, C. Freeman, R. Nelson, G. Silverberg, & L. Soete (Eds.), *Technical change and economic theory* (pp. 349–369). London: Frances Pinter.

Massey, D. (1978). Regionalism: Some current issues. *Capital and Class, 6,* 106–125.

Massey, D., & Meegan, R. (1982). *The anatomy of job loss.* London: Methuen.

Maurice, M., Sellier, F., & Silvestre, J.-J. (1986). *The social foundations of industrial power: A comparison of France and Germany.* Cambridge, MA: MIT Press.

Nelson, R. (Ed.). (1993). *National innovation systems: A comparative analysis.* New York: Oxford University Press.

Ohmae, K. (1993). The rise of the region-state. *Foreign Affairs, 72,* 78–87.

Porter, M. (1990). The competitive advantage of nations. *Harvard Business Review, 68,* 73–93.

Reich, R. (1991). *The work of nations.* New York: Knopf.

Richardson, H. (1973). *Regional growth theory.* London: Macmillan.

Rosenberg, N. (1976). *Perspectives on technology.* Cambridge: Cambridge University Press.

Rosenberg, N. (1982a). *Inside the black box.* Cambridge: Cambridge University Press.

Rosenberg, N. (1982b). Technological progress and economic growth. In N. Rosenberg

& L. Jörberg (Eds.), *Technical change, employment and investment* (pp. 7–27). Lund, Sweden: Department of Economic History, University of Lund.

Science Council of Canada, (1992). *The Canadian machinery sector* (Sectoral Technology Strategy Series, No. 10). Ottawa: Supply and Services Canada.

Smith, C., & Meiksins, P. (1995). System, society and dominance effects in cross-national organisational analysis. *Work, Employment and Society, 9,* 241–267.

Sorge, A., & Warner, M. (1986). *Comparative factory organisation: An Anglo-German comparison of manufacturing, management and manpower.* Aldershot, UK: Gower.

Storper, M. (1992). The limits to globalization: Technology districts and international trade. *Economic Geography, 68,* 60–93.

Storper, M., & Walker, R. (1989). *The capitalist imperative.* Oxford: Basil Blackwell.

Stowsky, J. (1987). *The weakest link: Semiconductor production equipment, linkages, and the limits to international trade.* (Working Paper 27, Berkeley Roundtable on the International Economy). Berkeley: University of California at Berkeley.

Streeck, W. (1991). On the institutional conditions of diversified quality production. In E. Matzner & W. Streeck (Eds.), *Beyond Keynesianism: The socio-economics of production and full employment* (pp. 21–61). Aldershot, England: Edward Elgar.

Teubal, M., Yinnon, T., & Zuscovitch, E. (1991). Networks and market creation. *Research Policy, 20,* 381–392.

von Hippel, E. (1988). *The sources of innovation.* New York: Oxford University Press.

Walker, R. (1978). Two sources of uneven development under advanced capitalism: Spatial differentiation and capital mobility. *Review of Radical Political Economics, 10,* 28–37.

CHAPTER 3

Strategic Localization

THE MYTH OF THE POSTNATIONAL ENTERPRISE

Andrew Mair

True internationalization of production is not at all the path these [Japanese automobile] firms identify as being in their best interest.
—SINCLAIR (1983, p. 68)

By the end of the 1990s, the following conditions are very likely: . . . The emergence of new forms of "postnational" or "global" corporations able to operate successfully in a world of regions. . . . Japanese firms will play the pioneering role in creating new global forms of organization.
—WOMACK (1989, p. 6)

Eventually this will mature into a "global supply network" which will flexibly respond to the diversification of demand and the unique circumstances of each country. This approach transcends the conventional concept of manufacturing in a particular area simply because demand exists. But the most vital aspect is that each Honda organization will lay its roots deep into each locale to become a responsible corporate citizen.
—HONDA MOTOR CO. (1992, p. 14)

FROM MULTINATIONAL ENTERPRISE TO POSTNATIONAL ENTERPRISE?

In the literature on international business, companies with substantial operations in more than one country have traditionally been labeled "multinational," "multidomestic," or "transnational" enterprises (see Dunning, 1993; Pitelis & Sugden, 1991). Notwithstanding debates and differences of viewpoint, it is fair to say that these concepts describe a common family of international companies. Such companies follow a model that has three core characteristics. First, they replicate their home country activities abroad ("top to bottom," including manufacture, sales, research and development [R&D]; the word "clone" is sometimes used). Second, international management structures are based on devolution of control to separate subsidiaries. Third, separate subsidiaries are linked largely in terms of (1) financial flows depending on investment needs and variable market conditions across subsidiaries, (2) circulation of home-based managers ascending their career ladder, and (3) trickle-down of processes (including capital equipment deemed out-of-date in the home country), of products, and of power from the corporate center. In sum, while clearly operating internationally, the companies described by this literature remain focused primarily on their home country (in terms of output and sales turnover, locus of most innovation, and leadership mentality) with relatively weak strategic and operational linkages among countries.

During the late 1980s, a new and very different vocabulary emerged. The emphasis appeared to be diametrically opposed to that of the traditional literature. The language shifted from multinational or transnational to *postnational, stateless,* or *global* enterprises, said to be operating in a "borderless world," terms meant to capture the practices and structures of a new generation of international companies that no longer focused primarily on their home country and that had developed very strong international links to the point where their internationalism outweighed their roots in any one country (Borus, 1990; Ohmae, 1989; Womack, 1989).

The new literature reflected a perceived fundamental shift in the nature of international companies, or at least the "best" of these companies; the idea being that the market would force competitors to follow suit, a process which the authors of the new arguments were "aiding." Indeed, much of the literature was deliberately and strikingly normative in approach, appearing to describe an inevitable "ideal type" or future state. As the phenomenon first emerged, it became common to portray the phenomenon of "global production" with maps of continents or the world showing crisscross flows of components and finished products (Bloomfield, 1981; Sinclair, 1983) or lists of the multiple countries from which a product's components originated (Bluestone & Harrison, 1982). Now there were theories of emergent postnational enterprises, which were developing and implementing strategy at the global scale. The new breed of international company was simultaneously taking into account both its markets in various countries (demand side), and the facilities it had available throughout the world to meet market needs (supply side). Replacing self-sufficient separate subsidiaries producing for local markets, global integration was proceeding a very significant step further, toward the *global integration of the production process.* Indeed, suggestive evidence was offered by flows of finished products and components manufactured in various countries across the globe as the corporate headquarters marshaled its resources to meet market needs at the global scale.

The business, management, and semipopular literature describing the new phenomenon was quickly picked up in the nonbusiness social science disciplines: geography, planning, political science, and sociology. It appeared to confirm and indeed explain (from "respectable" sources that remained largely unquestioned) the experience of many local communities in the traditional industrial areas of the advanced economies during the late 1970s and early 1980s that "capital was fleeing the community" in a process of "deindustrialization." A significant literature developed to examine the local, regional, and national consequences of the "global corporation," the "globalization of capital," and the "new era of globalization" more generally (for instance, Bluestone & Harrison, 1982; Thrift, 1986; Trachte & Ross, 1985). This set of interrelated concepts also emerged into the wider political debate in both North America and Europe.

But were the proponents of the postnational enterprise concept swinging the pendulum too far when they emphasized the global aspect of international business? Was too much stress being placed on the apparently widening divide between the international company and its country of origin? Some were quick to respond in the affirmative, reiterating the importance of the national roots and the national socioeconomic supportive structures of the so-called global corporation (Porter, 1990), or restating the significance of national differences among markets that would effectively sabotage globalization strategies (Douglas & Wind, 1987).

Experience suggests that debates like this all too easily degenerate into an exercise in "talking past each other" (Kuhn, 1962) as proponents of "globalization" and proponents of "national difference" and "local context" state their respective cases with increasing fervor. How can the debate be moved forward? The fact that each side appears able to generate convincing evidence to support its case is suggestive. Perhaps each view is in fact correct, yet each side is only partially so: a case of both/and rather than either/or. This chapter attempts to steer a way through the globalization–localization polarity by following just this path. The methodology chosen is a sufficiently detailed investigation of one of the most advanced of the so-called postnational enterprises. The focus of attention here is on the automobile industry activities of the Japanese manufacturer Honda Motor Co. (see also Mair, 1994a, 1994b, 1996, in press). Precisely how is Honda organized at the global level?

The chapter is organized as follows. In the first part, the case for Honda as a candidate "postnational" enterprise is examined. In the second part, a series of dimensions of "localization"—the term the Japanese use for the establishment of company operations outside Japan—is examined as a window onto the issue at hand. These dimensions—product designs, research and development, manufacturing, components sourcing, production methods, employee hiring, terms of employment, and strategic decision making—give an overview of localization at Honda's automobile production operations in North America and Europe. The polar views that represent the new model (postnational) and the old model (multinational) of international business, respectively labeled *globalize* and *localize*, as they apply to that dimension, are introduced before the dimension is analyzed in depth for the Honda case. In the third part, these dimensions are brought together to draw out the lines of coherence and consistency that are the hallmarks of the overall process of *strategic localization*, the concept which, it is argued, best captures Honda's approach to organizing its international operations. A coda at the end of the chapter serves as a reminder of how important politics remains in this era of apparent globalization.

To anticipate the chapter's conclusions, it is argued that, if Honda's internationalization is to be properly understood, the strategic dimension of localization cannot be ignored. On the one hand, to describe the company as postnational, global, stateless, even, is inappropriate. On the other hand, neither has Honda's localization followed the path of the traditional model of multinational enterprise, which implies the establishment of operationally independent subsidiaries. Instead, each dimension of localization at Honda has "borne in mind" globalization, from which it cannot be separated; the form of each determining the form of the other. Not only does each localization decision frequently draw upon corporate resources from other world regions, but the localization processes are themselves designed so that they can contribute in turn to Honda operations in other world regions: hence the term *strategic localization*. The resultant *global local corporation* (Mair, 1994b) is extraordinarily sensitive to local variations in markets and production conditions and yet is also able to function as an integrated unit at the global scale.

HONDA AS A CANDIDATE FOR POSTNATIONAL ENTERPRISE STATUS

The new Japanese international manufacturers have played a significant role in the development of the postnational enterprise concept. Yet as recently as the early 1980s, this would have seemed unlikely to many observers. Reflecting the newfound competitiveness of Japanese manufacturers in international markets, their organizations, operations management, corporate strategies, human resource management, and product development processes had become the focus of considerable attention in the West. Yet only 15 years ago it was being claimed—both in Japan and in the West—that, notwithstanding the undeniable successes of Japanese manufacturers in export markets, Japanese companies and Japanese management techniques would never function successfully outside Japan, for reasons to do with the uniqueness of the Japanese business environment and the inward-looking character of Japanese management culture. In short, there would be no successful Japanese multinationals, as the citation from Sinclair (1983) at the start of the chapter suggests (see also Dohse, Jürgens, & Malsch, 1985; Ohno, 1983; Trevor, 1983). A mere decade later, Japanese manufacturing companies, particularly in the automobile and consumer electronics sectors, were being held up as examples of successful global companies, not merely catching up with their Western counterparts but now providing lessons for Western companies in the realm of global organizational forms, as suggested by the citation from Womack (1989) at the start of the chapter. But was this argument based on solid analysis of international Japanese companies?

Honda, with its rapid penetration of the North American market from its Japanese export base in the 1970s, followed by its massive investments in North American productive capacity and its complex relationship to the European carmaker Rover during the 1980s, has been one of the pioneer "postnational enterprises," breaking the mold of the traditional multinational enterprise both in reality and in perception. Honda is certainly a promising candidate for postnational status, and figures prominently as an outstanding case in discussions of the new model (Borus, 1990; Ohmae, 1989; Womack, 1989). In the well-known report of the results of the International Motor Vehicle Program (Womack, Jones, & Roos, 1990), Honda replaces Toyota as the paradigm company when "lean production" becomes internationalized. It is not difficult to see why. Honda's founders Soichiro Honda and Takeo Fujisawa enshrined an "international viewpoint" in the company from the 1950s onwards, in a country where the wider business culture remained almost uniformly isolationist. By 1958, Soichiro Honda was racing motorcycles internationally to test his engine technologies against the world's best. During the 1960s, he followed suit with Formula II and Formula I racing cars. By the early 1960s, Honda had become the first Japanese automotive industry company to successfully establish a U.S. distribution network (for motorcycles), and was the first Japanese manufacturer to establish a manufacturing plant in the West (the Aalst, Belgium, motorcycle plant opened in 1963). During the 1970s, Honda automobiles (the Civic and Accord models) enjoyed remarkable success in the North American market with their low pollution, high-fuel economy engines, attractive designs, and high build quality. The company deliberately sacrificed market share in Japan by ceasing production of its most popular model (minicar), assigning production capacity to meet booming demand in North America. By 1979, Honda had built the first Japanese automotive industry manufacturing plant in North America (in Ohio, for motorcycles), followed in 1982 by the first Japanese automobile assembly plant in the West (adjacent to the motorcycle plant).

Honda became one of the first Japanese companies to break with the policy by which assignment of a Japanese manager to an overseas operation spelled the end of career progress; indeed, the best young Honda managers were deliberately sent to work in North America. Already by the late 1980s one in five top managers in Japan had spent lengthy periods working in North America, and they formed a powerful voice in strategic decision making. Meanwhile, Honda had begun to establish itself in Europe through a complex working relationship with the British company Rover Group (formerly British Leyland).

By the early 1990s, Honda was by far the most internationalized of all the world's major automobile producers in terms of sales (three-quarters outside its home region); was second only to Ford, which had long-standing European investments, in the proportion of manufacturing outside its home region (two-fifths); and was now expanding production operations in a fourth world region, Southeast Asia. In 1995, Honda became the first Japanese automobile producer to manufacture more than half its automobiles outside Japan. Including its automobile, motorcycle, and power products (such as lawn mowers or outboard motors for boats) divisions, Honda owned 83 factories in 40 countries worldwide. So dependent had Honda been on its North American markets for 20 years that analysts had openly speculated that the company would move its headquarters from Tokyo to the United States as part of a corporate reorganization.

Honda appeared to be a clear-cut case of a company breaking its ties with its home base, both in terms of sales and in terms of production activity, and considering the whole world as its theater of operations.

DIMENSIONS OF STRATEGIC LOCALIZATION

This part of the chapter examines the full logic behind Honda's overall global structure by analyzing a series of dimensions of strategic localization. Our interest lies not so much in Honda's development trajectory over time as in bringing to the surface the underlying organizational logic that permits Honda to function effectively at the global scale. To introduce each dimension, the globalize–localize polarity (respectively representing the postnational and multinational perspectives) as it applies to that dimension is briefly discussed to set the context for examination of the Honda case.

Localization of Product Designs

The globalization model is represented by the "world product" (for instance, "world car") concept, in which the same product is produced for sale in all (or at least many) world markets. The alternative localization model involves production of distinct products for each market, which was the traditional pattern in the automobile industry.

During the 1970s and 1980s, Japanese carmakers, with Honda playing a lead role, were responsible for a significant shift toward the "world car" that their Western counterparts had been unable, or had not sought, to achieve. The superiority, in terms of high quality and low cost, of vehicles produced by the Japanese allowed them to override a number of previous differences between world regions; hence, smaller cars were introduced in North America, and there was partial globalization of front-wheel drive technologies. Until the late 1980s, Honda adopted a strategy of conquering the "most difficult" markets first with its automobiles, in the expectation that the others would follow "naturally." The company's view was that the United States was the most difficult market in the world until the mid-1980s, and that Japan took its place in the late 1980s. Within Europe, Germany was seen as the most difficult market. However, this strategy, a derivative of the product life-cycle approach and a close relative of the globalization model, began to cause Honda problems. The company's internationalization had started with automobiles designed initially for Japan which found favor in North America (the Civic in 1972, then the Accord in 1976). During the 1980s, these cars were redesigned in steps with a clear focus on American market tastes, but as the Accord model became increasingly "Americanized" (much larger, and with gentle design lines), it began to fail in the Japanese market, where it was perceived as uninspiring in the late 1980s bubble economy atmosphere of euphoric consumption.

Moreover, there were persistent problems in Europe. Honda found it difficult to understand the subtle differences among European markets. Further, unlike their American counterparts, European competitors already offered high-quality, small, and low-cost products (though not always in the same vehicle). These factors, combined with lower levels of Honda sales in Europe (11% of global turnover in the early 1990s) than in Japan (33%) or North America (43%), meant that fewer resources were devoted to product development for Europe. Even by the mid-1990s, Honda's European distribution network, unlike North America, did not receive any Honda cars fully designed for Europe. Instead, basic Japanese products, of similar general size—though slotting uncomfortably in-between the actual size classes used by European producers—were tinkered with, the first being a partially successful 1992 Accord for Europe, the second being a more successful 1995 Civic for Europe (although this tinkering produced improvements over the Ballade and Concerto models that Honda had asked Rover Group to manufacture for it during the 1980s). Neither did the automobiles Honda had designed for North America fare much better In Europe. The 1989 Accord was not very successful in Europe as a near-luxury car because its midsized 2.0l engine proved underpowered in Germany. Thus while Japan was an important enough market to warrant its own products, and so was North America, Europe was not, and was accordingly fed an ill-fitting range of products designed and produced in Japan for Japanese and American markets or designed and produced in the United States for North American markets (niche derivatives of the Accord and Civic).

How did Honda attempt to overcome these problems without undermining either global economies of scale or capacity to meet local requirements?

From the late 1980s, the central theme of Honda's global car design process became the "total car concept." The 1993 Accord model exemplifies the outcome. In North America, the Accord had now evolved into a large car with a clearly American-oriented design. A smaller automobile was developed for Japan (Accord Inspire/Ascot). This product became the basis for the "spin-off" Accord for Europe (seats, suspensions, and some other features altered for European tastes). The same automobile, with a more radical body redesign, became the Rover 600, produced and marketed by Rover Group. At the same time, four-door, coupe, and estate/station wagon variants of the American Accord were exported to Europe for sale alongside the smaller (family resemblance, but still different) Europeanized Accords, and to Japan as a new and different model. Moreover, Honda's first minivan recreational vehicle was designed as a direct spin-off from the American Accord, sharing 50% of its components.

In this process of creating a *global local car*, similarity of design lines and sharing of components is taken as far as possible. The various aspects of car design are logically separated into (schematically) (1) the power train technology (engine and transmission), (2) the engine compartment (which gives the dimensions of the front of the vehicle), (3) the basic design shape (aesthetics), (4) detailed aspects of seats, suspensions (handling characteristics), and (5) other expensive components like instrument panels and exterior lights. The engineering and managerial puzzle, and hence the key issue in the strategic localization of product design, is to put all the pieces together for each local market in a way that both meets requirements in that market—fitting the demands of localization—and also permits economies of scale and acceptance of the product in other Honda regions—fitting the demands of globalization. Thus an American model, for instance, may share power train technology and expensive components with a Japanese model but differ in all other respects. Or a European model may share everything but handling-characteristic components and minor style cues with a Japanese model.

Localization of Research and Development Operations

The globalization model implies that research and development operations are centralized at company headquarters and their outcomes dispensed to dispersed subsidiaries, either through a trickle-down/product life-cycle approach or more evenly across international subsidiaries. By contrast, the localization model implies separate research and development facilities that feed their results directly into each separate subsidiary.

The key to understanding the global organization of research and development that has emerged at Honda also lies in identifying the different processes that constitute the activity. These include (1) basic research (on the properties of materials or combustion technologies, for instance); (2) design and development of core product technologies (principally engines, together with other mechanical components ranging from transmissions to suspension systems to antilock brakes); (3) product design (aesthetic aspects; vehicle handling characteristics, including components that vary according to different road systems and customer expectations; in general, customer interface aspects); (4) marketing research (including pricing, advertising, development of car "concepts"); and (5) the new product development and introduction process (the interface of research and development with production engineering, manufacturing, employee training, product distribution networks, and so on). Further complexity arises from the fact that in Honda's case, each of these processes also involves a number of suppliers of components and materials.

Starting in the early 1970s, when all these processes were still concentrated in Japan, Honda steadily developed a global research and development organization. A California design studio, located near Los Angeles, opened in 1973. This facility was involved in market research and in design of products targeted at the North American market, beginning with activities such as customer feedback on the Civic and Accord models and specific input into the first CRX sporty version of the Civic (1983), designed in Japan for the North American market with significant advice from California.

By the later 1980s, the California facility was playing a lead role in the design of niche variants of models for the North American market that would be manufactured in North America too: the Accord coupe (1987), Accord Aerodeck (1990), and Civic coupe (1992). The work was now undertaken in liaison with a product development and introduction team located at an Ohio research and development facility (adjacent to the manufacturing plants), which had opened in the mid-1980s. By the early 1990s, Ohio research and development operations included both liaison with manufacturing to get the niche variants into production (including prototype manufacture), and liaison with suppliers located in North America (domestic and Japanese transplants) to design components, including establishment of centralized facilities for suppliers to utilize. By 1995, the California and Ohio research and development operations were collaborating to design and develop a complete new automobile model (a further step beyond responsibility for niche variants of existing models), albeit one that, like most Honda products, would share perhaps 50% of its components with another model.

Honda has therefore progressively built up the various aspects of a research and development capability in North America. This is a rich and deep process, and has included sending American employees to work in Japan for long periods (several months to several years) to learn Honda methods; the research and development processes that are being localized in North America are being established thoroughly so that they will be able to operate independently of Japan. However, this does not yet include all the different aspects of research and development identified above.

In Europe, Honda established a branch of Honda Research and Development at a small office near Frankfurt in 1985. Parallel to its choice of a California location in North America, Honda selected what it considered to be the most challenging market in the region. By the late 1980s, this facility was purchasing what Honda perceived to be the best cars in Europe—all German plus Peugeot—and test-driving them in European conditions. By the early 1990s, the facility had progressed to participate in product development programs run by Honda Research and Development in Japan to design particular components for Europe's Accord and Civic versions: suspension, seating, and the first design to incorporate the possibility of fixing a tow-bar to the Accord for the caravans of Northern European consumers, for instance.

Honda Research and Development established an office in the United Kingdom, too, for liaison with Rover while that company made Honda vehicles. There was close collaboration with Rover over links with suppliers. Development engineers also oversaw launch of the Accord for Europe in 1992, and continued to teach supplier companies Honda methods. However, in the mid-1990s, European research and development activities remained coordinated and controlled from Japan, whereas in North America the degree of independent interaction between California and Ohio was already marked. This organizational form paralleled the strategy for localization of product design previously discussed, with separate models for North America but European models derived from Japanese vehicles.

Are there some research and development processes that will not be localized in North America or Europe according to the current trajectory? Thus far, the most basic research and development of Honda technologies has remained concentrated in Japan. The products of these processes tend to be invariant across the world and thus there does not appear to be a particular benfit from localization. Moreover, the processes themselves are very costly to replicate. Yet when Honda withdrew from Formula I automobile racing in the early 1990s, it simultaneously entered the American equivalent, Indy Car racing, and assigned a new American team to work on the engine technology, suggesting that by the early 21st century deeper technology-oriented capabilities, too, might be expanded in North America.

Localization of Manufacturing

The globalization model suggests that manufacturing is to be centrally coordinated so that production sites across the world are utilized according to supply-side characteristics—low factor costs, presence of particular production skills, economies of scale—in a manner unrelated to the markets in which they are located: a world car or "global sourcing" model. The localization model, by contrast, suggests that each regional subsidiary should make its own products for its own markets, which is the dominant historical pattern in the automobile industry.

In North America, Honda has focused its production on its two best-selling models in that market, the Civic and the Accord, including the niche variants of each (coupes, station wagons) which are only produced in North America, for sale primarily there but also exported to Japan and Europe. Overall exports from North America accounted for nearly 15% of output by the mid-1990s. As the basic four-door Accord evolved into a vehicle with low demand in Japan, all production was shifted from Japan to Ohio. In Europe Honda contracted Rover Group to manufacture three car models—the Ballade, the Legend (only small numbers of each), and the Concerto—prior to opening its own assembly plant in 1992. Rover production of Honda models was due to end in 1995, even prior to BMW's purchase of Rover Group from its owner, British Aerospace in 1994. In 1992 Honda started to make the Europeanized Accord in the United Kingdom, and in 1995 added the five-door Civic model at the same factory.

Meanwhile, Honda factories in Japan graduated from focusing on Civic and Accord models for export during the 1970s and early 1980s to making a very wide range of vehicles. Some were for sale only in Japan, such as the small Today, the Beat sports car, and an evolving range of spin-off versions of the Accord and the Civic sold under different names. Others were for sale worldwide but for very small niche markets, such as the NSX sports car, and others again were for larger scale export to North America, Europe, and beyond (the Prelude, Legend, and Del Sol/CRX sports car).

There was, therefore, no fixed pattern of globalization and localization in terms of production locations that could be said to apply to all, or even most, Honda automobiles. The pattern is really only discernible through a vehicle-by-vehicle examination. The best generalization that might be made is that production for local markets of the larger volume midrange cars, the Accord and the Civic, was increasingly localized in North America and Europe, at the same time as these cars were designed distinctly (as already discussed, to varying degrees) to meet local market needs, and in a global pattern that paralleled their design differences. Meanwhile, production of lower output niche models remained in Japan, for sale both in Japan and internationally. The picture was complicated by production of niche variants of the Accord and the Civic in North America, including for export to Japan and Europe, and by the mid-1990s addition to North American production of a third, larger model, the Vigor, previously exported from Japan. As this pattern emerged, exports from Japan to North America switched dramatically, from nearly all Accords and Civics in the early 1980s, to nearly all models *except* Accords and Civics by the mid-1990s.

Economies of scale clearly played a fundamental role in determining the global pattern. So too did another vital feature of Honda's production system which has a bearing on the company's localization strategy: the company's policy of developing its production sites as "flexifactories" (Mair, 1994a). This policy means that the company deliberately retains the same sites, work forces, and capital equipment (as far as possible), even as product mixes and even product types evolve over time, rather than seeking new locations and work-forces at times of structural change in markets. This policy is related to a de-sire to retain highly trained employees who understand the "Honda Way"; the reverse side of the coin is that it permits employees to be retained for the long-term. The classic case of the flexifactory is the company's main Suzuka auto-mobile plant in Japan. Originally built as a motorcycle factory in the late 1950s, Suzuka was for many years the world's largest motorcycle plant. Grad-ually, however, the factory shifted from motorcycle production, which was transferred to peripheral and overseas plants, to automobile production, and by 1992 was no longer making motorcycles.

Following the same principle, Honda's factories in North America and Europe are also very flexible. Since the mid-1980s, they have been the only automobile assembly lines in North America capable of introducing model changes without stopping production for a single day. Each of the North American production lines can manufacture a range of automobiles, and allo-cation of products to lines has continually been rejigged in order to maintain full capacity utilization. In Europe, the Belgian motorcycle factory was con-verted, step by step, into an automobile components plant during the early 1990s. The flexifactory policy clearly has significant implications for the con-cept of capital relocation and the supposed "hypermobility" of global capital sometimes associated with the postnational enterprise concept. In Honda's case, global operations go hand in hand with *hyperfixity*, not hypermobility.

Localization of Components Sourcing

The globalization model implies a global flow of components crisscrossing the world, each manufactured at the most advantageous site in production terms, and then exported to appropriate sites for final assembly. In the localization model, each subsidiary is self-sufficient, independently purchasing all the ma-terials and components it needs in the country or world region in which it op-erates.

In North America, Honda built up a broad and deep components-mak-ing infrastructure composed of both Japanese-transplant components manu-facturers and domestic companies supplying basic materials. The Japanese transplants selected locations in or around Ohio. Following a slow build-up of local sourcing between 1982 and 1986, a wave of transplant investments had followed the mid-1980s appreciation of the yen and the simultaneous quadrupling of Honda's North American production capacity between 1984 and 1989. By the mid-1990s, official measures suggested local content levels, by value, for Honda automobiles made in North America to be over 80%. Some Japanese-transplant components makers were also exporting significant quantities of components, such as window glass, back to Honda plants in Japan.

In Europe, by contrast, Honda developed a components-making infrastructure prior to starting its own automobile manufacture, in alliance with Rover. Honda shared most of its suppliers with Rover, since the Concerto and the Rover 200/400 were close twins, as were the Accord for Europe and the Rover 600. This aided both companies considerably in terms of economies of scale, permitting Honda to increase its own production capacity by steady steps rather than target a 200,000 vehicles per year output level that the market would not support. The relationship with Rover also helped Honda to reach 80% local content 18 months after Accord production commenced, and over 90% local content, with a small but rising proportion of components sourced from North America, by 1996.

Honda's strategic localization of components sourcing at its North American operations can be best understood by disaggregation into types of components. In general, sophisticated components, such as electronics, were brought in from Japan, while manufactured and customer-visible components were purchased from Japanese-transplants in North America, and basic materials (for Honda and for components-maker transplants) were purchased from domestic companies.

Honda pursued a different strategy in Europe. The links with Rover were vital, and there was no wave of incoming Japanese-transplant components makers. The Japanese components makers instead entered in a series of "strategic partnerships" ranging from direct investment in domestic companies to technology-transfer deals with domestic companies. Honda deliberately sourced some components from major European components makers, whereas their North American counterparts were shunned.

Overall, Honda's localization strategy for components purchasing has varied by region and by particular component type. Likewise, despite a high degree of localization, the principal economic advantage of which was to shift added value production into the final market region, some components remained resistant to localization outside Japan, such as high-value electronics, while a new set of geographically concentrated components plants, such as glass factories, was also emerging in North America.

Localization of Production Methods

The globalization model implies the imposition abroad of production methods that have proved successful at the home base. A variant is a life-cycle approach in which outmoded equipment and methods are transferred to overseas facilities. The localization model implies adoption of local, or certainly hybridized, production practices. These might be influenced by expectations of "normal practice" by employees and domestic companies with which the international company is doing business, expectations that might include proper roles for employees, such as job flexibility, "indirect" tasks, quality standards, and communication, or might include business practices for companies, such as delivery schedules, quality control, and contractual arrangements.

Honda's North American and European factories and their production equipment were built as cutting-edge Honda facilities, as advanced, sometimes more so, as those in Japan. The Marysville (Ohio) assembly plant was established by a team from the Sayama factory in Japan, and the East Liberty (Ohio) assembly plant was based on the Suzuka factory in Japan. When Honda Engineering, the company's production technology subsidiary, was developing new production technologies at the same time that Honda was building overseas plants during the 1980s, the innovative equipment was installed immediately in the overseas plants prior to installation in Japan. The overseas facilities were therefore planned to be as close as possible to those in Japan in terms of production technologies and physical layouts, with the exception that somewhat more space was used for buildings and large tracts of land were purchased in North America and Europe, to overcome some of the negative impacts of space restrictions in Japan, such as awkward internal logistics and difficulties in expanding production capacities.

Honda also took great pains to adopt the same logistics and quality relationships with its components makers in North America and Europe as in Japan. Indeed, it was the considerable difficulties Honda experienced in persuading domestic components makers to adopt its operations systems—for instance, delivering precisely at the hour requested—that encouraged the first waves of components makers from Japan to set up operations in Ohio. In fact, a more reliable logistics system has been set up in North America than is possible in congested Japan, through the establishment of a coordinated "just-in-time region" of components makers (Mair, 1992; Mair, Florida, & Kenney, 1988).

In Europe, after early problems, especially when it had been Rover that was responsible for dealing with components makers, by 1992, when the Accord was first built in Europe, management and production innovations from Japan had become much better accepted by European components makers. A number of technology-transfer deals between European and Japanese companies involved the transfer not only of product designs but of processes and (Japanese) capital equipment to make the products.

The organization of work at Honda's international facilities was also modeled on Japanese practice. Production workers were to concentrate basically on their physical work, flexibility in accepting assignments, and mental tasks directly attached to physical work, such as quality control, together with contributioning innovations in areas peripheral to main production activities, such as waste disposal or conditions of employment, through combinations of quality circles ("NH circles") and suggestions schemes. However, the reward systems for these innovations were designed locally, and they varied. In North America, rewards were certificates and a points-accumulation scheme leading to free use of a Honda car or in rare cases ownership of a Honda car. In Europe, there were at first no rewards and no formalized suggestions schemes, but by the mid-1990s, items of clothing were being given as token rewards.

Largely because Honda was able to introduce the principles, embedded in Japan, of assignment flexibility and willingness to learn new tasks and approaches into North America and Europe, indigenous social structures did not interfere with the transfer of production techniques. In terms of adaptions necessary for localization, perhaps the most significant was that the transfer of Honda management and operations philosophies overseas required that they be made explicit and written down or made into films to make them comprehensible to Western workers, a process that had never been necessary in Japan.

Hence the key distinction that is required to understand the strategic localization of production methods divides "hard" technologies and operations management principles, including related organizational principles, from the most "human-related" aspects. Honda has introduced globally uniform hard technologies and operations management, but has adapted the most "human-related" aspects to mesh with local cultures.

Localization of Employees

The globalization model might suggest assigning most, if not all, managers and engineers from home base. No one proposes bringing production workers from home base; the dividing line might be at frontline supervisory level, where supervisors might be sent from the home base temporarily to train local production workers but then be replaced by local employees. Potentially, a cadre of managers and engineers would emerge, including nationals from other countries—"global managers"—who become effectively "postnational" and are able to work in various international operations. By contrast, the localization model suggests that all employees be hired locally, including production workers, engineers, and managers; perhaps only the managing director would be sent from home base.

In Honda's case a very large cadre of managers and engineers, varying over time around 300–350, was sent from Japan to North America. Japanese employees were often sent for 3- to 5-year assignments. Their goal was to transfer technical skills and to firmly implant the Honda philosophy both in locally recruited production workers, who were the easiest group to deal with given the lower intellectual content of their work, and in a growing cadre of counterpart American managers and engineers, who were the more challenging group because of the higher intellectual content of their work. At the same time, by making service overseas part of the normal expectation of Japanese managers and engineers, Honda broke with the Japanese norm by which to be posted abroad effectively constituted demotion. With large numbers of Japanese staff gaining considerable experience abroad, a certain "globalization" of Japanese managers and engineers was emerging.

At the same time, a clear division of labor was established within the managerial ranks between high-level local managers on the one hand, and Japanese managers on the other hand, with local nationals rising to high positions in areas of personnel management and general factory and facility management, without necessarily possessing prior automobile industry experience. Technical functions ranging from process engineering to quality control to technical relations with components makers remained firmly in Japanese hands.

North American and European employees were sent to Japan for short courses and training, a process which by the early 1990s had extended to lengthy stays accompanied by families for American research and development engineers, as previously mentioned. This was a selective "globalization" of Western managers and engineers. Over the coming 2 decades, it is quite possible that a cadre of local North American (and perhaps European) managers and engineers will emerge to be given high-level responsibilities in Japan or at other Honda international operations.

Disaggregation of employee roles into production worker, engineer and manager, and further disaggregation in terms of general and human resource management on the one hand, and technical functions on the other, permits the strategic localization of employee hiring and assignment at Honda's international operations to be deciphered. At one extreme, production workers are localized. At the other extreme, senior managers and technical experts are globalized, but thus far are all Japanese. Between the extremes lie a series of complicated arrangements including twinning, where Japanese and Western staff share responsibilities.

Localization of Terms of Employment for Production Workers

Globalization of terms of employment implies the diffusion of a panoply of Japanese practices (which are shared by Honda) ranging from enterprise unionism to individualization of wages. Localization of terms of employment implies either of two opposite approaches. The first is the wholesale adoption of existing local practices, such as relations with trade union organizations and linkages between status, wages, categories, and job demarcations. The second is the invention of a new local system consistent with local culture and tradition but different from the dominant model.

The central plank in Honda's strategic localization of terms of employment in North America and Europe was indeed the design and adoption of a new single-status system consistent with a significant vein of Western ideology and culture, emphasizing fairness, equality, information sharing, and organizational transparency but rarely if ever adopted in the West. This system, with its equal wages for all production workers, shared car parks and canteens for all employees, and private healthcare paid for all, was also foreign to Honda in Japan. The focus on equality of opportunity, a certain "classlessness" (in the sense of status), and recognition of pride in work was adopted in both North America and Europe. However, there were some subtle variations in the single-status system between North America and Europe. One difference was the argument made in Europe that the provision of company cars to top managers was appropriate in the United Kingdom because it was in tune with British management practices, making the British factory the only Honda facility in the world to adopt this practice.

Trade union representation of workers was strongly and successfully resisted in both North America and the United Kingdom, with Honda officially neutral on the question but opposition not far below the surface. By contrast, there has been a Honda enterprise union in Japan since the early 1950s. Moreover, Honda negotiates with trade unions who represent workers at the motorcycle/automobile components plant it established in Belgium in 1963.

Hence, terms of employment at Honda are localized in a marked and striking way. This stands in significant and logical contrast to Honda's rigid adherence to a globally invariant manufacturing system. Extending the earlier discussion of the transfer abroad of production methods, these human-related organizational structures that support the labor process were subject to considerable variation. In fact, the objective of local human resource managers was precisely to design structures able to build a *coherent bridge* linking Honda's fixed labor process requirements, such as very low absenteeism, good discipline, assignment flexibility, and willingness to suggest improvements, with the local cultural and social environment. Honda's requirement that production techniques be globalized uniformly meant that strategic localization of terms of employment for production workers had to involve considerable variation among regions, but existing local structures were seen as inconsistent with Honda's production system, and considerable inventiveness was therefore required to create the appropriate bridges.

Localization of Strategic Decision Making

Globalization of strategic decision making requires all strategic decisions concerning product ranges, market niches, or appropriate investment policies to be centralized at a single global headquarters. Localization, by contrast, permits each regional subsidiary to determine its own strategic development as it sees fit, with the main influence of headquarters being felt through the appointment of a top manager and to- and-fro flows of investment capital.

Starting from a concentration of all strategic decision making at Honda's Tokyo headquarters, the company has attempted to systematically feed back information from the frontline of marketing and distribution networks, or research facilities (such as California or Germany)—a policy that has included requiring top directors to meet with frontline employees. This is not to suggest that the company has always been directly and flexibly responsive to information from the front line. Honda's manufacturing strategy of being able to building different models on the same production lines was in part responsible for a reluctance to diversify the product range into the popular, but less physically similar to other products, minivan segment in North America in the late 1980s and early 1990s, despite strong demands for such a vehicle from the American dealer network.

Since the mid-1980s, however, there have been clear moves toward a localization of strategic decision making to other regions. Decentralization has been built on the basis of the growing operational independence described earlier. North America provides the clearest case. By 1987, Honda had created an umbrella organization to help manage all its North American operations. By the mid-1990s, the operational capability that had been created to research, design, develop, and manufacture whole vehicle models was permitting Honda North America the strategic capacity to run a whole new product project, from selection of an appropriate market niche through product design, development, and manufacture and on to distribution and to recycling of sales income. This clearly strategic activity had therefore been largely localized.

Indeed, the evolution of Honda's global organizational structure pointed toward an extended localization of strategic decision making. In 1994, the company formally adopted a four-region organizational structure based on Japan, North America, Europe, and Asia/Oceania. Each region contained automobile, motorcycle, and power product operations, and each region was now to report its accounts separately.

At the same time, other elements of strategic decision making remained in Japan, where much of the strategy for Honda operations across the world was formulated, despite the rumors that Honda would move its headquarters to North America. Similarly, the focus of basic research and the most technically advanced new product introductions remained rooted in Japan, suggesting strong parallels between the strategic localization of strategic decision making and that of research and development.

Again, the pattern of strategic localization in strategic decision making becomes clear once its various elements are disaggregated. A certain localization, of model design and niche targeting, is taking place, as is a localization of financial reporting, but these developments are emerging within a framework of other elements that remain firmly centralized at the global level.

STRATEGIC LOCALIZATION REQUIRES CONSISTENCY AND COHERENCE AMONG DIMENSIONS

This review of strategic localization at Honda has not, of course, examined all possible dimensions; corporate finance, product distribution, and marketing, for instance, might be subjected to similar analyses. The focus has been squarely on dimensions related to product design and to production, dimensions that were not organized globally in the traditional multinational enterprise, but ones that, according to the postnational enterprise thesis, are globalizing now.

In sharp contrast to some reductionist analyses of international business, to follow the path of strategic localization is clearly a highly complex endeavor. Even the disaggregation of activities into the series of dimensions analyzed in this chapter did not yield straightforward models. Each dimension had to be further disaggregated before the patterns were revealed. The first intellectual process for the analyst, and, before that, for Honda strategists, is to visualize this complexity.

The second intellectual step for the analyst is to begin to put the pieces of the puzzle together again; for Honda this step had to be undertaken simultaneously with the first. Reintegration of the disaggregated dimensions requires a process of *logical paralleling* that matches up the patterns of strategic localization across dimensions so that they are consistent with each other. To take the simplest of examples, it is logically consistent to locate the manufacture of component α in country β if component α is unique to products manufactured in country β. In fact, two *clusters* of logical paralleling of strategic localization dimensions can be observed in the Honda case. One cluster focuses on the product and its components: research and development, product design, location of production, components sourcing. The second cluster focuses on the production process: work organization, production technology, recruitment of production employees, terms of employment. Within each cluster, decisions along one dimension must be consistent with decisions along the other dimensions if strategic localization is to produce a coherent organization. The flexifactory concept provides the vital pivot between clusters.

The search for consistency and coherence that is the hallmark of strategic localization at Honda is characterized by the innovative resolution of apparent paradoxes, problems, and tensions (Mair, 1996). Some are easier to resolve than others. Two examples of difficult issues can be given. The first is the significant question of the internationalization of research and development activities by Honda's components makers, many of which are small companies unable to justify separate research and development facilities at their manufacturing transplants in North America or Europe that could parallel Honda's own research and development activities there. Part of the solution in North America has been for Honda to design its own facilities in such a way that these companies can utilize them, too, sharing overheads. Another part of the solution has been for Honda itself to become deeply involved in evaluating, selecting, and procuring the raw materials used by components maker transplants. A second example of a difficult problem relates to the differing expectations regarding terms of employment held by Japanese and Western managers and engineers. The most significant personal interaction between Japanese and Westerners takes place at these levels rather than involving the production work force. There are tensions to be managed over acceptable working hours, or over conventions about the level of employee choice in new postings to other Honda facilities. This is a particularly thorny problem. Hypothetically, Japanese and Western managers and engineers could maintain their national cultural expectations even when working side by side. But would Westerners then be at a disadvantage when it came to promotion because of shorter working hours, reluctance to engage in after-hours social activities, and unwillingness to accept short-notice reassignment to other countries? Alternatively, Japanese cadres posted abroad might adopt Western habits, raising problems in terms of their relationships to Japanese counterparts in Japan; working abroad might make them "lazy." What solutions might be found for dilemmas like these?

Traditional ideas about localization by international companies already accept that it is a very difficult process, for well-known reasons related to unfamiliarity with new local environments and mismatches between company practices at home base and what is acceptable or possible in other countries. Indeed, it is these traditional concepts that have led to the establishment of subsidiaries that are operationally separate, each consistent with its own environment but not with subsidiaries elsewhere.

The concept of strategic localization, by contrast, suggests that localization must not only seek consistency with the local environment, whether market, industrial infrastructure, or culture/society, but do so in a way that is also consistent with the company's strategy and operations in other regions of the world. As previously suggested, this means developing patterns of consistency and coherence across clusters dimensions of activity. It also means developing patterns of consistency and coherence across space and across time. Moreover, the Honda case reveals that strategic localization is not simply a case of "fitting in" to existing local environments. Indeed, these latter may have to be inventively molded if company operations and strategy in one region are not to become inconsistent with those in other regions. Hence, in North America Honda has altered standards and norms in terms of products (including quality, cost, and acceptance of smaller front-wheel drive vehicles), in terms of components supply infrastructure (effectively bringing its own with it when the existing infrastructure proved inadequate), and in terms of cultural and social expectations for terms of employment (including refusal to accept trade unions, and adoption of the single-status system). This is what Setsuo Mito (1990, p. 102) meant when he perceptively suggested that "Honda may even discover an America that has not yet been discovered by Americans."

Far from creating a postnational company, strategic localization at Honda has meant the adoption of a series of new nationalities, as suggested in the citation from Honda itself at the start of the chapter. Some of these nationalities are themselves being reinvented along the way, delivering that cutting edge of sociopolitical and economic change for which multinational enterprises have long been well known. Set against this deeper understanding, simple and reductionist ideas about postnational enterprises and global corporations operating in borderless worlds do not offer very helpful interpretations of Honda's international strategy. Moreover, other potential routes to globalization of operations, such as the "world car" and global sourcing strategies pursued by some of Honda's Western rivals during the 1980s and 1990s, have run into serious difficulties (Hoffman & Kaplinsky, 1988). Honda's new global local corporation, by contrast, helped the company to weather the storm caused by the collapse of the Japanese bubble economy in the early 1990s (Mair, in press). Further investigation and analysis of the *underlying logic* behind Honda's internationalization—as suggested in this discussion of the company's *strategic localization*—offers a promising route to clarifying how a global corporation can be made to work.

At the theoretical level, this suggests that of the all the analyses ventured since the rise of the so-called global corporation, it is the approach taken by Bartlett and Ghoshal (1987) that remains the most promising. For Bartlett and Ghoshal, the successful organization of what they call a transnational organization requires that account be taken of the complex interplay among a number of abstract dimensions, including symmetry–differentiation, dependence–independence, and control–coordination. They challenge company strategists to rise to the task by developing within themselves a complex "mind matrix" capable of grasping all the dimensions simultaneously. This is precisely what Honda's strategists have done in creating their global local corporation. Set against this process, the thesis of the postnational, stateless, or global enterprise operating in a borderless world appears hopelessly simplistic.

CODA: GLOBAL COMPANY, LOCAL POLITICS

This chapter has deliberately focused on strategic localization with little direct reference to the power of the nation-state, since otherwise it might have been tempting to suggest that only political pressures oblige otherwise "globalizing" companies to invest in the localization of their operations, and such an interpretation would be quite misleading. In fact, as we have seen, the localization of the global corporation is a response to geographical variation in the operating environment that goes well beyond the political domain, incorporating variations in consumer demand (over time and product types), in local industrial infrastructures, and in local cultures and social structures.

It is nonetheless important to examine briefly the overt political influences on Honda's internationalization, for there have been several. Hence, in North America Honda was subject to the same protectionist pressures that affected all the Japanese automobile producers in the years around 1980. However, Honda had in fact been studying the possibility of production in North America since 1974, and as early as 1977 had started constructing the motorcycle plant that would be the seed of its Ohio production complex. Thus, Honda was the first Japanese company to open an automobile production plant there, in 1982. The establishment of deeply rooted operations in North America, however, did not prevent the company from being overtly attacked by U.S. government agencies during the 1992 Presidential election campaign for alleged low local content in its North American automobiles. A 1995 decision to set up a small assembly plant in Mexico was planned far more carefully than domestic North American companies would need to do. The plant was to produce the Accord model, thus allaying fears in Canada that production of the Civic in Canada would be transferred to Mexico, and, despite the North American Free Trade Agreement (NAFTA), the plant would not export products to the United States. While in a changing political climate Honda was able to establish nonunion factories in the early 1980s, it was unable to impose hiring policies that appeared to avoid hiring nonwhite, older, or women workers, being forced to change its policies by a U.S. government agency. As these examples make clear, Honda still has to tread very carefully in North America.

Similarly, in Europe, Honda did not invest in its own car manufacturing plant until the political situation surrounding the establishment of a single European market in the early 1990s became clearer. Moreover, Honda sought two forms of political "protection." First, the company positioned itself as the "savior," rather than "destroyer," of the indigenous British automobile industry through its technology transfers to Rover Group. Second, Honda came to an agreement that the British government would certify that the company had reached its target of 80% local content after 18 months of production. The British government acted as a shield against potential European critics; and indeed, the French government had openly discussed refusing to permit Honda products built in the United Kingdom or the United States entry into France on the basis of their supposed high Japanese content.

On the other hand, Honda has been able to utilize its North American production base, and the implicit protection of the U.S. government, to export products to markets where importation from Japan would not be possible. Hence Israel, subject to an Arab embargo supported by Japan, is serviced from North America, as is Taiwan, which restricts imports from Japan. Indeed, it is politics that explains why the partner of the Taiwanese company that jointly owns Honda's manufacturing subsidiary in Taiwan is not Honda Motor (Japan) but Honda North America. When the French government suggested that it might restrict entry of Honda products made in North America, it was the U.S. government that protested in Honda's defense, claiming high North American content (a different government branch from the one that was simultaneously criticizing Honda's low local content for domestic political reasons!). The supposedly stateless corporation must deal directly and indirectly with the demands and power of the nation-state, but can utilize its influence, too.

It is appropriate to bring this discussion of political contexts to a close on a cautionary note. While academic analysts and consultants may have successfully shifted the theoretical ground towards the idea of a postnational enterprise, the dominant ideas in the "real world," including the real world in which Honda operates, have lagged behind. Thus, while in this chapter Honda has been compared empirically with the postnational enterprise thesis, in reality Honda has been contending with political environments where expectations about the behavior of international companies have remained rooted firmly in the traditional multinational enterprise model. Nowhere has this been more striking than in the political debate over local content in North America, where industry and political commentators appeared to be convinced that Honda would keep its local content as low as possible, since they firmly believed that the Ohio production complex could only ever be a branch plant that would assemble components imported from Japan. This conviction derived not from some postnational vision but from one version of a traditional multinational enterprise model. Since, as has been argued here, Honda was following a quite different strategy based on a quite different model, the critics were unable to respond effectively and misinterpreted Honda time and again (for a full analysis, see Mair, 1994b, Chapt. 4). A more sophisticated analysis of the new organizational forms of international business is urgently needed in both theory and practice.

REFERENCES

Bartlett, C. A., & Ghoshal, S. (1987, Fall). Managing across borders: New organizational responses. *Sloan Management Review*, 43–53.

Bloomfield, G. T. (1981). The changing spatial organization of multinational corporations in the world automotive industry. In F. E. I. Hamilton & G. J. R. Linge (Eds.), *Spatial analysis, industry and the industrial environment: Vol. 2. International industrial systems* (pp. 357–394). Chichester: Wiley.

Bluestone, B., & Harrison, B. (1982). *The deindustrialization of America.* New York: Basic Books.

Borus, A. (with Zellner, W., & Holstein, W. J.) (1990, 14 May). The stateless corporation. *Business Week,* pp. 52–60.

Dohse, K., Jürgens, U., & Malsch, T. (1985). From "Fordism" to "Toyotism"? The social organization of the labor process in the Japanese automobile industry. *Politics and Society, 14*(2), 115–146.

Douglas, S. P., & Wind, Y. (1987, Winter). The myth of globalization. *Columbia Journal of World Business,* 19–29.

Dunning, J. H. (1993). *Multinational enterprises and the global economy.* Wokingham, UK: Addison-Wesley.

Hoffman, K., & Kaplinsky, R. (1988). *Driving force: The global restructuring of technology, labor and investment in the automobile and components industries.* Boulder, CO: Westview Press.

Honda Motor Co. (1992). *Guide to Honda.* Tokyo: Author.

Kuhn, T. S. (1962). *The structure of scientific revolutions.* Chicago: University of Chicago Press.

Mair, A. (1992). Just-in-time manufacturing and the spatial structure of the automobile industry: Lessons from Japan. *Tijdschrift voor Economische en Sociaale Geografie, 83*(2), 82–92.

Mair, A. (1994a). Honda's global flexifactory network. *International Journal of Operations and Production Management, 14*(3), 6–23.

Mair, A. (1994b). *Honda's global local corporation.* London: Macmillan.

Mair, A. (1996). Honda Motors: A paradoxical approach to growth. In C. Baden-Fuller & M. Pitt (Eds.), *Strategic innovation* (pp. 435–461). London: Routledge.

Mair, A. (in press). The Honda Motor Company, 1967–1995: Globalization of an innovative mass production model. In M. Freyssenet, A. Mair, K. Shimizu, & G. Volpato (Eds.), *One best way? Trajectories and industrial models of the world's automobile producers, 1970–1995.* Oxford: Oxford University Press.

Mair, A., Florida, R., & Kenney, M. (1988). The new geography of automobile production: Japanese transplants in North America. *Economic Geography, 64,* 352–373.

Mito, S. (1990). *The Honda book of management.* London: Kogan Page.

Ohmae, K. (1989, May–June). Managing in a borderless world. *Harvard Business Review,* pp. 152–161.

Ohno, T. (1983). Foreword. In Y. Monden, *The Toyota production system: Practical approach to production management* (pp. i–ii). Atlanta: Institute of Industrial Engineers.

Pitelis, C. N., & Sugden, R. (Eds.). (1991). *The nature of the transnational firm.* London: Routledge.

Porter, M. (1990). *The competitive advantage of nations.* New York: Free Press.

Sinclair, S. (1983). *The world car: The future of the automobile industry,* London: Euromonitor.

Thrift, N. (1986). The geography of international economic disorder. In R. J. Johnston & P. J. Taylor (Eds.), *A world in crisis? Geographical perspectives* (pp.12–67). Oxford: Blackwell.

Trachte, K., & Ross, S. (1985). The crisis in Detroit and the emergence of global capitalism. *International Journal of Urban and Regional Research, 13,* 31–42.

Trevor, M. (1983). *Japan's reluctant multinationals: Japanese management at home and abroad.* London: Pinter.

Womack, J. P. (1989). A postnational auto industry by the year 2000. *JAMA Forum, 8*(1), 3–7.

Womack, J. P., Jones, D. T., & Roos, D. (1990). *The machine that changed the world.* New York: Rawson.

CHAPTER 4

The Informational Content of Financial Products and the Spatial Structure of the Global Finance Industry

Gordon L. Clark
Kevin O'Connor

INTRODUCTION

The current structure of the global financial economy reflects powerful forces of centralization and decentralization, notwithstanding often-made claims that geography does not matter. Such claims seem to be based upon substantial improvements in global communications and the remarkable mobility of people and goods at the end of the 20th century. Relevant technological improvements include international direct dialing, real-time electronic networks linking sites across the globe, and high-speed and high-capacity global intermodal transport networks. So pervasive are these improvements that some commentators presume the "end of geography," at least in the area of international finance (O'Brien, 1992).[1] And yet, notwithstanding the significance of places like London and New York with respect to the volume and structure of global financial transactions, global financial centers coexist with other smaller national and regional centers. Despite dramatic improvements in information transmission, there is no systematic evidence that the global financial system is either collapsing to a point or fragmenting into a "thousand pieces of geography" scattered randomly across the globe.

This chapter moves beyond simple empirical observations about finance and geography and focuses upon the informational content of financial products to show why (logically speaking) geography still matters. It matters because it embodies key factors in the production process of financial products, even if these products are increasingly processed and distributed to consumers from remote sites (Sanford, 1993). These key factors include locally specific information networks of producers and the monitoring of firms' financial and investment performance. This chapter shows how these dimensions have a geographical logic and, in turn, why geography remains essential to the global financial industry. We begin by showing that even with a financial product as apparently transparent and homogeneous as gold, there are significant differences between London's and New York's daily closing prices. These differences are unpredictable and are an opportunity for market agents like arbitragers to make a profit in the short run, and sustain their role in the market over the long term. At a more fundamental level, this chapter shows that the production of financial products can be profoundly influenced by the location of the provider.

We argue here that the significance of location is felt through the creation and management of information related to the design and structure of financial products, to the benefit of larger established places that have institutional structures that facilitate information (and funds) transfer. It is argued, via a typology of financial products, that the nature of information varies in systematic ways according to the characteristics of products; hence, a critical dimension of this institutional structure is the role of markets not simply as locations of trading but as centers of information collection and the formal exchange places of specialist expertise (Thrift, 1994). The effect of geography is to be found in the impact of particular markets in the production process of financial services. Like Martin (1994), our chapter challenges the notion that "money will escape the confines of geography" (O'Brien, 1992, p. 2). We suggest that the geography of places shapes the operation of finance markets and the global economy primarily because of the geography of information that is embedded in the provision of specific financial products. There is, in effect, a robust territoriality to the global financial industry.

We make, however, one qualification to this argument, which should be acknowledged from the outset. While we are convinced there is a logical spatial hierarchy inherent in the production of financial products, it is clear that the regulatory context in which the production process takes place can be very important in determining the nature and availability of investment products in local markets (Roberts, 1994). Evidence abounds about the advantages and disadvantages of different jurisdictions with respect to investment firms' management of financial products. Not surprisingly, trading nations like Britain are very sensitive to differences between domestic and other jurisdictions' regulations and how those differences promote (or otherwise) local firms' (and places') competitiveness (Smith, 1992). Note also recent attempts of the French government to insulate domestic firms against competition from U.S.-based global finance firms in the interests of developing an indigenous investment management industry. By virtue of their regulatory regimes, nation-states could affect the relative standing of their financial centres in the global economy.[2] We deal with this issue only incidentally. Formal analysis is left to another occasion.

CONCEPTS AND TERMINOLOGY

In order to understand our argument, let us set out the logic of our analytical world—that is, the concepts and terms that underpin our analysis. Here, we are most concerned with the institutional market for financial services. By this we mean the Anglo-American international, national, and regional markets for financial products bought and sold by institutions on behalf of their clients. These clients may be other institutions and first-order financial intermediaries like banks, but are in the end, more often than not, pension plan beneficiaries. Clearly, this focus means excluding sections of the financial market, like individual investor segments of markets, that are important to the total volume of nations' financial transactions. At this point, we wish to simply focus on one part of the market in the interests of clarity. Note an important consequence of our focus on institutional investors: embedded in our analysis is a presumption in favor of expertise. We assume the existence and persistence of firms like J. P. Morgan is due (in part) to their superior (relative to competitors) ability to collect, sort, and value information with respect to decision-oriented norms of risk and return for clients around the world.

A second, and, related, organizing principle used in this chapter is that institutional investors manage clients' investments in accordance with modern portfolio theory (MPT) mediated through common law and statutory conceptions of fiduciary responsibility (Jobling, 1994). MPT shows that an optimally diversified portfolio of securities will have a temporal profile of returns that exactly matches their systematic risk. The seminal papers are by Markowitz (1952) on MPT and Sharpe (1964) on the Capital Asset Pricing Model (CAPM; see Merton, 1994). By invoking MPT, we do not mean to imply that we believe MPT to be a comprehensive and complete depiction of the functional performance of Anglo-American finance markets. Quite the contrary. The evidence suggests, in fact, that as a practical matter there is no cross-sectional (and international) relationship between risk and return, the principal prediction of Markowitz's MPT and Sharpe's CAPM (see Fama, 1991; Roll & Ross, 1994). We believe (an empirical claim), however, that many institutional investors use MPT as the basis of their routines or practices of managed investment (Clark, in press). In this respect MPT is, at the minimum, an heuristic device—a commonly accepted language used in the financial services industry to describe to one another and to their clients what investment firms should do and how they might do it. Risk and return are the basic building blocks of a developed and internationally accepted but variously interpreted nomenclature.[3]

For all the virtues of O'Brien's (1992) book, we find it surprising that he supposes (albeit implicitly) that the Anglo-American financial world can be described as an efficient and wholly integrated system of markets. This idea is surely at the heart of his argument, even if not explicitly described as such. By the "end of geography" he must mean the efficient spatial–economic integration of the global financial system. In this respect he seems to reference the ideal world of Black and Scholes (1973) and assumes an equivalence between their ideal world and reality. Recall that Black and Scholes, and the international asset pricing models that follow their logic, assume global equity, bond, and futures markets are all perfectly integrated in just the same way that Sharpe (see Sharpe & Alexander, 1990) defined financial markets to be strongly efficient: that is, given the uniform availability of information between and within markets about asset prices, price changes can only be random.

Of course even Sharpe does not, now, as a practical matter subscribe to this strong efficiency thesis. He would now say that markets are weakly efficient, in that current security prices reflect their (weighted) previous prices. Sharpe allows for time lags, mismatches and the like so that parameters on the previous values of a security's price are statistically significant: there are spatial and temporal transmission effects that structure the global efficiency of financial markets. Note, though, that an efficient spatially integrated system of markets would, in the strong sense we associate with O'Brien, be a system in which location does not matter. In effect, he implies that it does not matter where institutional investors are located: all information, past and present, public and private, about security prices are available everywhere and anywhere so that no investor can profit by virtue of their particular location. As a corollary, in the spatial context the strong efficiency hypothesis would suppose that current security prices in one market (say New York) fully reflect local past prices *plus* other markets' (London, Tokyo, etc.) past and current security prices, so that each market's prices are a random walk and so that events in one market are immediately and completely integrated into the price structure of other markets. Put slightly differently, the strong efficiency hypothesis supposes no systematic differences in markets' prices—no differences that would mean being located in a specific, distant market is an advantage in trading international securities.

How plausible is O'Brien's (implicit) strong efficiency claim with respect to spatial–economic (intermarket) integration? At the most general level, Roll (1977) has shown that it is impossible to directly test the predictive power of MPT.[4] More recently, he (Roll, 1992) has shown that it is also very difficult to assess the extent of integration of international security markets given their very different rules and regulations, varying underlying economic structures, and differing trading technologies. In fact, it is problematic to specify what would be an adequate measure of intermarket economic (price) integration, ignoring for argument's sake the theoretical complexities of MPT (Chen & Knez, 1994). Nevertheless, J. P. Morgan (1994) has provided a set of tests or measures by which we can evaluate integration (market and intermarket efficiency). Their *RiskMetrics* methodology for quantifying market risks emphasizes three related tests: (1) the extent to which price changes are serially autocorrelated; (2) the extent to which price changes have an underlying trend or identifiable periodicities, and (3) the extent to which an asset's price changes can be reasonably approximated by a normal distribution. By their empirical assessment, many asset prices (and changes between markets) show evidence of serial autocorrelation, periodicities, and skewness (or bias) with respect to a normal distribution. In other words, there is comprehensive evidence of *systematic* price changes and differences within and between markets with regard to commonly traded securities.[5]

But what if there were securities whose price changes within and between markets could be characterized as a random walk? What if there were no systematic or predictable differences between markets in these securities' prices? What would that imply for O'Brien's thesis of global financial centralization? Figure 4.1 portrays the daily differences (1993–1994) in gold prices between London (Metal Exchange) and New York (COMEX). Gold, like silver but unlike most other metals, is essentially a global store of value; its value is principally as a short-term hedge against changes in other asset prices rather than being in its use as an input to production (Ng & Pirrong, 1994). As a pure speculative product, homogeneous in character and transparent as a

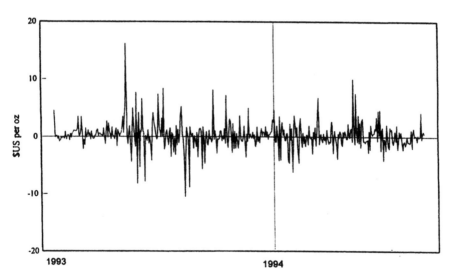

FIGURE 4.1. Closing prices for London and New York gold markets: January 1993 to September 1994.

traded commodity, we might suppose, a priori, that at least this asset could be typified as a spatially integrated security. In fact, our analysis of gold price differences between London and New York leads us to conclude that they can be characterized as a random walk (no serial autocorrelation) with no evident trends or periodicities (a stationary, stochastic process) and a distribution of observations (differences) consistent with a normal distribution. See the Appendix for details of our time series analysis.

Actually, while the distribution of observations (differences) appears "normal," there is evidence of what J. P. Morgan terms as *leptokurtosis* (a peak around the mean higher than predicted by a normal distribution). More than 35% of all differences in the daily closing prices for gold between London and New York are 0, while the average difference is just 22¢, a tiny proportion of the price of gold per ounce which currently trades around U.S.$380–400.[6] In essence, it can be reasonably assumed that there are no systematic differences between the London and New York gold closing prices, and it can be assumed that traders are able to assign a known probability distribution to those differences in closing prices that do occur on a random basis. Does this mean, though, that there is no value to geography, as O'Brien seems to suggest? Is there any reason to suppose that a trading company should have both a London office *and* a New York office? Why not centralize all gold trading in just one place? Our judgment is that such a decision would be inefficient—a trading company that used such a strategy would lose money relative to a company (all things being equal) that had an office in London *and* New York (or, for that matter, offices distributed around the world).

Why? For one simple but profound reason: the London Metals Exchange opens before COMEX in New York. The difference in closing prices, while not systematic in any fundamental sense (reflecting, say, local economic structure), *is* systematic in the sense that it must reflect unanticipated information available *in* New York *after* the London market has been trading for the day. Now it is possible, of course, that a global trading company could operate its London office as long as the New York market is open, thereby, in effect, acting as if it were local to both London *and* New York. But to do so would imply that the London office is as efficient in collecting, sorting, and valuing information from New York as a New York office would be. This is a crucial assumption underlying O'Brien's thesis. We can now see why he makes such a strong connection between intermarket efficiency and innovations in communications technology. However, we are not convinced that a London office would be enough; we believe based upon interviews with global funds managers that a decentralized trading system would be relatively more efficient than a centralized trading system.[7] We would also hypothesize that inter-market differences in daily closing prices for gold become more pronounced as time/space increases from the London market. Even if the differences in daily closing prices for gold between, for example, London and Tokyo are normal, we would hypothesize that the *mean* and *variance* of differences increases with time and space as more new information becomes available thereby increasing the importance of collecting, sorting, and valuing additional *market-specific* information.

We would suggest then, that even with respect to evidence consistent with O'Brien's thesis, his claims are quite misleading, even misguided, given the existence of time and space. Moreover, evidence for and against intermarket integration is generally inconsistent with his argument. But we should also acknowledge that he argues that those who claim the continuing significance of geography confuse the production of financial products with their "marketing and delivery" (p. 75). Our next argument is that geography matters for the design and production of financial products. In effect, our argument denies O'Brien's spatial–economic strong efficiency hypothesis at its very core (the production of investment products). In making this second argument we do not rely on time–space differences between markets, systematic differences in countries' economic structures, or differences in regulatory regimes to generate intermarket arbitrage opportunities. Rather, we argue in the next section that financial products often have a distinct spatial configuration of information embedded in their design.

TYPOLOGY OF FINANCIAL PRODUCTS

In the previous sections of this chapter we have advanced two basic claims. First, with respect to the spatial configuration of the global finance industry, we suggested that any analysis of the finance industry must be able to account for the coexistence of centers like London and New York with national and regional finance centers like for example, Chicago and Los Angeles. It may be the case that the U.S. finance industry is centralized around New York, just as places like Chicago have come to dominate adjacent centers like Minneapolis. What we contend, however, is that O'Brien (1992) was incorrect to argue that the global finance industry is inevitably being concentrated in just a few sites; an adequate analysis of the industry must allow for spatial differentiation and decentralization against the forces that promote centralization. The second claim we have made is that even with respect to the trade of a homogeneous and transparent product like gold (the kind of financial product that most clearly fits into O'Brien's thesis), there remain important reasons not to centralize trading. Even if markets were strongly efficient in the sense that they were comprehensively and completely spatially and economically (price) integrated, arbitragers with local market-specific information can still make a profit.

We now take this set of arguments further by providing a logical explanation of the continuity and coexistence of various regional, national, and international finance centers.[8] As noted earlier, the continuity and coexistence of various kinds of financial centers could be explained with reference to factors external to the industry or, as O'Brien obliquely suggests, by factors more related to the processing of financial transactions than related to the nature of financial products. In essence, he assumes financial products to be universal in much the same way we described gold. To appreciate why O'Brien is misleading is complicated; we require the reader to understand the design and structures of three common types of financial products. These types of products are found throughout the Anglo-American world and are representative of the product domain in which financial institutions find themselves either as producers or as purchasers of these products. Following Ross (1989) and Merton (1993), each type of product is listed and described in the following sections (including an illustrative example).

Transparent Products

As in our gold example, these types of products are those whose qualities and dimensions (including relationships to other products) are so well known or simply and cheaply observed that institutions can trade in/out of positions just on the basis of observed past and current prices. While these products may not be, after all, representative of spatial–economic integration in the strong sense, they are products that can be bought and sold throughout the Anglo-American world from just a few sites. While the local price of such products may not exactly replicate the global price, it is more than likely that local investment houses would have sufficient expertise to execute trades so that local clients are not systematically disadvantaged over the long term by virtue of their peripheral location (in relation to New York and London). At the same time, the transparency of these products means that they are so homogeneous—functionally and spatially—that it is very difficult to make more than an average (compared to the relevant bench mark) return. Indeed, because of their transparency, these kinds of products deliver a relatively low risk-adjusted return. The upper and lower bounds around the appropriate benchmark returns are so very well known that, in normal circumstances, perhaps the only way to improve on an average return is to use a trading routine that is very cost-efficient.

Translucent Products

These are commonly traded and produced products whose particular characteristics are deliberately designed by institutions to be different from the standard, industry reference product. In a sense, translucent products are variations on products whose standard properties are well known in the industry (at the global level), but whose specific qualities are only known in the local market. For instance, while most financial institutions know how to design and trade a pooled investment product like a balanced equity product, its particular characteristics reflect both the sectoral and size composition of the target industry sector (or sectors) *and* the skill of the finance institution's research staff in selecting particular stocks with respect to the performance targets of the balanced equity product. In some respects, balanced equity products are increasingly thought of as transparent products in the sense that, over time, the basic principles involved in their design and functioning have become so well known as to have been generalized or standardized. Indeed, computer programs now exist that allow anyone with sufficient knowledge of the market to select, bundle, and trial (with respect to performance) hypothetical balanced equity products against those offered in the market. The existence of surveying companies like Morningstar have likewise promoted product standardization. Nevertheless, balanced equity products remain translucent, perhaps even opaque, rather than transparent because performance is a combination of firm-specific expertise, knowledge of particular stocks, and standardized trading routines. There is, as a consequence, an inherent geography in balanced equity products. But there is also a geography (a spatial specificity) in the information by which they are produced.

One implication of this argument is that these kinds of products vary both with respect to their observed risk and their actual returns. Because firm-specific expertise cannot be directly observed by most institutions, and because knowledge of firm performance (that is, the performance of firms' securities that are selected into balanced equity products) is highly differentiated over space and time, buyers of such products face a wide array of products whose performance can only be estimated with a margin of risk.[9] As a consequence, assuming institutions (and their clients) to be risk averse, institutions will buy and sell those balanced equity products for which they have more information than less information. It is not surprising, then, that countries have their own institutions that offer balanced equity products comprised of local stocks. Put more directly, Fidelity's mutual funds have a certain geography in terms of their scope and in terms of their market penetration around the globe because, to be effective with respect to performance, product designers must be close to the primary market of the selected stocks *and* because, to be effective with respect to institutions' assessment of their likely risk-adjusted returns, institutional investors must be close to the designers of the funds themselves. This does not mean that translucent products are always local. Rather, the proper implication to be drawn is that any investment in a translucent product requires first an investment in information to judge the risk and return of an investment. Local markets are often the best and most cost-effective source (in terms of obtaining, sorting, and valuing) that information.

Opaque Products

These are products whose design and execution are premised upon the existence of asymmetrically distributed information. In essence, opaque products are built on private information (or what we could term as transaction-specific information) as opposed to public information (or third-party and market information), the latter being either available in the local market at a price, as is the case with translucent products, or generally available between markets by virtue of the information embodied in prices (Grossman, 1989), as is the case with transparent products. There are two dimensions to this issue of information which should be emphasized at this juncture. First, while the asymmetry of information may be the litmus test for product designers, the inability of financial institutions to directly observe the internal logic or elements of these products means that investors must rely on product designers for the requisite information by which to make their investment decisions. Immediately important in this context is the perceived (and actual) honesty of the product designers and managers (witness the Barings debacle). To make an assessment of honesty requires: (1) independence of the financial institutions' managers from the product designers; (2) knowledge of the product designers' reputations, and (3) a long-term relationship with the product designers over a series of events that could be used to assess their veracity directly. Thus, the second dimension of the information issue is this: opaque products are a form of relational investing, something that modern Anglo-American financial institutions are uncomfortable with, but a form of investing a few global financial institutions now actually specialize in and make a core component of their business.[10]

Not surprisingly, opaque products require a significant and essential component of specialist expertise. The designers of these products, assuming their interest in a long-term market position, must be able to design a product that can meet financial institutions' qualms about the potential for corruption, investors' needs for continuous reporting on products' performance, and investors' interests in a relatively high (relative to other financial products that are either transparent or translucent) risk-adjusted return given the common practice of diversifying clients' investment portfolios (and sometimes investment managers) across a range of types of investment products.

On the other hand, opaque product designers also have an interest in keeping hidden (or private) their special knowledge base, which is the basis of their comparative advantage over financial institutions offering comparable products. For companies like CS First Boston, competing around the world for clients that have an interest in such specialized products, how they make up opaque products has become an issue of intellectual property. Not surprising, these types of firms are very secretive about how such products are designed, albeit they have to be open enough to gain the confidence of clients.

Here, notions of personal trust and firms' reputations are very important for firms with a long-term interest in producing and marketing opaque products. At another level, less related to advanced mathematics and proprietary software, opaque products can also be easily described by reference to examples like private placements, property trusts, and the like. In Australia and the United States, property trusts (or real estate investment trusts—REITs) are a common form of this kind of opaque product.[11] Elsewhere, in the United States and Europe, designer-driven derivative products are perhaps more important. In essence, of course, opaque products are both heterogeneous in design *and* subject to enormous variety with respect to their risk-adjusted returns.

To summarize, Table 4.1 details the basic elements of the three different types of investment products. Note that where we make an assessment of market scope—global, national, and local—what we mean is the extent to which a financial institution is able and willing to allocate resources to that investment product by virtue of its origin. We would argue that many financial institutions are able and willing to take positions on transparent international equity products like stock market indexes (including the Standard and Poor's 500) because there is sufficient information in observed price movements to make a reasonable bet about future performance, even at a distance. Translucent products are more often national in scope because they require detailed knowledge of local companies, their performance and potential. Notice, though, these are only national products in the sense of the costs of information collection and verification. To the extent that such information can be produced, bundled, and sold on the international market at a competitive price (compared to local products), then international financial institutions may be willing to cross over boundaries to buy these products. In a sense, this is what is happening with the rise or significance of "emerging markets" for international investment companies.[12] At the same time, we would argue that once financial products rely upon trust and long-term relationships then it is inevitable that the probable market for such products is local. This does not mean that all consumers must be "local" in the sense of being located in a

TABLE 4.1. Summary Characteristics of Three Types of Financial Products

Financial product type	Probable market scope	Information intensity	Specialist expertise required	Perceived risk-adjusted return
Transparent	Global	Ubiquitous	Low	Low
Translucent	National	Third party-market specific	Significant	Medium
Opaque	Local	Transaction specific	Vital	High

particular city. Rather, "local" means that it is produced at a particular site relying upon transaction-specific clients.

A final point to be made about this typology of products is about their longevity in any one category. That is, we could imagine that financial products have a life cycle beginning in the opaque category and ending at the transparent category. Indeed, we could also imagine that firms like CS First Boston occupy certain product niches rather than others as a matter of corporate strategy and have, as a consequence, a significant role in promoting product innovation in the whole industry. For instance, while we have argued that CS First Boston has specialized in opaque products like derivatives, swaps, and options, it is also clear that as the design of these types of products has become increasingly understood in the market, other firms have begun to offer these same kinds of products in a more generalized form. In essence, transaction-specific information has become diffused through market networks, allowing other firms to design competing products using third-party market information (see Thrift, 1994). Much the same has happened in the balanced equity product market. As financial institutions have become more knowledgeable about balanced equity products and the like, and as some of the markets have offered trading facilities for investors wishing to trade in/out of these funds, they have tended to move from the opaque category to the translucent category, and even the transparent category as market intermediaries have developed sophisticated reporting systems and performance evaluation systems.

TYPOGRAPHY OF FINANCIAL MARKETS

The next stage of the Chapter illustrates how the structure and informational content of financial products have shaped the geography of the world's finance markets (compare with ter Hart & Peirsma, 1990). Implied by the previous discussion is an assumption that the current pattern of activity is not a seamless global system; rather, it remains organized in a spatially differentiated manner—the product of the informational content of products and the role of information in the production of these products. These links reflect especially the availability of information. In addition, consumption, even though often seen as a global activity, contributes to this structure of finance, as some places have special advantages in the trading process. The geography of the world's finance industry, as evidenced by the spatial distribution of financial transactions between global, national, and regional finance centers has been described by Reed (1981) and specified as a "hierarchical structure" by Daniels (1993, p. 141), who relied upon the study of banking centers prepared by Noyelle (1989). The hierarchy described by these authors has been discussed in many places, and is a well-understood pattern, reappearing in the discussion of "world cities" and the global nature of service activities (see Sassen, 1991). In this section, we outline an ideal geography, illustrating the links between financial products and location. This ideal geography is, however, disputed in the penultimate section of the chapter.

Transparent Products—Global Centers

The foundation of the hierarchical structure of the global finance industry is laid at the transparent end of the spectrum. As discussed earlier, the design of a gold or gold futures product typically involves sophisticated arrangements of information processing and complex trading mechanisms that cope with futures contracts and foreign currency exchange. Given the complexities of trading, transparent products are produced where the trading volume is large enough to make economical the repetitive small market that which are associated with this form of trading. These turnover efficiencies are only met in the larger global centers, so that the design and production of transparent products provides the apex of the world's financial system. New York and London are an essential part of the system. The daily trading volumes and the instantaneous information systems in these centers allow transparent products to attract considerable funds from a wide set of locations. Indeed, compared to other products and centers, New York and London dominate in sheer volume the total volume of all financial transactions across the globe. Not surprisingly, these centers are also the dominant employment centers in the global financial industry.[13]

Translucent Products—National Centers

The design and production of a translucent product, like a balanced equity product, draws upon a different set of factors and creates opportunities for a second (national) level of financial centers. There are many different types and forms of balanced equity products, typically differentiated by country of origin. They all require skills in design to structure them so as to maximize returns, spread risks, and maximize product differentiation in order to give such a product an edge in the competition with other funds. Hence, there are opportunities for local operators and local markets. However, the costs of assembling and maintaining the information systems necessary to identify and monitor the various investments within a fund, and the skilled personnel required to market them, relies upon significant scale economies. These scale economies limit the effective diffusion of these products to smaller, third-level financial centers and provide the larger national centers with an important source of business.

In addition, success in attracting institutional funds to these products involves, in part, minimizing transaction costs and maximizing market share.

These transaction costs can be minimized by concentrating the administration and organization of the flow of funds, providing a further reason for the role of the first- and second-level centers; market share can also be maximized by location in these places, as companies can use their globally distributed networks of offices (needed to assemble the information on performance of potential stocks) to funnel funds to the large markets in these cities. The costs of the global networks become another source of scale economies available in the major markets. Hence, the large global centers and some of the big national markets have special roles to play in these activities. In effect, a second level of centers like Chicago, Frankfurt, Hong Kong, and Sydney can be added to the hierarchy.

Opaque Products—Subnational Centers

Finally, there are products where the design and production is shrouded in some mystery to the outsider, and local knowledge is essential for confident trading.[14] These are opaque products, like the REIT or property trust, where a set of properties are packaged into a product that can be sold in units or shares. The market success of the product will depend on attracting consumers desiring higher returns and confident about the apparent risks because of their access to local network-specific information. Property trusts will often be produced by firms with access to local markets as the information about them is so specialized, thereby providing the third layer in global financial geography. But, of course, these products may be consumed at distant locations. Places like Boston and Melbourne, for example, illustrate this type of city. Some products that incorporate high-profile properties in a number of cities may be traded across a national market. They may be produced by firms that also design translucent products and may aspire to the same level of market acceptability. If this happens, the role of the national-level cities in the financial hierarchy will be strengthened against subnational financial centers.

We have sought to show that the structure of the products is reflected in a structure of places. While our discussion has emphasized production, it is important to consider the pattern of consumption. As indicated earlier, this is technically possible from almost any location, and the more transparent the product the greater the probability that remote location dealers will be able to participate in central markets. However, there are some dimensions of consumption that reinforce the hierarchy of places rather than create a dispersed structure. One very significant factor is that much of consumption is now done by large funds on behalf of groups of investors (superannuation or pension funds especially). These consumers need a scale of market commensurate with their scale of turnover; in many countries the latter has been rising rapidly in recent years. Big buyers seek out big markets, and so contribute to the role that middle and larger centers play in the spatial hierarchy, while bypassing lower levels. The individual and smaller institutional trader may be able to operate effectively on the smaller national and regional markets but could be attracted by better information and trading systems toward larger places. Hence, the consumption of financial products contributes to the geography of financial centers, without necessarily focusing all activity in one place.

In essence, the spatial pattern of products and places reflects other dimensions of economic activity among markets, based on the range and threshold of the products themselves. The scale economies of transparent products means in effect they have a high threshold, and can only be effectively supplied from the global centers of the world. The need to maintain a diverse mix of instruments within translucent products, and the need to spread risk as widely as possible means that the producers of these products balance local knowledge and global sourcing where possible. In effect, then, these products have a wide range, and there are few places that can effectively provide the scope of the information the producers need. In contrast, smaller scale, localized opaque products have a lower threshold, and can be produced in smaller markets. Just as with a set of retail centers, where differences in range and threshold lead to hierarchies of outlets, so in the production of financial instruments the hierarchical pattern reflects supply-side considerations. The interdependent set of financial centers distributed across the globe reflects the characteristics of the different products and the location of their producers. The size and activity of each center reflect the mix of products that are available and the size of the markets that are accessible to producers. The hierarchical pattern may be undergoing change with the advent of communication technology (just as has happened in retailing), but the pattern retains structural rigidities and lacks the forces needed to produce the homogeneity implied by O'Brien (1992). The world's finance markets may be integrated in terms of consumption, as he suggests, but that integration need not produce a globalization or an implosion to just a few centers.

Geographical differentiation could also be understood as an opportunity set or map of markets and institutions that, by virtue of their heterogeneity (itself a product of history and path dependence) offer discrete opportunities for profit. Put another way, the problem with transparent products is that, for almost all investors, it is very difficult to make a *net* profit (after accounting for trading costs, etc.). Market segmentation, on the other hand, is a means of locating or isolating profit opportunities away from the core of the financial market system. In this sense, the continuing existence of spatial differentiation is a vital ingredient in any global financial firm's portfolio of investment opportunities. For these companies, translucent and opaque products built around distinctively different markets (and their industries, sectors, and investment opportunities) promise higher-than-average returns (albeit at a higher risk). Firms that specialize in these types of products, also, inevitably have distinct economic geographies. To the extent they are able to retain a firm-specific knowledge of these types of products (and their geographies), their operations remain separate from the transparent core of the global finance industry.

As noted earlier, it is the case that what may begin as opaque products may end up as transparent products. The packaging of global equity markets into tradeable index products by Barings, Morgan Stanley, and other companies is an instance where local knowledge of the peculiarities of emerging markets have been bypassed by a transparent type of financial product, which, by its very nature, discounts the relevance of local knowledge by spreading the risk of holding local stock across a large bundle of geographically diverse, market-specific stocks. These types of products, in effect, homogenize geography by discounting or pooling "local" risk. On the other hand, we should be wary of supposing that these types of index products effectively exclude other information-intensive (local) products. This does not seem to be the case. Rather, transparent, translucent, and opaque products coexist, drawing upon different consumer tastes and providing different kinds of risk-return profiles for clients. In this sense, they are equally a map of investment opportunities—from the core of the global financial system (where all three types of product are produced and consumed) out to the (subnational) periphery (where only opaque products are likely to be produced). With this in mind, it should be apparent that O'Brien's (1992) thesis is only plausible (empirically speaking) at the *core* of the global financial system, where a few transparent products dominate the total volume of investment transactions.

CUSTOM AND CONVENTION

Our discussion of financial products and their spatial logic was underpinned (albeit implicitly) by assumptions of rational optimizing behavior. The typology of products and the hierarchy of places rely upon firms acting in ways that sustain a logical ordering of the industry. As argued, it seems inevitable that products and places—the manifestations of firm behavior—should evolve together in such an efficient manner that the structure of the international financial industry comes to reflect the global configuration of products, costs, and benefits. In play, one way or another, is an evolutionary metaphor of selection and competitive survival quite in keeping with Alchian's (1950) notion of an evolving long-term equilibrium but at odds with recent models of financial firm behavior that tend to stress the contingent nature of interfirm competition (Clark, in press).

One advantage of this analytical strategy was that it allowed us a broad, integrative perspective matching in substance the breadth of debate apparent in discussions of the global city (compare with O'Brien, 1992, with Sassen,

1991). It would be misleading, however, to leave the reader with the impression that the logic apparent in the foregoing discussion of products and places is an adequate and sufficient representation of the structure of the financial world. More specifically, it should be obvious that the logic of the previous discussion of products and places is quite insensitive to history and geography—perhaps in keeping with O'Brien's thesis of the "end of geography." He seems to imply that the revolution in communications technology is so profound as to obliterate the past. Less profoundly, it may be that the new communications technology makes the past so inefficient relative to the near future that Alchian's evolutionary metaphor can be invoked to explain the necessary direction (if not rate) of adjustment and transformation. Notwithstanding the rhetorical scope of his vision, we would argue that there is no evidence for such a systematic shift against the complex topography of the financial world toward a new, stripped-out, centralized financial world.

There are a variety of ways of explaining the persistence of the global map of the financial industry against O'Brien's inexorable tendencies of centralization. Here, we explained persistence by invoking the informational content of financial products. The spatial economic hierarchy is, then, a consequence of the informational content of different types of products. Even so, our map of global financial industry is as rational as O'Brien's, even if differentiated. If geography and history are invoked as causes rather than as consequences of global financial differentiation (as previously suggested), we also have to account for the persistence of geography and history against the homogenizing or centralizing competitive forces of the international economy. This is a huge topic, and beyond the immediate scope of this chapter. Nevertheless, it is useful to briefly consider how and why geographical differentiation may persist over time.

One way of proceeding is to return to the issues initially ruled out of our analysis: that is, return to institutional differences between markets, differences of economic structures, and differences due to regulatory frameworks as reasons for the continuing relevance of history and geography. Here, a number of arguments might be made. It could be suggested that such differences between markets persist (and translate into global financial differentiation) because of their local value as opposed to their global efficiency. Put slightly differently, it might be reasonably imagined that because nations have different economic structures, reflecting in part differences in comparative advantage *and* imperfect price competition between nations (Cooper, 1994), nations' financial markets are differentiated according to the local value attributed to different types of financial products. For instance, countries and regions specializing in agricultural commodities for export may, in effect, demand transparent types of financial products rather than opaque products as hedging devices. Regulatory frameworks, to the extent they reflect the product interests of local financial elites would then reinforce differentiation between markets.[15] It might also be argued that as local demand is slowly overtaken (in some markets, if not all markets) by demand for a range of transparent financial products, geographical differentiation would diminish (Alchian's [1950] argument in another guise).

A way of avoiding this tendency toward homogenization (in theory and in effect) is to scrutinize more closely the implicit optimizing assumptions that underpin most financial analysis. We could argue, for example, that geographical differentiation persists in the global financial industry because local customs and conventions persist. How is that possible, given the overarching risk-return logic by which we began the chapter? Here, there are two related answers. First, the logic of risk and return is, itself, a social practice subject to local interpretation and the preferences of local clients. This does not mean that local interpretations are necessarily stable, nor does it mean that local interpretations exist totally separate from other interpretations in other jurisdictions. Given the intrusion of global finance companies into virtually all competitive securities markets, any local interpretation of risk and return is likely to be subject to rival interpretations. Second, the logic of risk and return is entirely theoretical; there is no dominant empirical recipe that has been shown to produce predictable and consistent results either by firm or by market. This is a profound empirical finding, now commonly recognized in the global finance industry. Not surprisingly, clients are very wary of grand claims of unique firm-specific or market-specific expertise. But because there are few common and stable reference points by which to judge the efficiency of the process of global investment management, local (firm-based and market-based) customs and conventions persist *and* flourish (Clark, in press).

In this context, it is difficult to accept any argument (inspired by Alchian-type reasoning) to the effect that history and geography are being systematically stripped out of the global finance industry. Indeed, quite the contrary. The fact that theory has not translated into practice in a comprehensively successful way has encouraged financial analysts to view local customs and conventions as systematic, albeit irrational in the strict sense attributed to the original MPT and Sharpe's versions thereof (Thaler, 1993).[16] For instance, Zeckhauser, Patel, and Hendricks (1991) identify four behavioral traits apparent in the U.S. investment management industry which seem systematic and yet irrational with respect to MPT. In summary terms, these are *barn door closing* where, against the logic of the efficient markets thesis, investors use past, apparently successful investment practices even though past success appears to be no guarantee of future success; *expert and reliance effects*, where local investors rely on advisers they know best, often forming long-term relationships, against the theoretical assumption in favor of diversification of expertise; *status quo bias* where, against the evidence of declining relative performance, investors tend to stay with underperforming advisers; and, *illusions, framing, and data packaging*, where investors tend to look at local performance relative to local bench marks as opposed to global performance.

Our point in citing this material is entirely provocative. Whereas writers such as Lash and Urry (1994) and McDowell and Court (1994a, 1994b), amongst many others, rightly observe that the finance industry is a complex social structure, differentiated by gender, class, and power, they nevertheless tend to imagine that what they observe in one market (for instance, London) or in a related complex of domestic and international firms is illustrative of a process of homogenization throughout the global industry. While accepting entirely their arguments about the significance of social differentiation, we believe that the investment process is itself spatially differentiated in part because of the scope for local interpretation of rules of investment behavior like risk and return. In this sense, we can see why institutional differences between markets, differences in countries' economic structures, and differences in their regulatory regimes may persist; these differences, like their associated social configurations, contribute to and reflect upon the significance attributed by many investors to local investment customs and conventions.

CONCLUSION

In this chapter, we provided a rationale for the existence of a hierarchy of places in the international finance industry. This rationale was framed with particular reference to (but against) the logic of O'Brien's (1992) thesis of the "end of geography." He argued that geography has all but disappeared (or will disappear) as an organizing principle explaining the structure of finance markets around the globe. We suggest he is mistaken. He is mistaken empirically and theoretically. There is no evidence that the global finance system is systematically centralizing to a point or fragmenting into a thousand pieces. A more plausible scenario is one in which international financial centers coexist with national and regional centers. Granted, coexistence may be tense and contested: New York competes directly with Chicago for national and international trading business, though few would suggest, we would guess, that New York dominates Chicago in the same way Chicago dominates the older midwestern financial markets like St. Louis and Minneapolis. We accept there are competing pressures for centralization and decentralization. But we do not accept O'Brien's notion of the accelerating (and in the end) obliteration of geography.

This empirical argument was, however, just the point of departure for the chapter. In fact, much of the chapter was devoted to a theoretical rationale for the continuing significance of geography in the global financial industry. Here, we emphasized the design of financial products, arguing that different types of products have a logical location in the global economy. Rather than identify particular of products according to their location of consumption, we concentrated upon a typology of products differentiated by virtue of their information intensity. Transparent products are those that require little in the way of particular information; we can buy these products from remote locations on the basis of reported prices (in the media). Many of these types of products are produced, however, in just a few places around the globe. Why? Because of the economies of scale inherent in securities trading *and* the comparative advantage of those places and the global finance companies located in those places. At the other end of the scale, opaque products are local in the sense of being network- or transaction-specific. They require heavy investment in terms of the collection, sorting, and valuing of information, and a degree of monitoring and surveillance that can only be efficiently done at the local level.

We have also noted, though, that this ideal match between types of products and levels of the global finance industry is an intellectual device. It is a means of demonstrating the status of geography in terms of the dominant logic of the international finance industry. As such, it is an argument that takes as given the logic that underpins O'Brien's thesis. While he is less than forthcoming about his theoretical assumptions, we have argued that his model seems to be built upon modern portfolio theory matched with recent innovations in communications technology, which (in combination) seem to suggest the existence of a hegemonic logic and global system of trading that collapses to a world dominated by just a few financial centers. Not surprisingly, in O'Brien's hands, there is no room for geography. We have shown that even by that logic the existence of different types of products produces geography, as different geographies imply different products.

We have also suggested that local customs, market behavior, and conventions sustain the persistence of spatial differentiation. Superficially, their significance may be attributed to momentary market or behavioral irrationality, to be stripped out of the system by global economic competition in a manner consistent with Alchian's (1950) model of (natural) economic selection. But we also suggest that there are reasons why these so-called irrationalities persist. The very foundations of global financial management—risk and return—are contingent upon interpretation and shared social practice for their meaning. In this context, the notion of a centralized global financial industry is, with respect to the process of institutional investment management, both a misnomer and an exaggeration. A more sophisticated explanation of the spatial structure of the industry should be able to account for, and respect, the persistence of local customs and conventions or, put slightly differently, the coexistence of large and small financial centers across the globe.

APPENDIX: STRUCTURE OF INTERNATIONAL GOLD PRICES

Here we report in more detail on the tests we undertook in evaluating the structure of London and New York day-to-day (1993–1994) gold closing prices. Following the empirical methodology in J. P. Morgan's *RiskMetrics*, three different set of tests were undertaken. First, we sought to determine the existence (or otherwise) of serial autocorrelation in the two price series (London's and New York's gold prices) and the day-to-day differences between the two markets' closing prices. This led us to the following observations and results.

1. As raw observations, the two markets' price series were not stationary, but after differencing $(X_t - X_{t-1})$ could be induced to be so.
2. There was no evidence from either the *acf* or the *pacf* of serial autocorrelation in the two markets' price series or the difference series.
3. In terms of serial autocorrelation, the price series were all random walks—that is, $X_t = X_{t-1} - \epsilon_t$.

Second, we also sought to determine whether the difference price series contained, hidden from the tests for serial autocorrelation, systematic periodicities. Here, a series of windows—weekly, monthly, 3-monthly, and yearly—were constructed to test for periodicities. This analysis led to a further finding:

4. There is no evidence of underlying, recurrent cycles in the structure of the difference price series.

Third, assuming then that the distribution of day-to-day differences in the two markets' gold prices is a normal distribution, we sought to establish statistically whether that was true. Notice that for J. P. Morgan, at any rate, this issue—normality—is very important in making an assessment of potential market risk. In this respect:

5. The distribution of price differences could be reasonably thought to be a normal distribution.
6. However, there was strong evidence of *leptokurtosis* but no evidence of skewness or distended tails of the normal distribution.

In essence, and quite unlike most other securities, the structure of gold price differences is as we would expect if finance markets are *strongly* efficient.

ACKNOWLEDGMENTS

This chapter was first presented at the North American Regional Science conference, Niagara Falls, November 1994, and was subsequently presented at the University of Auckland, Oxford University, and Seoul National Univerity. It reflects research done under a 3-year grant funded by the Australian Research Council. It is also linked to an ongoing project on superannuation (pension) investment strategies sponsored by the Australian Housing and Urban Research Institute. Data on London and New York gold prices were provided by Norwich Investment Management Ltd. (Melbourne). Debra Robertson and Benny Cheung, both of J. P. Morgan, provided the material *RiskMetrics*. Nigel Thrift, John Evans, Robert C. Merton, Kevin Cox, and Shirley Clark and seminar participants provided comments on previous drafts of the chapter. None of the above are responsible for any errors or omissions.

NOTES

1. We find it surprising that analysts like O'Brien (1992) insist that the global integration of the finance industry is a new phenomenon. Neal's (1990) study of the global nature of the finance industry during the 17th, 18th, and 19th centuries is a neat counterpoint to exaggerated claims of a new (late 20th century) epoch. He assembles quantitative evidence to show that global financial integration was an important aspect of the advanced world's financial system centuries ago.

2. At present, the best illustration of the significance of this issue has to do with the regulation of derivatives. Just as many countries are (notwithstanding the Barings debacle) liberalizing the regulation of their securities markets to allow for local firms to trade in these kinds of products, the United States is considering tightening its regulations in the hope of avoiding "sudden failure" and "liquidity problems in the markets" as well as potential threats to the financial integrity of "federally insured banks and the financial system as a whole" (Bothwell, 1994, p. 2). It is also the case that, given global competition amongst financial markets, any change in local regulations has to be matched against the map of related global regulation (if any) if local firms are to remain competitive in the industry. See Kane (1991) on the scope for domestic regulation of international finance.

3. To illustrate, Quinlivan's (1994) *Dictionary of Superannuation* published by the Association of Superannuation Funds of Australia (ASFA) and sponsored by a major funds manager, National Mutual, contains the terms and concepts of funds management commonly accepted in the United Kingdom, the United States, and Europe. Indeed, it is difficult to discern the national origin of some industry dictionaries; compare Quinlivan's with County NatWest (1994). Behind these dictionaries are international investment consultants like J. P. Morgan and Arthur Andersen (1994)—see their *Guide to Corporate Exposure Management*—equally at home in the Anglo-American world as well as France, Italy, and Germany (see the Geneva Stock Exchange's [1994] *Multilingual Financial Glossary*).

4. See also Patel, Zeckhauser, and Hendricks (1994) on the apparent shortcomings of Sharpe's (1964) CAPM and its progeny. They assert that the theory's predictions do not stand empirical scrutiny nor, most importantly, can the theory account for investor behavior that systematically flouts its essential tenets (like rationality).

5. For a related argument, see Cooper's (1994) review of the evidence against the so-called "law of one price": that, after adjusting for government import taxes, transport costs, and the like, there should be no real difference between countries' prices for given homogeneous commodities. Cooper argues that international commodity markets are not perfect, and that economists' obsession with commodities' real prices ignores the fact that nominal prices are actually very important in financial markets—witness the recurrent appearance of speculative bubbles.

6. Note that these results are consistent with Taylor's (1989) empirical analysis of

a select group of UK securities' price volatilities over a 20-year period. He shows that small but profitable arbitrage opportunities occur occasionally but that during periods of calm in the markets (no exogenous information shocks) those arbitrage opportunities disappear. He also provides evidence to the effect that over the 1970s and 1980s the size, frequency, and persistence of arbitrage opportunities have declined. We were not able to test this proposition (see Appendix).

7. Many investment houses trade gold and other commodities on a 24-hour basis. And many have central offices, versions of O'Brien's (1992) electronic world. But it is also clear that individual markets have their own *mentalities*: a sort of collective consciousness that is used to interpret and value global information in different ways between markets. We have been told by respondents a number of times that local firms dominated by central offices (say in London) often make mistakes about local conditions, believing, wrongly, that common data is the same as common information.

8. This argument about the coexistence of different financial centers, from core centers through to the periphery, has an analogue in arguments about the coexistence of spatially differentiated centers of manufacturing and trade. In Clark and Wrigley (in press) it is shown, in theory at least, why corporations may actively manage spatial differentiation as part of a larger risk management strategy (cf. Froot, Scharfstein, & Stein, 1993).

9. See a recent issue (Vol. 21, No. 10, March 4, 1994) of Morningstar's *Mutual Funds*. Therein, the editor complains about the lack of disclosure of most mutual funds regarding the actual management of those funds (firm-specific expertise). The editor argues that funds are deliberately obscuring the management process, who is in charge, and even the role of funds employees in the management process. More recently, a report in *Pensions and Investments* (Vol. 22, No. 21, October 17, 1994) accused some mutual funds of deliberately misclassifying their investment styles so as to achieve higher rankings by mutual funds performance valuators.

10. Relational investing is increasingly popular (again), at least in the academic literature. Columbia University's Center for Law and Economic Studies sponsored a major conference on the topic in 1993 based upon the supposition that, as the merger and acquisitions wave of the 1980s has receded, corporate governance has become more important as a means of sustaining shareholder value than the market for corporate control. In this context, relational investing is seen as a mode of institutional investing that aims "to enhance the quality, independence, and accountability of the board" in the interests of sustaining the long-term performance of corporations (Gordon, 1994, p. 127). Thus, following the experience of Japan and Germany, by this model institutional investors act, in effect, more like owners of the firm than "short term traders or arbitrageurs."

11. For a brief overview of the design and argued advantages of REITs in the U.S. context, see Gyourko and Nelling (1994). In theory, it is normally thought that REITs have a significant advantage over conventional asset classes because, by spatial and sector diversification of properties, investors are able to minimize systematic risk. Gyourko and Nelling dispute this assumption, and argue that sectoral diversification is more important than spatial diversification. Most important, though, in terms of the attractiveness of REITs as an asset class is the extent to which investors can "look through" the apparent structure of REITs to their actual operation and management.

12. The difference between an "emerging market" and a "less developed country" is difficult to discern in reading the trade literature. Recent issues of the *Emerging*

Markets Week include countries like Peru, Mexico, Vietnam, India, Poland, and China as emerging markets. In fact, the only countries not often listed as emerging markets seem to be African countries. Data on trading volumes in emerging markets' securities are difficult to find. According to the *Institutional Investor* (Vol. 28, No. 4, April 1994), in 1993 trading volume doubled in emerging markets driven largely by "yield-hungry U.S. investors" (p. 63). As a consequence, there can be extraordinary volatility in emerging markets as U.S. investors respond to rumors and advice in the market (witness the recent reaction to Mexican debt).

13. It is equally true that these kinds of places are intimately linked with what Roberts (1994, p. 92) identifies as a "series of little places"—the homes of all kinds of furtive capital whose offshore locations belie their close connections with the centers of global finance.

14. Here, we emphasize local knowledge and the costs of information acquisitions. This reflects our own methodological assumptions and empirical experience. Also important, however, are local and international business networks. These networks, if stable and self-governing, would be highly efficient mechanisms for sorting and valuing information, thereby allowing opaque products to have a wider spatial scope than we have suggested. See Thrift (1994) for an especially instructive instance (the City of London).

15. We were impressed by Cronin's (1991) historical geography of the emergence of the Chicago Board of Trade. His discussion documents the rapid evolution from individually labeled bags of wheat (opaque products) through to graded wheat accompanied by elevator delivery dockets that then could be traded as futures (translucent products). The role of institutions in grading wheat and regulating market membership, including channeling price information elsewhere, laid the foundations for a globally transparent commodity and product market.

16. Not all finance theorists are so enthusiastic about the new interest in nonrational market behavior. Jensen (1994), for one, while arguing for a richer conception of human behavior in economic modeling, is unwilling to abandon the joined actions of self-interest and utility maximization. It seems he is skeptical of other models of human nature which are not, at their core, based upon individual interests. Compare with Amin and Thrift (1992).

REFERENCES

Alchian, A. (1950). Uncertainty, evolution and economic theory. *Journal of Political Economy, 58*, 211–222.

Amin, A., & Thrift, N. (1992). Neo-Marshallian nodes in global networks. *International Journal of Urban and Regional Research, 16*, 571–587.

Black, F., & Scholes, M. (1973). The pricing of options and corporate liabilities. *Journal of Political Economy, 81*, 637–659.

Bothwell, J. L. (1994). *Actions needed to protect the financial system.* Testimony, House of Representatives (GAO/T-GGD-94-196). Washington DC: General Accounting Office.

Chen, Z., & Knez, P. (1994). *Measurement of market integration and arbitrage.* Mimeo, Graduate School of Business, University of Wisconsin, Madison.

Clark, G. L. (in press). Global finance and local investment: Competitive practice in the Anglo-American industry. In M. Gertler & T. Barnes (Eds.), *Regions, institutions, and technology: Re-organizing the economic geography of the Anglo-American world*. Montreal: McGill–Queen's University Press.

Clark, G. L., & Wrigley, N. (in press). The spatial configuration of the firm and the management of such costs. *Economic Geography*.

Cooper, R. (1994). An overview of (older) exchange rate theory. In R. Sato, R. Levich, & R. Ramachandran (Eds.), *Japan, Europe and international financial markets* (pp. 26–33). Cambridge: Cambridge University Press.

County NatWest (1994). *Dictionary of investment terms*. Melbourne: Author.

Cronin, W. (1991). *Natures's metropolis: Chicago and the Great West*. New York: Norton.

Daniels, P. (1993). *Service industries in the world economy*. Oxford: Blackwell.

Fama, E. (1991). Efficient capital markets II. *Journal of Finance, 46,* 1575–1617.

Fama, E., & French, K. (1992). The cross-section of expected stock returns. *Journal of Finance, 47,* 427–465.

Froot, K., Scharfstein, D., & Stein, J. (1993). Risk management: Coordinating corporate investment and financing policies. *Journal of Finance, 48,* 1629–1658.

Geneva Stock Exchange (1994). *Term finance: Multilingual financial glossary*. Geneva: Author.

Gordon, J. (1994). Institutions as relational investors: A new look at cumulative voting. *Columbia Law Review, 94,* 124–192.

Grossman, S. (1989). *The informational role of prices*. Cambridge, MA: MIT Press.

Gyourko, J., & Nelling, E. (1994). *Systematic risk and diversification in the equity REIT market* (Working Paper 11–94). Philadelphia: Rodney L. White Center for Financial Research, Wharton School, University of Pennsylvania.

Jensen, M. (1994). Self-interest, altruism, incentives and agency theory. *Journal of Applied Corporate Finance, 7*(2), 40–45.

Jobling, M. (1994). *A legal perspective on targeted superannuation investment: A comparison between the United States and Australia* (Working Paper 1). Melbourne: Australian Housing and Urban Research Institute.

J. P. Morgan (1994). *RiskMetrics–technical document*. New York: Author.

J. P. Morgan & Arthur Anderson (1994). *Guide to corporate exposure management*. London: Financial Engineering.

Kane, E. (1991). Financial regulations of market forces. *Swiss Journal of Economics and Statistics, 127,* 325–342.

Lash, S., & Urry, J. (1994). *Economies of signs and spaces*. London: Sage.

Markowitz, H. (1952). Portfolio selection. *Journal of Finance, 7,* 77–91.

Martin, R. (1994). Stateless monies, global financial integration and national economic autonomy: The end of geography? In S. Corbridge, R. Martin, & N. Thrift (Eds.), *Money, power and space* (pp. 253–278). Oxford: Blackwell.

McDowell, L., & Court, G. (1994a). Gender divisions of labor in the post-Fordist economy: The maintenance of occupational sex segregation in the financial services sector. *Environment and Planning A, 26,* 1397–1418.

McDowell, L., & Court, G. (1994b). Performing work: Bodily representations in merchant banks. *Environment and Planning D: Society and Space, 12,* 727–750.

Merton, R. C. (1993). *Operation and regulation in financial intermediation: A functional perspective*. (Working Paper 93–020). Boston: Harvard Business School.

Merton, R. C. (1994). Influence of mathematical models in finance on practice: Past, present and future. *Philosophical Transactions, Royal Society* (London), *347*, 451–463.

Neal, L. (1990). *The rise of financial capitalism: International capital markets in the Age of Reason.* Cambridge: Cambridge University Press

Ng, V. K., & Pirrong, S. C. (1994). Fundamentals and volatility: Storage, spreads, and the dynamics of metals prices. *Journal of Business, 67*, 203–230.

Noyelle, T. J. (1989). New York's competitiveness. In T. J. Noyelle (Ed.), *The challenge of globalization* (pp. 51–90). Boulder, CO: Westview Press.

O'Brien, R. (1992). *Global financial integration: The end of geography.* London: The Royal Institute of International Affairs.

Patel, J., Zeckhauser, R., & Hendricks, D. (1994). Investment flows and performance: Evidence from mutual funds, cross-border, investments, and new issues. In R. Sato, R. Levich, & R. Ramachandran (Eds.), *Japan, Europe, and international financial markets* (pp. 51–72). Cambridge: Cambridge University Press.

Reed, H. C. (1981). *The pre-eminence of international financial centers.* New York: Praeger.

Roberts, S. (1994). Fictitious capital, fictitious spaces: The geography of offshore financial flows. In S. Corbridge, R. Martin, & N. Thrift (Eds.), *Money, power and space* (pp. 91–115). Oxford: Blackwell.

Roll, R. (1977). A critique of the asset pricing theory's tests. *Journal of Financial Economics, 4*, 129–176.

Roll, R. (1992). Industrial structure and the comparative behaviour of international stock market indices. *Journal of Finance, 47*, 3–41.

Roll, R., & Ross, S. A. (1994). On the cross-sectional relation between expected returns and betas. *Journal of Finance, 9*, 101–121.

Ross, S. (1989). Institutional markets, financial marketing, and financial innovation. *Journal of Finance, 44*, 541–556.

Sanford, C. (1993). *Financial markets in 2020.* Wyoming: Federal Reserve Bank of Kansas City Economic Symposium.

Sassen, S. (1991). *The global city: New York, London, Tokyo.* Princeton, NJ: Princeton University Press.

Sharpe, W. (1964). Capital asset prices: A theory of market equilibrium of the conditions of risks. *Journal of Finance, 19*, 425–442.

Sharpe, W., & Alexander, G. J. (1990). *Investments* (4th ed.). Englewood Cliffs, NJ: Prentice-Hall.

Smith, A. D. (1992). *International financial markets: The performance of Britain and its rivals.* Cambridge: Cambridge University Press.

Taylor, M. (1989). Covered interest arbitrage and market turbulence. *Economic Journal, 99*, 376–391.

ter Hart, H. W., & Peirsma, J. (1990). Direct representation in international financial markets: the case of foreign banks in Amsterdam. *Tijdschrift voor Economische en Sociale Geographie, 81*, 82–92.

Thaler, R. (Ed.). (1993). *Advances in behavioral finance.* New York: Russell Sage Foundation.

Thrift, N. (1994). On the social and cultural determinants of international financial centres: The case of the City of London. In S. Corbridge, R. Martin, & N. Thrift (Eds.), *Money, power and space* (pp. 327–355). Oxford: Blackwell.

Zeckhauser, R., Patel, J., & Hendricks, D. (1991). Nonrational actors and financial market behaviour. *Theory and Decision, 31*, 257–267.

CHAPTER 5

Globalization and the Politics of Distribution

A CRITICAL ASSESSMENT

Kevin R. Cox

CONTEXT

The idea of the politics of globalization, at least as far as political economy is concerned, has emerged in the context of two interrelated sets of issues. Its dominant form has been distributional. There is also, however, a politics that is more concerned with the disintegration of economies as coherent objects of policy intervention; the focus here is regulation.

In the distributional politics of globalization there is a counterposing of capital which is mobile at diverse scales—international, interregional, and interurban—to what are variously described as communities, labor, residents. These tend, in turn, to be relatively *im*mobile. This counterposition, or so it is claimed, has given capital a bargaining advantage in determining the terms on which it enters and remains in particular locations. Communities, nation-states, cities, union locals, compete for employment by offering various concessions to business to locate there: tax concessions, loans at highly advantageous rates, generous land-use control consideration, the rewriting of labor law, wage concessions from unions. Apart from the concessions made to particular firms, there is a more general sensitivity to the demands of business. This sensitivity is registered in caution on raising taxation levels, in incurring debt, in extending welfare provisions, and in engaging in expansionary macropolicies.

The second form of the politics of globalization concerns the regulation of economies so as to achieve macroeconomic objectives. At the national level these typically include growth, a stable price level, and full employment. Globalization is a challenge to regulation, it is argued, due to the disintegration of national economies as coherent objects. The openness of national economies in terms of trade, capital flows, has led to what has become known as "territorial noncorrespondence": the agents and/or the social relations that those agents control and over which nations states need power if they are to regulate effectively either lie geographically outside their jurisdiction or can be so relocated. These agents are typically conceived of as firms and the relationships in question as their commodity chains.

The major emphasis of this chapter is that particular politics of globalization that has focused on the distributional. This is not to say that the distributional and the regulatory can be kept apart. For a start, macroeconomic regulation helps define the possibilities of distribution. In consequence, and at various points in the text, I will need to draw attention to some regulatory issues.

In this chapter I offer a critique of the distributional politics of globalization. This is not because of any skepticism regarding the existence of the processes and effects identified by it. Rather, I believe that their significance has been overestimated, and that while there are numerous instances in which they apply there has been a quite serious overgeneralization. But, and on the other hand, I do not wish my emphasis on overgeneralization to be misplaced. The critique I offer is only secondarily an empirical one. Rather, what I want to show is that the effects identified in the politics of globalization could not possibly be true as a general case. Furthermore, an attention to first principles, principles that have to do largely with concepts of capitalist development, facilitates an awareness of other effects that place the conclusions of the politics of globalization in a much more critical light.

THE SPATIALITY OF GLOBALIZATION

Dominant themes in the contemporary politics of globalization rest on certain quite basic assumptions as to the spatiality of that globalization. These refer to the respective mobilities of productive capital and of labor power. For diverse reasons it is believed that the range of substitutability of locations for industrial capital has greatly widened. These reasons include improvements in transportation and communications, both in terms of cost and time; and a deskilling of labor processes that has allowed industrial capitals to relocate production operations from higher wage to lower wage areas of the world[1]: Castells's (1983) space of flows.

There are no changing conditions, however, that might transform the mobility of labor power. Labor power, it is assumed, remains immobile. This has placed it at a disadvantage in bargaining for higher wages and improved work conditions. Industrial capitals will respond to increasing costs of operation by simply relocating elsewhere. Alternatively, they will go out of business as a result of the competition of those who have so relocated or from firms that have sprung up to exploit the newly accessible pools of cheap labor around the globe. Indeed, in order to retain industrial employment it may be necessary to reduce labor costs and to offer various inducements—changes in labor law, tax abatements—to persuade firms to continue investing there.[2] These pressures are particularly serious in First World locations where labor costs are already high, but even in some of the Newly Industrializing Countries (NICs) competition with cheaper labor elsewhere is already being experienced.

The enhanced locational substitutability that capital enjoys has also served to limit the regulatory powers of nation-states and their diverse agencies, both central and local. This is due to their own form of immobility. They experience problems of territorial noncorrespondence in trying to regulate all the relations pertinent to the national economy, or local economy, for that matter, simply because of the way those relations overlap jurisdictional boundaries. And to the extent that nation-states do not have jurisdiction, capitals have, when threatened by regulatory programs, a credible counterthreat. In consequence, state regulatory power has experienced a retreat. It is this which has led to calls for new regulatory mechanisms at supranational levels.

If this counterposition of relative mobilities is a constant theme in the literatures, there is less unity of opinion on the nature of the more concrete transformations of economic geography over which they preside. There are questions here of geographic scale, as well as, relatedly, the degree to which globalization can be reduced to, for example, a relation between the First and Third Worlds. In consequence, and before we turn to examining the question of relative mobilities, it would seem necessary to obtain a more precise idea of the particular arenas within which so-called globalization is occurring.

Geographies of Globalization

The changes in location usually considered under this rubric are by no means straightforward. Although the thesis of the New International Division of Labor is a highly visible and certainly publicized feature of the changes taking place they cannot be reduced to it alone. Much of the change occurring is between the more developed countries. It is, in other words, internal to the First World rather than involving a geographical reorganization of production across the First World–Third World boundary. The changes occurring in the geography of the automobile industry are well known, but there are many other cases of growth and a decline that is at least relative: the growth of international banking in London at the expense of Frankfurt and Paris; the emergence of a viable commercial aircraft industry in Western Europe and its relative decline in Southern California and St. Louis following the eclipse of McDonnel–Douglas; the growth of consumer electronics in Japan at the expense of American and British producers; the growth of the Japanese and German machine tool industries at the expense of U.S. firms; and so on.

The New International Division of Labor assumes a division between First and Third World sites. According to this, headquarters functions, research and development (R&D), and the more skilled production tasks remain in the more developed countries, while the more deskilled tasks are transferred to branch plants in Third World countries. But, in fact, many of these firm spatial divisions of labor are confined to the First World: the headquarters and R&D of the Japanese auto or consumer electronics firm remain in Japan, while branch plants are set up in small towns in the United States or in the depressed areas of Britain.

Just how significant the movements within the First World are relative to those between it and the Third World is difficult to calculate. Important questions, for example, are the degree to which First World imports are shifting from First World origins in the direction of Third World ones; and the degree to which First World investment is increasingly oriented away from the First to the Third World. Gordon (1988) has expressed extreme skepticism on both these scores. In a survey of the available evidence, he finds that in 1983 the developed market economies imported a smaller proportion of their total imports from the non-oil exporting Less Developed Countries (LDCs) than they had in 1959, and that even though the import penetration by the NICs had increased since 1966 it had barely regained the level enjoyed in 1959 (p.48). Likewise with investment, Gordon (1988, p. 50) states: ". . . it is difficult to sustain the conclusion that investment capital is racing away from the advanced economies, draining off our shores at an accelerating pace."[3]

Yet to highlight shifts between countries is again a serious oversimplification. To some degree this is recognized in many of the literatures that draw on images of globalization. Accordingly, the "global" can refer to anything from the metropolitan economy at one end, through the national to the international; while the "local" can refer to the city, the region, the nation, and even particular types of neighborhoods, like the inner city. First World countries have their own peripheries. These are the destinations not just for investments in branch plants coming from outside the country, but also for those coming from territorial production complexes within.

The constant element in all this is the maintenance of some sort of relational concept of scale rather than one that equates the global with the international and the local with the sub-national. Important literatures in the distributional politics include those of the New Urban Politics (NUP) (Cox, 1993, 1995) and that subscribing to the "capital versus communities" thesis of Bluestone and Harrison (1982). The particular "global" to which they relate is not always transparent. It could be competition for capitals that, while mobile, are confined to a national arena, or for capitals that are able to substitute between countries. An older literature, that relating urban poverty to suburbanization, clearly identifies the metropolitan as the global arena. On the other hand, the world cities literature, like that on the New International Division of

Labor, has been more emphatic on the international aspects of mobile capital and its implications for the politics of distribution.

The Mobility of Capital

The geographies frequently projected by the politics of globalization are nothing if not apocalyptic.[4] In a context of radical change in transportation and communication and the deskilling of labor processes, existing territorial production complexes melt away, to be replaced by back offices in small towns in respective national peripheries and by production facilities in Third World export processing zones. Concentration and immobilization in the First World, in metropolitan areas and conurbations there, is displaced by a dispersion of facilities. Existing locations have no stability, as firms move around seeking better conditions elsewhere.

The first thing to note here is that the conditions believed to be necessary for the enhanced locational substitutability implied by globalization arguments—the deskilling of labor processes, improvements in transportation and communication, and the vertical integration of labor processes within firms—are highly overgeneralized. They have occurred to variable degrees, and where they have occurred the effects of all three have been very uneven. Given the wide variety across industries in the concrete nature of products and conditions of production, this should not be surprising.

Deskilling is not nearly as universal or as inevitable as is implied by much of the literature. There is still a great deal of relatively skilled work, not learnt quickly, which would be difficult to relocate to a Third World or even Second World environment. Many of these labor processes are found in the so-called technology- or knowledge-intensive industries, and these have proven resistant to decentralization in the classic branch plant image. Moreover, the competitive position of many of these activities will likely be enhanced as a result of the growth in less developed countries of industries where deskilling *is* possible. This is because that growth in turn will resulted in increased demands for machine tools, water purification plants, steam turbines, transportation equipment, earth moving equipment, and the like.

Likewise, the needs of particular industries, firms, in terms of the cost, speed, and timeliness of transportation vary a great deal. With some products cost of transportation may be less significant than the achievement of speedier and smaller deliveries on a continual basis so that quality can be monitored and deficiencies quickly corrected. In this regard the transportation of subassemblies has to be subject to a different calculus from that applying to the transport of semirefined minerals or coal. This type of consideration has recently gained in importance with the interest in just-in-time forms of production organization. Cheap as transportation might be from a branch plant in a low labor-cost location, the time taken to deliver and the need to transport in bulk if cost economies are to be realized may be serious impediments to its establishment.

New communication technologies have been a precondition for the location of American back offices in Ireland and the Caribbean. Data inputs are delivered by overnight jet and the results beamed back to the United States by satellite for the beginning of the next business day. But much depends on the nature of the interaction. Video conferencing has its uses, but by no means can the communication important to the conduct of business be reduced to electronics. Indeed, it is hard to envisage precisely what would facilitate, at a distance, the sort of random, incidental, face-to-face contacts out of which insights about people, their trustworthiness, their personal strengths and weaknesses can be built up, or, alternatively, the generation of ideas for new products or ways of organizing the labor process. New modes of transportation and communication all have their possibilities for particular concrete forms of commodity and interaction, but their range of applicability is always circumscribed, sometimes quite seriously.

The third and final condition, sometimes, though less often, referred to in discussions of capital's hypermobility, is the vertical integration of labor processes. The argument here is that this emancipates the firm from the need to insert itself in a wider social division of labor for inputs or for markets for intermediate outputs. Instead of relying on another firm for parts and so having one's relative location structured accordingly, the labor process in question can be assigned to a branch plant. This assumes, of course, that the labor process has been deskilled and that there are no serious transportation constraints to location relative to the other parts of the firm's technical division of labor that might stand in the way of taking advantage of low-cost labor elsewhere. This means that the possibilities of integration are seen to depend on the satisfaction of the other two conditions commonly noted as necessary if globalization is to occur.

These widely held assumptions about the conditions for capital mobility can be placed in a broader theoretical context that ultimately, as we will see later in the chapter, can be referred to a particular view of capital as a social relation. Thus, to the extent that the politics of globalization in its distributional variant relies on notions of the increasing mobility of firms, then it depends on a particular conception of capitalist competition: that it is *cost reducing*. Firms move in the direction of deskilled labor because deskilled labor is cheaper. They are able so to move because transportation costs have come down to such a degree that the cost of bringing in parts or finished products from distant production points is not so high as to offset the gains from reducing labor costs. Obviously, firm competitive strategies can by no means be so reduced. Firms also compete through their products—their quality, reliability, novelty, costs of operation, ease of repair, durability.

But assuming for the time being that firms do indeed single-mindedly pursue cost-reduction strategies of competition, the first point that we should note is that deskilling and vertical integration are in no way inevitable outcomes or even objectives of that search. The precise form of a cheapening strategy is a contingent matter. It may indeed be achieved, as per the NUP, by deskilling or by vertical integration, but it may not be. It may be that, given particular combinations of machine–raw–material–skill–productivity, the cheapening strategy lies in *re*skilling. Likewise, although at a given point in time there may be economies from vertical integration, cheapening at other times may be a result of *dis*integration: uncertainties in product markets may emerge that discourage quasi-fixed expenditures and encourage alternative strategies of obtaining access to the technologies entailed by those expenditures, like subcontracting. Alternatively, labor market difficulties may suggest the advisability of spinning off operations, resulting in greater reliance on nonunionized subcontractors. The conclusion has to be therefore that there are no *secular* tendencies to deskilling or to vertical integration, and to the extent that arguments about hypermobility rely on the assumption that there are, then doubt is also cast on *that* particular thesis.

This is particularly interesting in light of the emphasis that Scott (1985) has given to vertically disintegrated labor processes in understanding the persistence of agglomerative effects in modern space economies. Far from melting away, as we might expect if the dire predictions of the effects of deskilling, firm integration, and reduced transportation costs were true, large agglomerations of interrelated firms persist.

The vertically disintegrated firm provides several advantages. Quite apart from it offering the maximal economies of scale given current technologies, it also means heightened firm specialization. Each firm focuses on a particular stage in an input–output chain, and this facilitates the learning process, an understanding of the technology and mode of organization of labor, and so the development of new ways of reducing costs. But if these advantages are to be secured, the individual firm has to be close to its suppliers and its clients. The smallness of vertically disintegrated firms means that they have difficulty taking advantage of the discounts that transportation firms offer for large orders. This is the origin of the agglomeration effect.

But as the agglomeration develops, new, reinforcing effects emerge. To the extent that the constituent firms are indeed able to descend a cost-reduction curve as a result of their specialization, this places firms elsewhere, less vertically disintegrated perhaps, at a disadvantage. The only place where production is economically possible becomes the agglomeration. As firms elsewhere die out, so too do the skills in those locations. The agglomeration that is now monopolizing those skills and associated knowledges grows further, therefore. New firms come into being. With this expansion, further vertical disintegration and hence further firm-specialization may be possible. The growth in demand may mean that market thresholds are reached for firms to further subdivide and relocate particular aspects of respective labor processes into new firms.

Much of this will be familiar. It is important to recognize, however, that it has a much wider applicability. Amin and Thrift (1992, p. 573) have referred to the recent consolidation of major metropolitan centers, though without elaborating on the reasons for it. But if industrial districts help to entrench particular roles in the spatial division of labor, then arguably similar forces are at work in the transformation of the scale division of labor (Cox & Mair, 1991), a transformation that has worked to the advantage of the metropolitan centers identified by Amin and Thrift.

This sheds a new light on the question of capital mobility. Mobilizing external economies of scale depends on the preservation of accessibility relations not just to one but perhaps to several other firms. Assuming the competitive logic just outlined, finding similar complexes of activities that could provide acceptable locational substitutes seems unlikely. Further, except for the largest firms that have strong market power the reconstitution of the cluster of firms in another location would be extremely difficult.

These conclusions are reinforced when we turn and examine the problem of firm mobility not from the standpoint of cost minimization but from that of product-based forms of competition. Instead of choosing to compete with other firms in terms of costs, firms obviously can and do compete in terms of the qualities of the product they offer: upgrading it, giving it some feature that no other product has, or simply replacing it altogether. In some industries, like pharmaceuticals, this is, of course, standard practice. This obviously applies also to intermediate products. Manufacturers of machine tools, of oil-refining equipment, of electric turbines and jet engines, all may, in fact almost certainly will, pursue product development and innovation strategies. Some of the products in question do not have the tangible quality that we typically associate with them. But the knowledges that, for example, consulting civil engineers, the designers of financial products, and architects draw on are also subject to conscious change with a view to obtaining a competitive advantage.

The point of immediate significance here is that the conditions under which product upgrading/transformation/innovation occur tend to be *locationally embedding*. This is because of the crucial role that *social learning* plays in the product development and innovation process. All production, of course, is the outcome of a process of social learning. But if the sort of learning that underlies product development and innovation is to take place—what Storper (1992) has termed "product-based technological learning"—then there has to be some stability in the locational relationships of those party to it: people have to be working together on a day-to-day basis for a sustained period of time, and firms working at different stages of the input–output chain have to be collaborating with each other; spatial separation can sever those arrangements.

Accordingly, firms with strong records of product development and innovation tend to be locationally stable and purposely exploit the advantages of that locational stability. They develop relations with other firms and exchange knowledge with them. These may be firms working on the same product or firms that actually consume the final product. It is important, for instance, that the producers of machine tools be in continual contact with the industrial firms that consume their products so that problems encountered in the running-in process can be eliminated, and new needs identified. In Chapter 2 of this volume, Gertler emphasizes the importance of close spatial relations between the producers of technology and their users. Recent empirical evidence is consistent with this view (Fagerberg, 1995). At another stage in the development of new products, their actual launching on the market, a spatial concentration again becomes important, owing to the intense and frequent personal communications and rapid decision making necessary at that stage (Patel, 1995, p. 152). Recent work on the introduction of new financial products underlines this point (Pryke & Lee, 1995).

On the other hand, the conditions for social learning and for the development of the division of labor can by no means be reduced to some ideal type of small, vertically and horizontally disintegrated firms. They may, rather, be as much within-plant and within-firm as they are between.[5] The fact of extremely dynamic firms dominating local economies but with little local synergy is exemplary. There are also those cases where territorial production complexes are dominated by one or two major firms which, while integrating much of the input–output chain necessary to their finished product, also subcontract to a range of satellite firms in the vicinity.

For technologically dynamic firms it is advantageous to have all stages of production (R&D, design, production) in the same location, because designing and developing new products can benefit from knowing just what the production possibilities are, what the skill limitations/possibilities are, and what the component suppliers are capable of. So while it might be possible in terms of the skills demanded to relocate some aspects of the production process elsewhere, there are also countervailing arguments in terms of the advantages of sharing knowledge.

Minimizing labor turnover is also significant. This is obvious in the case of formal research and development work. People work together on long-term projects, and the breakup of a research team can be a major problem for the employer in the sense of putting new products behind schedule. But it is also important in the production process proper. One of the important features of Japanese production technology has been the belief that the learning process on the production line is quite long and that workers can develop new insights about the product or about the way it is produced that can result in an upgrading of either the product itself or the way production is organized. This was one of the reasons that the Japanese auto companies for a long time were pessimistic about locating facilities in the United States: they realized that it would take a considerable period of time before they were able to exploit the same advantages of worker stability, even if they could accomplish that stability to begin with.

But if firms are to effectively mobilize the productive potential of their divisions of labor, internal and external, then there also need to be appropriate governance or regulatory mechanisms. At the level of the firm itself, internal labor markets are often important as a means of stabilizing the work force and harnessing the productive power of social learning. Between firms, territorially embedded forms of cooperation and coordination are significant, among other things, to the effective integration of divisions of labor and to the sharing of risk and reduction of uncertainty so as to facilitate the adoption of productivity-raising strategies. Relations of trust between agents become important if workers, let alone financial backers and component firms, are to commit themselves to a project. These relations in turn are the outcome of a social learning process as confidence is built up, tested, and strengthened. They can then become the basis of wider reputations, so that trust can be generalized among a large number of agents. These relations take time to form and depend on close, face-to-face interaction.[6]

Underpinning these relations may be other institutional forms, backed up by the power of the state. Advocates of the developmentalist state have shown a heightened interest in these regulatory forms. Indeed, an interesting feature of recent debates about competitive advantage/disadvantage under conditions of enhanced international competition is the increased attention devoted to national regulatory systems. These analyses commonly contrast Germany and Japan with the United States and the United Kingdom. They draw attention to such features as training systems (Lane, 1988), and state orchestration of markets to limit uncertainty (Grahl, 1991; Grahl & Teague, 1989).

Swyngedouw (1992) has referred to territorial organization as the dialectical unity of a social relation and a force of production. Accordingly, territorial coherence is defined as a specific combination of the form of territorial regulation with a concrete form of the valorization process that generates a relatively stable pattern of "territorial development." In other words, the exploitation of the properties of spatial arrangement as a productive force depends upon the sorts of governance and regulatory mechanisms identified earlier.

These arguments have important implications for the propositions advanced by mainstream arguments in the politics of globalization. Most obviously, the former suggest a reevaluation of the latter's distributional inferences. For if some capitals are indeed relatively immobile in the ways I have suggested, then this means that it is difficult to play one locality off against another and so drive down wages, social or otherwise. Furthermore, the advantages accruing from the collective commodity represented by spatial organization can signify quasi-rents or superprofits, so that the alternative to conceding to the superior leverage of labor is not that of going out of business. As Storper (1992, pp. 67–68) argues: "Quasi-rents (from a high price-cost margin) can be distributed in the form not only of high returns to capital and further physical capital accumulation through reinvestment, but also in the form of high-wage jobs in the labor markets where technologically dynamic industries are present." Moreover, provision for wage increases is often built into the modes of regulation internal to dynamic firms. This is because one of the points of internal labor markets is to provide incentives for work force stability and so allow the firm to recoup its investments in worker skill.

This does not mean to say that all involved in the production process will gain to the same degree (Cox, 1995, pp. 220–222). In a complex of vertically disintegrated firms, some have greater bargaining power than others: the designers in the garment industry as opposed to the sweatshop workers, for instance, though the squeeze on the suppliers can be moderated somewhat by the need to build up relations of trust. Likewise, the gains to labor can be bid away in the form of increased housing prices, so that it is the developers who gain from the enhanced competitive position of some spatially embedded firm in the locality's economic base rather than the employees. Nevertheless, this is a very different bargaining situation at the point of production from the sort postulated by "capital versus community" or world city arguments, or those of the NUP. There is, of course, empirical evidence for the sorts of situations that have been highlighted by those literatures. But, and in light of the underlying social relations emphasized here, it has to be highly selective evidence, and there have been serious tendencies toward overgeneralization.

Likewise, the bleak conclusions of those who see the possibilities of some collective regulation evaporating with the globalization of markets also seem premature. Indeed, the emergence of regulatory institutions and practices in industrial areas and the exploitation of regulatory advantages existing at the national level are important to the development of the productive forces: a development, that is, which is rooted in particular places and which opens up the possibility of redistribution to labor.

Recognition of capital as characterized by tendencies toward not just mobility, but also immobility, has implications for the broader regulatory question as well as for distribution. Arguments about the decline of national economies as meaningful objects of intervention require some qualification. While these may continue to have some applicability in the case of macroeconomic aggregates, the case is less clear-cut when, for example, it comes to state support of a more microeconomic character. This is consistent with the continuing relevance of national regulatory institutions for competitive performance: institutions like those governing labor training, the collaboration of firms one with another, employer–employee relations, and the relations between finance and industrial capital that encourage long-term as opposed to short-term investment horizons.

Hirst and Thompson (1992, p. 371) have also argued this point: "While national governments may no longer be "sovereign" economic regulators in the traditional sense, they remain political communities with extensive powers to influence and sustain economic actors within their territories. Technical macro-economic management is less important, but the role of government as a facilitator and orchestrator of private economic actors remains strong." They argue in particular for the need to construct what they call a distributional coalition, in which the distribution of income and expenditure is consistent with promotion of competitive manufacturing performance and involves particular allocations to physical and social infrastructure and a framework for controlling wage settlements. They also talk about the need for "adequate balance" in the nation-state's scale division of labor between more central and more local agencies.

Perhaps more controversially, they refer to the nation-state's need to create a social consensus to underpin these arrangements culturally. I say "more controversially" because they also see the maneuverability of different nation-states in this regard quite severely hampered by historical legacies: one of the competitive advantages that acquires new significance under globalizing markets and to which I referred earlier.[7] This suggests that while regulation is by no means dead, its possibilities vary considerably from one situation to another.[8]

The Mobility of Labor

Alongside images of mobile capital continually shifting locations from one point of production to another are images of workers as equally *im*mobile. It is this combination of relative mobility–immobility that provides the necessary condition for the regressive distributional effects identified in the politics of globalization. As we have seen, there are good reasons for being skeptical about claims regarding capital's mobility. This means that even if labor were immobile, it would have more leverage than is typically accorded it in the conventional wisdom. But, in fact, the immobility of workers is equally flawed as a fundamental assumption. Even if capital were as mobile as is argued, workers would not necessarily be immobilized in places of growing unemployment and deprivation and subject to the demands of firms looking for new locations. Indeed, it must seem odd to have to point out that wage workers are not immobile. But the tenacity of the assumption in much of the literature means that it is a bogey that needs to be laid to rest.

A major problem with the idea of labor's immobility is that it is not clear precisely what it means. Does it mean that workers are necessarily immobile or only contingently so? If the latter, then what is the historical geography of mobility on which that inference is based, so that the historicity of the distributional thesis can be correctly evaluated? Likewise, are workers undifferentiated? To whom does the sobriquet "immobile" apply? Finally, what scale are we talking about? Empirically it is clear that mobility is greater at smaller geographical scales than at larger ones, and within countries rather than between. It is not apparent, however, whether the strictures of the politics of globalization school are indeed to be confined to the international level. Certainly there are literatures, like that associated with the underclass literature, that locates the problem of immobility and unemployment at much smaller scales.

An important distinction in evaluating the immobility claim is that between sponsored or contract migrants on the one hand and speculative migrants on the other.[9] Contract migrants are those who know they have a job before they move. They have been interviewed, a job has been offered, and terms agreed to; moving expenses may be paid for and some help with procuring housing offered. In contrast, speculative migrants move residence without the certainty of a job at the other end; they are literally speculating on an offer being forthcoming. Not surprisingly, most migrants are of the contract variety. In Britain, 83% of long-distance movers already had a job before moving. In the United States, in 1967 at least, only 30% of moving heads of household did not have a job before moving (Gordon, 1995).

The distinction is in part between different levels of skill and/or trainability. Contract migrants tend to be those who can offer a relatively scarce skill and/or in whom the firm intends to make a large investment with a view to them staying. Given the commitment that the firm intends to make and the significance of the recruit to the overall profitability of the firm, a good deal is invested in the recruitment process. The scarcity of skills in these markets also suggests that the local pool will be quite thin. Not only are firms willing to recruit at a distance, but they may have to. Accordingly, positions are likely to be advertised in national newspapers and in trade and professional journals.

Speculative migrants tend to be in a different sort of labor market. This is altogether a lower skill market and one in which, from the firm's standpoint, labor turnover is less critical. Recruiting is carried on locally either by word of mouth of existing employees or through local newspapers. The large number of workers with the quite minimal job skills required means that recruiting does not have to take place on a larger geographic scale. In consequence, labor markets are highly localized.

Even so, migration, even of the speculative type, does occur, and in such a way as to enhance the leverage of labor. As Gordon (1995) has noted, it is the speculative migrant that is most typically assumed in the migration literature, and this literature is quite clear on the directional characteristics of migration. Rates of out-migration tend to be fairly constant across different places, but what makes the difference is that in-migration rates vary quite substantially, so that stagnating or contracting local economies do indeed show some movement toward respective labor market equilibria. Moreover, some are more mobile than others. Speculative migration shows its own social biases. Not surprisingly, it is concentrated among those most able to absorb the risk: the young, the renters, those without children and those inserted in those sorts of flows mediated by earlier migrants—friends and relatives, perhaps—and known as chain migrations.

If things were otherwise, it would be surprising. Capitalist relations of production mean that owners of labor power are free to move between employers. On the other hand, their divorce from the means of production means that access to means of subsistence is dependent on capital's geography. Given the unevenness of that geography over both space and time, at least some workers will have to act on their power to relocate. Who moves, the directions and distances over which they move, and the geographic scales at which they move, however, are, from the standpoint of the laws of motion of capital, a contingent matter. This means that for those left behind, their leverage with respect to capital is enhanced.

Current argument about the distributional consequences of globalization is, therefore, from the viewpoint of the mobility–immobility of labor, unjustifiably alarmist. Globalization is having effects on the spatial restructuring of production, but these effects by no means signal a draining out of productive activity from major urban centers to the internal peripheries of the First World, let alone to those of the Third World, in a way that would portend a long-term convergence in living standards. Rather, most of the migration that is necessitated by the changes set in motion can be within national boundaries. Some of it will be from declining to growing places, relieving the pressure on those left behind to cede to the demands of the branch plants. Most of it will be sponsored, suggesting once again that the changes going on are thoroughly contradictory with respect to the power of workers relative to employers.

CONCEPTS OF CAPITAL

I now want to move on and consider the broader, more conceptual implications of these arguments for the various literatures dealing with the politics of globalization. The major point I wish to make is that in the debate stimulated by those writings, it is contrasting concepts of capital that are important. Dominant in the politics of globalization mainstream is a conception of capital as an exchange relation. This can be put in useful critical context by comparing and contrasting it with a view of capital where the stress is on the social relations into which people enter in order to produce. The implications of these two conceptions for understanding the politics of globalization are quite different.

Seen as an exchange relation, what is important are the prices at which commodities exchange. Globalization of markets has produced new possibilities of locational advantage through exchange: cheaper labor power, cheaper raw materials, a narrowing of transportation cost advantages, and so on. Yet this is to privilege the costs of inputs as opposed to how they are deployed within the workplace so as to maximize productivity: aspects of labor process design; particular configurations of workers and fixed capital, not just within but between plants, as in just-in-time systems and vertically disintegrated labor processes of the sort Scott (1985) has highlighted; and the use of internal labor markets to limit turnover, facilitate social learning, and so enhance productivity.

What this points to is the importance of spatial organization as a productive force rather than as a geography of input costs.[10] This is true whether one is talking about the organization of the factory itself, that of an industrial district, of firms arranged with respect to each other so as to take advantage of just-in-time forms of organization, or the spatial relations of firms at larger geographical scales, including the physical infrastructure of highways, airports, railroads, and airline services, and utility lines through which they are connected.

This in turn implies a different relation between production and location: a relation in which not all the advantages accrue to a ready mobility but one in which an embeddedness with respect to suppliers, skilled workers, and the like is important to the development of profitability. Immobility weakens in the sense that it takes away a source of leverage over input costs: the leverage loudly proclaimed in the politics of globalization. But lowering input costs is not the point: profitability is the ultimate objective, and reducing input costs is only one of the strategies possible.

A related distinction is between what Storper and Walker (1989) have called "weak" competition and "strong" competition. In weak competition the conditions of production—products, forms of labor process, raw materials, and the like—are given exogenously: change in the forces of production is external to capital, therefore. Their change creates new possibilities of profit through a subsequent change in the firm's market relations, but those possibilities rapidly contract as other firms exploit them. In strong competition, on the other hand, those conditions themselves become an object of competition as firms strive to change them to their own advantage: introducing new products, developing new process technologies and raw materials, and the like. In contrast to weak competition, strong competition creates the conditions for superprofits of a more enduring nature. It is for competitive advantage of a strong nature, therefore, that firms necessarily strive, though they do not all succeed.

The world of weak competition is one in which it is exchange relations that are crucial. In strong competition, on the other hand, inputs are combined in innovative ways to produce an existing array of products or entirely new ones. It is, in other words, what employers do with their workers after they have hired them that is of central importance: the degree to which they are able to exploit the social learning process by stabilizing labor turnover. Likewise, relations with suppliers can be more than mere market relations. They can also be ones in which firms collaborate on the design and development of new products and inputs.

This is not to say that weak forms of competition do not exist. Clearly as, and to the extent that, labor processes become deskilled and products and inputs standardized, so one of the ways of enhancing profitability is through seeking out minimum-cost locations. But it is that very process of standardization of products and processes and the threatened elimination of superprofits that provides the incentive for strong forms of competition and the exploitation of space as a force of production.[11]

Moreover, without a concept of strong competition it is difficult to make sense of the distinction in the migration literature referred to earlier in this chapter: the distinction, that is, between sponsored (or contract) migrants and speculative migrants. Gordon's (1995) interpretation of the distinction is in terms of the labor market literature. He suggests that contract migrants are to be found largely in the primary segment of the labor market and are recruited into positions from which further movement is likely to be within the firm itself; that is, an internal job market will henceforth prevail. Speculative migrants are recruited into secondary labor market jobs, and from the firm's standpoint are part of its external labor market. Obviously, the links are not watertight, and Gordon is keen to dispel notions of constructing more embracing ideal types out of them.[12] But at the very least there are some interesting hypotheses here worth further investigation.

But what the distinction seems to underline once again is the importance of getting our concepts of capitalist social relations correct. The fact of contract or sponsored migrants depends on the presence of strong competitors who are in a position to operate an internal labor market and for whom it is of the greatest significance that they do so if they are to maintain their technological lead. Moreover, even if the firms were in a position to move, the thinness of the high-skill labor market on which they depend for the success of their core activities means that there is often nowhere they can so move and avoid the long-distance recruitment of the high-skill elements important to them. Strong competitors are able by virtue of their profitability to invest considerable sums of money in the labor recruitment process. That they have to do so in order to induce relocation is evidence once more of the leverage workers can enjoy—*pace* the distributional politics of globalization—in a world where the generation of superprofits has to be based on more than a simple manipulation of exchange relations.

In contrast, speculative migrants are evidence of segments of the labor market where exchange relations and hence weak competition *are* more important, so they lack the leverage that more skilled workers enjoy. The relatively low rate of speculative migration can be interpreted precisely as a result of their lack of leverage with employers. In this sense there is a limited truth to the claims of distributional disadvantage evident in the literature.

This discussion can be broadened out further into a consideration of wider debates in social theory. There is, for example, a deterministic element in exchange concepts of capital and related ideas of weak competition. Firms slide down price gradients in order to maximize profits, price gradients over which they have no control. In contrast, in production relations concepts, and to repeat, it is what capitalists do with their inputs after they have purchased them and how they relate to their suppliers above and beyond a simple exchange relation that are crucial. Without this sense of creativity and agency, then capitalism, albeit in the context of a set of production relations confronted by all, is neither transformative nor progressive.

CONCLUDING COMMENT

The major point I have tried to make in this chapter is that the conclusions of the various politics-of-globalization literatures follow to a substantial degree from the particular concept of capitalism they have—albeit implicitly—adopted. This is a concept that defines capital in terms of the commodity exchange relation. Conceptualizing capital as a production relation with its correlative concept of competition as not just "weak" but also "strong," allows us to redefine capital's relation to space. Spatial organization becomes a productive force rather than a discrete set of exchange opportunities and provides capital with competitive advantages. Accordingly, capital can become embedded in particular localities and dependent upon their reproduction. This alters its bargaining relation with labor, though this does not mean that the distributional gains will go to labor rather than to, say, the real estate industry, or to the local state for that matter.

When we turn and examine labor from the standpoint of these literatures, its supposed immobility is difficult to reconcile with *any* defensible conception of capital, and accordingly is hard to understand. Strong competition means that capitals actively mediate worker migration by facilitating the moves of the more skilled. Some of the less skilled, at least, *have* to move, and this alters the labor market leverage of those they leave behind. This is not to say that the politics of globalization is totally wrong. The banalization of products and of their labor processes means that capitalists cannot ignore the exchange relation, so there will indeed be some movement of plants in the search for cheaper labor, worker givebacks to preempt plant closure, and the like. It is, however, a serious overgeneralization.

Nevertheless, and despite their vulnerability to the sorts of arguments I have tried to set out here, the orthodoxy regarding the effects of the globalization of markets on distribution and regulation continues to have a remarkable tenacity. Trying to understand these beliefs should be an important issue. We can gain some clue as to what is happening here by adding to our earlier discussion of space, production, and exchange.

A symptomatic problem with the arguments of academics seems to be what I will call here the overspatialization of social relations. This is the tendency to misspecify the contingent nature of at least some spatial relations as necessary aspects of the social relations with which they are correlative: that, for instance, a search for maximizing profits costs will necessarily lead manufacturers in the direction of Third World locations. In other words, while space is a necessary aspect of social relations, it does not dictate particular strategies, either for labor or for business. At their most abstract, social relations define certain necessities and opportunities: the need to make a profit, to earn a wage, the possibility of shifting employment, and so on. But there is a considerable range of concrete sociospatial practices and strategies through which those social relations can be realized. Accordingly, there is always a variety of geographies that can come about. Globalization is but one possibility; another is the industrial district.

What seems to be implicated here, once again, are concepts of capital. As Marx showed, exchange concepts result in a fetishization of the commodity, so that it is the exchange relation that comes to be seen as the determinant, rather than the production of the immediate producers in and through each other. Whatever in this "thingified" view is correlated with, or seems to be correlated with, exchange relations can then be erected into a central principle of analysis. In the case of the politics of globalization it is space, so that the politics of globalization comes dangerously close to spatial fetishism. As I have tried to show in this chapter, there are good reasons for resisting this sort of reasoning and the alarmist conclusions which it generates.

NOTES

1. Cf. Burawoy (1985, p. 150):

It is now much easier to move capital from one place to another as a result of three phenomena: the generation of pools of cheap labor power in both peripheral countries and peripheral regions of advanced capitalist societies; the fragmentation of the labor process, so that different components can be produced and assembled in different places (sometimes at the flick of a switch); and the metamorphoses of the transportation and communications industries.

2. According to Burawoy (1985, p. 150): "The new despotism is the 'rational' tyranny of capital mobility over the *collective* worker. The reproduction of labor power is bound anew to the production process, but, rather than via the individual, the binding occurs at the level of the firm, region or even nation-state. The fear of being fired is replaced by the fear of capital flight, plant closure, transfer of operations, and plant disinvestment." Likewise, Streeck (1992, p. 518):

> With capital benefiting from unbounded opportunities to expatriate its interests into the larger, less socially integrated and politically regulated circuit of the world economy . . . the very substance of political-economic bargaining in the "bargained economies" of the West changed fundamentally. What in the past resulted, at least sometimes, in an imposition of social obligations on capital in exchange for labor and state cooperation with the requirements of accumulation, now began to generate obligations for the less mobile to behave in line with the need to attract and attach capital interests to their respective national economy.

3. This is echoed by Hirst and Thompson (1992, p. 366):

> Within the contemporary international economy the important relationships remain those between the more developed economies, the members of the Organization of Economic Cooperation and Development (OECD). Indeed these economies have increased in their relative importance over recent years in terms of their share of world trade and investment. In 1989, over 80% of world trade was conducted between the OECD economies and this rose to 85% if the ex-Eastern European and Soviet economies were included. The Group of Five (G5) main economies accounted for 75% of foreign direct investment. Thus for all practical intents and purposes it is the advanced industrial economies that constitute the membership of the "global" economy, if that entity can be said to exist. The LDCs, and even the NICs, still constitute a very small part of the international economy, however regrettable or disappointing that may be.

4. For example, given "a world-wide equalization of wage rates for work of equal low-skill content . . . only those in the elite high-skill workforces, particularly those able to partake via multinationals in the international rewards for skilled professionals, managers and technicians, will be able to command high and increasing wages. For the rest, a levelling-down to (the wages) received in the emergent developing nations is not so far-fetched in the long run" (Ashton, Green, & Hoskins, 1989, quoted in Leys, 1990, p. 121).

5. For an example, see Smith's (1994) discussion of minimills.

6. On the other hand, this is not to underestimate the diversity of empirical situations in which relations of trust can be formed and maintained. A recent paper by Clark (1993) suggests that it may well be possible, as a result of regular airplane connections, telecommunications, and a careful, mutual testing, over very long distances indeed. The case he refers to involves a small- to medium-sized brand-name clothing

manufacturer located in the Far East but with strong links to design expertise in each of the four markets, scattered around the world, in which it sells its products. Each of the nodes of activity so connected, however, is stable in its location, so one is left wondering about the nature of the social learning going on within those nodes and to what extent is it dependent on highly localized sociospatial relations that are difficult to reconstitute elsewhere, except at very great expense.

7. "States are . . . in considerable measure trapped by the legacies of social cohesion they inherit. Countries like the USA cannot just decide to adopt the more solidaristic and co-ordinative relations between industry, labor and the state characteristic of Germany and Japan" (Hirst & Thompson, 1992, p. 374).

8. The emphasis on distributional coalitions is echoed in a suggestive way by Glyn (1995, pp. 54–55, emphasis added.). The problem he addresses is that of expansionary policies where subsequent distributional conflicts create a problem of credibility in international financial markets and the reestablishment of unemployment as the means of moderating claims:

> . . . maintaining such credibility only rules out the expansion of employment if there are no means other than unemployment for regulating conflicting claims over distribution and control. Viable policies for expanding employment entail *costs which must be explicitly counted and willingly shouldered by the mass of wage and salary earners. Unless social democracy can formulate and gain support for such an alternative,* mass unemployment is set to continue as the mechanism by which distributional conflict and other challenges to capital are contained.

9. For a highly informative discussion of this distinction and some empirical examination of it, see Gordon (1995).

10. By emphasizing the role of space as a productive force in these ways, I do not want to marginalize the role of technology and worker skills. Rather, their effective use depends on the particular spatial configurations into which they are inserted.

11. Compare Storper (1992, p. 91) on the topic of strong competition: " . . . the image of the global economy as a sort of delocalized 'space of flows' of human, physical and financial capital controlled from major corporate headquarters, manifestly fails to grasp the nature of the new competition. It fails to grasp the complex ties among these global agents (especially the technology-based oligopolists) and the painstakingly constructed, territorially specific economic tissues without which they cannot function" (p.91).

12. "Contract migration is thus liable to be associated strongly with 'primary' labor markets, although only with certain sets of jobs within these markets" (Gordon, 1995, p. 142).

REFERENCES

Amin, A., & Thrift, N. (1992). Neo-Marshallian nodes in global networks. *International Journal for Urban and Regional Research, 16*, 571–587.

Ashton, D., Green, F., & Hoskins, M. (1989). The training system of British capitalism: Changes and prospects. In P. Nolan & F. Green (Eds.), *The restructuring of the UK economy* (pp. 131–154). London: Verso Press.

Bluestone, B., & Harrison, B. (1982). *The deindustrialization of America.* New York: Basic Books.

Burawoy, M. (1985). *The politics of production.* London: Verso Press.

Castells, M. (1983). Crisis, planning and the quality of life: Managing the new historical relationships between space and society. *Environment and Planning D: Society and Space, 1,* 3–22.

Clark, G. L. (1993). Global interdependence and regional development: Business linkages and corporate governance in a world of financial risk. *Transactions of the Institute of British Geographers, New Series, 18,* 309–326.

Cox, K. R. (1993). The local and the global in the new urban politics: A critical view. *Environment and Planning D: Society and Space, 11,* 433–448.

Cox, K. R. (1995). Globalisation, competition and the politics of local economic development. *Urban Studies, 32,* 213–224.

Cox, K. R., & Mair, A. J. (1991). From localised social structures to localities as agents. *Environment and Planning A, 23,* 197–213.

Fagerberg, J. (1995). User–producer interaction, learning and comparative advantage. *Cambridge Journal of Economics, 19,* 243–256.

Glyn, A. (1995). Social democracy and full employment. *New Left Review, 211,* 33–55.

Gordon, D. (1988). The global economy: New edifice or crumbling foundations? *New Left Review, 168,* 24–65.

Gordon, I. (1995). Migration in a segmented labour market. *Transactions of the Institute of British Geographers, New Series, 20,* 139–155.

Grahl, J. (1991). Economies out of control. *New Left Review, 185,* 170–183.

Grahl, J., & Teague, P. (1989). The cost of neo-liberal Europe. *New Left Review, 174,* 33–50.

Hirst, P., & Thompson, G. (1992). The problem of 'globalization': International economic relations, national economic management and the formation of trading blocs. *Economy and Society, 21,* 357–396.

Lane, C. (1988). Industrial change in Europe: The pursuit of flexible specialization in Britain and West Germany. *Work, Employment and Society, 2,* 141–168.

Leys, C. (1990). Still a question of hegemony. *New Left Review, 181,* 119–128.

Patel, P. (1995). Localised production of technology for global markets. *Cambridge Journal of Economics, 19,* 141–153.

Pryke, K., & Lee, R. (1995). Place your bets: Towards an understanding of globalization, socio-financial engineering and competition within a financial center. *Urban Studies, 32,* 329–344.

Scott, A. J. (1985). Location processes, urbanization, and territorial development: An exploratory essay. *Environment and Planning A, 17,* 479–501.

Smith, S. K. (1994). Internal cooperation and competitive success: The case of the US steel minimill sector. *Cambridge Journal of Economics, 19,* 277–304.

Storper, M. (1992). The limits to globalization: Technology districts and international trade. *Economic Geography, 68,* 60–93.

Storper, M., & Walker, R. A. (1989). *The capitalist imperative: Territory, technology and industrial growth.* Oxford: Blackwell.

Streeck, W. (1992). Inclusion and secession: Questions on the boundaries of associative democracy. *Politics and Society, 20,* 513–520.

Swyngedouw, E. A. (1992). Territorial organization and the space/technology nexus. *Transactions of the Institute of British Geographers, New Series, 17,* 417–433.

CHAPTER 6

Neither Global nor Local

"GLOCALIZATION" AND THE POLITICS OF SCALE

Erik Swyngedouw

THE POLITICS OF SCALE

In 1994, Deutsche Metallgesellschaft lost over U.S.$ 1.3 billion as a result of speculative activities in the financial derivatives market. The disastrous consequences of this debacle for the company's balance sheet necessitated a fundamental restructuring of its activities, including the manufacturing side. The net result was the loss of 10,000 company jobs throughout Germany (Verbraeken, 1994). In December 1994, Orange County, the county with the highest mean income in the United States, but with large pockets of poor neighborhoods, lost U.S.$ 2 billion in the derivatives market and went virtually bankrupt when it failed to refinance its highly leveraged investment fund with which it was deeply engaged in the interest futures market. The level of local public services (social, educational, environmental) is likely to be dramatically affected by this for years to come (*Orange County Register*, 1994). On 26 February 1995, one of Britain's oldest and most respected merchant banks, Barings Bank, collapsed in the face of an estimated total accumulated debt of £900 million. The event sent a shock wave through the City of London, and debate about the nature and characteristics of the international financial system heated up (*Collapse*, 1995). In April 1995, Mercedes–Benz announced a major restructuring in its corporate organization, which involved the loss of 13,000 jobs in Germany and a delocalization of some of its activities. The chairman referred to the combination of a high national wage settlement with the high value of the deutsche mark (DM) in the foreign exchange market to explain this restructuring drive (*De Morgen*, 1995).

These examples (and surely many more could be found) illustrate how the "local" and the "global" are deeply intertwined. They also suggest how local actions shape global money flows, while global processes, in turn, affect local actions. In short, the local and the global are mutually constituted, or so it seems. But of course, the preceding examples do not give indications of the intertwining of just local and global processes. Other spatial scales are also deeply implicated in these events as well.

Let us consider, for example, the case of the collapse of Barings Bank. As a result of increasing exposure to the Nikkei-225 stock exchange index on the futures market, the bank built up a debt greater than its own assets. One of its Signapore-based traders, Nick Leeson, had speculated on a rising Nikkei index, while the stock exchange was on a slippery slope downward. The consequences of the bank's bankruptcy are quite important in terms of the financial spatial geometry of power. In the aftermath of the collapse, the FTSE-100 index (of the Financial Times Stock Exchange) fell sharply, Barings clients in the United Kingdom and elsewhere worried about their investments, and other City banks were anxiously monitoring the effects of the collapse on money movements and on the stability of the financial system. In addition, money started to pour out of sterling into deutsche marks and Swiss francs, further destabilizing an already shaky European Monetary System. In combination with the Chiapas-induced crisis of the Mexican peso and its effects on the dollar, the Pound was sucked down and lost almost 10% in value terms against the DM and the yen. This, in turn, wiped out a significant amount of international buying capacity of the British population and, combined with the devaluation of sterling in September 1992, erased the "gains" the British economy had clocked up during the "manufactured" boom of the second half of the 1980s. These monetary shock waves worry European continental manufacturers, who see their export markets shrink while facing more intense competition from "cheaper" British goods and services. This, in turn, intensifies geopolitical tensions in Europe and reinforces calls for devaluationary beggar-thy-neighbor policies. In addition, the growing tensions within the European exchange rate system jeopardize the already hotly contested movement toward a European Common Currency. A few weeks after the collapse, a Dutch bank (ING) moved in to take over Barings, settled in the heartland of the City of London, expanded its business, and realigned itself strategically in the permanent reshuffling of global financial institutions.

In the plethora of explanations and analyses that were suggested during the days and weeks after the collapse, different groups strategically invoked different spatial scales as the preeminent sites to situate and "explain" the event. That of the individual male body proved the most popular and ideologically quite interesting scale of analysis. The devious behavior of an individual "rogue" trader with a dubious North London working-class background and less than satisfactory educational one, possibly (probably) conspiring with some of his mates, brought down a 233-year-old icon of the British establishment and symbol of a glorious imperial past. This deviant behavior was possible because of a clash of local cultures, that is, the clash between a traditional "old-boys," but hopelessly antiquated, banking elite, on the one hand, and a new, entrepreneurial, whizz-kid generation playing the high-tech and lucrative derivatives market in the "glocal" hyperspace of digital money flows, on the other. The latter delivered the highly valued goodies for the traditional elites—high profitability and massive bonuses. The combination of this constructed masculinity of an overambitious, money-hungry working-class boy lured by the glittering appeal of quick money with a decidedly new local banking climate that is out of step with the traditional highbrow City culture were considered to be the main culprits (both by the tabloid press and establishment circles—see Tickell, 1995) explaining the bank's failure and its consequences.

Another "local" explanation focused on the regulatory environment in Singapore, where the now defunct Southeast Asian Barings operations were located. Questions were raised as to why the purportedly highly regulated Singapore Money Exchange (SIMEX) did not intervene earlier, when Leeson began to accumulate massive losses. Still others invoked "nature" to explain the event. The "unexpected" earthquake in Kobe sent down the Nikkei-225 stock exchange index, the indicator in which the Barings trader was building up massive holdings. While Leeson speculated on a rise of the index, the Nikkei tumbled down.

Other accounts, in turn, stressed the regulatory failure of the Bank of England and the consequences of the 1986 Big Bang, which deregulated the British national financial system and reduced regulatory controls significantly. In addition to the scale of the body, the urban scale of the City's changing culture, the local event of a natural catastrophe, national policies, and regulatory systems were invoked as explanatory devices to account for the crash. Furthermore, the absence of a regulatory European central bank as well as the specific characteristics of the Southeast Asian market were also suggested as possible explanations for the unfortunate fate of Barings.

Precious little media attention has been paid to the nature of the derivatives trading system itself and to the characteristics of and conditions in the international financial markets. At the end of the day, the speculative global flows of money and the configuration of the global economy are surely "to blame" for the collapse of Barings. The collapse of the Bretton Woods system and the deregulation of the global money markets during the 1970s and 1980s changed the operation of the financial sector, as the increased volatility produced a rapidly expanding market for derivative instruments (which allow hedging against rapid changes between the financial indicators in different countries and over time, Swyngedouw, 1996). It is exactly speculative trading in these new instruments, it could be argued, that brought down Barings.

This example brings out how places and spaces at different geographical scales are invoked in attempts to account for dramatic events that have major local, national, and international implications. These "scalar narratives" provide the metaphors for the construction of "explanatory" discourses. Of course, it is not difficult to identify how scale-related explanations define and suggest different ideological and political positions. In addition, each of these scales contributes in some way to the processes that led up to the collapse, while the effects are equally felt in different ways at different geographical scale levels. Scale, it seems to me, is both materially and metaphorically central in structuring processes of the kind illustrated in the preceding examples. This multiplicity of scalar levels and perspectives also suggests that scale is neither an ontologically given and a priori definable geographical territory nor a politically neutral discursive strategy in the construction of narratives. Scale, both in its metaphorical use and material construction, is highly fluid and dynamic, and both processes and effects can easily move from scale to scale and affect different people in different ways, depending on the scale at which the process operates. Similarly, different scalar narratives indicate different causal moments and highlight different power geometries in explaining such events. Scale is, consequently, not socially or politically neutral, but embodies and expresses power relationships.

In this chapter, I shall argue that conceptualizing geographical change and restructuring in terms of an a priori given spatial scale is deeply problematic. In particular, concepts such as the "local" or the "global" are often merely speculative, discursive—but eminently powerful—vehicles that are used to order political, social, and economic processes in particular spatialized kinds of ways (see Amin & Thrift, 1994). Of course, there are local and global processes, but also processes that are regional, national, European, and so forth. The crux is not, therefore, whether the local or the global has theoretical and empirical priority in shaping the conditions of daily life, but rather how the local, the global, and other relevant (although perpetually shifting) geographical scale levels are the result, the product of processes, of sociospatial change (Cox & Mair, 1991; Smith, 1984). In other words, spatial scale is what needs to be understood as something that is produced; a process that is always deeply heterogeneous, conflictual, and contested. Scale becomes the arena and moment, both discursively and materially, where sociospatial power relations are contested and compromises are negotiated and regulated. Scale, therefore, is both the result and the outcome of social struggle for power and control.

SCALING THE "GLOCAL"

I insist that social life is process-based, that is, in a state of perpetual change, transformation, and reconfiguration (see Harvery, 1996). Starting the analysis, therefore, from a given geographical scale seems to me to be deeply antagonistic to apprehending the world in a dynamic, process-based manner (Howitt, 1993). Scalar spatial configurations, whether physical, ecological, in terms of regulatory order(s), or as discursive representations, are always already a result, an outcome, of the perpetual movement of the flux of sociospatial dynamics. The theoretical and political priority, therefore, never resides in a particular geographical scale, but rather in the process through which particular scales become (re)constituted. Struggling for the command over a particular scale can, in a given sociospatial conjuncture, be of eminent importance.

Spatial scales are never fixed, but are perpetually redefined, contested, and restructured in terms of their extent, content, relative importance, and interrelations. For example, the present struggle over whether the scale of social, labor, environmental, and monetary regulation within the European Union should be local, national, or European indicates how particular geographical scales of regulation are perpetually contested and transformed. Clearly, relative social power positions will vary considerably depending on who controls what at which scale. The struggle for equal rights in the European labor market for men and women is another example of a deeply scaled process. Consider, for example, how Britain's opt-out from the Social Chapter of the Maastricht Treaty leaves a whole range of social regulatory issues in the hands of a decidedly conservative English national elite and allows the intensification of a wage–cost-based competition within the European Union (EU). All this suggests that the continuous reshuffling and reorganization of spatial scales is an integral part of social strategies and struggles for control and empowerment. In a context of heterogeneous social and ecological regulations, organized at the the local, regional, or national level, mobile people, goods, and capital and hypermobile information flows permeate and transgress these scales in ways that are often deeply exclusive and disempowering for those operating at other scale levels.

In short, scale (at whatever level) is not and can never be the starting point for sociospatial theory. Therefore, the kernel of the problem is theorizing and understanding "process" (Smith, 1988a, 1988b). The ontological priority for a process-based view takes the focus away from both the "global" or the "local" as the starting point for analysis and explanation. It refuses to tackle global–local interplays in terms of a dialectic, an interaction or other mode of relating a priori defined things. Equally problematic is, of course, Howitt's (1993, p. 38) view arguing that "various scales are dialectically related," which is a typically reified way of grappling with scale, assigning motive, force, and action to pregiven geographical configurations and their interaction rather than to the struggles between individuals and social groups through whose actions scales and their nested articulations become produced as temporary standoffs in a perpetual transformative sociospatial power struggle.

A process-based approach focuses attention on the mechanisms of scale transformation and transgression through social conflict and struggle. As I have argued elsewhere, for example, recent political–economic transformations are characterized by a parallel and simultaneous movement to the smaller and the larger scale, to the local and the global (a "glocalization" process) (Swyngedouw, 1992a, 1992b). This process does not in itself assign greater validity to a global or a local perspective, but alerts us to a series of sociospatial processes that changes the importance and role of certain geographical scales, re-asserts the importance of others, and sometimes creates entirely new significant scales. Most importantly, however, these scale redefinitions alter and express changes in the geometry of social power by strengthening the power and the control of some while disempowering others (see also Swyngedouw, 1989). This is the process that Smith (1993) refers to as the "jumping of scales," a process that signals how politics are spatialized by mechanisms of stretching and contracting objects across space.

> This [stretching process] is a process driven by class, ethnic, gender and cultural struggles. On the one hand, domineering organizations attempt to control the dominated by confining the latter and their organizations to a manageable scale. On the other hand, subordinated groups attempt to liberate themselves from these imposed scale constraints by harnessing power and instrumentalities at other scales. In the process, scale is actively produced. (Jonas, 1994, p. 258)

These scales are, of course, not operating hierarchically but simultaneously, and the relationships between different scales are "nested" (Jonas, 1994, p. 261; Smith, 1984, 1993). Clearly, social power along gender, class, ethnic, or ecological lines refers to the scale capabilities of individuals and social groups. As power shifts, scale configurations change both in terms of their nesting and interrelations and in terms of their spatial extent.

I would, in sum, advocate the abolition of the "global" and the "local" as conceptual tools and suggest a concentration on the politics of scale and their metaphorical and material production and transformation. I believe that the vocabulary and heuristic devices suggested by the *Regulation Approach*, for example, may help to elucidate this. We shall attempt to illustrate this argument later in this chapter. First we need to turn and consider the role of place in a process-based theory and the importance of the politics of scale in the sociospatiality of life.

PLACING SCALE

Spatial Scales versus Sociospatial Theory

All social life is necessarily "placed" or "situated," and engaging place is essential to maintaining the process of life itself. This active "location" of life is, of course, the first sense in which "place" is essential. Engaging place is inevitably a contradictory process, as it necessarily implies some sort of "creative destruction" or "destructive creation" of nature/place. Furthermore, this transformation of nature/place is not an individual, atomistic, or isolated process. As Marx pointed out long ago, the Robinson Crusoe view of the world is a stubborn myth. Creative destruction is always an already social process: it is a metabolic transformation that *takes place* in association with others and extends over a certain space, as I will discuss.

However, this central importance of place does not offer the local as the preeminent site for the construction of sociospatial theory. Indeed, the obsession with the local in much of recent theoretical and empirical literature has been highly confusing in the sense that two fundamentally different processes and theoretical perspectives are mixed up. For some (see, for example, the CURS initiative), the local refers to already constructed and historically specific distinct geographical scales that exhibit a series of distinct historical–geographical characteristics in terms of political, social, cultural, economic, or physical conditions. (Cochrane, 1987; Cooke, 1987, 1989; Duncan & Savage, 1989). The latter are, in turn, considered as things and qualities that shape and affect the relationships between the locality and the wider geographical arena, while maintaining a highly differentiated, variegated, and unique landscape. The local(e) enters, then, as "the difference that space makes" in the formulation of social theory (Sayer, 1985, p. 49). This view, in turn, is contested by globalization theorists, who argue that the mundialization (global interconnectedness) of social life, particularly—although by no means exclusively—through money and capital circulation, has been the single most important sociospatial process, which, in turn, forces particular local(iti)es to adjust to the demands posed by a global economy, polity, and culture (Group of Lisbon, 1994; Taylor, 1982, 1989). In sum, a particular geographical scale is considered to be of preeminent importance in terms of theorizing sociospatial processes, while other scales either derive from the a priori positioned scale or express different realms in the process of social change. The global and the local then become sites for constructing contrasting methods of analysis (Lipietz, 1993), which are perpetually played off against each other in rather sterile ways (Amin & Thrift, 1994). Surely, attempts have been made to connect the local and the global (see, e.g., Amin & Thrift, 1992; Cooke, Moulaert, Swyngedouw, Weinstein, & Wells, 1992) in imaginative ways. But they, too, meander skillfully around the issue of scale and maintain the preeminent position of a bipolar (local–global) spatial perspective to account for sociospatial restructuring processes.

However, other theoretical perspectives start from a radically different ontological position, albeit that the two scales are often combined, confused, and eclectically intertwined. These perspectives argue that space is an integral element in the constitution of everyday life and its associated social processes or, put differently, everyday life is constituted in and through temporal–spatial social relations. There is no a priori assertion of the place of a particular geographical scale, but rather a recognition of the inevitable spatiality of everyday life. De Certeau (1984), Foucault (1980), Giddens (1984), Harvery (1996), Harvey (1985), Lefebvre (1974), Massey (1994), and Soja (1989), among others, explore in a variety of ways this sociospatiality of everyday life and its expression in the the production of space(s). Scaled spaces, then, become the embodiment of and the arena through and in which social relations of empowerment and disempowerment operate. Confusion often arises out of mapping the ontological importance of space in constructing social theory onto a particular and historically specific, that is, socially produced, material and metaphorical configuration of scale (the local, the regional, the global, and so on).

The observation that life is sociospatially constituted does not in itself give or assign priority to a given geographical scale. The sociospatial structuring of the everyday does not in itself offer the local, the global, or any other scale as the preeminent site for analysis. The role, importance, and position of each geographical scale results from the dynamics of sociospatial transformations. The role of particular geographical scales, their articulation and interpenetration, has to be theorized (and political mobilization has to proceed on this basis as well) and reconstructed as the result of the dynamics of sociospatial relations.

Place Matters, But Scale Decides

These social relations are always constituted through temporal and spatial relations of power with respect to the social and physical ecology that is being transformed. That is what Massey (1992, 1993) refers to as "the geometry of power," the multiple relations of domination–subordination and participation–exclusion through which social and physical nature are changed. This is the second sense in which place matters. Indeed, these social relations are "grounded" in the sense that they regulate (but in highly contested or contestable ways) control over and access to transformed nature/place, but these relations also extend over a certain material/social/discursive space. It is here that the issue of geographical scale emerges centrally. The sociospatial relations operate over a certain distance. In fact, scale emerges out of the sociospatial character of the perpetual transformation of places. The scaling of the everyday, as Smith (1993) insists, is expressed in bodily, community, urban, regional, national, supernational, and global configurations whose content and relations are fluid, contested, and perpetually transgressed.

The historical geography of capitalism exemplifies this process of territorial "scalar" construction of space and the contested production of scale. Friedrich Engels (1845/1968) already suggested how the power of the labor movement, for example, depends on the place where and the scale over which it operates, and labor organizers have always combined strategies of controlling place(s) with building territorial alliances that extend over a certain spatial scale (Harvey & Swyngedouw, 1993). Similarly, capitalists have always been sensitive to the geographical scale of their operations and to the importance of controlling greater spaces in their continuous power struggle with labor and with other capitalists. Scale emerges as the site for control and domination, but also as the arena where cooperation and competition find a fragile standoff. For example, national unions are formed through alliances and cooperation from lower scale movements, and a fine balance needs to be perpetually maintained between the promise of power yielded from national organization and the competitive struggle that derives from local loyalties and interlocal struggle. Similarly, cooperation and competition among capitals is also deeply scaled (Herod, 1991; Smith & Dennis, 1987). Tendencies toward cartel formation or strategic alliance formation point in that direction (Cooke et al., 1992). Clearly, these processes of alliance formation are cut through by all manner of fragmenting, dividing, and differentiating processes (nationalism, localism, class differentiation, competition, and so forth). Consider, for example, how firms may "home in" to insert themselves into a territorially embedded network that is finely tuned in terms of balancing competition–cooperation as part of a strategy to improve their competitive position at a greater spatial scale (Swyngedouw, 1991a). Similarly, negotiating national compromises (wage settlements, minimum wages, and the like) does affect competitive positions, as weaker firms may be forced to move out. In sum, as Smith (1984, 1993) points out, scale mediates between cooperation and competition, between homogenization and differentiation, between empowerment and disempowerment.

SOCIOSPATIAL RELATIONS, REGULATION, AND THE PRODUCTION OF SCALE

In this part of the chapter, I shall explore how the regulation approach implicitly captures these dynamics of the production of scale. The focus of Regulation Theory is surely on the dynamics of social relations or, rather, sociospatial relations. If indeed, capitalist society is rife with conflict, tensions, and power struggles along intraclass, class, gender, and ethnic lines, the practical and theoretical problem of political economy lies exactly in explaining why a restless, deeply heterogeneous, conflict-ridden mode of social organization maintains some sort of coherence while being intensely dynamic through the perpetual struggle for power and empowerment through which forms of domination and oppression are continuously (re)produced, changed, and/or transformed. The production and reconfiguration of scale is central to this process.

Regulationism fundamentally starts from a social relations interpretation of historical–geographical dynamics. As previously discussed, humans enter into relationships with others in a contradictory, deeply empowering/disempowering manner. These contradictions constitute the basis of historical–geographical dynamics, through which humans make their history on the basis of historically inherited conditions (Lipietz, 1985, p. 8). These relationships that define society are, therefore, simultaneously unifying and conflicting or, in other words, the unity is expressed in struggle and it is exactly this struggle that introduces change in time and space and produces concrete history and geography. As coherence suggests some sort of endurance and continuation in the face of conflict, each moment in time is characterized by a certain stand-off, a compromise that prevents chaos, revolution, or radical transformation and permits the continuation of everyday life. In other words, some form of cooperation and coordination is necessary to maintain some coherence in a social fabric whose continuation is predicated upon competition and rivalry. Scale represents exactly such a temporary sociospatial compromise that contains and channels conflict.

In capitalist societies, then, it is the intercapitalist struggle (competition), the capital–labor relationship institutionalized in the capital–wage nexus, and monetary exchange, institutionalized in various forms of market exchanges, through which the circulation and, hence, accumulation, of capital is organized. Such structured coherences, which exhibit a series of regularities at a variety of interpenetrating scales, are organized within a set of institutional–regulatory forms that canalize or codify those regularities. For example, the model of competition, of organization of the wage relationship, of regulating the distribution of value, of organizing exchanges within and between nations or other scales has to take concrete, formally or informally codified, forms and institutional settings.

Mode(s) of Regulation and Institutional Forms

Social relationships are incorporated in individuals in the form of habits, acquired routines, rules, and norms (cf. Bourdieu's [1977] notion of Habitus),[1] even if every player tries to ameliorate her or his hand in the game. This Habitus is always scaled, and every particular situated action embodies the interpenetration of various routines, rules, and norms that are regulated at a variety of always contested scales. For example, the money in my back pocket, the coffee I drink, or the personal computer I work with situate me in a local class, gender, and ethnic position, a national and international division of labor, a (still) nationally regulated set of wage relations, a variety of local, regional, national, and European redistributional mechanisms, the vagaries of the international financial system, and so forth.

Hegemony, then, can be defined as the capacity of a dominant group (or an alliance of class factions) to impose a series of social practices at a particular spatial scale that are to its (their) advantage, or, more generally, hegemony is the capacity of a model of social relationships to impose itself as the desired model on the rest of society and even on those societies that are not yet under its dominance. Gramsci's (1928/1971) seminal work on "Fordism and Americanism" documents the contested emergence and contradictory dynamics of such a series of hegemonic regular social practices developing partly from within and partly imposed as a hegemonic project from outside, but whose success is eventually conditioned by the struggle between classes and class fractions (and the alliances they forge through their struggle). These struggles and contestations reflect the interpenetration of scales (the body, the urban, the regional, the national, and the global) and the political production of new scales out of this contestation and struggle. Sexual, gender, and family relations, labor relations, production and consumption norms, the nation-state, the city and the countryside, the choice of products, production methods, and so forth are the product of rules and regularities, which are partly reproduced, but also—through struggle—continuously transformed.

As sociospatial relationships (norms, habits, attitudes) change and, thereby, transform and often transgress established norms and routines, the scale of their regulation also tends to change. Changing regulatory forms, therefore, imply altering sociospatial relations and, consequently, the scale at which they operate. Each "mode of regulation" is characterized by a series of formal or informal practices, embodied in the state or other scale-defined formal or informal institutions or levels of governance, through which the conflicting nature of social relationships is guided and negotiated and which assure the reproducibility of the relationships as well as their transformation. The mode of regulation can, consequently, be defined as the practices that assure the dynamic reproduction (thus including change) of social relationships, despite their inherently conflicting character.

Scale is hereby fundamental as it embodies a temporal compromise, solidifies existing power relationships, regulates forms of cooperation, and defines competitive and other power strategies. Scale reconfiguration, in turn, challenges existing power relations, questions the existing power geometry, and, thus, expresses the effects of sociospatial struggles. This "jumping of scale" can be horizontal and/or vertical; that is, scale configurations can move sideways as well as upward or downward.

Scaling Regulation

To put some flesh on these theoretical observations, we shall explore how regulation theory can elucidate the process of scale production and transgression, and identify the geometries of power through which this scaling

and rescaling process operates. Of course, the scaling of life is more complex than can be captured by the regulation approach. Nevertheless, we believe that this perspective provides a number of insights that allow one to illustrate the process of the production of scale and its contested
transformations.

The basis of regulation theory is schematically summarized in Figure
6.1. This skeletal vision of the circulation of capital as a chain of time–space-
structured commodity–money transformations is organized through millions
of individual transactions in which each individual is responsible for her or his
actions (i.e., for her or his value-in-motion). These actions are taken in the
context of a perceived landscape, and their success is only seen ex-post (expressed in either unemployment or nonsale of the produced commodity). The
formal possibility and probability of crisis is born out of the potential disequi-
libria between the accumulation imperative (structured by the production
norm) and the formation of wages and profits. It is the mismatch between the
expansion of capital-in-motion and the capacity to absorb this expanded capital through continuous money–commodity transactions that holds, among
others, the promise of breakdown and crisis. The regulation approach focuses
on the main elements that codify, organize, and regulate the social practices
that carry this flow of circulating capital, that is, (1) the capital–labor relationship (the wage nexus), (2) the forms of interfirm competition and cooperation,
at (3) monetary and financial management. These institutional forms are, fur-

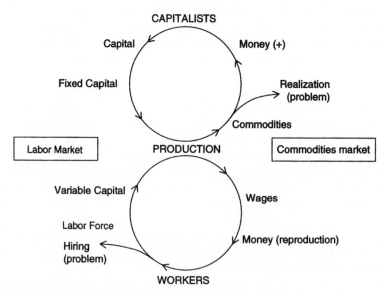

FIGURE 6.1. The double "helix" of the capital circulation process. From Lipietz
(1989, p. 30).

thermore, embedded in (4) forms of state or other formally or informally institutionalized configurations and forms of governance, and part of (5) a
world configuration (Lipietz, 1989, p. 32). Crises (i.e., the partial interruption
of the flow), then, are manifested in efforts to alter some or all of these key elements.

We shall briefly consider the role and importance of these institutional–regulatory forms (Boyer, 1986b, pp. 48–53) and the contested scaling(s) of
their operation:

The Capital–Labor Relationship (the Wage Nexus)

The definition of various specific forms of organizing the capital–labor relationship refers to the identification of the mutual relationships between the
form of organization of the labor process, the way of life, and the means of
reproduction of the labor force. The analysis of the wage nexus includes the
historically concrete analysis of the type of means of production; the form of
social, technical, and spatial divisions of labor, type and structure of mobilization and insertion of the labor force in the labor process; the determination of
direct and indirect income (wages); the gender and ethnic divisions, and, finally, the mode of reproduction, that is, the consumption norm (type of dominant consumption commodities and individual or collective services) (Boyer,
1986a, 1986c; De Vroey, 1984; Velz, 1983).

In the past, at least three types of distinct modes of organizing the wage
nexus can be identified. First is competitive regulation, characterized by a
very weak insertion of the labor force in the determination of the consumption norm and a highly localized, place-specific (usually individual) negotiation of wage levels, labor conditions, and work norms.

The second, Taylorist, is characterized by a fundamental restructuring of
the organization of the production process without significant alterations in
the consumption norm. Capital–labor negotiations are usually firm-based, although highly segmented and characterized by a stratified determination of
wage levels and work practices. Wage determination is usually locally/region-
ally tacitly agreed among employers. Finally, Fordist forms of wage determination codified a linkage between progression in the production norm and the
diffusion of new consumption norms (Boyer, 1983, 1988). The latter is regulated at a wider spatial level, often at the scale of the nation-state. In fact, the
conflictual development of Fordism is characterized by a continuous struggle
between labor and capital over the scale at which particular rules, regulations,
and conditions are set (Swyngedouw, 1989). Moreover, in addition to national
bargaining of the primary wage, secondary wage levels are also negotiated
and determined at the scale of the state. The determination of the wage
nexus, in short, is always scaled. Quite clearly, this scaling is of key importance
in terms of defining relative power positions between capital and labor, but

also shapes competitive strategies, degree of solidarity and co-operation with-in the labor movement, and so forth.

Thus, the organization of the capital–labor relationship depends on the institutionalized or (informally) practiced rules and codes within a particular space, which emerge historically through the development of class alliances and struggle in and over that space. Before Fordism, those relationships were eminently locally constructed; under Fordism, they became part and parcel of an institutionalized national compromise and embedded in the form of the nation-state. For example, in Belgium, during the 1950s and 1960s, several re-gional wage zones were agreed and maintained in the context of a neverthe-less nationally organized wage-bargaining system. Despite the union's relent-less struggle to abolish these spatial wage scales, they would last until the early 1970s when they were finally abolished and wages became nationally stan-dardized (Swyngedouw, 1991c).

The Form of Competition

The form of competition refers to the way in which the relations between au-tonomous and fragmented centers of accumulation are organized. For exam-ple, under competitive conditions, the validation of private labor takes place ex post on the market, while under monopoly[2] conditions, competition is characterized by a series of mechanisms that allow for some form of ex ante planning (advertising, cost-plus pricing, anticipated market expansion, medi-um-term [bureaucratic] planning, and so on) (Frantzen, 1990; Lipietz, 1986). In addition, the scale at which cooperation takes place shapes the type and practices of competition. While the post-war period was characterized by in-tense cooperation between the state and national capitals[3] to improve the competitive position of the latter in the world market and hence the nation-state's relative socioeconomic positions in the process of uneven geographical development, developments over the past 2 decades have seen an intense rescaling of such forms of cooperation and competition (see the following ex-tract). The form of competition is directly related to the structure of the "ter-ritorial configuration" of the accumulation process (see Swyngedouw, 1992b). Indeed, as Smith and Dennis argue in their discussion of the construction of regional scales:

> [W]e can conceive of regional differentiation as an inherent geographical compromise between opposing forces of competition and cooperation. Re-gional difference reduces internal competition among producers in favor of cooperation, while it increases external competition at the expense of coop-eration . . . employers in a region collaborate at varying levels in the use of physical infrastructure, manipulation of the state, determination of wage conditions and relations with employees, etc., while competing with other

firms in other regions over precisely the same issues . . . . The setting of geographical regions becomes a means (however volatile) of resolving the inherent anarchy of capital. (1987, p. 168)

Monetary and Financial Regulation

This refers to the various ways in which the monetary system is organized. Indeed, money as both the universal equivalent enabling the uninterrupted flow of the circulation of capital and a container of value expressing relative socioeconomic power simultaneously links, structures, and molds the relationship between the various centers of accumulation, the labor force, and other commodities. Depending on the way money structures these relationships (national vs. international, private vs. public, speculative vs. "real"), different modes of development of the circulation of capital are possible. This conceptualization shows the necessity of relating the organization of the monetary system (and its functioning) to the other forms of organization of socio-economic life (Aglietta, 1986; Aglietta & Orléan, 1982). In addition, it highlights the importance of the nature of money regulation and the spatial scale at which this operates. For example, the development of money has been historically related to the consolidation of the nation-state as the space in which national monetary exchanges are regulated and homogenized (Strange, 1994). This national money consequently resulted in a differentiation between internal and external (international) circulation of capital. In addition, it has been one particular currency (first sterling, then the dollar, currently an uncertain mixture of deutsche mark and yen)—the currency, that is, of the hegemonic (national) economy—which served as the value basis for relating various national spaces. The national regulation of money and the mode of constructing international rules and hegemony of a currency (or not as the case may be) are, therefore, part and parcel of the regulatory importance of money and credit.

These three key forms of regulation alert us to the importance and role of the "international configuration" and to the form of the state or other regulatory forms of governance.

The International Configuration

The international configuration refers to the way in which local, regional, national, and supranational spaces are articulated and how the relationships between them are constructed. This nested articulation of scale levels is defined by the mechanisms that regulate the relationship between spaces, both in terms of exchange relationships (e.g., the regulation of the monetary or trade system) and in terms of the localization of production and other investments (e.g., through direct foreign investment or the organization of credit and the financing of debt). In this way, places are inserted in an articulated nesting of spatial scales (see, for example, Boyer, 1986a; Cassiers, 1986; Lash & Urry, 1987; and Mistral, 1986, for national analyses).

Forms of the State and Other Forms of Governance

The state is interpreted as an "ensemble of institutionalized compromises" (Delorme & André, 1983)[4]. These (often uneasy, always precarious) compromises reflect the temporal crystallization of particular (allied) and often diffuse class interests within the state apparatus and create rules and regularities that operate almost in a semiautomatic form. The structure of the state budget, state revenue and expenditure patterns, the regulation of social and economic life, and so forth exemplify these compromises. In this sense, the form of the state and other institutional forms are closely interrelated. For example, the organization of the wage relationship or of competition is not independent of the institutionalized capital–labor compromise, of the organization of redistributive measures or of direct and indirect state intervention. Moreover, rules and laws influence the formation of particular institutional forms and contribute to the codification of certain social and economic practices. In addition, the spatial extent and level of the state's control largely influences the way in which other institutional forms operate. The importance of the form of the state for the organization of the mode of regulation implies that it is almost impossible to theorize the passage from one regime of accumulation to another without alteration in the form and the scalings of the state (Jessop, 1990). The state is, indeed, an indispensable element in the rise, consolidation, and demise of a regime of accumulation. Under Fordism, the *national* state became the preeminent site for regulating socioeconomic conditions, particularly those associated with capital–labor relations (although the regulation of gender, ethnic and cultural practices were implicated in the forms of state regulation—for example, through regulating child-care and benefits, parental rights, and the like). To be sure, other regulatory forms remained at local scales, such as, for example, the regulation of the gendered body within the household or the individual plant as the site for open class struggle (e.g., strikes). During the post-war period, supranational or global forms of governance saw the light of day and became increasingly more central in regulating socioeconomic and political practices: for example, the European Community, the World Bank, and the International Monetary Fund (IMF), the General Agreement on Tariffs and Trade (GATT), United Nations Educational, Scientific, and Cultural Organization (UNESCO), North Atlantic Treaty Organization (NATO), COMECON, and a host of others were put in place and nested themselves in a new set of scale articulations.

In the following section, I shall argue how over the past few decades, the articulation of and relative importance of various institutional scales have altered or, in Smith's (1987) description, how scales were jumped, how a new "gestalt of scale" (Smith, 1987) is being wrought in ways that have profound and often disturbing consequences for the geometries of sociospatial power.

CONTESTED SCALINGS: THE POLITICAL ECONOMY OF "GLOCAL" CHANGE

The key regulatory forms previously alluded to are continuously rescaled through the dynamics of sociospatial change. The rise of what would later be generically defined as Fordism,[5] for example, was paralleled by the formation of a new set of scale articulations and, in fact, the emergence of altogether new and significant institutional or regulatory scales. Throughout the contested development of Fordism, scale articulations changed, while the sharpening tensions within Fordism and its subsequent crisis manifested itself in a profound reworking of geographical scales.

The Fordist Production of Scale and Its Contradictions

The pivot of Fordist regulation was the national state. This was the preeminent scale at which both conflicts and tensions were negotiated (the corporatist State) and compromises settled (Altvater, 1993; Esser & Hirsch, 1989; Jessop, 1989, 1994a; Peck & Tickell, 1994). The foundations of the Fordist state resided specifically in the struggle of the labor movement to transcend the local shopfloor struggle and to jump scales through gaining increasing power at the level of the state. Similarly, the Keynesian view of macroeconomic policies resulted in the construction of a precarious but increasingly important bond between the state and private capital. An institutionalized tripartite setting was created, whose main focus was on treading a fine line between competition/struggle on the one hand and cooperation/compromise on the other, particularly around the productivity–consumption nexus.

Quite clearly, the command over the accumulation process remained firmly in the hands of private capital, and assumed an agglomerated urban–regional form, while the reproduction process became increasingly centered around the nuclear family and its associated sexual/gender divisions. Also at that scale, the family became a spatial arena of intense competition/struggle and cooperation/compromise, albeit at each level in a deeply uneven manner. The homogenization across national space of a series of socioeconomic aspects (wages, redistributive schemes, state intervention, socioeconomic norms, rules, and procedures) was articulated with a highly uneven and differentiated local and regional development process. Although the local state scale lost much of its power, it remained the arena for a whole host of centrally important community politics (Eisenschitz & Gough, 1993).

This state-based regulation altered the form and structure of competition, partly also as a result of the greater scale at which individual capitals began to operate. The productivity–consumption nexus allowed for a steady expansion of the national economy. However, the gradual internationalization of production and accumulation (Moulaert & Swyngedouw, 1989) contributed to a more intense competition in the international arena. This growing internationalization of production amidst a mosaic of nationally regulated consumption spaces would prove to be a fundamental dilemma. While capital jumped scales for the organization of production, consumption and reproduction remained fundamentally nationally regulated, despite feeble attempts to transnationalize redistributive schemes (such as, for example, through the establishment of the European Community or the Marshall Plan). In addition, the regulation of the various functions of money (see Swyngedouw, 1996) operated also at a variety of scales. During the interwar period, money was predominantly nationally regulated, while no international anchor value existed. The collapse of the financial system in the early 1930s reinforced calls for some form of international cooperation to prevent beggar-thy-neighbor devaluationary policies, without, however, sacrificing international competition. The Bretton Woods agreement embodied such a compromise, one which remained shaky, contested, and subject to change as the economic internationalization process accelerated during the postwar period. Only the hegemonic power of the United States could maintain some sort of relative cohesion. This compromise was anchored by the dollar–Gold Standard, which stabilized the international monetary system by providing a relatively secure container of value. However, while the regulation of the value of money was cemented in the rules of the Bretton Woods agreement and policed by the IMF (see Leyshon & Tickell, 1994; Swyngedouw, 1992a), the regulation of credit or the issuing of money, for example, remained firmly at the level of the nation-state. In short, different forms and functions of money were regulated at different scales. However, the differential scaling of regulating money would—as the scale of production and trade expanded—become riven with tensions and frictions and eventually break down[6].

In short, Fordism is not a condition or stable configuration. Rather, it refers to a dynamic, contested, and always precarious process of sociospatial change, during which a nested set of new or redefined spatial scales are produced. During the decades of the making and breaking of Fordism, new scale forms and new tensions between scales will gradually emerge. Out of this maelstroom, scales will be redefined, restructured and rearticulated.

The Reconfiguration of Scale and the Tumultuous Reordering of Sociospatial Power

It is of course impossible in this context to present a complete analysis of the politics of scale under Fordism/post-Fordism. We shall focus on some aspects of scale reconfigurations that relate to the five key elements of regulation presented earlier.

Some of the key scale-produced tensions that arose gradually as the postwar economy internationalized are the following:

1. The consolidation and increasingly more bureaucratic regulation of the wage nexus at the scale of the national state became more problematic as a significant part of the production system had become supernationalized. The supernationalization of production was itself a result of a process of jumping scales, through which some forms of capital sought to escape the harness of national regulation or tried to enhance their competitive position (see Swyngedouw, 1989). The power to jump scales is, of course, closely associated with hard and soft technologies that enable movement quickly from place to place, that "annihilate space by time," and is closely associated with social power (Swyngedouw, 1993). As Massey (1996, p. 112) put it in a recent article: "The power to move, and—the real point—to move more than others, is of huge social significance. Indeed, that it is *relative* mobility which is at issue is underlined . . . by the need of some, the relatively mobile/powerful to stabilise the identities of others in part by tying them down in place." This also happened with respect to the re-scaling of the state. Cox and Mair (1991, p. 204), for example, indicate how "the historical development of the welfare state in the U.S. . . . shifted from local and state governments before the New Deal to the national level during the 1930–80 era, and then returned to the local scale under Reagans's New Federalism, so that social services and homelessness programmes are now once again fought over locally rather than nationally."

2. The intensification of international competition was paralleled by a declining hegemonic position of the United States, which was challenged by the successful rise of Japanese and German capital. This internationalization process also questioned traditional forms of oligopolistic competition and inter-firm collaboration within nation-states, which was increasingly replaced by global strong competition between "glocalizing" companies.

3. The tension between money supply and credit regulation organized at the level of the nation-state and a fixed dollar–Gold Standard at the international level contributed to rising tensions in the Bretton Woods system, which had to give way. Of course, changing patterns of uneven development and reverse dollar flows (from the United States to elsewhere) accentuated these tensions.

4. The tension between a set of decidedly local/regional cultures and identities in a homogenizing global cultural landscape and consumption norm resulted in more intense (local) contestations of the imposed cultural norms (Robertson, 1995).

Through this process of growing tension between nested scales, relative power positions changed or were challenged. This became particularly acute as a number of cities, regions, and countries became increasingly more uncompetitive and felt the sting of deindustrialization and crisis, while others prospered relatively in this shifting mosaic of unevenly developed places that made up world space.

What is generally referred to as "post-Fordism"—a problematic generic term that now seems to cover almost everything and thus nothing in particular (see Amin, 1994)—is a series of highly contested, deeply contradictory, and variegated processes and power struggles that often revolve around scale, control over particular scales, the content of existing scales, the construction of new scales, and the articulation between scales.

The so-called "crisis" of Fordism implies a significant rescaling of a series a regulatory practices (see Jessop, 1994a, 1994b; Moulaert, Swyngedouw, & Wilson, 1988; Peck & Tickell, 1992, 1994). In particular, regulatory codes, norms, and institutions are spatially shifted from one scale to another. These rescalings are invariably highly contested, and the outcome varies considerably from scale to scale, both horizontally and vertically, depending on the type, degree, and content of the scale transgression, its downscaling or upscaling. The nature, substance, and configuration of the new scales and their nesting attest to the changing relative power positions of social groups and classes. The process of jumping scale is a central strategy in acquiring or strengthening control in the new geometries of social power. Nevertheless, the accumulation imperative (which is, of course, always place-bound) and the quest to sustain the circulation of capital seems to be of paramount importance, although the specific mechanisms through which this takes place can vary enormously from one scale to another. The overall pattern is one that I have termed elsewhere "glocalization" (Swyngedouw, 1992a, 1992b; see also Luke, 1994, 1995; Robertson, 1995), and refers to (1) the contested restructuring of the institutional level from the national scale both upward to supranational and/or global scales and downward to the scale of the individual body, the local, the urban, or regional configurations, and (2) the strategies of global localization of key forms of industrial, service, and financial capital (see Cooke et al., 1992).

The Glocalization of the State and Other Institutional Forms

Indeed, what seems to be of paramount importance is the changing position of the scale of the state. While this was, although by no means uniquely, the pivotal scale for the regulation and contestation of a whole series of socioeconomic and class practices in the postwar period, the relative position and importance of the state is shifting in decisive ways (Jessop, 1994a, 1994b; Swyngedouw, 1995). In a context in which the capital–labor nexus was nationally regulated, but the circulation of capital spiraled out to encompass ever larger spatial scales, there was a concerted attempt to make the market imperative the ideologically and politically hegemonic legitimation of institutional reform. This took shape through a variety of processes which combined (1) the hollowing out of the national state with (2) more authoritarian and often softly but sometimes openly repressive political regimes (Swyngedouw, 1991b).

Let us consider just a few of these key rescaling processes and identify the shifting power geometry associated with this glocalization of the state or other institutional or regulatory forms:

1. The devolution of capital–labor regulation from some kind of national collective bargaining to highly localized forms of negotiating wages and working conditions. The United Kingdom, for example, has moved a long way toward this, and continuous pressure is exercised to make unions and workers accept local pay deals. This practice is now widespread in a whole series of sectors. Similar movements have been documented elsewhere (see Cox & Mair, 1991), but, of course, depending on particular political configurations, resistance to these movements toward downscaling has been more successful in some countries, such as Sweden and Germany, than in others.

At the same time, attempts are made to supernationalize some of the issues related to the capital–labor divide. Particularly, but not exclusively, socialists and ecologists have fought for an upscaling of capital–labor and environmental regulations, respectively, to higher scale levels. For example, struggle over labor, safety, gender, and environmental regulation in Europe often revolves around the determination of the scale of regulation. Progressive movements generally fight for higher scale regulation to prevent that intensified interplace competition that might compel cities, regions, or nations to lower standards.

The "Schumpeterian Workfare State" (see Jessop, 1993; Peck, 1994) has either abolished a series of institutionalized regulatory procedures to leave them organized by the market (Christopherson, 1992) and, consequently, by the power of money, or replaced them by more local institutional and regulatory forms. In the latter instance, "local" can take a variety of spatial-scale forms, from local constituencies, cities or entire regions to a combination of them. Needless to say, this jumping of scales alters relative power positions, as interlocal cooperation is replaced by interlocal competition. This situation increases the power of those that can jump scales vertically or horizontally at the expense of those trapped in the confines of their local, community space.

2. The restructuring of, and often outright attack on, national welfare

regimes equally leads to a downscaling (in size and space) of money transfers, while privatization permits a socially highly exclusive form of protection, shielding the bodies of the powerful, while leaving the bodies of the poor to their own devices. In short, the hollowing out of the welfare state rescales relations to the level of the individual body through powerful processes of social, cultural, economic, or ethnic exclusion.

3. The interventionism of the state in the economy is equally rescaled, either downward to the level of the city or the region where public–private partnerships shape an entrepreneurial practice and ideology needed to successfully engage in an intensified process of interurban competition, (Harvey, 1989) or upward. The latter is manifested in the albeit highly contested and still rather limited attempt to create a supernational Keynesian interventionist state at the level of the EU. In a different sort of way are institutions such as the North American Free Trade Agreement (NAFTA), GATT, and others testimony to similar processes of upscaling of the state. Furthermore, a host of informal global or quasi-global political arenas have been formed. The Organization of Petroleum Exporting Countries (OPEC) may have been among the first and most publicized quasi-state organizations, but other examples abound: the G-7 meetings, the Group of 77, the Club of Paris, and other "informal" gatherings of world-leaders that attempt to regulate the global political economy. Of course, the competitive rivalry among these partners prevents some form of effective cooperation that could otherwise ultimately lead to some frightening form of a global authoritarian state.

4. In addition to the deeply uneven, sociospatially polarizing, and selectively disempowering effects of the jumping of scales that exemplifies this glocalization of the state or of other forms of regulating life, disturbingly undemocratic procedures characterize globalization. The double rearticulation of political scales (downward to the regional/local level, upward to the EU, NAFTA, GATT, and so on, and outward to private capital) leads to political exclusion, a narrowing of democratic control, and, consequently, a redefinition (or rather a limitation) of citizenship. Local or regional public–private initiatives often lack democratic control of any sort, while supranational institutions are notoriously autocratic (Swyngedouw, 1995). In short, the glocalization or rescaling of institutional forms leads to more autocratic, undemocratic, and authoritarian (quasi-) state apparatuses (Morgan & Roberts, 1993). Hegemony is pursued by invoking an imagined homogeneous territorial identity (which needs protection from the different outsider) and the portrayal of an apocalyptic future if an aggressive competitive stance is not vigorously pursued. The glocal quasi-states (appropriately called Quangos in the United Kingdom), in short, do not liberate or deregulate the market, but produce a set of new market environments and characteristics that empower some, but exclude many.

To be sure, this glocalization process does not proceed uncontested, and social movements organize around a variety of issues to tackle this thorny issue. However, recognizing the importance of the politics of scale has not yet resulted in the mounting of adequate scale strategies. We shall come back to this theme in the final section of this chapter.

The key question, in short, is not whether the state is globalizing or localizing, but rather what kind of struggles are waged and by whom, and how the rescaling of the state toward the glocal produces and reflects shifts in relative sociospatial power geometries.

The Glocalization of the Economy

The glocalization or rescaling of regulatory or institutional forms is paralleled by a variety of important rescalings of the circulation of various forms of money and capital.

In production, local or regional fillières, production and firm networks, deeply inserted in local/regional institutional, political, and cultural environments, cooperating locally but competing globally (Swyngedouw, 1991a) have become central to a reinvigorated—but often very vulnerable and volatile—local, regional, or urban economy. A variety of terms have been associated with such territorial economies, such as learning regions (Maskell & Malmberg, 1995), intelligent regions (Cooke & Morgan, 1991), "milieux innovateurs" (Aydalot, 1986), reflexive economies, and so on, while new organizational strategies have been identified (the "embedded" firm [Grabher, 1993], vertical disintegration, strategic alliances, and so forth). To be sure, such territorial production systems are articulated with national, supranational, and global processes. Similar processes can be identified in the service sector (Moulaert & Djellal, 1990). In fact, the intensifying competition on an ever-expanding scale is paralleled exactly by the emergence of locally/regionally sensitive production milieux. Quite clearly, "glocalizing" production cannot be separated from "glocalizing" levels of governance. The re-scaling of the regulation of wage and working conditions or the denationalization of important companies throughout Europe, for example, simultaneously opens up international competition *and* necessitates a greater sensitivity to subnational conditions.

Perhaps the most pervasive process of glocalization and redefinition of scales operates through the financial system. The hotly contested and continuously postponed implementation of a European Common Currency exemplifies such contested rescaling, while the example of Barings from the introduction to this chapter illustrated how the gestalt of scale revamps the choreography of money power.

GOOD-BYE GLOBAL–LOCAL DISCOURSES, HELLO SCALE POLITICS

Engaging places, restructuring places, occupying places, transforming the physical and the social landscape takes places through conflicting sociospatial processes. The transformative continuation of sociospatial relations that operates through deeply empowering–disempowering mechanisms produces a nested set of related and interpenetrating spatial scales that define the arena of struggle, where conflict is mediated and regulated and compromises settled. Sociospatial struggle and political strategizing, therefore, often revolve around scale issues, and shifting balances of power are often associated with a profound rearticulation of scales or the production of an altogether new gestalt of scale. The sociospatial transformations that have characterized the past 2 decades or so are testimony to those scale restructurings through which older power relations are transformed. The disturbing effects of these recent glocalization processes suggest that the spaces of the circulation of capital have been upscaled, while regulating the production–consumption nexus has been downscaled, shifting the balance of power in important polarizing, or often plainly exclusive, ways.

The social struggle, therefore, that has been waged over the past decades revolved decidedly around scale issues, but it seems to me deeply disturbing to find the power of money and a homogenizing imperialist culture take control of ever larger scales, while very often the "politics of resistance" seems to revel in some sort of militant particularism (see Harvey, 1994) in which local loyalties, identity politics, and celebrating the different other(s) attest to an impotence when faced with the call to embrace an emancipatory and empowering politics of scale. To be sure, identity, difference, and place loyalty are central in any emancipatory project, but solidarity, interplace bonding, and collective resistance demand a decidedly scaled politics. In fact, empowering strategies in the face of the global control of money flows and the competitive whirlwinds of glocal industrial, financial, cultural, and political corporations demand coordinated action, cross-spatial alliances, and effective solidarity. Strategizing around the politics of scale necessitates negotiating through difference and similarity to formulate collective strategies without sacrificing local loyalties and militant particularisms.

In short, what is disturbing in the contemporary politics of resistance is not that the paramount importance of scale is not recognized, but rather that its protagonists have failed to transcend the confines of a militant particularism. The angst over negating the voice of the other has overtaken resistance to the totalizing powers of money and of capital.

Of course, some new social movements and, in particular, progressive ecologists, feminists, and socialists, have begun to struggle through the difficult process of formulating cross-spatial strategies that do not silence the other, exclude the different, or assume the particular within a totalizing vision. The politics of scale are surely messy, but they ought to take center stage in any successful emancipatory political strategy. The discourses on the global or the local, however intellectually stimulating and theoretically insightful they may be, seem to be increasingly out of step with the politics of scale, where the everyday struggle for power and control is fought out.

NOTES

1. Bourdieu (1977, p. 78, emphasis added) defines "Habitus" as "the durably installed generative principle of *regulated* improvisations. . . . The Habitus produces practices which tend to reproduce *the regularities* immanent in the *objective conditions* of the production of their generative principle, while adjusting to the demands inscribed as objective potentialities in the situation, as defined by the cognitive and motivating structures making up the Habitus."

2. "Monopoly" conditions for regulationists refer to what is commonly understood as oligopolistic competition.

3. National capitals in this context do not necessarily refer to capital of a particular national origin, but rather capitals that are present within a particular state, regardless of their national origin.

4. These "institutionalized compromises" can be interpreted as the institutional organization of the class alliances that are condensed within the state apparatus. This state analysis is very much indebted to Poulantzas's (1968) theory of the nation-state.

5. I use "Fordism" here as a discursive shorthand for a very dynamic, highly variegated and perpetually contested historical–geographical process that characterized the postwar period (see, e.g., Amin, 1994). I do by no means hold to a monolithic, homogeneous, and static view of Fordism. I hope to show, in fact, that Fordism as a process showed a continuous rearticulation of nested scales. At the same time, I insist that over the past 2 decades or so, a series of new scale articulations are in the process of being forged, aimed at among other things, transforming the particular power geometries associated with Fordism as a process.

6. See Swyngedouw (1996) for a fuller account.

REFERENCES

Aglietta, M. (1986). *La fin des devises clées*. Paris: La Découverte.

Aglietta, M., & Orléan, A. (1982). *La violence de la monnaie*. Paris: Presses Universitaires de France.

Altvater, E. (1993). *The future of the market: An essay on the regulation of money and nature after the collapse of "actually existing socialism."* London: Verso.

Amin, A. (Ed.). (1994). *Post-Fordism: A reader*. Oxford: Blackwell.

Amin, A., & Thrift, N. (1992). Neo-Marshallian nodes in global networks. *International Journal of Urban and Regional Research, 16*(4), 571–587.

Amin, A., & Thrift, N. (Eds.). (1994). *Globalization, institutions and regional development in Europe*. Oxford: Oxford University Press.

Aydalot, P. (Ed.). (1986). *Milieux innovateurs en Europe* (Groupement de Recherche sur les Milieux Innovateurs en Europe). Paris: Université de Paris I, Sorbonne.

Bourdieu, P. (1977). *Outline of a theory of praxis*. Cambridge: Cambridge University Press.

Boyer, R. (1983, October/December). L'introduction du Taylorisme en France à la lumière de recherches récentes. *Travail et Emploi, 18,* 17–42.

Boyer, R. (Ed.). (1986a). *Capitalismes fin de siècle.* Paris: Presses Universitaires de France.

Boyer, R. (1986b). *La théorie de la régulation: Une analyse critique.* Paris: La Découverte.

Boyer, R. (1986c). Segmentations ou solidarité, déclin ou redressement: Quel modèle pour l'Europe? In R. Boyer (Ed.), *Capitalismes fin de siècle* (pp. 207–304). Paris: Presses Universitaires de France.

Boyer, R. (1988). Formalizing growth regimes. In R. Dosi, C. Freeman, R. Nelson, G. Silverberg, & L. Soete (Eds.), *Technical change and economic theory* (pp. 608–630). London: Pinter.

Cassiers, I. (1986). *Croissance, crise et régulation en économie ouverte. La Belgique entre les Deux Guerres.* Bruxelles: Editions Vie Ouvrière.

Christopherson, S. (1992). *How the state and market are remaking the landscape of inequality,* (Mimeographed Paper). Ithaca, NY: Department of City and Regional Planning, Cornell University.

Cochrane, A. (1987). What a difference the place makes. *Antipode, 19,* 354–363.

Collapse of Barings—The A fallen star. (1995, 4 March) *Economist,* pp. 19–21.

Cooke, P. (1987). Clinical inference and geographic theory. *Antipode, 19,* 69–78.

Cooke, P. (Ed.). (1989). *Localities.* London: Unwin Hyman.

Cooke, P., & Morgan, K. (1991). *The intelligent region: Industrial and institutional innovation in Emilia-Romagna.* (Regional Industrial Research Report, 7). Cardiff: University of Wales.

Cooke, P., Moulaert, F., Swyngedouw, E., Weinstein, O., & Wells, P. (1992). *Towards global localization: The computing and communications industries in Britain and France.* London: University College Press.

Cox, K. R., & Mair, A. J. (1991). From localized social structures to localities as agents. *Environment and Planning A, 23,* 197–213.

De Certeau, M. (1984). *The practice of everyday life.* Berkeley: University of California Press.

Delorme, R., & André, C. (1983). *L'état et l'économie.* Paris: Le Seuil.

De Morgen (1995, 13 April). Duitse autosector herstructureert, p. 18.

De Vroey, M. (1984). A regulation approach of the contemporary crisis. *Capital and Class, 23* (Summer), 45–66.

Duncan, S., & Savage, M. (1989). Space, scale and locality. *Antipode, 21*(3), 207–231.

Eisenschitz, A., & Gough, J. (1993). *The politics of local economic policy.* Basingstoke, England: Macmillan.

Engels, F. (1968). *The conditions of the working class in England.* Stanford, CA: Stanford University Press. (Original work published 1845)

Esser, J., & Hirsch, J. (1989). The crisis of Fordism and the dimensions of a "post-Fordist" regional and urban structure. *International Journal of Urban and Regional Research, 13*(3), 417–436.

Foucault, M. (1980). *Power/knowledge.* Brighton, England: Harvester.

Frantzen, D. (1990). *Groei en crisis in het Na-Oorlogse Kapitalisme.* Antwerp: Kluwer.

Giddens, A. (1984). *The constitution of society.* Cambridge: Polity Press.

Grabher, G. (Ed.). (1993). *The embedded firm: On the socioeconomics of industrial networks.* London: Routledge.

Gramsci, A. (1971). *Prison notebooks.* New York: International Publishers. (Original work published 1928)

Group of Lisbon (1994). *Grenzen aan de Concurrentie.* Brussels: University of Brussels Press.

Harvery, D. (1996). *Justice, nature and the geography of difference.* Oxford: Blackwell.

Harvey, D. (1985). The geo-politics of capitalism. In D. Gregory & J. Urry (Eds.), *Social relations and spatial structures* (pp. 128–163). London: Macmillan.

Harvey, D. (1989). From managerialism to entrepreneurialism: The transformation in urban governance in late capitalism. *Geographiska Annaler Series B, 71B*(1), 3–18.

Harvey, D. (1994). *Militant particularism and global ambition: The conceptual politics of place, space and environment in the work of Raymond Williams* (Mimeographed Paper). Baltimore: Department of Geography and Environmental Engineering, Johns Hopkins University.

Harvey, D., & Swyngedouw, E. (1993). Industrial restructuring, community disempowerment and grass-roots resistance. In T. Hayter & D. Harvey (Eds.), *The factory and the city: The story of the Cowley automobile workers in Oxford* (pp. 11–25). Brighton, England: Mansell.

Herod, A. (1991). The production of scale in United States labor relations. *Area, 23*(1), 82–88.

Howitt, R. (1993). "A world in a grain of sand": Towards a reconceptualization of geographical scale. *Australian Geographer, 24*(1), 33–44.

Jessop, B. (1989). Regulation theories in retrospect and prospect. *Économies et Sociétés, Série R, "Théories de la Régulation," 23*(11), 7–62.

Jessop, B. (1990). *State theory: Putting capitalists in their place.* University Park: Pennsylvania State University Press.

Jessop, B. (1993). Towards a Schumpetarian workfare state? Preliminary remarks on post-Fordist political economy. *Studies in Political Economy, 40,* 7–39.

Jessop, B. (1994a). Post-Fordism and the state. In A. Amin (Ed.), *Post-Fordism: A reader* (pp. 251–279). Oxford: Blackwell.

Jessop, B. (1994b). The transition to post-Fordism and the Schumpeterian workfare state. In R. Burrows & B. Loader (Eds.), *Towards a post-Fordist welfare state?* (pp. 13–37). London: Routledge.

Jonas, A. (1994). Editorial. *Environment and Planning D: Society and Space, 12,* 257–264.

Lash, S., & Urry, J. (1987). *The end of organised capitalism.* Cambridge: Polity Press.

Lefebvre, H. (1974). *La production de l'espace.* Paris: Anthropos.

Leyshon, A., & Tickell, A. (1994). Money order? The discursive construction of Bretton Woods and the making and breaking of regulatory space. *Environment and Planning A, 26,* 1861–1890.

Lipietz, A. (1985). *Réflexions autour d'une fable: Pour un statut marxiste des concepts de régulation et d'accumulation.* Paris: CEPREMAP Couverture Rouge, no. 8530.

Lipietz, A. (1986). New tendencies in the international division of labor: Regimes of accumulation and modes of regulation. In A. J. Scott & M. Storper (Eds.), *Production, work, territory* (pp. 16–40). Boston: Allen & Unwin.

Lipietz, A. (1989). *De l'althusserianisme à la "théorie di la régulation."* Paris: CEPREMAP Couverture Rouge, no. 8920.

Lipietz, A. (1993). The local and the global: Regional individuality or interregionalism. *Transactions Institute of British Geographers, New Series, 18*(1), 8–18.

Luke, T. W. (1994). Placing power/siting space: The politics of global and local in the new world order. *Environment and Planning D: Society and Space, 12*, 613–628.

Luke, T. W. (1995). New world order or neo-world orders: Power, politics and ideology in informationalizing glocalities. In M. Featherstone, S. Lash, & R. Robertson (Eds.), *Global modernities* (pp. 91–107). London: Sage.

Maskell, P., & Malmberg, A. (1995, 6–9 May). *Localized learning and industrial competitiveness.* Paper presented at the Regional Studies Association Conference on "Regional Futures, Gothenburg, Sweden.

Massey, D. (1992). Politics and space/time. *New Left Review, 196*, 65–84.

Massey, D. (1993). Power-geometry and a progressive sense of place. In J. Bird, B. Curtis, T. Putnam, G. Robertson, & L. Tickner (Eds.), *Mapping the futures—Local cultures, global change* (pp. 59–69). London: Routledge.

Massey, D. (1994). Space, place and gender. Cambridge: Polity Press.

Massey, D. (1996). Tension in the city: Between anonymity and danger. In A. Merrifield & E. Swyngedouw (Eds.), *The urbanization of injustice* (pp. 100–116). London: Lawrence & Wishart.

Mistral, J. (1986). Régime international et trajectoires nationales. In R. Boyer (Ed.), *Capitalismes fin de siècle* (pp. 167–202). Paris: Presses Universitaires de France.

Morgan, K., & Roberts, E. (1993). *The democratic deficit: A guide to quangoland* (Papers in Planning Research, No. 144). Cardiff: Department of City and Regional Planning, University of Wales, College of Cardiff.

Moulaert, F., & Djellal, F. (1990, 22–23, November). *Les firmes de conseil en technologie de l'information: Des économies d'agglomération en réseaux.* Paper presented at the Conference on "Métropôles en Déséquilibre," Lyon, France.

Moulaert, F., & Swyngedouw, E. (1989). A regulation approach to the geography of flexible production systems. *Environment and Planning D: Society and Space, 7*, 327–345.

Moulaert, F., Swyngedouw, E., & Wilson, P. (1988). Spatial responses to Fordist and post-Fordist accumulation and regulation. *Papers of the Regional Science Association, 64*, 11–23.

Orange County Register, The. (1994, 7 December). O.C. seeks breathing room by filing bankruptcy, p. 1.

Peck, J. (1994). Regulating labor: The social regulation and reproduction of local labour markets. In A. Amin & N. Thrift (Eds.), *Globalization, institutions and regional development in Europe* (pp. 147–176). Oxford: Oxford University Press.

Peck, J., & Tickell, A. (1992). Local modes of social regulation? Regulation theory, Thatcherism and uneven development. *Geoforum, 23*, 347–364.

Peck, J., & Tickell, A. (1994). Searching for a new institutional fix: The after-Fordist crisis and the global–local disorder. In A. Amin (Ed.), *Post-Fordism: A reader* (pp. 280–315). Oxford: Blackwell.

Poulantzas, N. (1968). *Pouvoir politique et classes sociales I & II.* Paris: Maspéro.

Robertson, R. (1995). Glocalization: Time–space and homogeneity–heterogeneity. In M. Featherstone, S. Lash, & R. Robertson (Eds.), *Global modernities* (pp. 91–107). London: Sage.

Sayer, A. (1985). The difference that space makes. In D. Gregory & J. Urry (Eds.), *Social relations and spatial structures* (pp. 49–66). London: Macmillan.

Smith, N. (1984). *Uneven development. Nature, capital and the production of space*. Oxford: Blackwell.

Smith, N. (1987). Dangers of the empirical turn: Some comments on the CURS initiative. *Antipode, 19*(1), 59–68.

Smith, N. (1988a). Regional adjustment or restructuring. *Urban Geography, 9*(3), 318–324.

Smith, N. (1988b). The region is dead! Long live the region. *Political Geography Quarterly, 7*(2), 141–152.

Smith, N. (1993). Homeless/global: Scaling places. In J. Bird, B. Curtis, T. Putnam, G. Robertson, & L. Tickner (Eds.), *Mapping the futures—Local cultures, global change* (pp. 87–119). London: Routledge.

Smith, N., & Dennis, W. (1987). The restructuring of geographical scale: Coalescence and fragmentation of the northern core region. *Economic Geography, 63*(2), 160–182.

Soja, E. (1989). *Postmodern geographies*. London: Verso.

Strange, S. (1994). From Bretton Woods to the casino economy. In S. Corbridge, R. Martin, & N. Thrift (Eds.), *Money, power and space* (pp. 49–62). Oxford: Blackwell.

Swyngedouw, E. (1989). The heart of the place. The resurrection of locality in an age of hyperspace. *Geographiska Annaler, 71B*(1), 31–42.

Swyngedouw, E. (1991a). *Homing in and spacing out: Externalization of innovation, competitive practices and technology transfer* (Mimeographed Paper). Oxford: School of Geography, University of Oxford.

Swyngedouw, E. (1991b). Limburg: De dubbel(zinnig)e reconversie. *Planologisch Nieuws, 11*(2), 158–167.

Swyngedouw, E. (1991c). *The production of new spaces*. Unpublished doctoral dissertation, Department of Geography and Environmental Engineering, Johns Hopkins University, Baltimore.

Swyngedouw, E. (1992a). The Mammon quest; 'Glocalization,' interspatial competition and the monetary order: The construction of new scales. In M. Dunford & G. Kafkalas (Eds.), *Cities and regions in the new Europe* (pp. 39–67). London: Belhaven Press.

Swyngedouw, E. (1992b). Territorial organization and the space/technology nexus. *Transactions Institute of British Geographers, New Series, 17*, 417–433.

Swyngedouw, E. (1993). Communication, mobility and the struggle for power over space. In G. Giannopoulos & A. Gillespie (Eds.), *Transport and communication innovation in Europe* (pp. 305–325). London: Belhaven Press.

Swyngedouw, E. (1995, 14–18 March). *Exopolis and the politics of spectacular re-development*. Paper presented at the Annual Conference of the Association of American Geographers, Chicago.

Swyngedouw, E. (1996). Producing futures: International finance as a geographical project. In W. Daniels & W. Lever (Eds.), *The global economy in transition* (pp. 135–163). Harlow, England: Longman.

Taylor, P. J. (1982). A materialist framework for political geography. *Transactions Institute of British Geographers, New Series, 7*(1), 15–34.

Taylor, P. J. (1989). *Political geography: World-economy, nation-state and locality.* Harlow, England: Longman.

Tickell, A. (1995). *Making a melodrama out of a crisis: Interpreting the collapse of Barings Bank* (Mimeographed Paper). Manchester: School of Geography, University of Manchester.

Velz, P. (1983). Les entreprises et la stabilisation de la main d'oeuvre. *Révue d'Economie Régionale et Urbaine, 1,* 27–42.

Verbraeken, P. (1986, 16 April). Spekuleren in riskante niches. *De Morgen,* p. 34.

CHAPTER 7

Labor as an Agent of Globalization and as a Global Agent

Andrew Herod

INTRODUCTION

The geographic literature on the emergence of the global economy is marked by a curious omission—an almost total neglect of the international activities of workers and labor organizations. Whereas the internationalization of capital has been a topic of considerable interest to geographers—as a quick perusal of the recent literature will attest[1]—they have scarcely touched upon the internationalization of labor. Yet international labor organizations and international links between workers have existed in some form since the middle of the 19th century when, in response to the dramatic economic and political transformations associated with the geographical spread of the Industrial Revolution across Europe and North America, many socialists, anarchists, trade unionists, and others began to become increasingly concerned that labor protections in one country would be undercut by the lack of equivalent provisions elsewhere. Such concerns were particularly brought home to workers by the growing synchronization of economic booms and crises that became evident in the 1840s and 1850s (Hobsbawm, 1975), and the increasing use, especially by British employers, of foreign strikebreakers during periods of industrial unrest. Lattek (1988), for instance, has suggested that the first efforts to develop a formal structure to encourage internationalism among labor can be traced at least to 1844 and the founding by British Owenites and Chartists, together with refugees from France, Germany, and Poland, of the London-based "Democratic Friends of All Nations." During the 1850s and 1860s, some half-dozen international democratic and workers' organizations came into being, including the International Association (founded in 1855), the Congrès Démocratique International (1862), the Association Fédérative Universelle (1863), the Ligue de la Paix et de la Liberté (1867), and the Alliance de la Démocratie Socialiste (1868) (Devreese, 1988). And, of course, the 1864 founding of the International Workingmen's Association (the "First International") brought together trade unionists and socialists from several countries to discuss, among other things, strategies to facilitate international labor cooperation.

Prior to 1870, in what van der Linden (1988) has described as the "prenational phase" of labor internationalism, efforts to develop greater ties between workers in different countries were largely carried out by a relatively small number of political activists who, though deeply committed to the principles of international labor solidarity, were often unaffiliated with the trade unions in their respective countries. Through their endeavors they attempted to establish an international organization of workers before nationally structured trade union federations—which might fuel the growth of nationalist tendencies—had had the opportunity to consolidate themselves. However, the First International's decline and subsequent collapse in the 1870s, combined with the setting up in Western Europe and North America of permanent national trade union centers during the last three decades of the 19th century (the first being the British Trades Union Congress, established in 1868), marked something of a transitional phase in the history of international labor affairs.[2] Although rival institutions such as the Second International (founded in 1889) still sought to speak as the international voice of workers, after 1890 it was the various nationally constituted trade union movements that increasingly came to dominate the field of international labor affairs. Indeed, the three decades prior to World War I were marked by a veritable flurry of international trade union activities, which included the establishment of some 30 international trade secretariats (ITSs) designed to foster cooperation between unions in particular industries (Busch, 1983; Price, 1945; Segal, 1953) and the 1901 formation of the International Secretariat of Trade Union Centers to which national trade union federations could affiliate as a means to promote greater labor ties across national boundaries, to collect data of use to unions, and to deliver some modest financial aid during strikes (Sturmthal, 1950).[3] Such was the extent of these efforts to develop international labor links that van Holthoon and van der Linden (1988, p. vii) have described the 100 years prior to the outbreak of World War II as the "classical age" of working class internationalism.

During the 20th century, trade unions have developed international labor cooperation and contact primarily through three sets of institutions. First, workers have acted globally through the ITSs. Currently there are 14 such secretariats, of which the International Metalworkers' Federation (IMF), the International Federation of Chemical, Energy, Mine, and General Workers' Unions (ICEM), and the International Union of Food, Agricultural, Hotel, Restaurant, Catering, Tobacco and Allied Workers' Associations (IUF) have been most active in seeking to meet the challenge raised by the globalization of economic relations. Second, the national trade union centers in particular countries have affiliated with a number of international labor federations that serve to address broader economic and political issues affecting workers than do the secretariats whose activities are more focused on particular industries. During the post-World War II period, arguably the two most important of these have been the Western-oriented International Confederation of Free Trade Unions (ICFTU) and its Communist rival, the World Federation of Trade Unions (WFTU), although other similar global institutions have also played important roles—for example the religiously oriented Confédération Internationale des Syndicats Chrétiens (CISC).[4] These labor federations have also all set up their own regional organizations covering various parts of the globe. Third, trade unions have pursued labor and human rights issues through a number of intergovernmental bodies. Chief among these are the International Labour Organisation (ILO), the Organisation for Economic Cooperation and Development (OECD), and the Center on Transnational Corporations, all of which are specialized agencies of the United Nations (for more on the ILO see Alcock, 1971; Ghebali, 1989; Johnston, 1970).[5]

My purpose in recounting this activity is that it raises important questions about the process and implications of economic and political globalization. Clearly, not only has capital become more global in its operations during the past century and a half but so, too, have workers. Given that the general theme of this book is to reevaluate globalization as it is typically presented, in this chapter I argue that an appropriate place to begin such a critical project is to address the omission of labor from the terms of debate in the geographic literature. Whereas the globalization thesis usually portrays the emergence of the global economy as capital's creation, the logical outcome of the expansionary nature of capital, and the new economic and political reality to which labor must respond, in this chapter I argue that such a view is problematic for (at least) two reasons.

First, it ignores the role that workers themselves have played in the actual genesis and subsequent integration of the global economy. Capital has not been the only actor operating at the global scale. Indeed, given the history just outlined, it might even be suggested that the formal transnationalization of labor in many ways predates that of capital, at least with regard to the arrival on the world stage of the transnational corporation and the global assembly line, two entities which are often seen as emblematic of globalization.

Second, there has been a tendency to portray workers as structurally defenseless in the face of a hypermobile, rapidly restructuring, and globally organized capital. However, while the transnationalization of capital has certainly presented workers with new problems, as they now frequently must negotiate with corporations whose operations are located in many different parts of the globe, I would maintain that labor's structural position is not always and necessarily that of the passive victim of globalization. Although their relative immobility in the face of more mobile global capital may make some workers that much more amenable to corporate arguments about the necessity for contract concessions and the like, theoretically we cannot concede the global scale of economic and political organization to capital and present labor as structurally confined to the local, regional, or national scale. Workers, too, have the capacity to act supranationally and, indeed, have a lengthy history of so doing.

The chapter itself is organized in three main sections. The first examines some of the international activities of the U.S. labor movement (particularly with regard to Latin America and the Caribbean), both in support of its own goals and in connection to U.S. foreign policy. I use this historical narrative to highlight the U.S. labor movement's complicity in bringing about the globalization of economic relations and how the movement was instrumental in structuring geopolitical discourse and practice after World War II. The narrative is intended to serve as a counterpoint to accounts that see globalization only in terms of the transnational activities of capital. In essence, *it allows a much more active role for workers to be written into analyses of the globalization of economic and political relations.* The second section discusses how some international trade union bodies have attempted to develop transnational strategies and structures to confront globally organized capital. This section, too, suggests that workers should not be conceptualized simply as passive flotsam driven by the powerful currents of global capital restructuring, but that *through their actions workers actively define and circumscribe the very possibilities for capital's global activities.* In sum, both sections serve to illustrate the active roles played by organized labor in shaping the historical geography of the global economy. The third section ponders some of the conceptual issues that these activities raise for the globalization thesis, particularly with regard to the genesis of the global economy and labor's structural position within it.

TOWARD AN UNDERSTANDING OF U.S. LABOR'S ROLE IN THE GLOBALIZATION OF ECONOMIC AND POLITICAL RELATIONS

The U.S. labor movement has been involved in international affairs since the last half of the 19th century.[6] The movement's foreign affairs have primarily been conducted by the leaders of the national trade union federations (the American Federation of Labor [AFL], the Congress of Industrial Organizations [CIO] and, since these federations' 1955 merger, the AFL–CIO) rather than individual national or local union affiliates.[7] The main exception to this has been a number of unions' activities in the various trade secretariats. A handful of unions, such as the International Ladies' Garment Workers' Union, the United Auto Workers, and the United Steelworkers of America, have also maintained staff on their own payrolls who are responsible for international affairs. Certainly, this list does not form an exclusive accounting of the international activities of U.S. workers and their organizations. Not all unions have historically been affiliated with these national federations and not all labor activists and workers operating in the international arena are members of AFL–CIO unions. Furthermore, AFL–CIO foreign policy has frequently been challenged by dissident elements within the labor movement and so should not be viewed as always and inevitably simply the product of the leadership's will (e.g., see Battista, 1991). Nevertheless, the making of the labor movement's "official" foreign policy has traditionally been the preserve of the President and Executive Council of the national trade union federation(s) and the Department of International Affairs, which they control.[8]

As we shall see, the U.S. labor movement's international activities during the 20th century have been shaped to a large degree by the United States' (dominant) economic position vis à vis other countries. The international activities of U.S. capital and labor have been conditioned, ultimately, by economic self-interest—an expanded market for U.S. goods abroad would generate profits for U.S. business and jobs for U.S. workers—and a belief that it is their historical mission to bring U.S.-style liberal democracy and modern capitalism to those parts of the world (especially Latin America) left economically and politically "backward" by European colonialism.[9] This belief itself is deeply ingrained in U.S. ideologies concerning American exceptionalism and Manifest Destiny, to which both U.S. capitalists and U.S. workers have frequently subscribed. It is nowhere illustrated better, perhaps, than in a statement by Samuel Gompers (who led the AFL for almost the first half-century of its existence): "The nation which dominates the markets of the world" Gompers suggested, "will surely control its destiny. To make of the United States a vast workshop [for the world] is *our manifest destiny*, and *our duty* . . . " (quoted in Scott, 1978, p. 92, emphasis added).

Thus, whereas the labor movement's goals have sometimes been at odds with those of the government and U.S. business, frequently they have been mutually reinforcing. Consequently, labor officials have played crucial roles in enforcing, and indeed shaping, U.S. foreign policy (Barry & Preusch, 1990; Hardy, 1936; Larson, 1975; Morris, 1967; Radosh, 1969; Scott, 1978; Simms, 1992). Equally, though U.S. labor has often virulently opposed the domestic actions of U.S. corporations, the AFL–CIO's Executive Council has frequently been prepared to work hand in hand with those very same corporations in the international arena. Representatives from the AFL and from the CIO were involved, for instance, in implementing the Marshall Plan, which so dramatically reshaped Europe's economic geography, and in reorganizing the trade union movements in postwar Germany, Italy, and Japan (Heaps, 1955; Maier, 1987; Windmuller, 1954). AFL–CIO officials have been active in supporting pro-U.S. trade unions in Latin America, the Caribbean, Asia, and Africa. This support has had a dual purpose. Certainly, AFL–CIO officials have sought to help weak local unions to become strong enough to provide services to, and to bargain on behalf of, their members. But their intervention has also been designed to oppose more militant labor activists and the perceived threat of Communist control over local unions (Cox, 1971; Spalding, 1988). Presently, with the apparent end of the Cold War, the AFL–CIO is working with various East European governments and labor officials in an effort to mold industrial relations and labor law in these countries in the image of U.S. trade unionism (see Herod, 1997).

Ideological Underpinnings of U.S. Labor's Foreign Policy

The often close relationship between AFL–CIO policy and that of U.S. capital and the federal government in the international arena stems from the underlying philosophy that has guided the labor organization's affairs both domestically and abroad, namely the acceptance of capitalism as, essentially, a munificent economic system for (U.S.) workers. Emerging, in part, out of the material conditions in which U.S. workers found themselves during the late 19th and early 20th centuries, especially the growing dominance of the United States in the world economic system, this philosophy became enshrined in AFL domestic and international policy and practice, largely through the efforts of Gompers to promote what he called "trade unionism pure and simple" (also sometimes referred to as "bread and butter trade unionism") in the face of the more militant and politically oriented brands of trade unionism advocated by various European and U.S. socialists. For Gompers, workers and capitalists were idealized as partners in progress, and so the purpose of trade unions was to ensure, through organization of the paid workplace, that workers gained the highest income and best working conditions possible within the given (and accepted) distribution of power in capitalist societies (Gompers, 1925). Although he sincerely believed in the principle of international links between national trade union movements and was often critical of European and U.S. government officials for pursuing colonial policies of outright territorial acquisition, Gompers was himself not necessarily opposed to U.S. economic expansionism abroad.[10] Rather, he believed that the international supremacy of U.S. capitalism, with its capacity to generate large quantities of relatively cheap commodities for both domestic and foreign consumption, would bring ever higher standards of living to both U.S. and foreign workers (Simms, 1992). Furthermore, the United States' "civilizing" mission would bring democracy and modernization to those workers of the world still toiling under the control of the various European imperial powers and/or local dictatorships.

The consequence of such a worldview during the 20th century has been a frequent correspondence in the international arena between the goals of U.S. organized labor and those of the U.S. government and big business, principally the defense of U.S. capital's interests abroad, opposition to militant "socialistic" organizations that threaten the hegemony of this capital, and the promotion internationally of a brand of trade unionism that takes capitalism as a given, rather than contestable, political and economic system. Although U.S. labor officials and representatives of business and the government may disagree on tactics, there is little fundamental disagreement on issues of basic philosophy: faith in the capitalist system and the need to make the world safe for U.S. investment.

Arguably, three elements have dominated U.S. labor's foreign policy during the past 100 years. First, the AFL–CIO has exhibited a certain ambivalence toward affiliation with international labor organizations, many of which it sees as too politically radical—particularly those that profess an anticapitalist agenda. Such ambivalence was evident at an early time. In 1910 the AFL somewhat reluctantly affiliated with the International Secretariat of Trade Union Centers which, under pressure from Gompers, soon thereafter changed its name to the International Federation of Trade Unions (IFTU).[11] This marked the first time the AFL formally participated in an international labor organization. However, by the end of World War I Gompers felt himself increasingly isolated from the more radical goals of several other member federations (especially concerning international labor policy toward the Versailles Peace Treaty) and, at his urging, the AFL in 1921 withdrew from the IFTU (see American Federation of Labor, 1921, for more reasons behind this decision). For most of the next 2 decades the AFL remained largely outside the ambit of the international labor movement.[12] Virtually the only organic link between U.S. organized labor and the international labor scene during this period remained the ITSs with which a number of individual AFL affiliates were still connected. Although in the post-World War II period the AFL–CIO has participated more fully in various international labor organizations, it has never really committed itself to the principle of ceding any of its own sovereignty to pursue collectively stated goals of the international labor movement, and continues to pursue an on-again–off-again relationship with such organizations.

Second, the AFL has often operated in close cooperation with the federal government in the international arena. Ideologically, the AFL has always been committed to the success of U.S. capital abroad since, until fairly recently at least, the success of U.S.-based firms in opening up foreign markets was usually a guarantee of employment for AFL members. This commitment is highlighted in a compact made between Gompers and President Woodrow Wilson's administration during World War I. In exchange for government recognition of the AFL's right to organize, Gompers worked to ensure that industrial production (particularly in munitions factories) would proceed unhindered by union-sponsored disruptions (Larson, 1975). Although during the 1920s Republican administrations broke this compact domestically and backed a corporate open-shop drive against the AFL, in the international sphere the AFL continued to receive federal support for its policy of exporting Gompers-style "trade unionism pure and simple" (Simms, 1992). Isolated from the IFTU and sharing many of the same international political and economic objectives as the U.S. government and big business, the AFL increasingly pursued the goal of implementing labor's own Monroe Doctrine in Latin America and the Caribbean. To achieve this goal, the AFL sought to destroy radical union and political organizations in the region, to fund labor organizations more favorably oriented towards U.S. geopolitical interests in the hemisphere, and, generally, to ensure the supremacy of U.S. capital. This policy has evolved into an interventionist labor stance that has often seen the AFL–CIO work hand in hand with the Central Intelligence Agency (CIA) to suppress movements (themselves often led by trade unionists) opposed to the spread of U.S. political and economic influence in the region and beyond, and to support the development of a form of trade unionism that more closely corresponds with the AFL's own view of unions' "proper" roles in capitalist economies (for more on this point, see Barry & Preusch, 1990; Morris, 1967; Radosh, 1969; Scott, 1978).

Third, since Gompers's time the AFL–CIO has pursued a virulently anti-Soviet policy that has fundamentally shaped international labor politics, especially in the post-World War II period. The outbreak of World War II weakened the IFTU significantly and, in late 1945, a new international organization, the World Federation of Trade Unions (WFTU), was established to replace it. Whereas the newly formed CIO played a leading role in creating the WFTU, the AFL rejected membership because, unlike the IFTU, the new organization included Soviet trade union representation. Although its refusal to join the WFTU left the AFL as the only major North American or European labor federation to remain unaffiliated, this did not mean it was inactive in international labor affairs. In light of the perceived Stalinist domination of the WFTU, the AFL's international policy after 1945 was increasingly structured by three objectives (Windmuller, 1954): (1) to oppose the WFTU wherever and whenever possible; (2) to maintain contact with the ITSs (which the AFL saw as less tainted by Soviet influence) and to build from within them an organization to rival the WFTU; and (3) to provide direct assistance to non-Communist unions and workers' organizations around the world, even to the extent sometimes of supporting socialists against Communists (Scott, 1978). These objectives were also largely supported by the U.S. State Department.

U.S. Labor and the Making of the Geopolitical and Geo-economic Order of the Cold War

In pursuing its anti-Soviet foreign policy, the AFL (and subsequently the CIO, too) played a significant role in fueling the Cold War and so in shaping the global geopolitical and geo-economic order of the post-World War II period. By 1948 the Cold War was gaining momentum and the national federations making up the WFTU had begun to ally themselves with either Washington or Moscow. A year later, most of the Western trade union federations withdrew from the WFTU, which they accused of having become simply an instrument of Soviet foreign policy, to form the International Confederation of Free Trade Unions (ICFTU) (Sturmthal, 1950).[13] The ICFTU's formation marked a clear political and ideological victory for the AFL. Not only had it achieved its international objective of splitting the WFTU into "free" trade unions and those sympathetic to the Soviet Union but, domestically, AFL leaders now asserted the moral superiority of their stance over the CIO which, they gloated, had been duped into believing it could work with Communist-dominated unions. Combined with the AFL's larger membership, this moral victory allowed the AFL to claim the position of chief architect of the U.S. labor movement's international affairs in the immediate postwar period. The CIO, somewhat more ambivalent than the AFL toward the ICFTU's goals and preoccupied with expelling several of its own more militant affiliates (Zieger, 1986), was prepared largely to concede this international leadership role to the AFL (Windmuller, 1954). This was significant not only for U.S. labor's international activities, for it left the generally more conservative AFL at the helm of foreign policy, but also for its domestic agenda. With the AFL once more the dominant voice of U.S. labor abroad, the AFL leadership, long critical of the CIO, felt that the time was now right for a rapprochement with its old nemesis that would allow the rival organizations to join forces in the looming struggle against the spread of Soviet Communism. Indeed, rapprochement in the international arena played an important role in laying the groundwork for the two labor organizations' eventual domestic merger in 1955.

Both the AFL and the CIO were eager participants in helping to secure U.S. postwar geo-economic and geopolitical interests around the globe as a means to ensure access for U.S. products to foreign markets. Perhaps one of the earliest indications of their commitment to this Cold War agenda, and hence of their role in facilitating the globalization of U.S. capital and culture, was the support they provided to the European Recovery Program (the "Marshall Plan"). The centerpiece of the newly articulated Truman Doctrine, the Marshall Plan was designed to prevent the further spread of Communist influence and to reintegrate Western Europe into a liberal capitalist international trade system dominated by the United States. Both the AFL and the CIO were called upon to play vital roles in undermining Communist-leaning and/or anti-U.S. labor groups, particularly in France, West Germany, Italy, Austria, and Greece (see Radosh, 1969, pp. 304–347 for more details).[14] By providing material aid and organizational support, all wrapped up in a major propaganda campaign extolling the virtues of U.S.-style economic unionism, the AFL and the CIO hoped to encourage the development of a pro-U.S. stance among European workers and labor leaders, an aim that often necessitated working closely and surreptitiously with the U.S. State Department and the newly formed CIA (for more on other labor links with the CIA see Langley, 1972; Morris, 1967). The AFL also encouraged its affiliate unions, which traditionally had not been that active in the ITSs, to step up their activities to ensure the secretariats remained non-Communist and supportive of the Marshall Plan (Godson, 1976). Through these activities, the AFL and the CIO were deeply involved in enabling the growth of U.S. political and economic influence in Western Europe and so of ensuring the emergence of a postwar economic system that marched to the tune of Bretton Woods and U.S. capital.

In its vision for remaking the postwar world under the aegis of the *Pax Americana*, the AFL was eager to see the ICFTU become the foremost international labor organization in the fight against Communism (e.g., see the tone adopted in American Federation of Labor, 1952, pp. 114–117). As part of this, the AFL urged the ICFTU to develop programs to preach the benefits of U.S.-style economic unionism geared toward workplace collective bargaining rather than broader political and social struggles, struggles that smacked of socialist agitation. To provide an ideological bulwark against domination of the ICFTU by more socialist-oriented European union centers, the AFL also encouraged closer ties with the predominantly Catholic CISC, while at the same time seeking to develop strong regional organizations that would prevent the concentration of power in Europe, a situation too reminiscent for the AFL of the prewar IFTU. Yet almost immediately these goals proved to be a source of disharmony in the new organization. European trade union officials appeared less committed to the fight against Communism than the AFL leadership desired and were even prepared at times to work with Communist-controlled labor organizations (such as the French Confédération Générale du Travail) in pursuit of common economic or political goals. Furthermore, whereas U.S. labor leaders saw Soviet Communism as the greatest threat to "free" trade unionism, European union leaders seemed more preoccupied with the threats posed by right-wing regimes in Spain, Portugal, Argentina, Venezuela, and elsewhere (Radosh, 1969). They were also more inclined to see the ICFTU as a vehicle for political agitation, whereas the AFL wanted to use the Confederation as a vehicle to propagate its ideas about Gompersian "bread and butter" trade unionism. Finally, European union leaders were concerned about U.S. control of the ICFTU's agenda and the possibility that the regional organizations would take power away from the central Confederation, thereby weakening its ability to implement coordinated international labor policy.

Throughout the 1950s and the 1960s, the AFL–CIO maintained a strained relationship with the ICFTU, and U.S. labor leaders continued to clash with their counterparts abroad (particularly those in the unions beginning to form in postcolonial Africa, Asia, and Latin America) over the ICF-TU's position on several matters: its stance toward the Soviet Union and contact with Communist-dominated unions; the balance of power within the ICFTU; economic versus political unionism; the role to be played by AFL–CIO-controlled regional labor organizations such as the American Institute for Free Labor Development (AIFLD) (discussed later); and whether such organizations should be subject to ICFTU dictate (see International Confederation of Free Trade Unions, 1958, for more on the Confederation's position regarding some of these matters). After nearly 20 years of tense relations, in 1969 the AFL–CIO formally disaffiliated from the ICFTU.[15] Although it reaffiliated in the early 1980s, during the past 3 decades the AFL–CIO has largely pursued its foreign policy through its own Department of International Affairs and the four regional labor institutions that it has established in Europe (the Free Trade Union Institute), Latin America (the American Institute for Free Labor Development), Africa (the African-American Labor Center), and Asia (the Asian-American Free Labor Institute).[16] These regional organizations have funded a number of projects designed to strengthen pro-U.S. forces abroad, including supplying technical assistance, grants and training to local unions, and supporting political campaigns (see American Federation of Labor–Congress of Industrial Organizations, 1987a, 1987b, for official statements concerning its foreign policy and organs working in the international arena). Although all the AFL–CIO's regional institutes have been active in this regard (e.g., see Foner, 1989; West, 1991), given the value of U.S. investments in Latin America it is perhaps not surprising that none has been more so than the AIFLD.[17]

Making the World Safe for (U.S.) Capitalism:
Latin America and the Caribbean

The AFL has a long history of intervention in Latin America and the Caribbean. Under the guise of putting an end to old-style European colonialism in the region (and in the process making way for new-style U.S. economic hegemony), Gompers and others on the AFL's Executive Council actively supported anti-Spanish labor activities in Cuba, Puerto Rico, and elsewhere in the 1880s and 1890s. When war with Spain finally came in 1898 William Randolph Hearst may have supplied the headlines, but it was the AFL that provided moral and technical support to U.S. military operations in the Caribbean. However, it was the outbreak of World War I that really served as the catalyst to the AFL's deep intervention in the region in tandem with U.S. capital and the U.S. State Department. As the war disrupted trade between Europe and Latin America, Woodrow Wilson saw an opportunity to expand control over the region's economies. The AFL took a leading role in this regard. Working with members of the Confederación Regional Obrera Mexicana (CROM), Gompers played a key part in helping to establish in 1918 a new regional labor organization for the region—the Pan-American Federation of Labor (PAFL)—which, he hoped, would secure U.S. interests in the hemisphere in the face of more radical anticapitalist labor movements in countries such as Argentina, Chile, and Uruguay (Snow, 1964).[18]

Publicly, Gompers averred that the PAFL was designed to encourage solidarity between all Latin American workers—and, indeed, in his mind this was probably true. But it soon became clear that the PAFL had been established largely with the goals of U.S. labor in mind. There is evidence to suggest, for instance, that Gompers's preliminary efforts to promote such a regional labor federation under AFL tutelage were designed to undermine attempts by the Industrial Workers of the World to create a similar, though more radical, organization. The PAFL would also be a way to control German influence in Mexico during the war.[19] Furthermore, by organizing workers (particularly in Mexico) the AFL hoped to discourage U.S. capital from locating in the region to take advantage of cheap labor. Finally, the PAFL would serve as a mechanism, Gompers hoped, to stabilize Mexico in the wake of the 1910 revolution and his fears that the revolution might radicalize along the lines of the recent Bolshevik actions in Russia (Andrews, 1991). For their part, the corporatist-minded leaders of the CROM saw the PAFL as a way of easing growing tensions between the United States and Mexico (particularly in light of General Pershing's 1916 invasion) and of trying to improve conditions for Mexican migrant workers in the U.S. A number of Latin American trade unions refused to join the PAFL, however, arguing that it was little more than an arm of the U.S. government (which had provided substantial financial support for its establishment) and an instrument of the *monroismo obrero* practiced by the AFL.[20]

Although the PAFL continued in existence on paper until the 1940s, Gompers' death in 1924 and the loss of most of its U.S. financing following the crash of 1929 were essentially death knells for the organization. In its place a far more militant Latin American-led regional organization, the Confederación de Trabajadores de America Latina (CTAL), emerged in 1938. The CTAL's agenda was much more radical than was that of the PAFL. CTAL officials advocated massive land redistribution programs, nationalization of foreign-owned facilities, a more clearly class-based politically oriented labor politics that called for proletarian internationalism, and opposition to U.S. imperialist designs on Latin America (e.g., see Barbash, 1948, for examples of the tone of CTAL's language; also, Radosh, 1969, pp. 360–368). Arguing that Latin America needed to develop free from U.S. interference, the CTAL leadership specifically excluded the AFL from the new organization (it did, however, develop closer links with the CIO). Although the CTAL was initially quite ideologically diverse, within a short time Communist elements came to dominate the organization, something which the AFL found particularly distressing. As a result, the AFL stepped up efforts to oppose the CTAL.

The outbreak of World War II saw increased U.S. labor activity in Latin America as both the AFL and the CIO worked to secure essential raw materials. Close links were forged between the AFL and the CIO on the one hand, and the U.S. Office of Inter-American Affairs (OIAA) headed by Nelson Rockefeller—whose family owned vast holdings in Latin America—on the other. The U.S. government channeled funds through the OIAA to aid efforts by the AFL and the CIO to undermine the CTAL. As part of these efforts, the AFL took the leading role in founding in 1948 a new regional body—the Confederación Interamericana de Trabajadores (CIT)—to rival the CTAL. The CIT, however, was relatively short-lived. When the World Federation of Trade Unions split in 1949, the CIT made provisions to dissolve itself and to reconstitute as the IFTU's Organización Regional Interamericana de Trabajadores (ORIT).[21] Through the ORIT AFL leaders hoped once again to use a regional labor organization as cover to encourage the formation and growth of Latin American trade unions that were more favorably inclined toward U.S. economic influence and/or disinclined toward Communist politics in the region. While the ORIT primarily carried out its task through a wide range of organizational and training activities, it did also engage in more clandestine operations. ORIT members, for instance, participated in the 1954 Guatemalan coup that toppled the government of Jacobo Arbenz after he nationalized much of the country's land (including some owned by his family) and redistributed it to the local peasantry—whereas giving his own land to peasants was one thing, giving away land owned by the United Fruit Company was, clearly, quite another.

Although the ORIT enjoyed several successes and was able to affiliate the majority of Latin America's largest unions into a non-Communist confederation, Castro's seizure of power in Cuba in 1959 greatly alarmed the architects of AFL–CIO foreign policy. Quickly, they came to believe that the ORIT was too independent a body to effectively prevent the further spread of Communism throughout the Western hemisphere, especially because some of its Latin American officials actually expressed support for Castro (Scott, 1978). Rather, what the AFL–CIO desired was a body that was totally accountable to its own Executive Council. It was with such a desire that in 1962 the AFL–CIO launched the AIFLD. Operating in conjunction with President Kennedy's Alliance for Progress initiative—which was itself designed to undermine radical anti-U.S. social movements in Latin America and the Caribbean—the AIFLD was set up to serve as the AFL–CIO's principal foreign policy arm in the region. Not only would the AIFLD gather intelligence for the U.S. State Department and the CIA, but it would also train Latin American unionists in the practices of U.S.-style "economic" unionism and oppose more militant social/political unionism, which was frequently anti-United States and anticapitalist in orientation (Barry & Preusch, 1990; Spalding, 1988).[22]

Initially conceived as a tripartite corporatist entity, the AIFLD included elements from organized labor, business (e.g., officials of W. G. Grace, United Fruit Company, Pan American Airlines, and other large U.S. corporations with interests in Latin America), and the U.S. government. However, after nearly 2 decades and continued criticism of this arrangement, in 1981 membership of the AIFLD's Board was limited to members of the U.S. and Latin American trade union movements. Nevertheless, several of the highest AIFLD officials have been, and continue to be, members of the Council of Foreign Relations and the Trilateral Commission, two bodies that are major players in formulating U.S. foreign policy. Furthermore, most of the AIFLD's funding continues to come directly or indirectly from the U.S. government in the form of grants from the Agency for International Development, the Department of Labor, the National Endowment for Democracy (NED), and the Inter-American Development Bank.[23] The AIFLD also works closely with the Council for Latin America, Inc., a business group founded by David Rockefeller, which seeks to further U.S. corporate interests in the region.

Primarily, the AIFLD sees its role as one "of trying to make the investment climate [in Latin America and the Caribbean] more attractive and more inviting to [U.S. corporations]" (AIFLD official, quoted in Spalding, 1988, p. 264). This goal is carried out by the AIFLD in a number of ways, including labor education programs (which usually focus on issues related to collective bargaining, labor movement structures, how to spot and counter "Communist propaganda," union finances, political theory from a liberal pro-capitalist perspective, labor legislation, and so on) and aid in setting up credit unions, workers' banks, producer–consumer cooperatives, and building housing for members of pro-U.S. local unions (Romualdi, 1967). However, Latin American and Caribbean trade unionists who have been trained by AIFLD representatives either in their country or at the AIFLD's school in the United States have also been involved in several coups against leftist governments—including those in the Dominican Republic (1963), Brazil (1964), and Chile (1973)—and other political activities aimed either at destabilizing regimes seen to be anti-United States or at supporting pro-U.S. regimes.[24] Although the 1980s saw growing rank-and-file opposition in the U.S. labor movement to official AFL–CIO foreign policy in Latin America, such opposition has not yet been sufficiently powerful to fundamentally reorient the AFL–CIO's objectives abroad. As a result, the AIFLD's activities continue to serve to make Latin America and the Caribbean a much safer place for U.S. multinationals to invest, a policy that has undoubtedly encouraged the movement of capital out of the United States and into the region.

In this section of the chapter I have attempted to do three things. First, I have examined the U.S. labor movement's basic philosophy regarding the position of workers in a capitalist economic system and sought to suggest that this philosophy owes much to the economic dominance enjoyed by the United States during much of the 20th century. Second, I have shown how this philosophy has led the AFL–CIO to work hand in hand with U.S. capital and the federal government in the international arena, especially in the fight against Communism and anti-U.S. political activity. Third, I have tried to raise the issue of labor's role in the globalization of economic and political relations. The AFL–CIO was not simply taken along for the ride by U.S. corporations as they sought to expand operations in Latin America and the Caribbean. Rather, the AFL–CIO's own philosophy has led it to adopt an interventionist role in the pursuit of its own political and economic agenda, namely implementation of a workers' Monroe Doctrine. The AFL–CIO and U.S. capital were, I would argue, truly partners in the expansion of U.S. economic and political influence in Latin America and the Caribbean. Not only were U.S. corporations responsible for processes of economic and political globalization, particularly with regard to Latin America and the Caribbean, but so, too, was the U.S. labor movement. Such international activities by the AFL–CIO, its surrogate organizations, and other labor bodies suggest that a much more active role should be accorded workers in explanations of the genesis of the global economy.

LABOR AND THE CHALLENGE OF THE TRANSNATIONALS

As we have seen, during the post-World War II period the U.S. labor movement's fear of the spread of Communism has dramatically shaped its foreign policy. However, this has not been the only concern driving U.S. labor's international activities. As many corporations have shifted their production overseas to previously unheard of degrees, and as growing imports threaten jobs domestically, in recent years U.S. unions have increasingly turned to the international trade secretariats to network internationally (Uehlein, 1989). While some AFL–CIO officials, perhaps wary of the waning of their own political influence, have expressed fears that growing involvement with the ITSs might "reinforce [not] a common policy for the AFL–CIO but one that is fragmented" (quoted in Gershman, 1975, p. 72), many have come to recognize the potential role the secretariats can play in confronting globally organized corporations. Paradoxically, a further stimulus in the United States for strengthening the secretariats has come from dissident elements within the labor movement who see the possibility of using them to challenge official AFL–CIO foreign policy. After the United Auto Workers (UAW) broke with the AFL–CIO over the latter's support for U.S. involvement in the war in Vietnam, for instance, the UAW increasingly used the International Metalworkers' Federation (IMF) as the conduit for its foreign aid contributions (Foner, 1989; Windmuller, 1970). Additionally, the AFL–CIO's disaffiliation from the ICFTU and the United States' withdrawal from the ILO in 1977 encouraged many individual unions to step up their activities in the secretariats as one of the few means left open to maintain organic links with workers in other countries.[25]

Arguably, the secretariats' organization on the basis of industrial structure rather than territoriality makes them best suited of all the international labor bodies to confront transnational corporations' global production structures and strategies.[26] The most active secretariats have pursued four main policies to counter the effects of the growth of transnational production. First, they have had some success in developing a degree of international coordination in the realm of contract bargaining. In 1969, for instance, the old International Federation of Chemical, Energy and General Workers' Unions (ICEF) (now the ICEM after its 1995 merger with the mineworkers' ITS) trade secretariat played a key role in coordinating contract negotiations between the French glass manufacturing giant Companie de Saint Gobain and local unions in France, Italy, West Germany, and the United States, in the process ensuring that the company bargained on the basis of its global profits rather than national conditions in each of these four countries (Cox, 1971). This success undermined the company's efforts to play these local unions against each other during collective bargaining talks. In the mid-1980s West German unionists lobbied executives at the chemical transnational BASF to settle a dispute with workers locked out of one of the company's plants in Louisiana (see Bendiner, 1987, pp. 62–102, for more on this and other such examples; also, Barnet & Muller, 1974, pp. 312–319).[27] More recently, a group of steelworkers locked out of their aluminum smelting plant in the United States successfully used the IMF, the ICEF, and the IUF to articulate a global corporate campaign that forced the company to allow the union back into the plant (Herod, 1995).

Second, although ITSs recognize that economic conditions around the globe realistically preclude establishing uniform wage rates, they have argued that such differential conditions should not prevent workers from enjoying similar health and safety conditions at work, nor rights to union representation and collective bargaining. Beginning in the mid-1960s, the IMF established World Auto Councils (WACs) at each of the large producers to pressure them to adopt a number of policies concerning union rights and working conditions throughout their plants worldwide. Similar world councils have subsequently been extended to other industries. Through these WACs the IMF's various national affiliates are able to provide information on contracts and conditions to their fellow autoworkers in different countries.[28] In 1971 the IMF WACs initiated a campaign to harmonize some nonwage issues in an effort to discourage manufacturers from playing workers in different parts of

the globe against each other in a continuous process of downward concessionary whipsawing. However, this strategy is not without its problems. Cultural
differences between Japanese, European, and North American auto workers,
particularly concerning attitudes toward work and labor–management cooperation (e.g., the "team concept"), have made it difficult to pursue such harmonization to the fullest extent. Also, whereas auto production until fairly recently was characterized by relatively integrated production systems
concentrated in North America and Europe, the spread of production into
low-wage countries such as Mexico, South Korea, and Brazil, combined with
the auto producers' assault on national bargaining in North America (Herod,
1991b) and elsewhere, have made it increasingly difficult to secure more har-
monized contracts. Furthermore, different groups of workers have different
pressing needs. Latin American and Southeast Asian delegates to IMF WAC
meetings have consistently stressed the need to ensure basic trade union rights
in the face of authoritarian regimes, whereas in North America and Europe
job security, wages, and shorter working hours have often been the priority
(Bendiner, 1987). Nevertheless, the WACs do see harmonization as the most
viable strategy for confronting the growing transnational challenge.

Third, several secretariats have encouraged mergers between unions in
particular industries as a means to present a more unified position against
management, especially in countries such as Britain and Japan, where several
different unions might be present in a single manufacturing facility. In 1972,
for instance, the IMF undertook a campaign to promote the merger of several
Japanese auto unions (Curtin, 1973). Despite some success, this, too, has
proved problematic because the varying ideological and political affiliations of
the unions representing workers in particular industries often limit cooperation, let alone the possibility of mergers. Even in cases where politics and ideology are not issues, particular unions' unwillingness to concede their autonomy to other unions can also be stumbling blocks.

Fourth, the secretariats have invested time and money in developing
databases to provide affiliates with information on corporate operating and
bargaining practices in different parts of the globe. The IMF Economic and
Social Department, for instance, maintains files on more than 500 multinational companies (International Metalworkers' Federation, 1991). Such information has proven particularly valuable to IMF affiliates seeking to implement campaigns (increasingly global in extent) against corporations. Indeed,
it is somewhat ironic, perhaps, that international communication between
workers has been greatly facilitated by unions' use of the very same new technologies by which transnational corporations coordinate their global operations. Whereas many of those who write about the global economy have argued that the telecommunications revolution has now made possible the
micromanagement of distant operations by corporate decision makers, few
seem to appreciate the fact that electronic mail and bulletin board systems

also allow workers in different parts of the globe to exchange information about strikes, contracts, and working conditions almost instantaneously (e.g., see *Labor Notes*, 1994; Herod, 1997). Access to this type of information has proven vital for unions seeking to trace patterns of corporate ownership and control as a starting point for political campaigns and for coordinating international activities (cf. Herod, 1995).

In order to concentrate their efforts on these four issues, the secretariats have delegated to the ICFTU many of their traditional activities concerning propagating trade unionism and representing workers' interests before intergovernmental agencies (Casserini, 1993).[29] By working with agencies such as the ILO, the OECD, and the United Nations' Center on Transnational Corporations, the ICFTU has tried to regulate corporations' international activities by exerting influence on the shaping of international economic and social policies. Trade union representatives, for instance, have pushed hard for inclusion of a social clause guaranteeing basic labor and human rights in the General Agreement on Tariffs and Trade (GATT). Although the unions have successfully managed to incorporate a number of guidelines and codes into several international agreements and resolutions (e.g., formulation of the OECD's "Code of Conduct" for transnationals), the lack of an effective enforcement mechanism has sometimes limited the practical effects of such regulations. Nevertheless, a number of corporations have agreed voluntarily to adopt such regulations, largely out of concern that failure to do so might damage their corporate image and hence ability to market their products (Weinberg, 1978).

Whereas some labor dissidents in the United States have turned to the ITSs as an alternative to official AFL–CIO foreign policy, still others have tried to develop international connections at the shop level, bypassing altogether the secretariats, which they see as too often beholden to the bureaucracies of their various national affiliates. The past 2 decades have seen a number of such organizations spring up. One of the most important has been the Transnationals Information Exchange (TIE). Composed of some 40 research and activist labor groups, the TIE tracks transnationals and disseminates information concerning their activities. In 1981 24 top AFL–CIO officials and hundreds of rank-and-filers formed the National Labor Committee in Support of Democracy and Human Rights in El Salvador to oppose official AFL–CIO policy toward Central America. Because many of the officials on the Committee head large AFL–CIO affiliates, they have been able to use the size of their membership to initiate some debate concerning the foreign policy goals of the Federation's Executive Council and Department of International Affairs, particularly concerning support for U.S. military intervention in Central America. In the mid-1980s several labor-led, grassroots antiapartheid groups also emerged in efforts to build links with the growing number of black trade unions in South Africa, and apartheid was an issue in a number of strikes in the United States against transnationals that had operations in that country (Moody, 1988). A number of grassroots labor groups in the United States have also developed contacts with workers in the Philippines (Johns, 1994) and several other less developed countries. Although such groups are usually lacking in funding and are often relatively small, they do nevertheless represent an increasingly important challenge to official AFL–CIO foreign policy and an alternative means by which rank-and-file workers can communicate with and support one another globally (for other examples of grassroots international labor cooperation, see Hecker & Hallock, 1991).

To summarize, in this section I have highlighted a number of ways in which workers in various countries have attempted to develop transnational structures to coordinate their activities globally. As this all too brief account suggests, they have been quite active in seeking to build structures and organizations to challenge *at the global scale* the operations of transnational corporations. Although bodies such as the trade secretariats have a long lineage, during the past 3 decades they have become particularly important as capital has become transnational to a degree never before seen. Equally, numerous new worker networks are being formed in the wake of the telecommunications revolution. Through the ITSs and other mechanisms, such as the Internet, workers across the globe have been able to network with their confederates and to organize several successful transnational labor campaigns. These efforts raise important conceptual issues about how globalization is frequently represented in the literature, particularly with regard to the presumed impotence of workers in the global economy (cf. Gibson-Graham, 1996).

IMPLICATIONS OF INTERNATIONAL TRADE UNION ACTIVITIES FOR THE GLOBALIZATION THESIS

The international activities on the part of U.S. and other workers previously outlined raise three further issues that have broader bearing on the question of globalization: (1) how the economic and political context within which various social actors find themselves affects the ways they behave, (2) workers' roles in shaping the (international) division of labor, and (3) workers' roles in shaping the geography of capitalist uneven development in the global economy.

The Contingent Nature of Capital–Labor Coalitions

U.S. unions have generally subscribed to a view that their historical mission on the global stage is to help bring "modernization" and liberal democracy to precapitalist and/or authoritarian societies, with both gifts to be delivered under the umbrella of U.S. economic hegemony. However, this belief has had different implications at different times. U.S. labor had much to gain in the first half of the 20th century by paving the way for U.S. economic expansion-ism in Latin America and the Caribbean at a time when production was orga-nized nationally and the United States was the dominant global economic power. As long as these conditions prevailed, U.S. workers could enjoy rela-tively secure, well-paid jobs producing commodities that were ultimately des-tined for export and consumption south of the border. Yet, in working fre-quently hand in glove with capital to destroy militant anti-U.S. trade unions and precapitalist economic systems, ironically the U.S. labor movement itself played a significant part in changing these very conditions and, ultimately, in undermining this accord. By helping to make Latin America and the Caribbean safe for U.S. investment, labor's foreign policy actually encouraged and facilitated the spread of offshore production by U.S. corporations. In turn, this has meant that instead of U.S. workers producing commodities for consumption in Latin America and the Caribbean, workers in Latin Ameri-can and Caribbean countries are increasingly producing commodities for consumption by U.S. workers. Combined with the decline of U.S. economic power generally, this transformed economic situation has encouraged many U.S. workers to turn to the trade secretariats and other grassroots internation-al organizations during the past few years as a means of trying to save their own jobs by bringing pressure to bear on the global operations of U.S. transnational corporations.

This change in relative emphasis in U.S. workers' international activities suggests a number of things.[30] First, there is clearly a need to be historically and geographically specific when seeking to understand the political and eco-nomic decisions made by workers and their organizations. Rather than imput-ing a universal behavioral trait to particular social groups because of their structural relationship to other groups—labor is automatically assumed to be opposed to capital because it is, in terms of the extraction of surplus value, exploited by the latter—behavior can in fact be dramatically influenced by contingent factors (e.g., a nation's relative economic strength at particular his-torical junctures). Whereas U.S. labor and capital have often fought bitter bat-tles domestically during the 20th century, the United States' global economic dominance meant they both had a vested interest in working closely interna-tionally to secure common objectives. This suggests that not only may social relationships between the same actors take different forms in different places (home vs. abroad, for instance) but that as the political and economic environ-ment changes so, too, may the relationship between those actors. The transnationalization of U.S. capital has redefined the boundaries within which U.S. workers once lived. In turn, this is leading many U.S. workers to seek to develop new relationships with workers abroad.

Second, the existence of such a capital–labor accord in the international arena contradicts much of the literature on globalization, which sees unions attempting to "go global" in an effort to match the transnationalization of capital and so to maintain some degree of economic and political leverage vis à vis corporations. Not only did U.S. labor first begin to go global *in collaboration with* U.S. capital, but much of the impetus to do so came as a result of labor's efforts to stop the spread of Communism internationally and to secure U.S. geopolitical interests, rather than from the transnationalization of capital. Indeed, U.S. labor's international activities during the first three-quarters of the 20th century probably had as much, if not more, to do with foreign and domestic political concerns (the fight against Communism, and rivalries between the AFL and the Industrial Workers of the World concerning creation of a pan-American regional labor organization, and between the AFL and the CIO concerning membership of the IFTU and the WFTU) as it did with the emergence of the global assembly line. This suggests a need to integrate more closely economic explanations of labor's attempts to go global (the need to confront transnational capital) with political concerns (e.g., the geopolitical intrigue of the Cold War).

Third, the literature on Fordism and the apparent emergence of a post-Fordist mode of regulation has made much of the importance of the domestic capital–labor accord as a prop for the emergence of a mass production–mass consumption economic and political system in the United States (and elsewhere). The existence of such an accord in the international arena suggests that the argument may be extended geographically in potentially fruitful ways. In particular, it raises questions concerning to what extent U.S. Fordism was based on the United States' dominant position within the global economy and the ability of U.S. capital and labor to get foreign workers to consume U.S.-produced goods, and to what extent it was based on factors internal to the United States. Equally, the collapse of the domestic capital–labor accord in the United States and the transition to what some have called a post-Fordist system appears to have an international aspect to it, as the interests of U.S. capital and labor are increasingly diverging abroad and as many U.S. workers have begun to develop new cooperative relationships with foreign workers.

Labor and the International Division of Labor

The division of labor is one of the most fundamental social structures that defines any economic system. The transnationalization of capital, particularly during the past 3 decades or so, has augured a dramatic transformation in the organization of capitalist production and brought with it a new international division of labor (Fröbel, Heinrichs, & Kreye, 1980). Many writers on this topic conceive of the forces that have led to this unprecedented transnationalization of capital and new international division of labor as deriving from the internal logic of capital itself. It is the "tendencies inherent in the nature of capitalist development," so the argument goes, that have led to the emergence of "multinational corporations [as] the dominant institutions of advanced capitalism" (Peet, 1987, p. 42). Competitive pressures (including, often, the desire to avoid well-organized labor in the core capitalist countries) have forced many companies to go global by enlarging the geographical scope of their operations in search of new markets and sources of raw materials, cheaper labor, less regulated environments in which to do business, and generally lower production costs. In this interpretation, transnational corporations are seen as the agents of contemporary globalization, while workers are seen as (usually) passive bystanders in this process.

Such a focus on the activities of capital as the primary agent bringing about the globalization of economic relations has a long lineage. Classical trade theory, for instance, was largely concerned with examining the international flow of capital in the form of traded commodities and portfolio investments. Classical capital theory sought to explain international flows of capital in terms of interest rate differentials. Marx (1867/1967) examined the roles played by colonies as providers of working capital for European industrialization, suggesting (though not in so many words) that the economic crises inherent to capitalism to some extent could be geographically displaced to other parts of the globe through the process of capital becoming global in its operations. Equally, Lenin's (1900/1939) analysis of imperialism focused on the role played by cartels and multinational financial capital as an integrating and globalizing force. Similar sentiments are expressed in the contemporary geographical literature both by radical analysts and by more mainstream writers (e.g., Barnet & Muller, 1974; Dixon, Drakakis-Smith, & Watts, 1986; Dunning, 1971; Hymer, 1979; Palloix, 1973; Taylor & Thrift, 1982). Thus, whereas for Peet (1987, p. 18, emphasis added) "opposition from labor in [the core capitalist countries] is a powerful force propelling *capital* towards internationalized operations," for Dicken (1986, pp. 4–5) the "new global system of production and trade is being created by the actions and interactions of two major sets of institutions ... the transnational corporation ... [and] ... nation-states."

Two points are important here. First, the historical narrative outlined in the first part of the chapter illustrates that workers, too, have played an active role in shaping the new international division of labor. They have done this both indirectly and directly. Indirectly, workers in the industrialized economies have helped propel capital toward transnationalized operations by organizing (as recognized by Peet). Directly, workers have actively shaped flows of capital globally, either by encouraging/discouraging capitalist penetration into particular regions of the world or, alternatively, by organizing to prevent capital from leaving particular localities. This suggests that analyses that portray the spatial and social division of labor as evolving in response solely to the way *capital* needs to organize the production process in particular ways are problematic, for they marginalize workers' roles in this process. In contrast, the international activities previously detailed suggest the need to conceptualize workers as active participants in the creation of the (international) division of labor and the shaping of the geography of foreign direct investment (cf. Herod, 1995).

Second, the contemporary actions of some North American and European workers relating to the trade secretariats raise interesting questions concerning the intersection of class relations and spatial relations within the international division of labor. On the one hand, workers in the industrialized economies have increasingly been trying to use the secretariats to encourage the organization of workers in the less developed countries so that such workers may protect themselves against the predations of transnational capital. This practice can be seen as a *class*-based response to transnationalization, with the secretariats attempting to develop global links between workers as a means to limit corporations' ability to play different parts of the globe against each other in a downward concessionary spiral. On the other hand, however, it is clear that the impetus for many workers in the industrialized nations to develop such global campaigns often comes from their desire to protect their own particular niches in the international division of labor. In this sense, developing global links through the secretariats and other organizations can be read as a *geographical* response to capital flight and restructuring by which North American and European workers are simply attempting to preserve their own industrial spaces in the face of the globalization of production. This raises significant questions concerning political strategy and the extent to which geography may cross-cut class-based social structures (cf. Herod, 1991a, 1994, especially pp. 91–93; see also Johns, 1994). It especially suggests the need to pay closer attention to how class practices are geographically constituted and how space is infused with class relations. Any attempt to develop a class politics clearly must be sensitive to issues of geographic variation between places. Equally, geographic variation between places has profound implications for the process of class formation and the articulation of class politics.

Labor and Uneven Development

The third issue raised by the examination of workers' international activities concerns the link between these activities and the uneven development of capitalism. Typically, the uneven geographical development of capitalism is seen in one of two ways (Smith, 1990). The first and most widespread view in the geographic literature is to see uneven development as simply inevitable, given the impossibility of *even* development. However, this conceptualization is highly problematic and has little explanatory power because it presents uneven development as an ahistorical, universal process—everywhere develops unevenly all the time. The second approach portrays uneven development as inherent to the dynamic of capitalism. In this view (Smith, 1990, p. xiii) "uneven development is the systematic geographical expression of the contradictions inherent in the very constitution and structure of capital. . . . [It is] structural rather than statistical" and is seen to emerge from the internal dynamic of capital itself.

Certainly, there are definite theoretical advantages to be gained by conceptualizing uneven development as an expression of deeper structural forces at work under capitalism rather than as simply an ahistorical inevitability. For instance, by doing so it becomes possible to make powerful theoretical links between the dynamics of capitalist accumulation and the production of economic landscapes in ways that the more traditional concept of uneven development does not allow. However, the international activities of workers outlined earlier suggest that explanations that see uneven development solely as an expression of contradictions within capital alone do need to be revised. U.S. workers, I would argue, played an important role in maintaining Latin America and the Caribbean in a state of dependent development vis à vis the U.S., both by helping to undermine political organizations that have challenged this dependency and by ensuring that markets remained open to U.S. goods and services. In this sense, they were active players in the underdevelopment of the region. Furthermore, they played this role in their own right in pursuit of their own economic and political agenda (principally, job creation in the United States) rather than as simply adjuncts to U.S. capital. Equally, by seeking to restrict the flow of capital out of the industrialized nations and to maintain their own niche in the new international division of labor, North American and European workers are at the moment actively engaged in trying to maintain present levels of economic development in their own economies. At the same time, workers who are organizing themselves in the less developed countries are also shaping patterns of production and consumption and thus, ultimately, of global (uneven) development.

Recognizing that workers play active roles in producing the unevenly developed geography of capitalism opens up a number of important theoretical and empirical avenues. Much Marxist work has argued that capital needs to create particular landscapes in order for accumulation to occur (Harvey, 1982; Lefebvre, 1976, 1991; Smith, 1990). Thus, Harvey (1982, p. 415), for instance, asks whether there is a "spatial fix" to capital's crises, and what the role of geography is "in the processes of crisis formation and resolution." Lefebvre, too, suggests that the production of space in particular ways is critical to the accumulation process and the survival of capitalism. Portraying capital as the only active agent in the production of global uneven development, however, represents an undialectical approach to understanding the process, for it conceives of uneven development as arising simply out of the internal logic of capital. Instead, by seeing workers as actively engaged in the process of uneven development, it becomes possible to link workers' social practices with their efforts to develop particular spatial fixes of their own, which they perceive to be advantageous to themselves at specific historical junctures. In turn, this allows us to think about uneven development in a dialectical manner. Not only does capital need to produce geographic landscapes in particular ways for accumulation to occur and thus to be able to reproduce itself over time, but so, too, do workers need to mold the landscape in certain ways to ensure their own reproduction. This tension is at the heart of the social production of space. Thus, sometimes segments of capital and labor might have a vested interest in producing spatial fixes that are complementary of one another, such as when they join forces in local growth coalitions to encourage investment in particular localities or, as in the case of the U.S. labor movement for much of this century, in national coalitions designed to ensure continued economic and political dominance over regions abroad (e.g., Latin America). At other times, these segments of capital and labor may seek to develop very different spatial fixes to ensure their own reproduction, such as when workers attempt to keep capital invested in particular localities but corporate decision makers wish to move their facilities elsewhere. Equally, different fractions of labor may themselves seek to create quite different spatial fixes, such as when workers in one location (e.g., the industrialized countries) attempt to keep capital in their own locality at the expense of workers elsewhere (e.g., in the less developed countries). The struggle in which each of these actors engages to ensure that its own spatial fixes are realized is, at heart, a geographical struggle to shape the economic landscape in decidedly different ways. Examining how workers construct such spatial fixes not only illuminates the tensions incorporated in any geographical landscape, but it also suggests that understanding the making of the geography of capitalism requires paying close attention to the spatial practices of workers.

CONCLUSION

In this chapter I have tried to do two things. First, I have suggested that workers have been actively involved in the processes which have brought about the globalization of economic and political relations. Although I have focused much on the activities of U.S. labor in this regard, I do not doubt that similar arguments can be made about the relationship between, for example, the various European labor movements and their own national governments' policies toward their (former) imperial possessions. The creation of organizations such as the ITSs and the various global labor federations, together with U.S. labor's activities relating to the implementation of its own version of the Monroe Doctrine in Latin America and the Caribbean, are indicative of workers' roles in shaping international geo-economics and geopolitics in the 19th and 20th centuries. Furthermore, whereas much of the literature on globalization avers that workers are now seeking to go global simply in response to the transnationalization of capital, the narrative presented here shows that this argument is problematic. Not only have workers been active in creating international labor organizations for over a century, but the impetus to do so frequently has had more to do with political concerns (e.g., anti-Communism) than with the activities of transnational corporations.

Second, I have attempted to show that rather than being *necessarily* structural victims of globalization, workers have often successfully challenged *at the global scale* the actions of transnational corporations. Thus, I would suggest, workers' immobility in the face of capital flight should not be conceptualized as *necessarily* leading to political impotence. While developing global solidarity is undoubtedly more difficult than developing national or regional practices of solidarity, it is nevertheless still possible. By building global networks to exchange information and provide material aid, immobile workers in different parts of the globe have, in fact, been successful in challenging more mobile capital's attempts to play them against each other. The much greater availability of information and ease of communications resulting from innovations in computer technology have, paradoxically, facilitated increased worker contacts around the globe. Although the greater variety of levels of development, legal structures, and cultural attitudes undoubtedly make it more difficult for workers and unions to confront corporations that are organized at the global scale than it does to confront those that are national or regional firms, such difficulties are not insurmountable (cf Herod, 1995). The ability of workers to further develop such contacts and links will have immense implications for international labor politics in the 21st century.

The issues raised in this chapter also lead to a broader theoretical question, namely, what are workers' roles in making the geography of global capitalism? Whereas economic geographers have traditionally relied on understanding the dynamics of capital to explain patterns of economic geography (e.g., theory of the firm, circuits of capital circulation, capital switching, and the like), the preceding analysis suggests the need to take labor's role in actively creating geographies much more seriously. Whereas many writers on the process and implications of globalization have tended to assume a priori that capital may act globally but that workers may not, the historical record does not sustain such a supposition. Workers, in fact, have a lengthy history of acting globally. In the process, they have helped to shape the economic and political geography of the global economy. Such activities demand a more inclusive account of workers' place in analyses of the process and implications of "globalization."

ACKNOWLEDGMENTS

I would like to thank Kevin Cox, Mike Renning, and Leyla Vural for comments on an earlier version of this chapter.

NOTES

1. For example, see Daniels, Thrift, and Leyshon (1989); Donaghu and Barff (1990); Fryer (1987); Langdale (1985); Mair, Florida, and Kenney (1988); Sayer (1986); Schoenberger (1985); Taylor and Thrift (1982); Thrift (1987); Warf (1989, 1991); and Wrigley (1989, 1993).

2. In the United States, the National Union of Labor was in fact established in 1860, but this was a relatively short-lived body, lasting only until 1866. The influence of the Knights of Labor, founded in the United States in 1869, was also relatively brief. The British Trades Union Congress is generally considered the earliest permanent national trade union federation. Similar federations were subsequently set up in other countries, including the American Federation of Labor in the United States (1886), the Unión General de Trabajadores (1888) in Spain, the General Committee of Trade Unions (1890) in Germany, the Nationaal Arbeids-Secretariaat (1893) and the Nederlandsch Verbond van Vakvereenigingen (1906) in the Netherlands, and the Canadian Labour Union Congress (1883) (van der Linden, 1988).

3. The precise number of international trade secretariats that had been formed prior to the outbreak of war in 1914 is disputed by a number of historical accounts. Busch (1983, p. 15) lists the number at 33, whereas a publication of the International Confederation of Free Trade Unions (1958, p. 19) lists the number as 28, 24 of which were headquartered in Germany. Windmuller (1980, p. 23) states that by 1914 "there were almost 30 International Trade Secretariats."

4. Inspired by Pope Leo XIII's encyclical *Rerum Novarum*, Christian trade unions had been organized in several European countries since the 1890s to counter the growth of socialist, anticlerical unions. The CISC was founded in 1920 as an explicitly Christian entity. However, during the 1960s it underwent a dramatic secularization as virtually all mention of Christianity was dropped from its basic constitutional documents and the organization renamed itself the World Confederation of Labor (WCL). These changes were part of an effort to reflect a more interdenominational basis for international trade union organizing. Furthermore, whereas the CISC was initially established for the purpose of opposing socialist domination of earlier international labor organizations, in the 1970s the reborn WCL adopted a program that rejected capitalism and argued for the socialization of the means of production and workers' control of industry.

5. These agencies are not dealt with in this chapter.

6. One of the earliest indications of interest in international affairs was the adoption of resolutions at the AFL's 1887 National Convention condemning British policies in Ireland and the persecution of Jews in Russia.

7. Although these three federations are not the only U.S. trade union organizations to have operated internationally (e.g., see Dubovsky, 1969, on the Industrial Workers of the World), they have been by far the most influential, and so it is their activities with which this chapter concerns itself.

8. Indeed, unless explicitly stated otherwise, this chapter refers primarily to the activities of the labor bureaucrats who make foreign policy, and in that sense it is largely an institutional account of U.S. labor's international activities.

9. This self-interest was made abundantly clear by John L. Lewis of the United Mine Workers of America in a 1939 Labor Day address, when he stated that "Central

and South America are capable of absorbing all of our excess and surplus commodities" (quoted in Scott, 1978, p. 201).

10. Scott (1978) suggests that despite acting as the AFL's spokesperson in the Anti-Imperialist League, Gompers did support U.S. territorial annexation, provided that the subsequent incorporation of large numbers of low-paid workers into the U.S. economic system did not threaten the living standards of AFL members. Thus, in reference to the war with Spain and the annexation of the Philippines, Gompers declared that it was vital to save "American labour from the evil influence of close and open competition of millions of semi-barbaric labourers in the Philippine Islands" but that "the government may annex any old thing as long as the laws relating to labour are observed" (quoted in Scott, 1978, pp. 93–94).

11. Gompers believed that the term "Federation" implied a more loosely organized body than did the word "Secretariat," a semantic shift that more closely followed his voluntaristic philosophy that the AFL not be obliged to follow policies with which it did not agree, even though they had been adopted by the international labor body. He argued instead that each country's labor movement should be free to "decide upon its own policy, tactics, and tendencies" (Gompers, 1910, p. 131).

12. The AFL rejoined the IFTU in 1937. Whereas publicly the AFL leadership portrayed its actions as a response to fascist intimidation of European unions, the growing challenge to the craft-based AFL's domestic political hegemony mounted by the industrially organized CIO was perhaps a more crucial shaper of the leadership's attitudes towards reaffiliation. In particular, IFTU rules permitted membership by only one trade union federation from each country. For the AFL, reaffiliating with the IFTU would shut out the nascent CIO and thereby preserve the AFL's right to speak as the sole voice of U.S. workers in this international arena.

13. The French Confédération Générale du Travail (CGT) and the Italian Confederazione Generale Italiana del Lavoro (CGIL), both Communist dominated, at this time remained affiliated with the WFTU.

14. Support for the Marshall Plan was a point of much contention in the CIO and led to a split between the Congress' left- and right-wing factions. However, with the expulsion of 11 more radical unions in 1949 and 1950, the CIO lined up solidly behind the Plan.

15. Although this split had been a long time in the making, the actual catalyst for it was the overtures made by the United Auto Workers concerning the possibility of joining the ICFTU as a trade union unaffiliated with its national center. The UAW had recently left the AFL–CIO over the latter's hawkish policy toward the war in Vietnam. The AFL–CIO leadership opposed the UAW's (ultimately unsuccessful) efforts and was outraged that the Confederation would even entertain such an idea.

16. Although primarily concerned with Europe, the Free Trade Union Institute (FTUI) also serves as an umbrella organization to distribute governmental monies to the other three institutes. The FTUI is the largest single recipient of funds from the National Endowment for Democracy, a Reagan-initiated body for strengthening pro-U.S. forces abroad, and between 1984 and 1988 received almost 50% of the dollar total of the Endowment's grants (Simms, 1992).

17. In 1992 some 63% of all U.S. investment in the Third World was in Latin America and the Caribbean (U.S. Department of Commerce, 1994).

18. Representatives from four Caribbean islands were also present at the PAFL's founding convention.

19. As it turned out, this secret aim was undermined by the signing of the Armistice in Europe 2 days before the PAFL's founding conference began.

20. Gompers himself described the PAFL as "based upon the spirit of the Monroe Doctrine" (quoted in Simms, 1992, p. 37).

21. The ORIT is now the ICFTU's regional organization for Latin America and the Caribbean. For a fairly uncritical account of early ORIT activities, see Hawkins (1965).

22. Although the AFL–CIO denies that the AIFLD effectively serves as a branch of the CIA, several ex-CIA operatives and Congressional hearings have provided ample evidence to the contrary. According to one ex-operative, "The real purpose of [AIFLD] was to train cadres to organize new trade unions or to take over existing ones, in such a way that the unions would be controlled, directly or indirectly, by the CIA" (Philip Agee, quoted in Barry & Preusch, 1990, p. 6).

23. During the 1980s, for example, the NED channeled several million dollars to the AFL–CIO for covert operations in Nicaragua and El Salvador.

24. Barry and Preusch (1990) provide an excellent summary of AIFLD activities in Guatemala, Nicaragua, El Salvador, Honduras, and Costa Rica. For other examples, see the autobiography of Serafino Romualdi (1967), who played a very active role in the AIFLD and in implementing the AFL's Cold War foreign policy more generally.

25. The U.S. withdrawal from the ILO came largely as a result of pressure from the AFL–CIO, which accused the Organisation of pandering to Soviet foreign policy and failing to criticize strongly enough Soviet human rights abuses. In fact, the Ford administration had made clear its intent to withdraw 2 years previously, as required by ILO bylaws. Thus, for all intents and purposes, AFL–CIO activities in the ILO had effectively ended sometime earlier. The United States rejoined the ILO in 1982.

26. The WFTU has its own version of trade secretariats organized on the basis of industrial sector, but with the end of the Cold War the WFTU has lost many of its former members and much of its influence, particularly in Eastern Europe (see Herod, 1997). Some former WFTU affiliates have joined ITSs, raising issues of the geographical expansion of the ICFTU and the ITSs into the countries of the former Soviet bloc.

27. The periodical *Labor Notes* frequently carries information concerning such international campaigns in its "Solidarity Network" section. *Labor Notes* is published monthly by the Labor Education and Research Project, 7435 Michigan Avenue, Detroit, MI 48210 (tel: 313–842–6262/ e-mail: labornotes@igc.apc.org).

28. The declaration (reproduced in International Metalworkers' Federation, 1991, p. 26) adopted by the WACs in Detroit on 3 June 1966 stated:

> Without neglecting the specially urgent problems that exist in specific countries and companies, we agree upon the need for coordinated worldwide concentration by the IMF affiliated organizations upon these problems that are of high priority:
>
> —full recognition of the right to organize and the right to bargain collectively
> —standardization of wages and social benefits at the highest level made possible by technological progress
> —immediate introduction of paid recreation and rest periods
> —ending of excessive overtime working and the introduction of adequate allowances for overtime

—payment of additional vacation allowance

—adequate retirement pensions

—guaranteed income for workers affected by production fluctuations and technological changes

—reduction of working hours without loss of earnings, more paid holidays, longer
vacations, and earlier retirement.

29. Though they are organizationally independent, the ITSs are themselves
closely linked with the ICFTU.

30. I do not want to give the impression that the spirit of internationalism has
broken out in all corners of the AFL–CIO. Nevertheless, there is a growing movement
within the AFL–CIO that is seeking to develop international links to pursue progressive policies of solidarity with workers abroad.

REFERENCES

Alcock, A. E. (1971). *History of the International Labor Organization*. New York: Octagon.

American Federation of Labor. (1921). *Report of proceedings of the forty-first convention of the American Federation of Labor, held at Denver, Colorado, June 13–25*. Washington, DC: American Federation of Labor.

American Federation of Labor. (1952). *Report of proceedings of the seventy-first convention of the American Federation of Labor, held at New York, New York, September 15–23*.

American Federation of Labor–Congress of Industrial Organizations. (1987a). *The AFL–CIO abroad* (Perspectives on Labor and the World Publication No. 182). Washington, DC: Author.

American Federation of Labor–Congress of Industrial Organizations. (1987b). *The AFL–CIO's foreign policy* (Perspectives on Labor and the World Publication No. 181). Washington, DC: Author.

Andrews, G. (1991). *Shoulder to shoulder: The American Federation of Labor, the United States, and the Mexican Revolution 1910–1924*. Berkeley: University of California Press.

Barbash, J. (1948, May). International labor confederations: CIT and CTAL. *Monthly Labor Review, 66*, 499–503.

Barnet, R. J., & Muller, R. E. (1974). *Global reach: The power of the multinational corporations*. New York: Simon & Schuster.

Barry, T., & Preusch, D. (1990). *AIFLD in Central America: Agents as organizers*. Albu-
querque, NM: Inter-Hemispheric Education Resource Center.

Battista, A. (1991). Political divisions in organized labor, 1968–1988. *Polity, 24*(2), 173–197.

Bendiner, B. (1987). *International labour affairs: The world trade unions and the multinational companies*. Oxford: Clarendon Press.

Busch, G. K. (1983). *The political role of international trades unions*. New York: St. Martin's Press.

Casserini, K. (1993). *International Metalworkers' Federation 1893–1993: The first hundred years*. Geneva: International Metalworkers' Federation.

Cox, R. W. (1971). Labor and transnational relations. *International Organization* (Special issue on "Transnational Relations and World Politics"), *25*(3), 554–584.

Curtin, W. J. (1973). The multinational corporation and transnational collective bargaining. In D. Kujawa (Ed.), *American labor and the multinational corporation* (pp. 192–222). New York: Praeger.

Daniels, P. W., Thrift, N., & Leyshon, A. (1989). Internationalisation of professional producer services: Accountancy conglomerates. In P. Enderwick (Ed.), *Multinational service firms* (pp. 79–106). London: Routledge.

Devreese, D. E. (1988). An inquiry into the causes and nature of organization: Some observations on the International Working Men's Association, 1864–1872/1876. In F. van Holthoon & M. van der Linden (Eds.), *Internationalism in the labour movement 1830–1940* (Vol. 1, pp. 283–303). London: E. J. Brill.

Dicken, P. (1986). *Global shift: Industrial change in a turbulent world.* London: Harper & Row.

Dixon, C. J., Drakakis-Smith, D., & Watts, H. D. (Eds.). (1986). *Multinational corporations and the Third World.* Boulder, CO: Westview Press.

Donaghu, M. T., & Barff, R. (1990). Nike just did it: International subcontracting and flexibility in athletic footwear production. *Regional Studies, 24,* 537–552.

Dubovsky, M. (1969). *We shall be all: A history of the Industrial Workers of the World.* Urbana: University of Illinois Press.

Dunning, J. H. (1971). *The multinational enterprise.* London: Allen & Unwin.

Foner, P. S. (1989). *U.S. labor and the Vietnam War.* New York: International Publishers.

Fröbel, F., Heinrichs, J., & Kreye, O. (1980). *The new international division of labour: Structural unemployment in industrialised countries and industrialisation in developing countries.* Cambridge: Cambridge University Press.

Fryer, D. W. (1987). The political geography of international lending by private banks. *Transactions, Institute of British Geographers, New Series, 12*(4), 413–432.

Gershman, C. (1975). *The foreign policy of American labor* (The Washington Papers, Vol. 3, No.29). Beverly Hills: Sage.

Ghebali, V. Y. (1989). *The International Labour Organisation: A case study on the evolution of U.N. specialised agencies.* Dordrecht: M. Nijhoff.

Gibson-Graham, J. K. (1996). *The end of capitalism (as we knew it): A feminist critique of political economy.* Cambridge, MA: Blackwell.

Godson, R. (1976). *American labor and European politics: The AFL as a transnational force.* New York: Crane, Russak.

Gompers, S. (1910). *Labor in Europe and America.* New York: Harper.

Gompers, S. (1925). *Seventy years of life and labor: An autobiography* (2 vols.). New York: E.P. Dutton.

Hardy, M. (1936). *The influence of organized labor on the foreign policy of the United States.* Doctoral dissertation, University of Geneva. Liège, Belgium: H. Vaillant-Carmanne, Imprimerie de l'Academie (Thèse No. 30).

Harvey, D. (1982). *The limits to capital.* Oxford, UK: Blackwell.

Hawkins, C. (1965). The ORIT and the American trade unions—Conflicting perspectives. In W. H. Form & A. A. Blum (Eds.), *Industrial relations and social change in Latin America* (pp. 87–104). Gainesville: University of Florida Press.

Heaps, D. (1955). Union participation in foreign aid programs. *Industrial and Labor Relations Review, 9*(1), 100–108.

Hecker, S., & Hallock, M. (1991). *Labor in a global economy: Perspectives from the U.S. and Canada.* Eugene: University of Oregon Labor Education and Research Center.

Herod, A. (1991a). Local political practice in response to a manufacturing plant clo-sure: How geography complicates class analysis. *Antipode, 23*(4), 385–402.

Herod, A. (1991b). The production of scale in United States labour relations. *Area, 23*(1), 82–88.

Herod, A. (1994). Further reflections on organized labor and deindustrialization in the United States. *Antipode, 26*(1), 77–95.

Herod, A. (1995). The practice of international labor solidarity and the geography of the global economy. *Economic Geography, 71*(4), 341–363.

Herod, A. (1997). Of blocs and networks: The end of the Cold War, cyberspace, and the geopolitics of labor at the *fin de millénaire*. In A. Herod, S. Roberts, & G. Ó. Tuathail (Eds.), *An unruly world? Globalization, governance, and geography*. London: Routledge.

Hobsbawm, E. J. (1975). *The age of capital, 1848–1875*. New York: Mentor.

Hymer, S. H. (1979). *The multinational corporation: A radical approach*. Cambridge: Cam-bridge University Press.

International Confederation of Free Trade Unions (1958). *Yearbook of the International Free Trade Union Movement 1957–1958*. London: Lincolns-Prager.

International Metalworkers' Federation (1991, 23–24, May). *The IMF and the multina-tionals: The role of the IMF world company councils* (Report). Lisbon: IMF Central Committee.

Johns, R. (1994). *International solidarity: Space and class in the U.S. labor movement*. Unpub-lished doctoral dissertation, Department of Geography, Rutgers University, New Brunswick, NJ.

Johnston, G. A. (1970). *The International Labour Organisation: Its work for social and economic progress*. London: Europa Publications.

Labor Notes (1994, August). Labor in cyberspace, p. 2.

Langdale, J. V. (1985). Electronic funds transfer and the internationalisation of the banking and finance industry. *Geoforum, 16*(1), 1–13.

Langley, D. (1972). The colonization of the international union movement. In B. Hall (Ed.), *Autocracy and insurgency in organized labor* (pp. 296–309). New Brunswick, NJ: Transaction Books.

Larson, S. (1975). *Labor and foreign policy: Gompers, the AFL, and the First World War, 1914–1918*. Cranbury, NJ: Associated University Presses.

Lattek, K. (1988). The beginnings of socialist internationalism in the 1840s: The "De-mocratic Friends of all Nations" in London. In F. van Holthoon & M. van der Linden (Eds.), *Internationalism in the labour movement 1830–1940* (Vol. 1, pp. 259–282). London: E. J. Brill.

Lefebvre, H. (1976). *The survival of capitalism: Reproduction of the relations of production*. New York: St. Martin's Press. (Original work published 1973, in French)

Lefebvre, H. (1991) *The production of space*. Oxford: Blackwell. (Original work published 1974, in French)

Lenin, V. I. (1900/1939). *Imperialism: The highest stage of capitalism*. New York: Interna-tional Publishers.

Maier, C. S. (1987). *In search of stability: Explorations in historical political economy*. New York: Cambridge University Press.

Mair, A., Florida, R., & Kenney, M. (1988). The new geography of automobile pro-duction: Japanese transplants in North America. *Economic Geography, 64*, 352–373.

Marx, K. (1867/1967). *Capital* (Vol. 1). New York: International Publishers.

Moody, K. (1988). *An injury to all: The decline of American unionism.* New York: Verso.

Morris, G. (1967). *CIA and American labor: The subversion of the AFL–CIO's foreign policy.* New York: International Publishers.

Palloix, C. (1973). *Les firmes multinationales et le procès d'internationalisation.* Paris: Maspero.

Peet, R. (1987). *International capitalism and industrial restructuring: A critical analysis.* Boston: Allen & Unwin.

Price, J. (1945). *The international labour movement.* London: Oxford University Press.

Radosh, R. (1969). *American labor and United States foreign policy.* New York: Random House.

Romualdi, S. (1967). *Presidents and peons: Recollections of a labor ambassador in Latin America.* New York: Funk & Wagnalls.

Sayer, R. A. (1986). Industrial location on a world scale: The case of the semiconductor industry. In A. Scott & M. Storper (Eds.), *Production, work, territory: The geographical anatomy of industrial capitalism* (pp. 107–124). Boston: Allen & Unwin.

Schoenberger, E. (1985). Foreign manufacturing investment in the United States: Competitive strategies and international location. *Economic Geography, 61*(3), 241–259.

Scott, J. (1978). *Yankee unions, go home! How the AFL helped the U.S. build an empire in Latin America.* Vancouver: New Star Books.

Segal, M. J. (1953, April). The international trade secretariats. *Monthly Labor Review, 76,* 372–380.

Simms, B. (1992). *Workers of the world undermined: American labor's role in U.S. foreign policy.* Boston: South End Press.

Smith, N. (1990). *Uneven development: Nature, capital and the production of space.* Oxford: Blackwell.

Snow, S. (1964). *The Pan-American Federation of Labor.* Durham, NC: Duke University Press.

Spalding, H. A., Jr. (1988). U.S. labour intervention in Latin America: The case of the American Institute for Free Labor Development. In R. Southall (Ed.), *Trade unions and the new industrialization of the Third World* (pp. 259–286). London: Zed Books.

Sturmthal, A. (1950). The International Confederation of Free Trade Unions. *Industrial and Labor Relations Review, 3*(3), 375–382.

Taylor, M., & Thrift, N. (Eds.). (1982). *The geography of multinationals: Studies in the spatial development and economic consequences of multinational corporations.* New York: St. Martin's Press.

Thrift, N. (1987). The fixers: The urban geography of international commercial capital. In J. Henderson & M. Castells (Eds.), *Global restructuring and territorial development* (pp. 203–233). London: Sage.

Uehlein, J. (1989). Using labor's trade secretariats. *Labor Research Review, 8*(1), 31–41.

U.S. Department of Commerce (1994). *Statistical abstract of the United States.* Washington, DC: U.S. Department of Commerce, Bureau of the Census.

van der Linden, M. (1988). The rise and fall of the First International: An interpretation. In F. van Holthoon & M. van der Linden (Eds.), *Internationalism in the labour movement 1830–1940* (Vol. 1, pp. 323–335). London: E. J. Brill.

van Holthoon, F., & van der Linden, M. (Eds.). (1988). *Internationalism in the labour movement 1830–1940* (Vol. 1). London: E. J. Brill.

Warf, B. (1989). Telecommunications and the globalization of financial services. *Professional Geographer*, *41*(3), 257–271.

Warf, B. (1991). The international construction industry in the 1980s. *Professional Geographer*, *43*(2), 150–162.

Weinberg, P. J. (1978). *European labor and the multinationals*. New York: Praeger.

West, L. A. (1991). U.S. foreign labor policy and the case of militant political unionism in the Philippines. *Labor Studies Journal*, *16*(4), 48–75.

Windmuller, J. P. (1954). *American labor and the international labor movement, 1940 to 1953*. Ithaca, NY: Institute of International Industrial and Labor Relations, Cornell University.

Windmuller, J. P. (1970). Internationalism in eclipse: The ICFTU after two decades. *Industrial and Labor Relations Review*, *23*(4), 510–527.

Windmuller, J. P. (1980). *The international trade union movement*. Deventer, Netherlands: Kluwer.

Wrigley, N. (1989). The lure of the USA: Further reflections on the internationalisation of British grocery retailing capital. *Environment and Planning A*, *21*(3), 283–288.

Wrigley, N. (1993). Retail concentration and the internationalization of British grocery retailing. In R. D. F. Bromley & C. J. Thomas (Eds.), *Retailing change: Contemporary issues* (pp. 41–68). London: University College London Press.

Zieger, R. H. (1986). *American workers, American unions, 1920–1985*. Baltimore: Johns Hopkins University Press.

CHAPTER 8

Social Democracy
and External Constraints

Ton Notermans

INTRODUCTION

Two years before his death, John Maynard Keynes argued in a speech to the British House of Lords that the toleration of free international capital movement might seriously compromise the ability of the government to pursue full-employment policies. Keynes's determination to "retain control of our domestic rate of interest, so that we can keep it as low as suits our own purposes, without interference from the ebb and flow of international capital movements or flights of hot money" (Keynes, 1980, p. 16; see also Keynes, 1973, p. 339) was widely shared at the time. The recognition that international capital flows needed to be strictly controlled both in the interest of international financial stability and domestic policy autonomy entered prominently into the institutions[1] and policies of the Bretton Woods era.

The first three decades after the World War II seemed to brilliantly confirm Keynes' views; international capital mobility was at a historic low and the world economy boomed. The Keynesian belief in the manageability of the economy, however, would not survive the 1970s and 1980s, when mass unemployment again became a constant and seemingly intractable problem in Western economies. After the first oil price crisis, but especially during the recession of 1979–1982, most developed countries experienced a substantial rise in unemployment. By the early 1990s, even the Social Democratic holdouts of Norway and Sweden had to report mass unemployment.

Simultaneously with the reemergence of mass unemployment, international capital mobility revived strongly. The exchange rate crises of the late 1960s and early 1970s, which eventually brought down the Bretton Woods system of fixed exchange rates, were only the prelude to even more extensive and volatile capital movements in the following decades. The amount of cross-border financial transactions virtually exploded since the late 1960s. As Helleiner (1994, p. 1) notes, daily foreign exchange trading in the early 1990s had reached a level of about $1 trillion, which is roughly 40 times the size of daily international trade. As many central banks have repeatedly experienced, the amount of short-term speculative capital flows dwarfs the resources they can muster for exchange rate defense (see, for example, Langli, 1993). In addition, the explosive growth of so-called Euromarkets meant that a substantial part of international financial transaction took place at a remove from national regulators.

The almost simultaneous appearance of these two phenomena has led many politicians and scholars to conclude that the reemergence of international finance undermined the Keynesian world in which governments could guarantee full employment by means of macroeconomic policies.[2] In theoretical terms, the "external constraints" view can be interpreted as an adaptation of the Keynesian position to the events of the last 25 years.[3] In contrast to the newly popular neoclassical interpretation, the external constraints view holds that macroeconomic policies in principle can be effective in durably influencing the economy, but that national governments have lost control over economic policy instruments. By maintaining, on the one hand, that macroeconomic policies do affect the economy in the long run, the external constraints view does seem to provide an explanation for the neoclassical puzzle of why growth and employment failed to recover after the disinflation of the 1970s and 1980s. On the other hand, the view that restrictive policies are forced upon reluctant governments by external forces seems to explain why macroeconomic policies are restrictive at a time of high unemployment.

Surveying the last 2 decades, the external constraints view seems able to draw from a rich reservoir of evidence. In a study of changes in economic policies in 11 countries, the Organization for Economic Cooperation and Development (OECD, 1988, p. 16) concluded: "In almost all the episodes considered, it was exchange-rate pressure that brought matters to a head and determined the timing of the introduction of comprehensive policy measures." The example of Mitterand's U-turn of 1982 features prominently in many accounts of external constraints on macroeconomic policies. In the United States, the shift to restrictive monetary and fiscal policies was preceded by a period of continuous capital outflows and a depreciating dollar. In Britain, the turn to monetarism was effectively prepared under the Labour government when strong downward pressures on sterling in 1976 led the government to take the humiliating step of applying for International Monetary Fund (IMF) assistance. Even the Bundesbank was not impervious to external pressures: Chancellor Schmidt's expansionary policies of the early 1980s led to massive capital outflows, which prompted the Bundesbank into drastic interest rate increases in February 1981. More recently, Bundesbank president Schlesinger deflected part of the political pressure to lower interest rates in the wake of unification by pointing out in an interview (*International Herald Tribune*, 1993) that interest rate reductions in Germany are constrained by the need not to destabilize exchange and credit markets.

For smaller countries, not surprisingly, many more examples can be found. In Austria the demise of the successful policy of full employment started in 1979, when the attempt to pursue a more expansionary monetary policy had to be abandoned in the face of massive capital outflows (see, for example, Scharpf, 1987, p. 91, and Unger, 1990). In Denmark two attempts in the mid- and late-1970s to pursue expansionary policies—by Social Democratic governments—floundered on a current account deficit and downward pressure on the currency (see, for example, Thygesen, 1982, and Mjøset, 1986). In Norway the Social Democrats' turn to restrictive policies in 1986, which was followed by the highest unemployment since the 1930s, was preceded by massive downward pressure on the krone, (see, for example, Qvigstad & Skjaeveland, 1994). With reference to both Sweden and Norway, Moses (1994, p. 142) concludes that "the current crisis of social democracy is a reaction to changes in the international economy."

However, especially when looking at the conduct of economic policies in a longer perspective, the claim that the emergence of global finance terminated the successful pursuit of growth and full employment policies is not very convincing. First, today's high level of international capital mobility is not without historical precedent, nor is the widespread belief that international capital mobility leaves countries no other option than to pursue restrictive policies. Whereas international capital mobility has indeed increased dramatically during the last 25 years, its present level is comparable to the situation before the Great Depression. Free flow of capital across borders constituted one of the main pillars of the classical Gold Standard, and, accordingly, the pre-1914 period was marked by very high capital mobility. Not unlike the 1970s and 1980s, the monetary history of the 1920s and 1930s is rife with examples of large speculative capital movements. Especially during the late 1920s and early 1930s, hot money flows frequently reached such proportions that they overwhelmed the resources of central banks (see, for example, Brown, 1987, Chap. 1). Reviewing the period 1920–1970, Zacchia (1977, p. 584) notes: "Short-term capital movements did not reach, in the post-war period, the dimensions of the 1920s, neither did they produce such disruptive effects." Zevin (1992, p. 51–52), examining the empirical evidence on financial openness, comes to the conclusion that "every available descriptor of financial markets in the late nineteenth and early twentieth centuries suggests that they were more fully integrated than they were before or have been since."

Examining the degree of convergence of average long-term real interest rates between 11 countries,[4] Bordo and Jonung (1994) found that convergence during the most recent period (1974–1990) was only slightly stronger than during the prewar Gold Standard (1881–1913) and at the same level as during the Bretton Woods period (1946–1970). Moreover, comparing the periods 1959–1970 and 1974–1990, real interest rate convergence actually decreased, albeit minimally. In a study of the degree of financial integration of the

Swedish economy, Oxelheim (1990) reached a similar conclusion. Surveying the differentials of real long-term interest rates between Sweden and a host of other countries, total financial integration[5] seemed rather to have decreased in the early 1980s. "Whatever perspective we adopt in relation to real interest rate developments, the conclusion is that during the first half of the 1980s total financial integration decreased compared with the immediately preceding period" (Oxelheim 1990, p. 344). For Norway, Dammann (1991, pp. 54–56) has shown that both the real and nominal interest rates for Norwegian and U.S. state bonds moved very closely together up to roughly 1980. After 1980, however, large interest rate differentials appear.

In view of the high level of capital mobility, many governments, especially from the early 1920s up to the demise of the Gold Standard in the early to mid-1930s, held that expansionary policies necessarily would falter due to external constraints. Consider, for example, the experience of the second Labour government under Ramsay MacDonald. MacDonald's government fell in 1931 because the Labour Party and the Trade Union Congress (TUC) were not willing to accept further cuts in unemployment benefits, which were required to balance the budget and thereby defend the parity of the pound. Yet given that Britain had both a current account and a budget deficit, that the pound had been under pressure from international capital flows almost continuously since 1928, and that the state carried a large short-term debt which it needed to revolve, MacDonald thought he had no choice. Failure to balance the budget in such a constellation, let alone enact expansionary policies, would undermine confidence in the pound and reduce international investors' willingness to lend to the British government. Most of those who presently argue that expansionary policies are impossible due to external constraints would have to agree that MacDonald indeed did not have a choice. Similarly, in Germany leading Social Democratic politicians like Rudolf Hilferding in the early 1930s rejected expansionary policy proposals advanced by the trade unions because such policies would undermine confidence in the currency and destroy the creditworthiness of Germany.

Second, the historical record does not provide strong evidence that the presence of extensive cross-border financial flows will require countries to pursue restrictive macroeconomic policies. Obviously, MacDonald and Hilferding were wrong in believing that there were no alternatives. Within a few months of assuming office, the so-called National Government, which succeeded the second Labour government in 1931, abandoned the Gold Standard and embarked upon a policy of "cheap money," which lay at the root of Britain's recovery from the Great Depression. In contrast to the German Social Democratic Party (SPD), the Swedish Social Democrats in 1932, after the currency had been cut loose from gold, put into practice their trade unions' proposals for expansionary policies. Indeed, postwar Keynesian scholars have interpreted MacDonald's and Hilferding's attitudes as a prime example of how attachment to erroneous liberal (MacDonald) or Marxist (Hilferding) theories served to aggravate the depression (see Skidelsky, 1967, on the United Kingdom, and Gates, 1973, on Germany).

In more recent times, several countries have been able to pursue a more expansionary policy course despite high capital mobility. While many European countries were complaining that Paul Volcker's restrictive policies forced them to do the same, Japan defended a more expansionary policy orientation by means of an aggressive devaluation. In Europe, the Social Democratic governments in Sweden and Norway for a long time defended their commitment to full employment by staying outside the European Monetary System (EMS). Moreover, after the breakdown of the narrow EMS band in late 1992, it has again become difficult to argue that the effect of increased capital mobility is to require fixed exchange rate policies in order to maintain the confidence of financial markets. It is noteworthy that the Swedish Riksbank felt it necessary to charge an interest rate of 500%—from 16 to 21 September 1992—when it was desperately trying to defend a fixed exchange rate, and not after it had let the krona float downward.

Moreover, it would also appear rather surprising that at a time when governments are allegedly under increasing pressures from international capital flows, economic policies seem to aim at increasing the international financial exposure of domestic economies rather than reducing it. Whereas the massive capital flows of the interwar period led many governments, during the 1930s and after the World War II, to impose exchange controls, governments in the 1970s and 1980s have been abolishing restrictions on cross-border capital flows. At present even moderate proposals to limit international financial speculation, like the so-called Tobin tax[6], fail to arouse interest in most countries.

Third, it is somewhat peculiar that the conviction that full employment policies have fallen victim to external constraints historically tends to gain political popularity at the same time as many governments hold that expansionary macroeconomic policies are in fact undesirable because they merely lead to higher inflation, and that consequently external constraints constitute a welcome obstacle to inflationary domestic policies.[7] Whereas many Keynesians at present bemoan that external constraints preclude expansionary policies, the demise of Keynesian policies started in the 1970s when several governments became convinced of the monetarist critique that such policies merely create more inflation and cannot reduce unemployment. The Bundesbank's turn to restrictive policies since 1974 was obviously not prompted by external constraints but by the desire to quell domestic inflation. Nor was Margaret Thatcher forced by external constraints to pursue restrictive policies. Like the external constraints view, the view that expansionary policies only create inflation is not new. As Kindleberger (1987, p. 6) has pointed out, the debate between neoclassics—or monetarists as he labels them—and Keynesians "did not have its origin in the 1920s or 1930s, as many students of the subject think, but can be traced back to the seventeenth century and beyond." The decision of the early 1920s to liberate capital flows and tie the currencies of the developed countries to the fixed exchange rate arrangement of the Gold Standard was mainly inspired by the belief that the expansionary policies pursued immediately after the World War II had caused massive inflation.

Finally, while it is correct that the successful pursuit of growth and full employment since the late 1930s was closely linked to a macroeconomic policy stance, a countercyclical Keynesian policy pattern was a rare case indeed. Keynesian policies were absent in response to the Great Depression and largely irrelevant during the so-called Golden Age from the mid-1940s to the early 1970s. In effect, Keynesian countercyclical demand management policies were only pursued in Germany during 1926 (see McNeil, 1986, Chap. 4, and Hertz-Eichenrode, 1982), and on a broader scale during the 1970s. Such policies generally proved to be unsuccessful and short-lived. But if neither the recovery from the Great Depression nor postwar growth can be attributed to Keynesian policies, the alleged emasculation of such policies due to international capital mobility cannot serve as an explanation for the termination of full employment.

In sum, because the present level of international capital mobility is not historically unprecedented and because countries have managed to steer an alternative course despite high capital mobility, it is not very convincing to argue that no room for policy choice exists due to external constraints. Instead, it will be argued here that the general turn to restrictive policies, both during the last two decades and in the early 1920s reflects the inability of governments to contain inflation in any other way than by creating recession and unemployment. Within 2 years of the end of World War I, most countries were confronted with a constellation of rapid growth, tight labor markets, rapidly increasing inflation, and massive financial speculation, which made a turn to restrictive policies inevitable. The subsequent resurrection of the Gold Standard, which linked all currencies rigidly together, was primarily an effort to prevent a resurgence of inflation by institutionalizing powerful external constraints. Similarly during the last two decades, the majority of Western countries have found that income and price policies could no longer successfully contain inflationary pressures. As a result, restrictive policies proliferated throughout the western world. As Layard (1986, p. 29) argued: "The only reason we have unemployment is that governments are using it to contain, or to reduce, inflation." Similar to the developments in the 1920s, the continued emphasis that countries have come to place on "sound" macroeconomic policies is primarily inspired by the fear that expansionary policies will lead to a resurgence of inflation rather than being a dictate of internationally mobile finance. Put differently, it is widespread fear among policymakers of renewed inflation, and not the presence of internationally mobile capital, that presently prevents a turn to policies promoting growth and employment.

The structure of the chapter is as follows. The following section reviews some theoretical arguments advanced in support of the external constraints argument and sketches an alternative view. The three subsequent sections examine the three radical breaks in macroeconomic policymaking in this century: the return to the Gold Standard in the early 1920s, the emergence of a growth-oriented policy regime during the 1930s and 1940s, and the advent of a disinflationary regime in the last two decades. The final sections draws these lines of argumen together in a concluding analysis.

As a survey of all West European countries would exceed the space limits of the present chapter—as well as the time and knowledge of the author—the historical sections will mainly focus on Germany, Great Britain, Norway, and Sweden. Special attention will be paid to the economic policies of Social Democratic countries. By selecting two large and two small economies, it will be possible to explore the topic of the differential impact of external constraints according to the position of the respective country in the international hierarchy. Since Social Democratic governments are generally seen to attach prime importance to full employment, an examination of their policies should more clearly reveal the limits of national autonomy.

INFLATION, DEFLATION, AND INTERNATIONAL FINANCE

The topic of external constraints on domestic policy autonomy arises mainly within a Keynesian approach to political economy. Neoclassics hold that expansionary macroeconomic policies cannot create growth and employment but will merely lead to inflation. As mentioned earlier, fixed exchange rates and free capital flows according to this perspective are seen to constitute welcome safeguards against domestic inflationary policies.

To arrive at the conclusion that capital mobility has evaporated domestic policy autonomy, it is necessary, in a Keynesian perspective, to argue that exchange rate changes cannot be used as a policy instrument. If a country has to maintain a fixed exchange rate, domestic policy autonomy is indeed very limited. But if a more flexible management of exchange rates is possible, different policy strategies may coexist in the international system. In that case, countries with more restrictive policy preferences would allow their currency to appreciate while, conversely, countries with a higher preference for growth and full employment would pursue a soft-currency policy. The route through which Keynesians have generally arrived at the conclusion that there is no more domestic policy autonomy is by arguing that devaluations will easily become cumulative under capital mobility. In this view international investors interpret a devaluation as a commitment to unsound policies and hence come to expect further devaluations. The result is a flight out of the domestic currency that can only be stopped by turning to restrictive policies. Yet while confidence is easy to loose it is difficult to gain. Countries with a history of devaluations and expansionary policies will be suspect in the eyes of financial investors, and their distrust will need to be compensated for by higher interest rates in order to convince them to hold the domestic currency. But if devaluations and expansionary policies inevitably lead to exchange crises and higher interest rates for a long time to come, then the best service a government can perform for the economy in the macroeconomic field is to give absolute priority to a fixed exchange rate and institutionalize this priority in such a way that investors will have no reason whatsoever to suspect a rekindling of expansionary policy experiments.[9]

However, it is not obvious at all why a devaluation should be considered the prelude to further devaluations rather than the correction of an unrealistic exchange rate level. Nor, therefore, is it clear why economic policy should have to adjust to a fixed exchange rate rather than the exchange rate to economic policy. To argue that a country that corrects an overvalued exchange rate by means of devaluations will necessarily disrupt the confidence in its currency is like arguing that someone who visits a physician must be expected to become ill more often rather than to be cured. It would seem quite plausible that a country with a strong political preference for full employment, which is committed to maintaining a fixed exchange rate to a much more restrictive neighbor, would find its exchange rate coming under pressure exactly because it is considered politically unviable. Rather than further reducing confidence in the currency, a devaluation would make the new exchange rate more viable politically and hence more credible economically.

Yet soft-currency strategies can, and historically have, become unfeasible at the point when they are seen to signal a political unwillingness to combat domestic inflation. If the confidence in the domestic currency is already disrupted because its value is continuously undermined by inflation, then a soft-currency strategy can only serve to disrupt it further, both because devaluation leads to additional inflationary pressures through higher import prices and because it allows governments to continue pursuing more expansionary policies. Historically, it has been the presence of domestic inflationary problems that has doomed soft-currency strategies. Compare, for instance, the benign neglect with which the Federal Reserve treated the depreciation of the dollar in April 1995 to the fall of the Dollar in 1978–1979, which prompted a radical shift in U.S. monetary policies. In 1978–1979 the United States, suffered from a serious inflationary problem, but not in 1995. In the opposite case of a falling domestic price level (deflation), a soft-currency strategy may even be a precondition for domestic economic recovery. In contrast to a still-widespread conviction, the currency depreciations during the first half of the

1930s were not an instance of "beggar-thy-neighbor" policies that tried to improve export competitiveness at the cost of other countries, but rather they constituted one of the measures designed to halt a fall in the domestic price level.

To argue that historically the shifts to restrictive policy regimes have been prompted by domestic inflationary problems is to beg the question why governments, especially Social Democratic ones, should not treat inflation with benign neglect and concentrate on growth and employment instead. Keynesians have long assumed that governments can choose between high inflation or high unemployment. Even monetarists argue that inflation stimulates the economy in the short run, while being harmless in the long run.

The historical evidence suggests that governments in the longer run have been unable to treat inflations (and deflations) with benign neglect because they tend to become cumulative. If inflationary and deflationary forces are self-reinforcing, governments will eventually have no choice but to intervene, even if this implies, as in the case of disinflationary policies, creating recession and unemployment.

The argument that nominal price movements may tend to become cumulative has a long lineage. In the first part of this century authors like Wicksell (Wicksell) and Keynes (1937) developed it, while at present authors like Tobin (1980), Dow and Dow (1989) and Riese (1986) advance similar views. The starting point of the analysis is that the monetary and financial system, rather than being a veil that one has to pierce in order to arrive at the "real" driving forces of the economy,[9] determines the development of the real economy. At the center of the analysis stands the dynamics of portfolio allocation, that is, the behavior of wealth holders, as the choice between financing productive assets and holding money or investing in speculative real or financial assets sets the limits on the level of economic activity and hence is the most crucial determinant of growth and employment.

Inflation initially exerts a stimulating influence on economic activity. For industrialists inflation increases profits because it reduces the burden of real debt and increases their price-setting ability. For wealth holders, inflation reduces the attractiveness of holding money relative to financing productive investment. The expansion due to the initial investment, in turn, is apt to increase the entrepreneurs' optimism about future conditions as well as to increase wealth-holders' willingness to part with their money as the risk of debt default decreases, thereby leading to a further stimulation of economic activity. As economic activity increases, labor markets come to play a crucial role in propelling a cumulative inflationary process, as an increased demand for labor tends to lead to an escalation of nominal wages.[10] Therefore, in a continued inflation the stimulative effect is only temporary. Inflation does by nature undermine the value of money holdings, and when wealth holders come to expect a continuation of inflation, holding speculative real assets must eventually come to seem a more promising way to safeguard the value of the portfolio than either holding money or financing productive investment. Allowing inflationary expectations to take hold in the financial system, hence, ultimately leads to an explosion of the financial system due to a pronounced willingness to hold debt and real assets and a refusal to finance productive assets and hold money. In the words of Herr (1994, p. 2): "The inevitable outcome (of unchecked inflation) is a collapse of domestic investment activity and economic growth because a flight into tangible assets implies a refusal to finance and participate in productive processes."

Deflations are very much a mirror image of inflations. A falling price level increases real debt and the attractiveness of hoarding money, thereby reducing the willingness to undertake and finance productive investment. The recession due to the initial contraction of investment may further strengthen entrepreneurs' pessimism about the future as well as wealth holders' fear of debt default. Again the labor market plays a crucial rule in propelling the cumulative process if unions react to rising unemployment with lower nominal wages. The endpoint is a flight into money marked by a pronounced desire to hold cash, the breakdown of lending activity, and the collapse of the financial system.[11]

It also follows that the presence or absence of international capital flows is not a factor that fundamentally changes the macropolicy options of domestic governments. Because of their peculiar habits of analyzing only those financial flows that cross borders and neglecting the dynamics of domestic financial transactions, the proponents of the external constraints view fail to realize that the absence of international capital still does not allow governments to continue "unsound" policies. Continued inflation in an open economy will most likely prompt domestic wealth holders to switch to a more stable foreign currency, thereby creating an exchange rate crisis. Yet this exchange crisis is simply the manifestation of a desire to change portfolio allocation, which would have taken place in other forms if the option of acquiring assets denominated in foreign currencies had been effectively barred. In a closed economy, such a desire manifests itself in a flight into debt and real estate and an explosion of financial markets. In such a constellation, effective exchange controls, rather than increasing policy options, can be counterproductive as they contribute to a domestic "financial greenhouse" climate. Moreover, while the notion that a policy of currency devaluation may give rise to a cumulative momentum is right, this momentum arises only to the extent that devaluations are seen as an attempt to avoid combating domestic inflation. If, indeed, domestic wealth holders have come to doubt the future value of the domestic currency because they suspect a continuation of inflation, a devaluation can only serve to strengthen that conviction. But again, the ensuing exchange crisis is a manifestation of a domestic inflationary constellation rather than the result of the presence of international capital flows. In the absence of domestic inflationary pressures, governments can be more sanguine about pressures on the currency.

Conversely, the deflationary situation of the Great Depression required a relaxation of external constraints. It is not surprising that governments in the 1930s, after more than a decade in which maintaining the confidence in the currency reigned supreme on the political agenda, displayed a strong urge to break free form these constraints. Continued adherence to the Gold Standard implied a continued adherence to domestic deflation. The consequent flight into money posed an acute threat to the financial system and the rest of the economy. Consequently, only a credible end to the policy of deflation could bring about a turnaround, and this required a credible end to the Gold Standard commitment.

In sum, whereas the external constraints view argues that the limits on domestic policy autonomy derive from the fact that in an international system in which many currencies coexist each single government can only have limited control, it is argued here that the limits on policy autonomy primarily derive from the decentralized character of decision making in a monetary economy.[12] In other words, in decentralized economies coordinated by the medium of money, economic policies must necessarily accord priority to maintaining relative price stability[13] in order to ensure the coherence of the system (see Riese, 1987).

THE 1920s: ABORTED SOCIAL DEMOCRACY

Historically, Social Democracy occupies the middle ground between liberalism and socialism. On the one hand, it rejects the socialist planned economy as both economically inefficient and undemocratic. On the other hand it also rejects the liberal demand for government abstinence and the acceptance of market outcomes, as it holds that those outcomes are normatively unacceptable. Socialists, who at times formed a significant part of Social Democratic party membership, have traditionally tended to interpret Social Democracy as a political movement that does share the same goals but rejects the revolutionary route in favor of a democratic one. In retrospect it has become clear that a "socialist revolution" has only been a historically relevant option in less developed economies with a radical peasant movement instead of in highly developed economies with a strong labor movement. In developed industrial states, Social Democracy has shied away from traveling the road toward a socialized economy. As Social Democrats soon found out socialization was not only unpopular with parties to its right but also with its own electorate. In Sweden, for example, the strong emphasis on socialization in the election of 1920 led to disappointing results for the Social Democratic Party (SAP) (see Tilton, 1991, p. 91). and more than 6 decades later many in the SAP's rank and file failed to be convinced of the proposal for collective ownership through union-managed wage earner funds.

At the end of the World War I, no Social Democratic party had developed concrete plans for socialization and, once the issue was researched more thoroughly, socialization seemed to create more problems than it would solve. While from a shopfloor perspective, expropriating the owners might seem a solution to the problems workers encountered in wage bargaining, the perspective looked quite different for those Social Democrats in charge of economic policies. Socializing firms in times of crisis would, initially at least, create even more economic dislocations. By itself, socialization would not create more demand nor improve competitiveness, but rather would place more burdens on the budget by having to support ailing firms. Especially in open economies dependent on foreign demand, it was difficult to see how a change in the ownership of domestic firms would improve economic conditions. Finally, to socialize firms would imply that decisions concerning wages and employment would become internal political problems for the labor movement. But as the active participation of Social Democratic Parties in the regulation of the wartime economy had shown, the administration of scarcity increased internal tensions both in and between the party and the unions. To a political movement dependent on an appeal to workers in general, political viability and unity required that such divisive issues remained external. The fate of the Swedish Socialization Commission is representative of the general reluctance of the European left to proceed with nationalization after World War I. The commission was established in 1920 by a minority SAP government in order to develop concrete plans for the socialization of industry and natural resources. In the end the commission devoted 15 years to this task without being able to come up with substantive answers.

Historically, therefore, it is not very surprising that World War I was not followed by a socialist revolution, or any substantive progress on the road to socialization. Rather, it would seem much more puzzling that within 3 years of the end of hostilities virtually all Western countries had embarked on severely restrictive policies at great costs to growth and employment. The political constellation at the end of the war would seem to have been very conducive to a policy of promoting growth through cheap money, which came to be characteristic of Western countries in the wake of the Great Depression. And as happened after the Great Depression, buoyant growth would then provide the necessary distributional space to facilitate the effort to reduce the budget deficit and to expand welfare arrangements. In short, given the political situation at the end of World War I, it must seem puzzling that the settlement reached in Europe between the mid-1930s and late 1940s did not take place 15 years earlier.

Relations between capital and labor were very tense after the war. The hardship in the trenches and at home had radicalized many, and as a result trade unions and Social Democratic parties generally recorded a rapid growth in membership. Moreover, the advent of general (male) suffrage in many European countries further strengthened the position of the left. While postwar elections nowhere produced a majority for Social Democrats, liberal and conservative politicians clearly saw the need to appease the labor movement.

Apart from the fear of working class unrest, most non-Social Democratic parties also felt sincerely that the soldiers should not be greeted by recession and unemployment when coming home. The desire of a Liberal prime minister like Lloyd George "to make Britain a fit country for heroes to live in"[14] were quite representative of the feelings of most politicians of the time. In addition, 4 long years of wartime destruction and insufficient investment created a need for growth policies. Furthermore, restrictive monetary policies would make funding and servicing the huge debts of the belligerents more difficult. Finally, stimulating domestic growth would help reduce budget deficits, while a restrictive policy would further aggravate the deficits.

Indeed, immediately after the World War I, most countries embarked on a policy of low interest rates (see Eichangreen, 1992, p. 106). In Britain, Lloyd George resisted repeated calls from both the Bank of England and the Treasury to raise interest rates and implement policies that would allow a return to the Gold Standard for fear of provoking unemployment and industrial unrest (Howson, 1974, p. 91). Accordingly, the bank rate remained at 5% until November 1919 and was only raised again in April 1920 (Eichengreen, 1992, p. 111). But while the Bank of England had consistently, though without result, advocated a restrictive policy, central banks in other countries seem to have been more worried about the prospects for the real economy. Norges Bank lowered the discount rate after the World War I and kept it there until December 1919. Norges Bank director A. Sandberg argued that to pursue a restrictive policy in order to stop inflation and stabilize the currency would be to put the horse behind the cart. First the productive resources of the economy should be allowed to recover, and only then it would be possible to achieve a stable currency and price level (Sandberg, 1919). In Sweden, the Riksbank lowered its discount rate in April and June 1919, and its board declared that its aim was to keep industry going at all costs and to avoid a crisis (quoted in Östlind, 1945, p. 310). Similarly, German governments felt that a recovery of production had to enjoy absolute priority, and the Reichsbank largely shared this view (see Feldman, 1993, pp. 156–157, 214–215, and Veb, 1989, pp. 23–25, 120, 122). The discount rate was kept at 5% from late 1914 to mid-1922.

While stimulating domestic production by a policy of cheap money, governments at the same time tried to remedy their budget problems by contractionary fiscal policies. The budget for 1919 was generally still dominated by military expenses. Yet as demobilization and the termination of wartime contracts proceeded, the budget situation improved. In Britain the budget showed a surplus already in the fiscal year 1919–1920. "In other words, budgetary measures were operating against the boom throughout its duration" (Howson, 1975, p. 23). In nonbelligerent Sweden, the budget was already in surplus in 1919 (see Östlind, 1945, p. 310). Norway and, especially, Germany, however, were less successful in fiscal retrenchment. In 1920 the German deficit was halved with respect to the previous year as a result of reduced spending and increased revenues, and again in 1922 as a result of the Erzberger Tax reforms of 1919–1920. Yet domestic political problems as well as reparations and the autonomous effects of inflation itself meant that massive fiscal deficits became a continuous feature after the war.

But whereas the parliamentary political situation pointed toward a growth regime, the labor market and economic situation pointed in a rather different direction. Rather than having to confront the feared mass-unemployment, the combination of stimulative monetary policies and a postwar restocking boom meant that governments had to confront a situation of tight labor markets and domestic inflationary pressures. In such a constellation only two possible options existed. Either governments managed to contain the price-wage spiral by means of microeconomic measures like prices and incomes policies, or central banks had to break the inflationary cycle by creating recession and unemployment.

Under the conditions of the postwar years, it was both institutionally and politically impossible to pursue nominal incomes policies aimed at reducing inflation. Unions had generally experienced the restrictions on wage bargaining as a restriction of their market power, and they favored a return to free bargaining after the war. Governments likewise wished to abolish price regulations as quickly as possible, but without regulated prices an attempt at incomes policy would be completely illusory in the boom conditions following the war. Not even Social Democratic governments seemed to have an advantage in enlisting the cooperation of the unions. At a meeting of the leadership of the LO trade union 28–29 April 1919, SAP minister of finance Thorsson argued that unions should show some moderation in their wage demands, but his suggestion was not greeted enthusiastically.[15] More importantly, governments generally recognized no clear need for an incomes and price policy after the war. In good neoclassical fashion, the inflation after the war was initially interpreted as the reflection of an abnormal scarcity of supply. By speeding up the recovery of supply, a policy aimed at stimulating domestic demand could hence be expected to lead to an abatement of inflationary pressures.

The institutional and political impossibility of the first solution and the political unattractiveness of the second meant that most governments hesitated for some time and decided to accommodate the market pressures for inflation. But when inflation, contrary to expectations, continued to increase rapidly rather than to recede in response to the recovery of production, currencies depreciated, nominal wages escalated ever more rapidly, and the financial system started to show the typical signs of a massive explosion of speculative lending activity, governments eventually decided to provoke a recession and unemployment. The turn to restrictive policies in the early 1920s created a recession that in many cases was worse than the Great Depression.

In the end, only Germany failed to give priority to combating inflation. The resulting hyperinflation impressively shows the results of a political inability to orient economic policies toward the inherent priority of price stability. Historically, the German hyperinflation has been interpreted primarily in two contending ways (see Hardach, 1973). For the balance of payments school, the reparations demands of the allies depressed the exchange rate of the currency and thereby initiated a cumulative depreciation–inflation spiral. From the quantity theory perspective, the political inability of the German polity to reconcile the labor claims, business, and the Allies on the German national product resulted in budget deficits financed by way of the printing press.[16] Yet neither of these views seems entirely accurate (see also Riese, 1986, pp. 214–231, and Eichengreen, 1992, pp. 125–127). As Jaeger (1988, p. 92) points out, the currency was eventually stabilized without a cancellation of reparations demands. And as the example of countries like Britain and Sweden shows, budget deficits were no necessary precondition for inflationary pressures. Postwar restocking and the realization that governments would prioritize growth led to an endogenous upswing in demand, which soon led to scarcity in labor and goods markets. Currency depreciation did certainly contribute to inflationary pressures, but ultimately it was the domestic labor market situation that allowed depreciation to translate into a cumulative inflation spiral. The budget deficit doubtlessly contributed to demand pressures, but to instead attribute the inflation solely to government deficits reflects a theory that fails to recognize the possibility of market-driven inflation and conceals its theoretical shortcomings as policy failures (see Riese, 1987).

The German hyperinflation was not initiated by a government that could not find a durable solution to a domestic distributional crisis. Rather, it was the presence of a domestic distributional crisis that led the government to accommodate the upswing and inflation rather than to embark on a restrictive course that would have had severe consequences in terms of growth and unemployment.[17] Looking across the border to, for instance, Britain, German policymakers could observe the severe crisis caused by a macroeconomic disinflation strategy.[18] Such costs seemed politically intolerable in the unstable situation of Germany's postwar years.

Initially, the German government's refusal to initiate a stabilization crisis meant that, during the early 1920s, the German economy performed better in terms of growth and employment than its neighbors (see Laursen & Pedersen, 1964, Chap. 7, and Hanisch, 1979, pp. 254–267). But when the currency was disrupted to such an extent that it would not serve as a medium of credit contracts any more, toleration of inflation would not allow Germany to avoid crisis and unemployment any longer. Under hyperinflation, unemployment rose from 3.5% in July 1923 to 19.1% in October of the same year (Riese, 1986, pp. 217–218). With the subsequent currency reform and the linking of the Reichsmark to gold, German economic policies finally converged with those of its neighbors.

Governments in the 1920s, as today, did not interpret the decision for a macroeconomic anti-inflation regime as a simultaneous decision to reduce growth and create durable unemployment. Rather, in an inflationary constellation in which the government seemed to be rapidly losing control over the economy and no other policy instruments were available, the postulate that a policy of tight money has no durable effects on growth and unemployment exerted an irresistible attraction. In line with this interpretation, the irresponsible attempt to mitigate domestic distributional conflicts by recourse to the printing press now came to be held responsible for the inflationary mayhem. In order to prevent a repetition of inflation, removing monetary policies beyond the reach of politics by granting the central bank independence and by tying the currency irrevocably to gold became generally accepted. Because macroeconomic policies were interpreted not to affect employment, the durable unemployment of the 1920s hence had to be due to microeconomic distortions.

Eventually Social Democrats also embraced this view. They did not interpret inflation as a problem that had its roots in the labor market. Unlike their political opponents, who blamed budget deficits on the government's desire to appease labor, Social Democrats instead frequently interpreted inflation in class-struggle terms. Inflation, in this interpretation, was an attempt to reduce real wages. In line with this interpretation, Nils Karleby (1921), the SAP's most prominent theorist, argued that deflation was beneficial to labor as it would increase real wages. The SAP itself, which was in power from 1917–1920 and in 1921, played a crucial role in getting deflationary policies adopted. Yet the emergence of mass unemployment did not lead Social Democrats to a revision of their macroeconomic policy views. Rather, the crisis was interpreted as proof of their postulate that capitalist economies are inherently crisis-prone. However, since the Social Democrats lacked an alternative policy, such an argument could not be employed to political benefit. In effect, this view meant that Social Democrats had become structurally unable to govern because, on the one hand, they accepted the need for Gold Standard policies, while, on the other hand, they were politically unable to sustain the social and economic consequences following from such policies.

The radical reduction in policy autonomy that was achieved through the resurrection of the Gold Standard was hence initially viewed not as an unwelcome restriction imposed by external forces, but as a self-imposed constraint required to prevent a repetition of inflationary mayhem. The theme that external constraints imposed unduly restrictive policies would only blossom lat-

er, in response paradoxically, to capital movements that threatened to undermine the self-imposed constraint of the Gold Standard. International capital
flows had been quite extensive before the war and reemerged afterward. Giv-
en the uncertainties surrounding the Gold Standard, hot-money flows remained a constant feature during the 1920s and into the 1930s. Since not all
countries returned to the Gold Standard at the same time, some speculative
gains could be made by anticipating when a country would undertake the final spurt to bring up the currency to par, as was the case, for example, with
the pound in 1925 and the krone in 1928.

More importantly, as deflation spread toward the end of the decade and
its mounting economic and political costs cast doubts about the gold parity,
hot-money flows became ever more intense. It is easy to understand how the
misunderstanding that internationally mobile capital imposed unduly restrictive policies might arise. As the economic crisis intensified, international finance reacted to every development that might indicate that the domestic
costs of maintaining the Gold Standard were becoming too high. In such a
situation, a higher than usual budget deficit or increased public means to
combat unemployment and support the unemployed could easily lead to capital flight. Most affected were evidently those currencies that figured prominently in international portfolios. In Britain the second Labour government
fell in 1931 because the Labour party refused to agree to the substantial cuts
in unemployment benefits that the government held to be essential in order to
reduce the budget deficit and thereby restore confidence in the pound. In the
end, not only public policies but the public display of opposition to austerity
policies could spark off capital flight. Apparently, international finance could
only be appeased by strict adherence to austerity policies. Yet this whole argument rested on the belief that the self-imposed constraint of the Gold Standard was a necessary safeguard against inflationary mayhem. As the Great
Depression would show, it was the opposite that was true.

THE GREAT DEPRESSION: STABILIZATION OF PRICES
AND THE BIRTH OF SOCIAL DEMOCRACY

Restrictive policies in combination with the resurrection of the Gold Standard
successfully eliminated inflation, but they did so at the price of creating a deflationary bias in the international economy. Given the inflation of
1914–1921, the decision to return to the prewar parity in itself implied the
need for substantial deflation. Moreover, by rigidly tying currencies to gold,
domestic austerity and deflation would be the only available adjustment
mechanism in times of balance-of-payments imbalances. Because exchange
restrictions were ruled out, as international capital flows were considered to
function as a welcome safeguard against inflationary policies, the emergence

of serious external imbalances due to speculative movements was an ever-present possibility.

What gave the Great Depression its particularly catastrophic character was that the decade of the Gold Standard had weakened those institutions that could provide a safeguard against excessive downward nominal flexibility. The wage bargaining position of most trade unions had been weakened seriously after a decade of mass unemployment. Similarly, a decade of recession and falling prices seriously undermined the agricultural sector. Finally, the policies of the 1920s had also weakened the banking sector. Many countries had already experienced bank failures during the deflation of the early 1920s, and the policies of the rest of the decade were not conducive to a recovery. In short, the resurrection of the Gold Standard on the basis of a restrictive policy regime meant that the threat of a cumulative cycle of deflationary policies was ever present. The disaster was just waiting to happen.

The downward slide of the world economy was initiated by restrictive policies in Germany and the United States during 1926–1928. The Reichsbank had become increasingly worried about large capital inflows into Germany, in particular because the favorable balance-of-payments situation undermined Germany's claim that she could not pay reparations. The ensuing monetary contraction had already caused a stock market crash in Germany in 1927. In the United States, instead, the Federal Reserve worried about domestic speculation and engineered its own monetary contraction in 1928. The American policy in particular, by drying up capital flows to the rest of the world, forced other countries into restrictive policies in order to maintain the gold parity of respective currencies. Hardest hit initially were less developed primary producers dependent on capital inflows. Their effort to increase exports only increased deflationary pressures (see Eichengreen, 1992, pp. 222–223). By 1931, banking systems started to collapse under the pressure of deflation, first in Austria, followed closely by Germany. In March 1933, the newly elected president Roosevelt had to declare a bank holiday in the United States.

The deflationary constellation determined the character of the emerging new regime. Despite wide cross-national variations, the new regime came to rest on three pillars: (1) proliferation of institutional devices designed to promote downward nominal rigidity, in particular agricultural price stabilization agreements and cartels backed up by tariffs, and, in some countries, a deliberate effort to strengthen the wage bargaining power of the trade unions; (2) the abandonment of the Gold Standard and the stabilization of the domestic price level instead of the exchange rate; and (3) a policy of cheap money.

The Gold Standard regime did not give way in one piece. Just as in the early 1920s, when the domestic policy reorientation had taken place first, followed by the resurrection of the Gold Standard, so in the Great Depression the first clear break with the principle of the old regime occurred on the domestic level, while the external shell of the Gold Standard lived on for some time. Under the Gold Standard regime, price flexibility was deemed crucial both because it was seen to reduce the real effects of monetary restriction and because it was required as an internal adjustment mechanism to defend the fixed exchange rate. Yet as deflation threatened more and more sectors of the economy, governments changed course from combating to promoting nominal rigidities. The general pattern consisted of government assistance to sectoral producers to enter into price stabilization agreements. Since many sectors would find it difficult to maintain a cartel on a voluntary basis, governments granted sectoral boards of producers the right to impose the agreements on reluctant producers. In open economies, successful price stabilization also required preventing undercutting of prices through imports. Accordingly, another pillar of the Gold Standard regime, namely, free trade fell victim to deflation. Finally, in industry, successful price stabilization also required that individual firms should not be able to gain an advantage by lowering the wage of their work force. The advent of microeconomic price stabilization, hence, introduced a contradiction in the Gold Standard regime. While the continued macroeconomic adherence to the Gold Standard required that domestic prices be lowered in order to defend the parity, microeconomic policies started to actively stabilize prices. The only way to solve this dilemma was to abandon gold.

The new policy regime set the stage for the domestic political accommodation that had eluded most countries during the 1920s. While in an anti-inflation regime governments necessarily had to be skeptical with respect to collective organizations of economic interests, the deflationary constellation meant that such organizations could now be seen as performing a stabilizing role. The logic of microeconomic price stabilization entailed that the unions' ability to enforce sectorwide collective agreements was a desirable feature. Moreover, exchange rate management was now subordinated to domestic policy, and central bankers lost much of the autonomy they had gained since the early 1920s.

Although Social Democrats generally did not initiate the new policies, they were to reap the electoral and ideological benefits. In Scandinavia the logic of halting deflation already brought Social Democrats and farmers together in a new governing coalition in the 1930s, After World War II Social Democrats would occupy the government benches in many more countries. After the cataclysm of the Great Depression, Liberals had to pay the price for labeling the interventionist policies of the Gold Standard a "free market" regime, while at the same time Social Democrats could claim that history had shown their postulate of the need for political regulation of a capitalist economy to be correct.

Many contemporaries, with such episodes as the fall of the second Labour government in mind, held that short-term capital flows were damaging as they introduced a restrictive bias into the system. In effect, international capital flows in the early 1930s played a positive role. Given the sanctity of the parity, capital outflows indeed would prompt more restrictive policies. But by eventually forcing many countries off the Gold Standard and by thereby showing that abandoning Gold did not spell disaster, the hot-money flows of the 1930s speeded up the decline of a policy regime that perpetuated low growth and unemployment.

According to the orthodoxy of the early 1930s, and of the present, a lack of confidence in the currency could only be remedied by means of domestic austerity. As those countries that desperately tried to cling to the Gold Standard after 1931 experienced, quite the opposite was true. Continued adherence to deflation only served to undermine the economy. As a result the Gold Bloc countries,[19] rather than those that had floated their currencies and pursued cheap money policies, were confronted with massive and highly erratic currency flows.

The speculation against the British pound during the late 1920s and early 1930s was obviously not inspired by the fear of expansionary policies but by a general belief that the pound had been reestablished at too high a parity and that British society was less and less likely to bear the costs of such a commitment. Even the fall of the second Labour government and the presentation of a balanced budget by the National Government on 10 September 1931 failed to calm financial markets. Instead, a relatively harmless protest of Navy sailors against pay cuts, known as the mutiny at Invergordon, on 14 September 1931, caused sheer panic on exchange markets. After the decision to cut the pound loose from gold on 21 September 1931, however, no cumulative downward run on the pound developed. During November and December there was downward pressure on the pound, and on 3 December it reached a low point of $3.24 (Sayers, 1976, p. 422). While the Bank of England stayed aloof, downward pressure on sterling abated. From March 1932 onward, wterling instead came under strong *upward* pressure. The announced twilight of the civilization did not follow the end of the Gold Standard; instead, the British economy started its slow ascent toward recovery.

After the devaluation of the pound, Sweden and Norway experienced large capital outflows as financial markets apparently perceived their commitment to the Gold Standard to have become noncredible. The initial reaction of both Norges Bank and the Riksbank was to defend the old parity. Being unable to procure foreign currency loans, devaluation became inevitable within 1 week of the British decision. Again, after devaluation, speculation against both currencies largely abated. No flight out of the Swedish krona occurred after the SAP came to power in 1932 on the basis of an explicitly reflationary program. Nor did Norway experience an exchange rate crisis when the Social Democratic Nygaardsvold government took office in 1935.

In the Netherlands, which desperately tried to cling to the Gold Standard, the credibility of the exchange rate waned as more and more countries devalued and the depressing effects of deflationary policies to neutralize the overvaluation of the exchange rate became more pronounced. Especially from 1933 to 1936, the Dutch Central Bank continuously had to ward off speculation against the guilder. Large outflows occurred in response to the devaluation of the yen (31 December 1931), the devaluation of the dollar (March 1933), the devaluation of the belga, and in May 1936, after the victory of the popular front in France. Whenever a change in the domestic political situation seemed to imply a weakening of support for the gold parity, capital flowed out. When, for instance, it seemed in September 1935 that the government did not have a majority for the proposed budget cuts, the guilder came under massive pressure and markets calmed only after the proposals were approved. As was the case in Britain, the depreciation of the guilder in 1936 restored rather than destroyed confidence in the currency.

During the Great Depression, therefore, the presence of massive short-term capital flows was no hindrance to establishing an expansionary policy regime. Yet the skepticism with respect to free capital flows born in this period would play a useful role in stabilizing the new regime in the years immediately following Word War II. Shortly before or after abandoning the Gold Standard, many countries had installed emergency exchange controls, but as financial markets calmed after devaluation, the need for exchange controls proved less urgent than many governments had feared. With the exception of Germany,[20] far-reaching exchange controls were only installed during the run up to the World War II. After the war, these controls would be maintained for a considerable period. Apart from the abortive attempt to return the pound to convertibility in July 1947, most European currencies remained inconvertible up to 1959. Moreover, the use of exchange controls was explicitly envisaged in the articles of the IMF. The main reason for maintaining controls after the war was that policymakers had drawn the lesson from the Great Depression that free capital flows would compromise the ability to pursue a cheap money policy. But since the determination to pursue cheap money policies was quite widespread in the Western world after World War II, exchange controls were probably not all that crucial in defending a cheap money policy. They did play a useful role, however, in weathering the inflationary pressures of the immediate postwar years. For individual countries, massive capital outflows in response to inflation could easily have led to currency devaluation, thereby exacerbating inflationary pressures, yet the main contribution to containing postwar inflation came from the domestic front.

In contrast to the late 1910s and early 1920s, Western governments in the years following 1945 successfully managed to contain inflationary pressures, thereby obviating the need for macroeconomic anti-inflation policies. Being able to maintain their commitment to growth, the postwar boom eventually came to last almost three decades. Unlike after 1918, there was to be no bonfire of controls after 1945. Price controls, which had been used during the war to reduce inflation, as well as administrative rationing of consumption, imports and investment were generally kept in force for several years (for Norway, see, for example, Bjerve, 1989). In addition, many central banks developed selective credit rationing instruments that would allow them to restrict credit to overheated or less essential sectors of the economy, without having to resort to a general monetary contraction and high interest rates.

Most important, after the war it proved possible to enlist the cooperation of trade unions in nominal wage policies. Politically, such policies were facilitated because in many countries political parties sympathetic to labor held power. In the United Kingdom, Sweden, and Norway Social Democrats enjoyed an absolute parliamentary majority. More important than the political hue of the party in power, however, was the changed outlook of both the Social Democrats and the trade unions. Both organizations had come a long way from the radicalism of the 1920s.

Germany again proved somewhat of an exception to the general pattern, as the experience of the Nazi regime led both the employers and the trade unions to place great emphasis on government noninterference in wage bargaining (*Tarifautonomie*). Yet this lack of an incomes policy instrument was largely compensated for by a massive influx of refugees from the lost territories in the East. As a result, the German economy could grow at a rapid pace without the emergence of severe inflationary pressures due to tight labor markets.

THE 1970s AND 1980s: EXTERNAL CONSTRAINTS AND THE DECLINE OF SOCIAL DEMOCRACY

In essence, the viability of the growth regime during the postwar era depended on the ability to contain inflation by means of microeconomic policy measures, like prices and incomes policies.[21] In practice this meant increasing reliance on incomes policies because the price and quantity controls of the immediate postwar period could not be continued indefinitely. Despite their primary orientation to growth, macroeconomic policies did provide some assistance to the microeconomic efforts aimed at containing inflationary pressures. Brief periods of macroeconomic contraction could temporarily ease labor market pressures and thereby reduce the strain on incomes policies.[22] Moreover, in a constellation where functioning incomes policies could be relied on to support a macroeconomic growth orientation in the long run, these brief periods of macroeconomic restriction would be interpreted as just that, rather than as a regime change. Accordingly, such policies could be employed without negatively affecting the engine of private sector growth: positive expectations about future growth prospects. As Tobin (1980, p. 19) put it: "As

Keynes also knew, protracted underproduction and under-utilization severely damages the marginal efficiency of capital. In mild and short-lived recessions investment is buoyed by the belief that high employment and prosperity are the long term norm. Once this confidence is destroyed, as contemporary events again demonstrate, it is terribly difficult to revive it."

However, relying on incomes policies to some extent always is a precarious strategy. Ultimately, trade unions are organizations designed to benefit their members in wage bargaining and not to function as an additional instrument in macroeconomic policies. As became clear during the late 1960s, the strategy of relying on microeconomic policies to contain inflation would come into conflict with the organizational logic of trade unions. The replacement of the growth regime by a disinflationary regime during the last two decades is, in consequence, primarily a story about the disintegration of the ability to contain inflation by microeconomic means rather than a story about the emergence of external constraints.

The rapid increase in cross-border financial transactions since the late 1960s is to a considerable extent a—direct and indirect—consequence of mounting inflationary pressures. With low inflation and a credible commitment to fixed exchange rates there was little incentive for massive short-term capital flows. The dollar, in fact, was "better than gold" because it not only provided stability but also earned a yield. As inflationary pressures in the United States mounted, dollar holdings became less attractive. This new situation was first manifest in the exchange crises leading up to the end of Bretton Woods. The advent of flexible exchange rates, by itself, introduced another element of uncertainty and hence an additional incentive for short-term capital flows.

Given the lessons policymakers drew from the Great Depression, one might have expected a proliferation of exchange controls in response to the reemergence of capital flows, especially since, in contrast to the Great Depression, international capital flows now seemed to pose an acute threat to an expansionary policy regime. During the late 1960s and early 1970s a tightening of exchange controls could indeed be observed, but this development soon gave way to widespread deregulation. In general, this policy of promoting the openness of the domestic economy to international financial flows was based on two considerations. Those governments that switched to a macroeconomic disinflation strategy had no use anymore for an instrument designed to isolate the domestic economy from a more restrictive international environment.[23] Rather, exchange controls would now come to be considered a source of microeconomic inefficiency and an impediment to the international competitiveness of domestic financial institutions. In addition, promoting free capital flows could help stabilize the new regime, just as (the threat of) capital outflows could serve as a powerful hindrance—political and economic—to more expansionary policies.

The first country to switch to a regime of macroeconomic disinflation, with its ensuing mass unemployment, was Germany, to be soon followed by the Netherlands. Germany led the way not because it was confronted with the most serious inflationary pressures, but because the political commitment to a growth regime was most precarious there. Due to the tradition of *Tarifau-tonomie* Germany lacked an important policy instrument. The Social Democratic government of the late 1960s did attempt to institutionalize tripartite consultations on wage prices and policies but, as Scharpf (1987, p. 157) notes, the *konzertierte Aktion* soon degenerated into a mass meeting at which the leaders of the participating groups read prepared statements to the press. In addition, the extreme hesitation in revaluing the German mark (DM) in the 1960s, and the drying up of immigration from the East put increased strains on the labor market. The humiliating defeat of the government in the 1974 bargaining round with the public sector union strengthened the Bundesbank in its resolve to combat inflation by means of radically restrictive monetary policies. The policy of announcing monetary targets, which was introduced by the Bundesbank in 1974, incidentally had the full support of SPD chancellor Schmidt.

But while, in the interwar period, Germany (until 1933) and the Netherlands (until 1936) were fighting a losing battle by clinging to restrictive policies, in the 1970s they were the pioneers of a regime that came to be generally accepted in the next decade. The first set of countries to follow their lead were those—like the United Kingdom, the United States, France, Denmark, and Belgium—which, while displaying a political desire to continue a macro-economic growth regime, lacked the microeconomic means for doing so.

While Britain did not practice Keynesianism either in the interwar period or in the 1950s and 1960s (see Matthews, 1968), it did do so in response to the first oil price crisis. Largely because many other countries did not do so, a sizable current account deficit developed (see, for example, Healey, 1989, p. 393). Devaluing the pound could, in the medium term, have solved the United Kingdom's current account problem, but the downward drift of sterling exacerbated the decisive problem, namely, the increasing inability to control domestic inflation. Quite in keeping with the principle of the growth regime, monetary policy was subordinated to the overall policy orientation (see Dimsdale, 1991, p. 125). Under expansionary fiscal and monetary policies, containing inflation had to rely on prices and incomes policies, but due to the general outlook of the trade unions as well as their high degree of decentralization, conditions were very unfavorable for such a policy. Wilson's Labour government in 1974 had initially placed its hopes on voluntary wages restraint but had to resort to statutory policies in 1975. Such a policy, however, was highly unpopular with the rank and file, and it completely collapsed in the notorious "winter of discontent" of 1978. Domestic inability to control inflation could only serve to undermine the confidence in the pound. In this constellation both Chancellor Healey and the Bank of England saw no alternative to a switch to "monetarist" policies. As Gordon Richardson, Governor of the Bank of England, argued: "In times past other features of the economic system, such as a fixed exchange rate or Gladstonian budgetary principles, were thought to provide some guarantee of stability. These restraints have now gone. The main role therefore that I see for monetary targets is to provide the framework of stability within which other policy objectives can be more easily achieved" (Bank of England, 1978, p. 34) While the basic shifts in policy assignments had already taken place before 1979, Labour, due to the high costs in terms of unemployment, remained reluctantly "monetarist." It was left to Margaret Thatcher to fully develop the new regime.

While more and more Western countries submitted to a disinflationary regime, Norway and Sweden maintained their course of giving priority to full employment. Here not only the political will for full employment was more pronounced, but also the institutional preconditions seemed ideally suited for such a strategy. Ever since the mid-1930s Social Democrats had presented themselves as the guarantor of employment and prosperity. Given the political dominance of Social Democracy, full employment also became the highest priority for non–Social Democratic parties. Also Norway and Sweden had implemented far-reaching exchange controls in the period immediately prior to World War II. In the postwar period these controls were further extended and refined, with the result that by the mid-1970s the isolation of domestic financial markets from developments abroad was probably stronger than for any other developed industrial nation. In particular the system of credit rationing by which the government tried to control the amount of credit to (specific sectors of) the economy without relying on interest rate changes dictated that a high degree of isolation of domestic financial markets be maintained. In terms of the microeconomic ability to contain inflation, both countries also compared favorably to most OECD economies. The combination of a hegemonic social democracy and strong and centralized trade unions implied that the ability and willingness to use prices and incomes policies was rather pronounced.

Despite the regime change in Germany, both Norway and Sweden initially decided to participate in the European Snake exchange rate arrangement.[24] In Norway the potential conflict between membership in the Snake and the commitment to full employment was not expected. After the unprecedented growth period under the Bretton Woods system, the move to more flexible exchange rates was rather interpreted as a threat to international trade and growth. The Norwegian government considered the doubling of the bandwidth of the Smithsonian versus the Bretton Woods agreement to contribute to uncertainty, and it welcomed the so-called "snake in the tunnel" exchange rate arrangement. Initially, participation in the Snake rather seemed to pose a threat to the ability to pursue restrictive policies domestically. With low unemployment, high price and wage increases, and the North Sea oil wells coming on line in the mid-1970s, large current account surpluses and strong domestic demand was expected. Against the majority of the business community, but with the support of the LO trade union, the government on 15 November 1973 decided to revalue the krone by 5%. The single most important factor in this decision was the goal of dampening domestic inflation (see Dobloug, 1992, pp. 53–54, and Lie, 1987, p. 87).

But tying the currency to Germany's led to an undermining of external competitiveness due to a positive inflation differential. Instead of adjusting their domestic policy to a fixed exchange rate, starting in 1976, both countries decided to leave the Snake and adjust the exchange rate to domestic policies. Between 1976 and 1986 the Norwegian krone was devalued seven times, while Sweden devalued six times between 1976 and 1982.

Up to the early 1980s the more flexible approach to exchange rate management was primarily defensive in nature, that is, the currencies were devalued in order to compensate for higher domestic cost and price increases. The fight against unemployment during this period came to rest primarily on the so-called "bridge building policy." In essence, this policy involved fiscal expansion so as to maintain the level of Gross Domestic Product during a trough in export demand and in domestic private investment activity. At the same time higher domestic inflation was to be contained by a stronger reliance on tripartite incomes policies (see Dahl, 1989, and El Vander, 1988).

The policy of bridge building involved the typical Keynesian mistake of treating private investment activity as an exogenous cyclical factor rather than an endogenous factor critically determined by the nature of the policy regime. The international downturn during the 1970s and 1980s was not the reflection of a cyclical, that is, temporary downturn in investment demand but the result of the decision of the majority of OECD economies to stamp out inflation by reducing growth and creating durable mass unemployment (see Riese, 1987, and Layard, 1986). Accordingly, the expected international upswing did not take place and, therefore, the bridge-building policy also had to fail in the medium term. Although successful in terms of preventing open unemployment, a policy that created jobs in the public sector while private sector activity remained slack eventually had to shipwreck on the rocks of simultaneous current account and budget deficits.

By the early 1980s it had become clear that a change in course was unavoidable. In principle two options existed. Both countries might decide to follow the example of Danish Prime Minister Poul Schlüter and prescribe a "potato diet" to the population. By means of a combination of a hard-currency policy and fiscal retrenchment, the Schlüter government managed to reduce inflation as well as the current account and budget deficits. The unpleasant effect of such a strategy was the emergence of durable mass unemployment. Alternatively, one might decide to stimulate private investment rather than to compensate for the lack of private investment by means of fiscal expansion. Successful expansion of the private sector would not only mean higher tax receipts but would also allow for cuts in fiscal spending without jeopardizing full employment. Given the policies of the rest of the OECD countries, such a strategy would also imply giving domestic industry a decisive advantage, both in order to prevent the restrictive condition in the international environment from dragging down the domestic economy and to reduce the current account deficits. Both countries choose the latter course.

Starting in 1982 the newly elected SAP government, under the direction of minister of finance Kjell-Olof Feldt, started a new strategy labeled "the third way." The centerpiece of this strategy consisted of a massive devaluation, by 16 %, announced on the government's first day in office. The devaluation was intended to give a major boost to the private sector. A the same time the extensive subsidies to industry, which had been introduced under the previous "bourgeois" governments were to be abolished. While the devaluation remedied the current account deficit, the budget deficit was to be tackled by means of increased revenues and reduced spending. In order to prevent devaluation from merely leading to more inflation, the government proclaimed a price stop and reached an agreement with the unions that the increase in import prices would not be compensated for by higher nominal wages (see Feldt, 1991, especially pp. 59, 65, 124).

The Norwegian government was not forced to take such dramatic measures. While restrictive policies abroad in the wake of the second oil price crisis clearly had negative consequences for the domestic economy, the rise in oil prices itself implied a strong improvement in export earnings and government revenues. Despite some attempts at fiscal retrenchment during the early 1980s, the oil price increase allowed Norway to continue its course of fiscal expansion, using monetary policy and mainly microeconomic initiatives to contain inflation. Although successful in terms of full employment, this strategy also meant that inflation continued at a higher pace as compared to most European countries.

The explicit choice of continuing the employment-oriented regime after the early 1980s meant, in consequence, that market participants in Norway and Sweden would have to expect a continuation of high inflation rates. In addition to the impulse imparted through devaluation or oil price increases, the adjustments of economic behavior in response to expectations of continued inflation provided for a strong expansion of the domestic economy. While expectations of continued inflation did make real investments more attractive, it eventually also made debt, and debt-financed speculation with real assets, seem the most attractive way to safeguard and increase wealth. As a result of a macroregime that allowed expectations of inflation to become ingrained and hence created incentives for a flight out of money, the system of domestic credit regulation would come under pressure. Given the incentive for holding debt, the governments' and central banks' attempt to administratively restrict access to credit was confronted with increasing evasion. The increasing problems with making controls effective plus the perceived need for higher interest rates led governments to dismantle the domestic system of credit regulation.

Given the following credit explosion, the deregulation is now considered by many to have been a fatal mistake. Yet, although dismantling credit regulations has an expansive impulse irrespective of the macroregime (as banks scramble for increased market shares), the unique credit explosion that resulted in Scandinavia was ultimately the result of the orientation of the macroregime. The advent of widespread evasion since the late 1970s showed that credit expansion did not have to wait deregulation but was already underway. It is difficult to see how central banks could have maintained control over regulated financial systems as long as macroeconomic regimes effectively served to undermine them. Credit deregulation without a radical change in macroeconomic policies led to an explosion of the financial system and a complete loss of control over the economy. The main elements in the disintegration of the Scandinavian model are described in Figure 8.1.

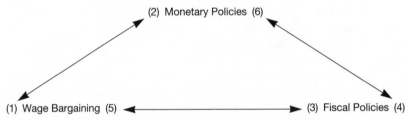

FIGURE 8.1. The unraveling of the Scandinavian model. (1) The failure to check the growth of credit to the economy contributes to labor scarcity and high profits, which in turn increase the incentives of local wage earners as well as employers to defect from centrally negotiated wage bargains. Furthermore, the emergence of a "speculation economy" with high profits and wages in the financial sector makes trade unions, especially blue-collar ones, less willing to support wage moderation. (2) Inflation due to high wage settlements in tight labor markets increases the overall demand for and supply of debt and increasingly makes both the credit rationing system as well as more market-based monetary policy instruments ineffective. (3) Labor scarcity and high wage increases in the private sector make it difficult to contain wage demands in the public sector and thereby lead to increased public spending. (4) Strong monetary growth makes it increasingly difficult to find political support cuts in public spending at a time when high incomes are earned in the "speculation economy." (5) The failure to check fiscal spending contributes to labor scarcity and high profits, which in turn increase the incentives of local wage earners as well as employers to defect from centrally negotiated wage bargains. (6) The failure to contain fiscal spending increases the government's borrowing requirement, adds to the liquidity position of the economy, and thereby counteracts the efforts of the central bank to control the volume of money. Furthermore, buoyant demand in the economy overall as well as inflation increase the overall demand for debt and increasingly make both the credit rationing system as well as more market-based monetary policy instruments ineffective.

The new restrictive policy regime was hence not forced upon the Scandinavian Social Democrats by the forces of international finance but rather constituted an effort to contain domestic inflation. Rather than trying to avoid restrictive impulses from the world economy, both countries since the early 1980s were desperately seeking to cool down their domestic economies. In the early 1980s both countries enforced a ban on foreign borrowing by public authorities. As Swedish deputy minister of finance Erik Åsbrink (SAP) argued, the purpose of this policy was to increase constraints on the domestic economy: "There are many indications that (the policy of public foreign borrowing) has tempted, in a longer perspective, a too expansionary fiscal policy. Due to the state's foreign borrowing it has been possible to have a deficit on the current account year after year without the negative effects becoming sufficiently clear. When the state started to borrow abroad in 1977 to cover the current account deficit a natural corrective mechanisms was abolished" (Åsbrink & Heikensten, 1986, p. 27, my translation). In a further attempt to cool down domestic demand, tax deductibility of interest payments were reduced. In Norway, subsidization of interest rates decreased due to the reduction of the share of state banks in the credit market. All these measures indicate that not external constraints but domestic overheating was the main policy problem.

Further, the abolition of foreign exchange controls during the 1980s must be interpreted in terms of a strategy to increase the external constraints on an overheated domestic economy. Given the importance that the advocates of the external constraint view should attach to exchange controls, it is surprising that Social Democrats in both countries treated external deregulation as a fairly unimportant issue. Under conditions of acute domestic overheating, maintaining regulations that had been created to protect a more expansionary domestic policy stance were not considered crucial. Moreover, exchange controls in an inflationary constellation rather tended to become counterproductive as they closed off capital outflows and hence redirected funds into domestic financial speculation (see, for example, Dammann, 1991, pp. 72–73).

But as none of these measures by itself was sufficient to prevent a further escalation of domestic inflation, even Scandinavian Social Democrats saw no alternative but to implement macroeconomic disinflation along the lines now common in the developed world. As a clear sign of the new policy preferences, both countries tied their currency to the European Currency Unit (ECU) in the early 1990s. Even after the narrow EMS arrangement has declined in the wake of the massive capital flows of late 1992, both governments have made it clear that the involuntary floating of the currency should form no pretense for pursuing more expansionary policies.

Even though both countries experienced a cycle of boom and bust that had no counterpart abroad (see also Stelgum, 1994, pp. 19–26), this did not preclude external constraints from being blamed for much of what went wrong. Apparently heeding the principle that external constraints provide a convenient scapegoat, two main arguments have emerged in retrospect in order to explain the failure to contain the speculative frenzy of the 1980s. First, international financial integration was seen to undermine the credit rationing system by giving lenders access to foreign funds. Second, financial integration was argued to have made more restrictive monetary policies impossible because higher interest rates would merely lead to capital inflows, and a revaluation of the currency would not be credible and hence not feasible.[25]

But even within the neoclassical model from which it originates, the argument that revaluation was impossible is not valid. If the differential between domestic and international interest rates is indeed determined by the degree of confidence in the chosen domestic exchange rate level and if a revaluation would have led to an exchange rate level that was not deemed credible, domestic interest rates would have had to rise, and the ability to pursue restrictive policies would have increased.

Rather, the hesitation with which both governments reacted to domestic overheating was due to a deeply ingrained reluctance to accept the fact that in a monetary economy, and if only macroeconomic means are left to combat inflation, full employment and growth will have to be sacrificed. While restrictive monetary policies were certainly possible, both governments hesitated to use them because they would hit private investment while leaving the public sector relatively unscathed. In a situation where the diagnosis was that the private sector had to be stimulated and the public sector was too big, such a policy seemed perverse. Yet as Scandinavian Social Democrats eventually had to realize, any economy that is allowed to run under prolonged inflation for a long period of time will become uncontrollable.

CONCLUSION

It is no coincidence that the neoclassical view that macroeconomic policies cannot positively affect growth and employment and the external constraints view have become popular simultaneously. Although the proponents of the respective views generally consider themselves to belong to quite opposite theoretical and political camps, they both arrive at the same policy conclusion, namely, that restrictive macroeconomic policies are inevitable and that a return to growth and full employment will depend on microeconomic measures (see Garrett & Lange, 1991, and Cerny, 1990, Chap. 8).

In effect, the reemergence of both the neoclassical and the external constraints view must be understood as the ideological mechanism by which a democratic polity adjusts to the policy priorities of a monetary economy. The democratic constitution of the polity requires, as a rule, that politically viable economic policies must be presented in terms of benefiting the overall performance of the economy. A policy that creates a recession and mass unemployment in order to eliminate inflation does not conform to that normative requirement, but because, as has been argued, in a decentralized economy that is coordinated through the medium of money, governments have only a very limited direct influence on the behavior of market participants, such economies may, in specific constellations, become prone to a cumulative dynamic. In such a constellation economic policies will eventually have no alternative but to restore the coordinating and allocative functions of money by stabilizing the price level. As continued inflation confronts governments with a galloping loss of control—manifested mainly by rampant financial speculation, exploding financial markets, depreciating currencies, and escalating nominal wages—the need to combat inflation is impressed on them ever more clearly. In such a situation the neoclassical position that macroeconomic policies can only affect inflation and that combating inflation will have no costs in terms of growth and employment becomes well-nigh irresistible.

And exactly because the regime shifts in the early 1920s and during the last 2 decades were primarily informed by the goal of eliminating inflation, the fact that the neoclassical promise of a nondiscretionary policy with no negative effects on growth and employment is not fulfilled, does not lead to a change in the basic policy orientation.[26] Ever since the first suspension of Peel's second banking act in 1847, it should have been clear that non-discretionary monetary policies are impossible in a monetary economy (see Herr, 1993, p. 215). Monetary policies were decidedly discretionary during the Gold Standard. In recent times, the monetarist prescription of strict adherence to a money growth rule has proven to be unworkable from its inception.[27] Although perhaps more extreme, the experience of the Thatcher government nevertheless was typical. While firmly committed to the control of monetary aggregates, the Thatcher government, to its great embarrassment, was confronted with a massive overshoot of its £3M target during its first 3 years in office.[28] In fact, monetary policy activism has probably increased in comparison with the first two decades after World War II.

More important, as might have been clear already after the experience of the 1920s, a restrictive monetary regime leads to durable and not transitory mass unemployment. The fear of a resurgence of the recently conquered inflation, however, prevents governments from changing their macroeconomic course in response to its emergence. Instead of interpreting it as evidence that restrictive macroeconomic policies do have long-term effects, its reemergence is therefore attributed to microeconomic deficiencies.

For the political left, the neoclassical position is generally unattractive because it tends to blame (Social Democratic) policy mismanagement, welfare state arrangements, and the trade unions for inflation and unemployment. The initial reaction to the (re)emergence of mass unemployment and monetarism consisted of embedding Keynesian concepts in a corporatist framework. This position, quite correctly in principle, argued that macroeconomic policies could only concentrate on full employment if most of the fight against inflation could be delegated to labor market institutions. Because of their centralized trade unions and tradition of tripartite bargaining between state, employers and unions, corporatist countries like Austria and Sweden for some time during the late 1970s and early 1980s were held out as the examples to emulate. But as these countries also submitted to the new regime this interpretation became untenable. Instead, the external constraints view gained popularity because it allowed the left to maintain its Keynesian convictions, and to shift the blame for the restrictive policies actually pursued to the anonymous financial markets and the structural progress of telecommunications and computing technology. This way of defending the historical correctness of the policies of the past is not only wrong, but also comes at the price of a loss of political initiative and vitality. While neoclassics can enthusiastically argue in favor of the adoption of a set of new policies, the left seems to be reduced to the position of preaching grudging acceptance of what is considered undesirable but inevitable.

If only because of the politically unattractive fatalism implied in the external constraints view, the left also is driven to focus attention on microeconomic policies. Again, the present debate is reminiscent of the 1920s. As a counterweight to the "conservative" supply-side views of deregulation, wage cutting, and welfare state retrenchment, the left-wing version of supply-side policies maintains that high (real) wages and strong trade unions are beneficial as they promote productivity and competitiveness (see, for example, Matzner & Streeck, 1991). But whatever the respective merits of these two positions, it is fundamentally impossible to return to growth and full employment by way of microeconomic policies as long as monetary and exchange rate policies are informed by the goal of maintaining unemployment so as to prevent a resurgence of inflation.[29]

As should be clear from the preceding, the view that external constraints have become insurmountable is not an argument promoted by some political groups in order to push through unnecessary restrictive policies. If a country finds itself in an economic constellation where it is no longer possible to contain inflationary pressures by microeconomic means, a stabilization crisis is inevitable. To the extent that the neoclassical and external constraints view facilitate the adoption of such a policy, they must be considered to play a necessary political role. Rather, the danger of attributing the need for restrictive policies to free international capital flows is that it deflects attention from the real problem and perpetuates a restrictive regime even at times when the labor market situation does not require it.

The crisis that stands at the cradle of a new regime constitutes a trauma that continues to inform policymaking. The desperation with which many nations clung to restrictive policies for fear of renewed inflation during the Great

Depression when the world economy was collapsing under the weight of deflation is perhaps the most telling example of the inertia of regimes. For a more recent and less dramatic example, consider also the lengths to which the Swedish government and the Riksbank went to defend the krone in November 1992 because they feared the reemergence of inflation under a floating currency. Yet at a time when mass unemployment reigns and banks have become very conservative in their lending behavior, due to the recently experienced crisis, it would be very difficult indeed to create an inflationary spiral. Rather than resulting in inflation, the floating of the currency in 1992 in fact meant that the pressure of international financial flows led to a considerable improvement in the position of the exposed sector of the economy against the determined wishes of the government.

In response to the devaluation of sterling in September 1931, Labour MP Tom Johnson is said to have remarked: "They never told us we could do that."[30] Apparently Labour had internalized the alleged insurmountability of the external constraint to such a degree that its abolition came as a complete shock. I hope that we do not need to experience another Great Depression before it is realized that the international environment leaves us with many more policy options than commonly thought.

NOTES

1. The articles of the International Monetary Fund (IMF) in particular.

2. See, for example, Garrett and Lange (1991, pp. 542–543), who argue that during the 1950s and 1960s

> . . . leftist governments were able to pursue the interventionist policies of the full-employment welfare state—epitomized by countercyclical fiscal and monetary policies—without fear of undermining macroeconomic performance. . . . Thus, even if today there are still strong domestic incentives for governments to pursue distinctive partisan strategies . . ., these interdependence arguments suggest that such incentives are now overwhelmed by international constraints.

See also, Huber and Stephens (1992, p. 6): "National sovereignty over economic and social policy was lost due to the internationalization of capital markets," as well as Stewart (1983), and Scharpf (1987, Chap. 11).

3. External constraints are not an important topic in neoclassical economics because macroeconomic policies, even in a (hypothetical) closed economy, are considered unable to durably affect growth and employment. Rather, free capital flows are considered desirable as a protection against domestic inflationary policies. See, for example, Calmfors (1985).

4. The countries are the United States, Britain, Germany, France, Japan, Canada, Italy, Belgium, the Netherlands, Sweden, and Switzerland.

5. A situation of total financial integration would be characterized by cross-na-

tional equality of real interest rates. For this condition to obtain, not only financial markets but also goods markets have to be fully integrated. An observed reduction in total financial integration can hence be due to either reduced financial and/or reduced goods market integration.

6. Tobin (1978, p. 153) proposed an "internationally uniform tax on spot transactions across currencies."

7. See, for example, James Callaghan's famous pronouncement at the 1976 Labour Party conference: "We used to think that you could spend your way out of a recession and increase employment by cutting taxes and increasing government spending. I tell you in all candour that that option no longer exists, and that insofar as it ever did exist, it only worked on each occasion since the war by injecting a bigger dose of inflation into the economy, followed by a higher level of unemployment in the next step" (quoted in Callaghan, 1987, p. 426).

8. For an illustration of this argument, see, for example, Skånland (governor of Norges Bank 1985–1993) (1993, pp. 13–14).

9. The conviction that money and finance ultimately are irrelevant is shared by Marxist and neoclassical thought.

10. The exact relation between nominal wage increases and increased demand for labor will depend on the specific organization and outlook of trade unions and employers' associations and the specific skill composition of the demand for and supply of labor. But as the experience of the 1980s shows, at the point where acute labor scarcity arises, even highly centralized trade unions in a Social Democratic polity will be institutionally unable to prevent an escalation of nominal wages.

11. While short-term bank deposits are usually counted as money, they do carry a risk of default and therefore really are a form of credit. Normally obscure, this point becomes very clear in periods of severe deflation when the public attempts to withdraw its deposits for fear of bank default. See also Spahn (1986, p. 167).

12. This is of course, not to imply that a centralized, planned economy could be managed with superior economic outcomes. The historical record quite convincingly shows the opposite.

13. Relative price stability does not mean the complete absence of any change in the overall price level. Cumulative processes emerge only if market participants come to expect deflation or inflation to be durable and adjust their decisions accordingly. A fairly high, one-shot increase in prices which is clearly seen to be caused by exceptional short-term conditions will generally prove fairly harmless. In the words of Alan Greenspan: "For all practical purposes, price stability means that expected changes in the average price level are small enough and gradual enough that they do not materially enter business and household decisions" (quoted in Skånland, 1993, p. 16).

14. Lloyd George election campaign speech, 24 November 1918 (quoted in Boyle, 1967, p. 467).

15. Lo Archives, Sekretariatet Representantskapsprotokoll, Box A2A:2.

16. In essence, this was of course a highly political debate. In the first interpretation the blame for the hyperinflation lies with the Allies, while in the second interpretation the German polity must carry the responsibility.

17. "The inflation in Germany until 1923 was not the result of a policy, but rather a lack of policy" (Laursen & Pedersen, 1964, p. 123). See also Webb (1989, p. 7), who notes that the Reichsbank pursued an accommodating policy.

18. Conversely, observing the spectacle of German hyperinflation strengthened other countries' commitment to restrictive policies.

19. France, Belgium, the Netherlands, Switzerland, Italy, and Poland.

20. Germany decided to maintain the gold parity of the Reichsmark. Since it also pursued an expansionary policy since 1933, this meant that the Reichsmark effectively had to be turned into a nonconvertible currency.

21. Former Conservative Chancellor of the Exchequer Nigel Lawson captures the nature of the new regime quite accurately:

> The conclusion on which the present Government's economic policy is based is that there is indeed a proper distinction between the objectives of macroeconomic and microeconomic policy, and a need to be concerned with both of them. But the proper role of each is precisely the opposite of that assigned to it by the conventional post-War wisdom. It is the conquest of inflation, and not the pursuit of growth and employment, which is or should be the objective of macroeconomic policy. And it is the creation of conditions conducive to growth and employment, and not the suppression of price rises which is or should be the objective of microeconomic policy (1993, p. 414–415)

Yet to expect a revival of growth and employment from microeconomic policies under a macroregime which discourages investment is illusory. As in the 1920s such "supply side" policies during the last 2 decades have disappointed the hopes originally placed in them.

22. In Britain this policy is generally known as stop-and-go. British stop-and-go policies commonly are interpreted in a negative light. Yet in terms of growth and employment, this was one of the most successful periods in British economic history. For a description of the short-term policy cycles in Sweden, see Martin (1985) and Swenson (1989, pp. 144–147).

23. Strictly speaking, embracing monetarist policies provides an incentive for maintaining exchange restrictions because, as Kaldor (1983, p. 66) points out with respect to the British deregulation of 1979, the volume of money is more difficult to control in a deregulated system. If one interprets the new regime as being primarily informed by the goal to stop inflation by means of restrictive macroeconomic policies, rather than by rigidly enforcing a money growth rule, Thatcher's decision is perfectly sensible. See also Lawson (1993, pp. 38–42, 82).

24. Norway joined the Snake in 1972, Sweden one year later.

25. The Swedish Riksbank especially has argued that it was not possible to combat the overheating of the 1980s by means of revaluation.

26. See also Healey (1989, p. 434): "I have never met a private or central banker who believed the monetarist mumbo-jumbo." Former Bundesbank president Otmar Emminger (1987, p. 439) argues that monetarism is severely deficient as an economic theory, but that it provides useful services in convincing the public of the need for restrictive monetary policies.

27. See Argy, Brennan, and Stevens (1990). Also Emminger (1987, p. 439, my translation): "The development of the volume of money is an important auxiliary indicator, but I have learnt very quickly—from our own experiences of 1975–76 and from foreign experiences—that the relationship between the volume of money and total demand can be unstable or even distorted, also from one year to the other," and

Lawson (1993, p. 454): "Had there been a monetary aggregate with a clear and predictable causal connection with inflation, I should certainly have used it. The problem was that no such aggregate existed."

28. The £M3 targets for the years 1979–1980, 1980–1981 and 1981–1982 were, respectively, 7–11%, 7–11%, and 6–10%. The actual outcomes during these years were 16.2%, 18.4%, and 12.8%, respectively. Source: Lawson (1993, p. 1079).

29. See also Norges Bank board member Tove Strand Gerhardsen's dissenting opinion to the Bank's letter of 19, October 1994 to the ministry of finance: ". . . active labor market policies together with incomes policies is, and should be the Norwegian road to low inflation and not an employment-reducing (*sysselsettingsbremsende*) macropolicy" (Norges Bank, 1994, p. 287, my translation).

30. Quoted in Kindleberger (1987, p. 332). The remark has also been attributed to Sidney Webb, a member of the second Labour government. See Temin (1989, p. 112), and the references given there.

REFERENCES

Argy, V., Brennan, A., & Stevens, G. (1990). Monetary targeting. The international experience. *Economic Record, 66,* 37–62.

Åsbrink, E., & Heikenstein, L. (1986). Valutaflödena 1985 och den ekonomiska politiken. *Skandinaviska Enskilda Banken Kvartalskrift, 1,* 21–27.

Bank of England (1978). Reflections on the conduct of monetary policy. *Bank of England Quarterly Bulletin, 18*(1), 31–37.

Bjerve, P. J. (1989). Strategiar for den "konomiske politikken i ettrekrigstida. In G. Hansen et al. (Eds.), *Mennesket i sentrum: Festskrift til Helge Seips 70–årsdag* (pp. 109–135). Oslo: Tanno.

Bordo, M. D., & Jonung, L. (1994). *Monetary regimes, inflation and monetary reform: An essay in honor of Axel Leijonhufvud* (Working Paper No. 16). Stockholm: Stockholm School of Economics.

Boyle, A. (1967). *Montagu Norman.* London: Cassell.

Brown, B. (1987). *The flight of international capital.* London: Routledge.

Callaghan, J. (1987). *Time and change.* London: Collins.

Calmfors, L. (1985). Valutaregleringen kan avvecklas! *Skandinaviska Enskilda Banken Kvartalsskrift, 4,* 88–93.

Cerny, P. G. (1990). *The changing architecture of politics.* London: Sage.

Dahl, S. (1989). *Kleppepakkene—Feilgrep eller sunn fornuft?* Oslo: Solum.

Dammann, A. (1991). *Fra penger og kreditt til gjeld og fallitt.* Oslo: Author.

Dimsdale, N. H. (1991). British monetary policy since 1945. In N. F. R. Crafts & N. W. C. Woodward (Eds.), *The British economy since 1945* (pp. 89–140). Oxford: Clarendon Press.

Dobloug, T. A. (1992). *Norsk Valutakurspolitikk 1971–90.* Oslo: Hovedoppgave i Statsvitenskap.

Dow, A. C., & Dow, S. C. (1989). Endogenous money creation and idle balances. In J. Pheby (Ed.), *New directions in post Keynesian economics* (pp. 147–164). Aldershot: Edward Elgar.

Eichengreen, B. (1992). *Golden fetters.* New York: Oxford University Press.

Elvander, N. (1988). *Den Svenska modellen* Stockholm: Allmänna.

Emminger, O. (1987). *D-Mark, dollar, währungskrisen.* Stuttgart: Deutsche Verlagsonstalt.

Feldman, G. (1993). *The great disorder.* New York: Oxford University Press.

Feldt, K.-O. (1991). *Alla dessa dagar . . . i regeringen 1982–1990.* Stockholm: Norstedts.

Garrett, G., & Lange, P. (1991). Political responses to interdependence: What is "left" for the left? *International Organization, 45*(4), 539–564.

Gates, R. A. (1973). Von der Sozialpolitik zur Wirtschaftspolitik? Das Dilemma der deutschen Sozialdemokratie in der Krise 1929–1933. In H. Mommsen, D. Petzina, & B. Weisbrod (Eds.), *Industrielles system und politische Entwicklung in der Weimarer Republik* (pp. 205–225). Düsseldorf: Droste.

Hanisch, T. J. (1979). Om virkninger av paripolitikken. *(Norsk) Historisk Tidsskrift, 58,* 239–268.

Hardach, K. (1973). Zur zeitgenössischen Debatte der Nationalökonomen über die Ursachen der deutschen Nachkriegsinflation. In H. Mommsen, D. Petzina, & B. Weisbrod (Eds.), *Industrielles system und politische Entwicklung in der Weimarer Republik* (pp. 368–374). Düsseldorf: Droste.

Healey, D. (1989). *The time of my life.* New York: Norton.

Helleiner, E. (1994). *States and the re-emergence of global finance.* Ithaca: Cornell University Press.

Herr, H. (1990). *Theorie der internationalen Geldwirtschaft.* Unpublished manuscript, Berlin.

Herr, H. (1994). *The international monetary system and domestic economic policy.* Unpublished manuscript, Berlin.

Hertz-Eichenrode, D. (1982). *Wirtschaftskrise und Arbeitsbeschaffung.* Frankfurt am Main: Campus.

Howson, S. (1974). The origins of dear money, 1919–20. *Economic History Review* (2nd ser.), 17(1), 88–107.

Howson, S. (1975). *Domestic monetary management in Britain 1919–38.* Cambridge: Cambridge University Press.

Huber, E., & Stephens, J. (1992, September). *Economic internationalization, the European Community, and the social democratic welfare state.* Paper presented at the annual meeting of the American Political Science Association, Chicago.

International Herald Tribune. (1993, 27 April).

Jaeger, H. (1988). *Geschichte der Wirtschaftsordnung in Deutschland.* Frankfurt am Main: Suhrkamp.

Kaldor, N. (1983). *The economic consequences of Mrs. Thatcher.* London: Duckworth.

Karleby, N. (1921). En prisfallsperiod och dess följder. *Tiden, 2,* 289–308.

Keynes, J. M. (1937). The general theory of employment. In D. Moggridge (Ed.), *The Collected Writings of John Maynard Keynes* (Vol. 14, pp. 109–123). London: Macmillan.

Keynes, J. M. (1973). *The general theory of employment, interest and money.* London: Macmillan. (Original work published 1936)

Keynes, J. M. (1980) Speech to the House of Lords, 23 May 1944. In D. Moggridge (Ed.), *The collected writings of John Maynard Keynes.* London: Macmillan.

Kindleberger, C. P. (1987). *A financial history of Western Europe.* London: George Allen & Unwin.

Langli, J. C. (1993). Sentralbankenes rolle i penge- og valutamarkedet: Nye institusjonelle forhold og nye aktörer. *Sosialökonomen, 11,* 10–15.

Laursen, K., & Pedersen, J. (1964). *The German inflation 1918–1923*. Amsterdam: North-Holland.

Lawson, N. (1993). *The view from No. 11*. New York: Doubleday.

Layard, R. (1986). *How to beat unemployment*. Oxford: Oxford University Press.

Lie, A. (1987). Det europeiske monet're system (EMS) og norsk valutapolitikk. *Internasjonal Politikk, 1–2*, 67–89.

Martin, A. (1985). Wages, profits and investment in Sweden. In L. N. Lindberg & C. S. Maier (Eds.), *The politics of inflation and economic stagnation*. (pp. 403–466). Washington, DC: The Brookings Institution.

Matthews, R. G. O (1968). Why has Britain had full employment since the war? *Economic Journal, 78*(311), 555–569.

Matzner, E., & Streeck, W. (1991). Introduction: Towards a socio-economics of employment in a post-Keynesian economy. In E. Matzner & W. Streeck (Eds.), *Beyond Keynesianism* (pp. 1–20). Aldershot: Edward Elgar.

McNeil, W. C. (1986). *American money and the Weimar republic*. New York: Columbia University Press.

Mjøset, L. (Ed.). (1986). *Norden Dagen Derpå*. Oslo: Universitetsforlaget.

Moses, J. (1994). Abdication from national policy autonomy: What is left to leave? *Politics and Society, 22*(2), 125–148.

Norges Bank. (1994). Det "konomiske opplegget for 1995. *Penger og Kreditt, 4*, 281–287.

OECD (Organization for Economic Cooperation and Development). (1988). *Why economic policies change course: Eleven case studies*. Paris: Author.

Östlind, A. (1945). *Svensk Samhällsekonomi, 1914–1922*. Stockholm: Svenska Bankföreningen.

Oxelheim, L. (1990). *International financial integration*. Berlin: Springer.

Qvigstad, J. F., & Skjaeveland, A. (1994). Valutakursregimes—Historiske Erfaringer og Fremtidige Utfordringer. In *Stabilitet og Langsiktighet: Festskrift til Hermod Skånland* (pp. 235–271). Olso: Aschehoug/Norges Bank.

Riese, H. (1986). *Theorie der Inflation*. Tuebingen: J. C. B. Mohr.

Riese, H. (1987). *Wider den Dezisionismus der Theorie der Wirtschaftspolitik*. Unpublished manuscript, Fachbereich Wirtschaftswissenschaft, Freie Universität Berlin.

Sandberg, A. (1919, 6 December). Saken som nu beskjaeftiger vor Handelsstand sterkest. *Verdens Gang, 304*, p. 9.

Sayers, R. S. (1976). *The Bank of England, 1891–1944* (3 vols.). Cambridge: Cambridge University Press.

Scharpf, F. W. (1987). *Sozialdemokratische Krisenpolitik in Europa*. Frankfurt am Main: Campus.

Skånland, H. (1993). *Economic perspectives*. Address by Governor Hermod Skånland at the meeting of the Supervisory Council of Norges Bank on 18 February 1993. Oslo: Norges Bank.

Skidelsky, R. (1967). *Politicians and the slump*. London: Macmillan.

Spahn, H.-P. (1986). *Stagnation in der Geldwirtschaft*. Frankfurt am Main: Campus.

Steigum, E., Jr. (1994). Nordisk Økonomisk Krise: Hvilken rolle kan finans—og pengepolitikken spille? In A. Sandmo (Ed.), *Perspektiv på Arbeidsledigheten* (pp. 19–60). Bergen: Fagbokforlaget.

Stewart, M. (1983). *The age of interdependence*. Cambridge, MA: MIT Press.

Swenson, P. (1989). *Fair shares*. Ithaca, NY: Cornell University Press.

Temin, P. (1989). *Lessons from the Great Depression*. Cambridge: MIT Press.

Thygesen, N. (1982). Monetary policy. In A. Boltho (Ed.), *The European economy: Growth and crisis* (pp. 329–364). Oxford: Oxford University Press.

Tilton, T. (1991). *The political theory of Swedish social democracy*. Oxford: Clarendon Press.

Tobin, J. (1978). A proposal for international monetary reform. *Eastern Economic Journal, 4*, 153–159.

Tobin, J. (1980). *Asset accumulation and economic activity*. Chicago: University of Chicago Press.

Unger, B. (1990). Possibilities and constraints for national economic policies in small countries: The case of Austria. *German Politics and Society, 21*, 63–77.

Webb, S. (1989). *Hyperinflation and stabilization in West Germany*. New York: Oxford University Press.

Wicksell, K. (1898). *Geld zins and güterpreise.* Jena, Germany.

Zacchia, C. (1977). International trade and capital movements 1920–1970. In C. M. Cipolla (Ed.), *The Fontana economic history of Europe: Vol. 5. The twentieth century—2* (pp. 509–602). Sussex: Harvester.

Zevin, R. (1992). Are world financial markets more open? If so why and with what effects? In T. Banuri & J. B. Schor (Eds.), *Financial openness and national autonomy* (pp. 43–83). Oxford: Clarendon Press.

CHAPTER 9

Representation Unbound
GLOBALIZATION AND DEMOCRACY

Murray Low

> In late-modernity, the nostalgic idealism of territorial
> democracy fosters the nostalgic realism of international
> relations and vice-versa. The nostalgia is for a time
> when a coherent politics of "place" could be imagined
> as a real possibility for the future.
> —CONNOLLY (1991, p. 463)

INTRODUCTION

When politics is viewed spatially it is, more often than not, characterized as a set of areal phenomena. The geography of states, from geopolitics to neo-Marxism, has been centered on a territorialized politics characterized by the construction of areal spaces by state organizations at various scales. Electoral geography, likewise, has focused the vision of political geography on the region, district, constituency, or locality as constitutive elements of the areal space of modern politics.

The metaphors of the arena or container have become common in geographically informed writings on politics. The arena as a space of direct physical conflict has long been irresistible as a representation of political conflict. Skocpol (1979) has drawn attention to this metaphor in her work on states, to try and sustain a conception of the state as an independent political actor, and to draw attention to how domestic processes and events are partly constituted by processes at the level of systems of states. Giddens (1981) speaks of states as "power containers," and Taylor (1994, 1995) has written on the implications of such a conception of "states as containers" in the geopolitical context. The use of areal metaphors in talking about states is a recognition of the importance of processes of spatial enclosure in modern politics: national states have (violently) constructed areal spaces within which territorial sovereignty operates. Nevertheless, there are a series of normative discourses that have become more or less implicated in this observation, that inform a wide range of work in the social sciences, and that are coming under increasing scrutiny.

Conceptualizing political spaces as areal, as a series of (mutually constitutive) arenas, privileges a way of thinking about political activity as a series of confrontations between agents. These arena occupants—which may be individuals or classes, groups, movements—square off, interact, struggle, compromise, constitute each other, and so on in academic writing as though mutually co-present. Moreover, they act in, through, and around the state, conceived of as a kind of center of this areal space constituting politics. This copresence of citizens, interest groups, classes, and so on within a definable areal space has come to seem an indispensable condition for democratic political institutions and practices. It is hard to imagine democracy without reference to bounded political communities, however divided internally.

A second ingredient of this areal view is that a series of spatial correspondences between political areas and those defined by economic processes and "cultures" is seen as a desirable, even necessary, condition for democracy. In the 20th century at least, democracy has been premised upon a congruence between cultural and political areas ("self-determination of nations") and between the area within which the state can act and key economic processes (macroeconomic management/social democracy/social citizenship).

When these two assumptions are given value as preconditions for democratic politics, we can speak, with Connolly (1991), of a "politics of place." Connolly is referring to a kind of politics that is centered on areal territorial units to which the identities of political communities can be unproblematically referred. Much democratic theory has been informed by a politics of place of this kind. Many accounts are structured around epochs of differently organized democracy, distinguished by the scale of the areas involved. These narratives of democratic development typically concern a scale-enlarging sequence running from the Greek city-state, via the modern national state, to some version or other of a contemporary transition to transnational democratic forms. In different ways, for example, the recent writings of Dahl (1990) and Held (1991, 1993) revolve around such narratives. The areal political communities involved may become larger and more complex, necessitating more mediated forms of democratic practice (Dahl identifies the transition from direct to representative democracy with the spatial expansion of the polity involved in the formation of national states), but it is clear that some form of polity which is areal, bounded, and hence encompassing a political community of some sort is assumed to be a prerequisite for democratic practices (Streek, 1992, p. 514).

"Globalization," it is usually suggested, disrupts bounded national communities and throws political, economic, and cultural processes out of congruence with one another. From the point of view of much thinking about democracy, therefore, processes of globalization are a matter of some concern: a politics of place no longer seems possible at the scale of the national state, and severe strain is placed upon the efficacy, even possibility, of democracy as usually conceptualized (Archibugi & Held, 1995; Held, 1991; Streek, 1992, p. 517). Much work suggests that in conjunction with heightened levels of capital and information mobility, changes in the international financial system, and associated reconfigurations of cultures and identities, the national state is becoming necessarily superseded by local, regional, and transnational forms of governance. The proliferation of functional (as opposed to territorial) modes of regulation via international regimes, a heightened profile for the United Nations, the General Agreement on Tariffs and Trade (GATT), and other global institutions, and seemingly greater economic responsibilities (if not powers) of local governments are compared to the apparent incapacity of national states to manage societies in the same manner as they did before the 1970s. The last 20 years of restructuring in the developed countries have been accompanied, in this sort of account, by a *scale* reorganization of governance (Guéhenno, 1995; Horsman & Marshall, 1993; Ohmae, 1993, 1995; Panitch, 1994; Preteceille, 1990).

Given the association of the national state with organized violence, exclusionary identities, and the ideological suppression of sub- and transnational interests, it is hard to imagine it being mourned. To the extent that there is deep concern about its decline, it is because of its role as a territorial anchor for modern democratic politics (Streek & Schmitter, 1991; Tilly, 1992, pp. 247–248; 1995). By the mid-1990s, many recent arguments about the deteriorating condition of Western democracy in general have come under greater scrutiny. In particular, there has been a reassertion of the continuing empirical importance of political parties and a more nuanced appreciation of party/social movement relations (Katz & Mair, 1994; Kitschelt, 1990; Maisel, 1994) after a stream of "decline of party" arguments and a flurry of interest in "new social movements" in the 1980s (cf. Lawson & Merkl, 1988; Sjoeblom, 1983). Prognoses about the impact of globalization on the efficacy of democratic arrangements, however, are proving quite resilient. This is so despite widespread skepticism about the more dramatic versions of decline-of-the-national-state arguments (Dunn, 1994; Gertler, 1988; Gordon, 1988; Hirst & Thompson, 1992, 1995; Thompson & Krasner, 1989), and despite arguments that contemporary problems of state and party legitimacy, welfare state decline and the erosion of citizenship rights have causes other than those related to globalization (Notermans, 1993; Zolberg, 1995).

Debates about the decline of the national state have settled into a pattern in which theses about the globalization and localization of politics are issued, at times without regard to the equally prolific literature suggesting that national institutions are (still) both uniquely capacitous and legitimate policy-making entities. The strangely static quality of these debates may be attributable to the fact that arguments are embedded in a conceptual system in which areal communities at different scales are privileged by different writers, but in which the focus on areal political communities and processes is accepted by all. The terms in which democratic futures are discussed—"the global," "the national," "the local"—do not change much from one argument to another, and can seem, even in the geographical literature, somewhat unexamined.

Moreover, where attempts are made to break out of this system of terms by redefining politics and regulatory structures as having "variable geometries" or articulating territorial and functional organizations at a number of levels and scales, the role of democratic procedures becomes more problematic than ever. Hirst and Thompson (1995), for example, argue that the creation of an effective system of global regulation out of a range of organizational and spatial forms has to take precedence over questions of democracy. This, indeed, appears to be the rationale behind the pattern of political development of the European Union (EU), a model to which Hirst and Thompson repeatedly return. Democracy appears indissolubly linked to areal spaces. If globalization undermines national-state capacities, local and global political democratic arenas can be imagined as alternatives, on condition that they are constructed by analogy with national states. If governance is redefined in nonareal terms, it appears that democratization is off the immediate agenda.

The first two sections of this chapter discuss two types of writing that seem to promise means of resolving this dilemma, or, rather, they suggest directions worth pursuing in *beginning* to resolve this dilemma, as the problem is immense. Just as the development of many of the widely valued forms of social and economic regulation associated with the national state would have been unlikely without formal and informal democratic pressures, the development of forms of regulation adequate to the configurations of a changing global space-economy seems unlikely if they are not shaped in the long run by democratic processes and institutions less "imprisoned" in areal spaces and the bounded political communities they harbor. Manuel Castells' (1989) arguments about the possible democratic regulation of economic networks are considered, but found to remain tied to a conception of political community that it is increasingly hard to sustain. The work of certain critical international relations theorists, which presents a direct critique of the centrality of bounded political communities in political thought is then considered. While they offer a valuable set of criticisms of Connolly's (1991) politics of place, and of the supposed coherence of national political communities, I argue that as a result of a preoccupation with state sovereignty rooted in their (proper) interest in international relations, they stop short of producing a vision of a democratic politics that is not organized around areal space and an account of mechanisms though which democracy could be constructed in nonareal forms.

The later sections of the chapter explore the politics of place as an ideology that obscures the variety of spatial forms assumed by democratic processes even in national states and that predicates democratic processes on truncated relationships of representation and mediation between political actors and states. Emphasis is placed, in particular, on recognizing the basis of democratic processes, and of processes of democratic representation in particular, in networks which in practice and in principle operate at cross-purposes to the areal spatial forms generally invoked by notions of political community.

SPACES OF FLOWS: ECONOMIC GLOBALIZATION

Areal forms of space are important in economic geography, both as units for the collection and aggregation of data, and in the form of substantive objects such as local labor markets, national economies, and industrial districts. These areal economic forms, however, are not generally regarded as closed or bounded to the same degree as are political spaces. They have to be supplemented with other forms of economic space, network spaces in particular, for analysis to proceed. In economic geography, globalization is not a matter of the construction of a "global" economic space or arena, but of the restructuring and extension of networks of flows (of money, goods, and people), and of their articulation with areal or "regional" spaces at different scales. Although it is possible to construct some recent work, that on industrial districts, for example, as presenting a vision of a developing patchwork of juxtaposed agglomerations of economic activity (Amin & Thrift, 1992), it is clear that as this literature evolves and whatever its demerits, it is concerned with neither localities nor "globalization" per se but with specifying the developing configurations of internationalized flows in networks as they intersect and form more or less sedimented nodes of investment, linkages and skills in particular locations (e.g., Storper, 1992). In this sense, the question as to whether emergent economic geographies should be viewed as congeries of regional specificities or as sets of interregional linkages seems rather forced (Lipietz, 1993). The economic geography associated with discussions of globalization considers both internationalized networks and their complicity with and embeddedness in particularly configured areal spaces.

Although there is an implicit set of arguments about the possibility of democratically informed policymaking in many writings about economic globalization, explicit formulations are rare. For an interesting example, consider this passage from Manuel Castells' (1989) *The Informational City*, which is structured around a basic distinction between "spaces of flows" and "spaces of places":

> ... [T]he ultimate logic of restructuring is based on the avoidance of historically established mechanisms of social, economic and political control by the power-holding organizations. ... The emergence of the space of flows actually expresses the disarticulation of place-based societies and cultures by the organizations of power and production that continue to dominate society without submitting to its control. In the end, even democracies become powerless confronted with the ability of capital to circulate globally, of information to be transferred secretly, of markets to be penetrated or neglected, of planetary strategies of political–military power to be decided without the knowledge of nations, and of cultural messages to be marketed, packaged, recorded, and beamed in and out of people's minds. (1989, p. 349)

Several things are worth noting. First, the desire and ability of firms to escape particular forms of national regulation, and the emergence of internationalized information flows, are used to suggest that the economy is increasingly evading national, and indeed in this case any kind of areal or place-based, control predicated on forms of territorial closure. "Spaces of places" are, in this world, real but thoroughly subordinated to the "space of flows." Second, *and because of this*, democratic forms of social control are incapable of managing the new situation. Third, as spaces of places go, systems of national states are *particularly* incapable of regulating this new order. Castells (1989, p. 352) describes them a little later on as "functionally powerless and institutionally bureaucratized," and this informs his predilection for local governments as nodes of a potentially effective network exercising a form of social control appropriate to the space of flows.

Finally, as in many discourses on globalization, national forms of democracy are credited (Castells' "*even* democracies") with powers in retrospect which it is unclear they had in the first place. The particular examples here are instructive. Where have democracies *ever* been able to stop capital circulating internationally? This is not the same issue as that of capital being unable to circulate for technological or infrastructural reasons, or because of economic conditions. Certainly there have been changes in the scope and speed of capital circulation, partly as a result of changes in the regulatory role of national states. However, these consequences of deregulation have been the results of policy action, and it would be misleading to suggest that they have occurred against some resistance from national states, democratic or not, rather than as part of a transformation of economic policy developed by national states singly and in concert since the 1970s. Since when has information *not* been transferred secretly, within or between democracies? Much of the difficulty in debates about "elites" in the literature of empirical democratic theo-

ry, for example, was that so much activity in democracies was transacted in secret that elitist theories of the state were "nonverifiable" in the terms of behavioral social science. It is not clear that democracy has been an effective
mechanism determining market penetration or neglect. To say the least, the
relationships between democracy and international political–military strategy
have been ambiguous, particularly as so much national policy in this area has
been conducted outside the public gaze. Democracy has not generally, despite
the importance of national states in cultural change, been able to control cultural messages, either. Perhaps this is not what Castells is arguing, and, indeed,
many of his comments make more sense when related to national states than
to democracy, but his argument does mirror others in implying that an age of
democratic social control at the national level is over and that this social control was (relatively) adequate to pre- late 20th century economic forms because those forms were place-based, embedded in areal space, and therefore
manageably congruent with the space of national democracy.

Castells does consider a way out of this crisis of control in a world regulated by the "placeless logic" he identifies. Again in common with a lot of recent literature, he sees the decline of national democracy as producing a new,
dual object of study. The internationalized space of flows has its counterpart
in weak and subordinated spaces of places constituted by the localities forming the nodes of informational networks. Local governments perforce become
crucial for reimagining democratic possibilities. Nevertheless,

> A growing social schizophrenia has resulted between, on the one hand, re-
> gional societies and local institutions and, on the other hand, the rules and
> operations of the economic system at the international level. The more the
> economy becomes interdependent on a global scale, the less can regional
> and local governments, as they exist today, act upon the basic mechanisms
> that condition the daily existence of their citizens. . . . The ultimate chal-
> lenge of this fundamental dimension of the restructuring process is the pos-
> sibility that the local state, and therefore people's control over their lives,
> will fade away, unless democracy is reinvented to match the space of flows
> with the power of places. (Castells, 1989, p. 347)

Much current writing revalidates "the local" as a means of revitalizing
democracy in current conditions beside, and in many ways complementary
to, the ever-growing work on local economic development strategies and increasingly proactive local governance structures. For Castells, however, the international space of flows calls not only for reinvigorated local or regional
democracy, but for networked forms of local or regional democracy (cf. Amin
& Thrift, 1995). This is important as it implies that areal political solutions per
se may be infeasible in terms of the democratic regulation of economic networks. In fact, in its stark contrast between the space of flows and spaces of

places, Castells' argument as a whole opens up the possibility of rethinking democracy and politics more generally in nonareal terms.

However, Castells' vision appears to involve democracy within places in conjunction with sets of intergovernmental linkages, rather than forms of democratic practice that are organized around networked forms of space. As a result, the outline solution remains at the level of strategic alliances of local and city governments, somewhat along the lines of the Hanseatic league or other city–state forms of the early modern period.[1] This solution takes the form it does because Castells cannot dissociate democracy (and perhaps politics in general) from the notion of place. This identification of democratic politics with place turns on the issue of identity, which it is argued can best be achieved through a reinvigoration of locally grounded community formation. Castells' recourse to the importance of local community as a source of identity raises several other interesting problems. First, the desirability of a place-based politics as a source of identity that is resistant to the space of flows appears to clash with the imperatives of political action within interlocal networks. On the one hand, local and regional identities are crucial in creating forms of social life that, because they are place-based, are *detached* from network-organized functional imperatives. On the other hand, local governments, closer to their communities than national states, can act more effectively in relation to international flows of money and information because they are able to quickly articulate local needs and "respond flexibly to the requirements of the flows of power, so identifying the best bargaining position in each case" (Castells, 1989, p. 352). It is not clear that the dilemma facing such local governments would be any different from that currently argued to be facing "spaces of places" at larger scales, where trade-offs have to be made between social needs and economic transactions. It is not clear that "closeness" to citizens would really make a great deal of difference to the difficulties encountered, and the articulation of localities with functional imperatives surely undermines their value as detached identity-forming havens in a world of flows.

Second, an analogy between small and middle-sized firms and local governments is at work, as suggested by the use of the idea of flexibility, and by the notion of networking as a means of mobilizing resources and organizing shifting strategies within a system of small, disintegrated contractors. In modeling a networked politics along the lines of emergent forms of interfirm cooperation, Castells avoids the trickier problems involved when trying to reimagine democracy when areal arrangements no longer seem to deliver workable solutions. Without suggesting that these problems are not important in the case of economic networks, especially in considering issues of democratizing corporate governance, the firms–governments analogy here is of limited utility in dealing with those questions of political identity and political community that Castells clearly wants to raise.

Third, the problem of the identity of political communities arises in relation to Castells' (1989, p. 350) question of "how to articulate the meaning of places to this new functional space?" The answer is that this could be achieved through shifting alliances of "organized, self-identified communities" (Castells, 1989, p. 352). The sorts of "self-identified communities" that Castells identifies as the "nodes" of these alliances have come in for a good deal of skepticism recently in disciplines like international relations, where there has been increasing unease about the degree to which theories depend on such entities, largely, but not exclusively, at the national scale.[2] It is not just that such a picture is in danger of overhomogenizing political communities by referring them to one particular local identity. To speak of such communities subsequently communicating transparently with each other, the argument would run, avoids facing up to the ways in which the interests, identities, and boundaries of such communities are, far from being readily identifiable by governments, constituted by all manner of interrelationships and flows between them. Such reservations apply equally to communities of a subnational type. In short, Castells invokes a model of communication between agents that have defined interests and identities prior to their external relations and communicative action, which may be problematic in general, let alone for communities and/or their local authorities (Derrida, 1982b).

Castells (1989, p. 353) refers to the tendential "deconstruction" of localities by "the placeless logic of flows-based organizations," but his attempt to recuperate democracy through networks of local governments and self-identified communities shares many characteristics with the old world of national spaces, where democracy was effective because of the (areal) copresence of political actors and the scale congruence of economic, political, and cultural processes. The difference is that in this new world there will be flexible copresence orchestrated by local governments "close" to their constituents and flexible congruity at the level of networks. The self-identified community, negotiating with its counterparts, facilitates all sorts of talk about how, despite the decline of the national political arena as an effective regulator of the economy by broader interests, democracy can be reconstituted locally, or interlocally, on the basis of similar forms of copresence of political interests and congruence of economic and political institutions.

It is difficult, however, to imagine alternatives in the face of such entrenched sets of ideas. Certainly, there are elements of Castells' arguments that are attractive and seem to be useful building blocks for a less place-bound set of conceptions. The mobilization of network concepts from economic geography seem particularly apposite, and will be taken up presently. In the following section, another literature is considered, which explicitly critiques the notion of political community. Does a literature that explicitly draws on notions from deconstruction and critiques of identity provide a more thoroughgoing response to the politics of place?

"THE PRETENSE OF REPRESENTATION": CRITICAL INTERNATIONAL RELATIONS THEORY

There has been a proliferation in recent years of critical literature on international relations that seeks to problematize, through a critique of state sovereignty, the sorts of areal closure of democratic politics discussed earlier (cf. Agnew & Corbridge, 1995, pp. 78–100). Through applications of poststructuralist theory, deconstruction in particular, the realist and idealist traditions in international relations are shown to be two sides of the same theoretical coin, and constituted as such by the elaboration of the notion of state sovereignty, which "fixes a clear demarcation between life inside and outside a centered political community" (Walker, 1993, p. 62) as the given of much modern work in the field.

State sovereignty has become the central focus of much contemporary critical work in international relations because it is the central concept in a network of discourses inside and outside the academy about modern politics (Ashley, 1995; Walker, 1987, 1991b; Walker & Magnusson, 1990). It guarantees a number of persistent dualisms. It permits a separation of "domestic" and "international" politics in theory, and also institutionally in the separation of international relations and "security" studies from the social sciences. It has structured the world's population into a global "humanity" and a set of mutually exclusive "citizenries." It has underwritten the seemingly endless counterposition of "realism" (as a body of work constructing international politics as an anarchic world that must be explained with reference to the national interests of states) and "idealism" (as a body of work arguing for the viability of consensual international decision making) as the (only) two major forms of international relations theory. These theories have dominated international relations for so long because the principle of sovereignty permits the imagination of a realm of experience to which the range of theories and arguments appropriate to social life inside states does not apply. As a result, a peculiar stasis in the way that international politics is conceived of and talked about, a stasis that permits talk about realist theory being equally applicable to Thucydides' Athens and the Cold War, can be reconciled with developmentalist ideas about social life inside states.

State sovereignty owes its tenacity in structuring so many aspects of political discourse to its intimate relationship to modern political institutions and because it is closely related to a stream of broader concepts in the Western tradition. Broadly speaking, theorists like R. B. J. Walker and Richard Ashley proceed by connecting the dualisms that are the stuff of political theory, and that permit the isolation of international relations theory from other bodies of work, to series of other dualisms, so as to try and undermine and disrupt the long unchallenged "common sense" of their discipline (Walker, 1993, pp. 8–9). State sovereignty can be seen as a way in which the broader dualisms of universality and particularity, identity and difference, are settled in political discourse. The sovereign state performs this settlement through its construction of political community as coextensive with its division of territorial space (Walker, 1990, p. 15). Without the mutually exclusive division of territory, and the production of political insides and outsides (Walker, 1993) that this division achieves, it is argued, the ways in which we think about political community and democracy might be rather different.

Walker locates the emergence of modern discourses about state sovereignty in the early modern period, where it formed an ideological resolution of contradictions between the universalist claims of the Church and the Holy Roman Empire and the apparent particularism of aspiring political–territorial jurisdictions at lower levels of the medieval hierarchy. Machiavelli is read as a thinker whose work is concerned above all with articulating the possibility of a (republican) city-state, a community founded upon civic virtue (*virtù*). This reading is partly opposed to the realist tradition, in that there Machiavelli is read as one of the original thinkers of international anarchy and the impossibility of ethical political life between states.

> To the extent that he was concerned with international relations and military affairs—and they certainly preoccupied him extensively—it is as a consequence of his account of the possibilities of political life within states. If it is useful to identify him with a tradition at all, it is a tradition concerned with the possibility of establishing a life of *virtù* within autonomous political communities. This reference, quite obviously, is to a classical conception of the *polis*, to a specific understanding of the location and character of political life within a bounded territorial space. Because the bounded space is identified as the location of political community, as the container in which republican *virtù* can flourish, the outside comes to be understood as the place where political community—as opposed to hegemony—cannot flourish (Walker, 1993, pp. 36–37).

The form of political community that emerged in theory and in the realities of state-building in the early modern period locates the possibility of political value, of ethical practice and aspirations, "universalist aspirations to the good, the true and the beautiful" (Walker, 1993, p. 62) *inside* spatially delimited territorial states. Realism assumes and reinforces "an impossibility of even conceiving an alternative to the account of political community that emerged in early-modern Europe" (Walker, 1993, pp. 15–21). As Connolly (1991) and Ashley (1987, p. 403) argue, this positing of community within sovereign boundaries and the absence of community outside is also an essential starting point for "idealist" or "utopian" theories expressing a yearning for integration or "perpetual peace" (cf. Rosenberg, 1994).

The "deconstruction" of these dualisms of inside–outside, idealism–realism, social science–international relations, ethical life–international maneuvering is pursued through links constructed with the critique of the subject developed in various forms of poststructuralist theory. The dualisms are underwritten by state sovereignty, which involves the invocation of "a speaking, writing sovereign subject" that "must stake its claim to truth and power on its ability to represent the objective reality of a homogeneous territory of vital and productive human labors" (Ashley & Walker, 1990, p. 367). The world of state sovereignty is a world of areal, bounded communities, the existence of which is conditional on the ability of states to position themselves as "subjects" capable of interpreting and representing the needs, interests, and desires of the populations within their territories. For domestic politics *and* international relations to be possible in such a world, national communities must be seen as autonomous and capable of articulating needs, interests, and desires that are representable by sovereign states, which in turn must be viewed as actors capable of autonomous decision making.

Much of this literature explores the problematic nature of these assumptions of self-identity and autonomy that states must constantly work at producing and giving institutional form in the face of what are much more messy realities. Ashley argues that realism is therefore shot through with conceptual instabilities, and that state sovereignty involves something akin to Derrida's *différance*, a combination of difference and deferral. By reducing ideas of community to politics within bounded areas, it institutes a play of differences (spatially) between communities. Boundaries take on a heightened significance in this type of critical analysis, as markers of difference between political communities, as limits of the political representation permitted by state sovereignty, and as sites of contestation (Ashley, 1987, p. 422). The achievement of community beyond these boundaries, at the level of the world, is always thinkable (and idealist theories turning on such notions are an integral part of the conceptual system associated with state sovereignty), but endlessly deferred into a receding future (Ashley, 1987, p. 413). Political practices ultimately turn on the tension between the form of community that state sovereignty institutionalizes, and the promise of a wider community that the same state sovereignty makes it possible to think of as a solution to the inevitable difficulties encountered when states represent themselves as autonomous subjects. This dual vision is inevitably a source of conflict over political identities and state activities, and political boundaries are "already visibly in the process of being imposed and resisted all at once. As a result, the pretense of representation, so crucial to the empowerment of any sovereign voice, simply cannot be sustained . . . " (Ashley & Walker, 1990, p. 367).

Just as with Castells' ideas about networked forms of democracy, the resources are present in these texts for approaches that might break with a politics of place understood as a political imagination centered on areal political communities:

> Thanks in large measure to realist practices, the "capitalist world" remains pluralistic. It contains multiple practical spaces, each granted its partial autonomy, its sovereignty, its effective claim on a right to a partially unique interpretation of the whole. It preserves spaces within its domain for alternative practices that are not reducible to mere variants of the same western rationalist tradition. These are practices that have until now escaped the totalizing normalization of western rationalist discourse. These are also resistant practices and movements that bear positive, productive potential—potential for the opening up of alternative spaces, for the constitution of alternative subjects, for the making of alternative worlds. (Ashley, 1987, p. 428)

The implications of these statements depend, in part, on the interpretation of the word "spaces," and hence the meaning that is to be attributed to capitalism's spatial pluralism. First, the preoccupation with the areal boundaries of sovereign entities, and with the *undecidability* of inside and outside that perpetually threatens to unravel the sovereign subject and the edifice of international relations theory, might mean that areal boundaries are put into question without discussion ever breaking out of a spatial language organized around national political communities. The model of sovereignty may be always already a "pretense" in its own terms, but the "deconstruction" of certain hierarchies and separations in this sort of account would not indicate their negation or dispensability. This sort of position may appear, on reflection, a little quietist, although it has the merit of avoiding the kind of exaggerated claims about boundary subversion and the dissolving effects of spaces of flows sometimes made in work informed by poststructuralist and postmodernist writings.[3] Connolly (1991) seems closer to this reading than Ashley and Walker, but it is compatible with many of their arguments about boundaries, which on this account would be perpetually "under erasure," so to speak, undecidably visible yet obscured, present yet absent, firmly drawn yet overwritten.

On another reading, the transcendence or subversion of these boundaries as one notion of what democracy might be can still easily involve the invocation of either global and/or local communities as alternative repositories of political value. Reasserting "the local" as the subordinated pole of the couple "national—local" as, for example, one quasi-deconstructionist argument would run here (Walker, 1991a, 1993, pp. 141–158), again reproduces the assumption that politics has to be centered around some or other set of areal communities, but this time at a different scale. The same could be said for arguments taking the privileging of "the national" (which connotes political community) over "the global" (which does not) as a critical focus. This possibility emerges in claims that some form of political community is ironically reconstituted in realist texts as a kind of international public sphere (Ashley, 1987, p. 421). In this context, a radical politics could involve "the violent and surreptitious appropriation of a realist community in order to impose a new direction, to bend it to a new will, to force its participation in a different game" (Ashley, 1987, p. 429). A desire to destabilize the discursive and practical relationships between political community and notions of sovereignty could lead to a result curiously parallel to that which is widespread in speculations about globalization: a production of global and local alternative objects for social science and political practice.

On this reading, we are back with possibilities entertained by Dahl, Held, and others, formulated here in terms of the question of scale shifting as political strategy. Smith (1993, p. 97) recognizes the problem here in suggesting that the "central obstacle" in talking about the politics of space is "the lack of any articulated language of spatial difference and differentiation."[4] In this light, yet another reading of Ashley's (1987) comments might see the spatial pluralism of capitalist politics residing not in a plurality of differently *scaled* areas or places, some sovereign, some sites of subversion of sovereignty. Rather, it might characterize democratic practices, as economic geographers characterize capitalist practices, as articulating different *forms* of space.

This avenue can be illustrated directly by referring to work that examines networked forms of political action. Without denying the areal dimensions of capitalist political practices, which are central to their view of how capitalism functions, writers influenced by world-systems theory have produced theoretical and empirical work on forms of political action that are not areal (national, local, or global) in any strict sense through a focus on "antisystemic movements" (Amin, Arrighi, Frank, & Wallerstein, 1990; Arrighi, Hopkins, & Wallerstein, 1989; Wallerstein, 1984). This interstate politics harks back to earlier socialist and other oppositional forms, apparently obliterated by state sovereignty and its imagined areal alternatives, and forward to new forms of politics less entrenched in areal territories (Taylor, 1994).

The theme of transnational movements has become a growth area in critical studies of the global system, much of it influenced not so much by world-systems theory as by the sorts of boundary questioning theory developed by Ashley, Walker, and others (e.g., Connolly, 1991; Lipschutz, 1992; Peterson, 1992; Rengger, 1992; Ruiz, 1991). Environmental movements, movements of indigenous peoples, AIDS-related movements, and international women's networks have received particular attention as constructors and users of transnational spaces constituted, in particular, through the development of globalized media systems (Held, 1995, pp. 124–125; Morley & Robins, 1995). To the extent that Castells' work moves in the direction of arguing that an effective democratic politics under contemporary conditions has to articulate both areal (place-based) and networked forms, work on transnational movements is empirically suggestive about what such a politics might look like when disembedded from issues of economic restructuring and flexible responses to it. It is also useful in mapping out the possibilities and limitations of an apparent resurgence of transnational pressures on states and intergovernmental organizations from networked constituencies other than capital.

Drawing attention to these new spatial movements, as we might call them, seemingly delinked as they are from a politics of place, is therefore one way in which critical international relations theory has sought to connect poststructuralist analysis of discourses on sovereignty and boundaries with emergent practices of political transformation without remaining hypnotized by the undecidable or slipping a politics of place in through the backdoor of "reasserting" local or global politics. How far does this take us in examining issues raised by debates about globalization and democracy?

The answer at this stage is, not surprisingly, a mixed one. It is easy to be skeptical about the extent and influence of transnational networks, about their representativeness of, and relationships with, wider constituencies, and about the way in which they can seem "tacked-on" to many theoretical arguments in search of a political referent for notions of destabilized or subverted boundaries. Even if we imagine that the influence of such networks will increase substantially, perhaps through sets of routinized relationships with organizations like the United Nations (cf. Commission on Global Governance, 1995, pp. 259–260), critical problems remain. While vigorous organization and mobilization through networks of social movements have always been necessary conditions for democratization, and essential mechanisms for producing political change through their interrelationships with the state and political parties thereafter, movement politics is not by itself sufficient for democracy as most participants in debates about globalization understand it. Democracy involves rights of involvement of more or less everybody in the political process, and we are still much better informed by this genre of work about the mechanisms through which most people are excluded from nonnational, nonareal forms of democratic politics than we are about how democracy, as opposed to movements per se, might escape them.

In the next section I consider the politics of place from the point of view of discussions about politics and globalization. The continuing relevance of a politics of place in a range of current work is a predictable "by-product" of the focus in globalization discussions on the decline of sovereignty and the national state, which is consonant with a series of more enduring schemata of social change. There are grounds, independent of discussions of globalization but prompted by them, for exploring alternative spatial structures of democracy. These depend, however, on a range of problems that will be considered in the closing sections of the chapter, but which can be fruitfully considered from the point of view of "domestic" politics, elections, and associated problems of representation about which the economic restructuring literature and critical international relations theory have not much to say.

THE POLITICS OF PLACE

"Place" is generally invoked to delimit a locale, usually restricted in scale, to which men and women attach meaning in their everyday lives and which facilitates the formation and reproduction of important forms of collective identity. The "politics of place" is used here, following Connolly (1991), to denote a range of discourses in which the meaning and identity of political actors are referred to a particular place, a portion of areal space, whether it be a neighborhood, a city, region, or national territory, and where as a result a certain degree of political closure is effected or at least reinforced. On this definition a politics of place occurs at all scales whenever an areal political community is posited and made the center of analysis and normative argument.

It is common in contemporary discussions about globalization to invoke a model of the national state that is retrospectively argued to have been an effective means of realizing democratic ideals and practices. Connolly is right to draw attention to the "nostalgia" associated with the politics of place. This is a phenomenon that is by no means limited to discussions of national states. Talk about the Greek *polis*, early Renaissance city–states, New England town meetings, "community," and other political entities important in arguments about democracy is regularly criticized for a similar retrospective idealization of the practices and capacities attributed to them. One important line of deconstructionist argument has focused upon the metaphysics of *presence* implicated in texts concerning themselves with idealized communities of one form or another (e.g., Derrida, 1976, pp. 101–140, 262–268; 1978), one result of which is that it is possible to imagine a whole series of coherent political forms embodying authentic or transparent intersubjective relations, on condition that they are perpetually constructed as *absent* (Derrida, 1976, p. 267). It is not necessary to subscribe to deconstruction to appreciate this point: many broad commentaries on social change that appear to be about forms of political community are, on closer inspection, really about the decline or emergence of such objects, things that are said to have been eroded or that are described as being in the process of formation. The problem with the politics of place is that it permits the seemingly endless recycling of assumptions about politics that depend on attributing value, and not merely convenience, to objects that are unsustainable as anchors for democratic aspirations because they are simultaneously constructed as unavailable as yet or in regrettable, but explicable, decline.

A familiar example would be the development of concepts of community in the social sciences of the late 19th and early 20th centuries. One reason why community has been central to normative social science accounts is because of the attributes of face-to-face negotiation (copresence) and an ability to consensually regulate local social life (congruence) it regularly carries. The notion that community is a more "authentic" mode of regulating social life than more mediated sets of relationships is rooted in these assumptions. Social science notions of community developed not in isolation, but as part of a system of conceptual terms from the late 19th century. "Community" was, and often still is, elaborated as a concept in relation to the developing "society" viewed as colonizing, undermining, or eclipsing it (or its latter-day companions, public space, the public sphere, the life world, and so on). This relationship was underwritten by the "individual," a constituent of both society and community, whose relationship to both these forms became a "problem" for social science theory and practice. Broadly speaking, the decline of community and the emergence of society, rather than community per se, was the "object" being theorized, and this process helped construct the modern sociological individual and society as the focus of newly institutionalized social sciences.

From the point of view of critical social science, the relationship between the local and the global is being produced as a similar field of tension to the individual and society around which to construct interdisciplinary work (Table 9.1). Again, this relation is being produced through positing the decline of an object of value. Just as community is not (usually) seen as an object of value in itself, neither is the national state per se, but, rather, the national state as a guarantor of the democratic political arena, a space where political actors of relevant kinds can be argued to have been copresent and where a governable congruence of political, economic, and cultural institutions and processes (a national "society") might be effected.

If it is even partially true that "society" was a concept produced through such a discursive process, then it should not be surprising to visit bookstores and libraries and get the impression that as "society" (the national state) is fading out as a shared focus of concern, the "global" and the "local" (or "place"), the latter a constituent of both the national and the global

TABLE 9.1. Continuities in the Politics of Place

	Declining or decaying object	Emerging object, or agent of decay	Linking or articulatory element
Early 20th century	"Community"	"Society"	"The individual"
Late 20th century[a]	"The national"	"The global"	"The local"

[a]These temporal categories are used for heuristic purposes—the "communitarian revival" of recent years is a good example of the continuing salience of discourses about the decline of "community." Whether current mobilization of "community" inserts it in the same system of terms as debates in the late 19th and early 20th centuries is, nevertheless, an interesting and open question.

which permits their articulation, are becoming constituted as objects of study across a broad set of disciplines. Certainly, an interdisciplinary reemphasis on geographical concerns has produced some necessary rethinking about modernist social science (e.g. Giddens, 1985; Mann, 1986). Nevertheless, the surge of writing both about lost community, which constitutes "society" and "the individual" as proper foci of knowledge, and about the loss of national democratic politics, which similarly constitutes "the global" and "the local," has reproduced a politics of place when it comes to the discussion of normative issues. The former discourse about community did this in a more indirect manner than discussions about globalization, by clothing what we now call local- and national-scale social forms in nongeographical language. Globalization discussions have achieved much the same result by premising discussion of the spatial organization of democracy explicitly on sets of areal spaces.

To suggest that the politics of place is pervasive and capable of renewal in novel permutations does not imply that everyone subscribes to the notion that globalization creates a need for democratizable local and/or global political arenas on analogy with national states. A more widespread problem is that if this sort of solution is rejected, as it often is, it is extremely difficult to imagine what democracy might look like outside these long-sedimented assumptions in social science argument. Without the politics of place, social and political life looks messy and uncertain. Policy and organizational change can be described and reconstructed in a pragmatic sort of way, especially in relation to policy areas where there is some consensus that national states can "no longer cope." But the democratization of resulting institutional arrangements is generally not an explicit focus because, as Walker (1993) suggests in his reading of Machiavelli, there are not well-developed notions of where political value and legitimacy come from outside the parameters of the politics of place.

Talk about the decline of the national state in social science, then, resonates with a series of ways of orienting discussions of desirable political arrangements around spatially congruent processes and the copresence, in areal spaces, of political actors. It is not surprising that contemporary writings on democracy seem much more content with what national democracy "was" than many writings of 20 years ago: it is not hard to attribute effectiveness to social arrangements once they are figured as being somewhere just out of reach, lately made inaccessible. Continuing to explore what is involved in democratic practices, their limits and potential for extension, and their spatial constitution, are desirable social scientific goals. But it is time to begin to detach this exploration from the "big" questions about globalization and the national state: if the national state is seen as declining, the result is a set of areal "solutions" or jeremiads about whether democracy is possible anymore; if it is not, then we are left with explicit or implicit acceptance that for all their faults, national sovereignty and political communities are constitutive of what democracy is, and talk of detaching it from these or developing it beyond its national form is academic.

In this light, and paradoxically, discussions of globalization may turn out to have been most useful in foregrounding problems in the social science analysis of politics that are important independently of the validity of claims that the world is "increasingly global" in a multidimensional way, or that the national state is in decline. Although at present it is hard to read anything on globalization and the national state without encountering references to the fact that the decline of the latter has been much exaggerated, contemporary debates about globalization have made useful steps in heightening awareness of a number of matters. Worries about the ideal–typical models used in discussions about the national state, for example, have moved beyond the stage of pointing out that states rarely coincide with nations, as some of the recent literature on sovereignty issues attests (Ruggie, 1993; Spruyt, 1994a, 1994b). The fairly recent emergence of a consolidated interstate system, which has in important ways always depended on the activities of institutions at higher scales for its competence and stability, has been highlighted, which begins to make the purported era of uncontaminated or autonomous national democracy look more and more like a vanishing point (Giddens, 1985; Milward, 1992). Above all, perhaps, the *geography* of liberal democracy has become an important issue, not only from the point of view of its "diffusion" from North America and Europe, but from that of the legitimacy and malleability of the spatial infrastructure of areal spaces undergirding it. Nowhere is this more evident than in the current efflorescence of work on citizenship in geography and other disciplines, which has focused in particular on issues of territorial justice at the core of the exclusionary practices and distinctions required by a democracy premised on a politics of place. Contemporary issues of immigration, migrant labor, steeply increasing refugee populations, and social marginalization within national communities surely make it crucial to reconsider in what ways democracy can be redefined and reorganized around less problematic notions of political community (cf., inter alia, Brubaker, 1992; Painter & Philo, 1995; Pincetl, 1994; Steenbergen, 1994).

Even if, in other words, skepticism about any model "preglobalization" national democracy is allied with an uneasiness at the level of the facts about the decline of the national state and a new globalizing era, there are independent grounds for exploring ways in which democracy could be detached from its association with areal spaces. In the last two sections of the chapter, I summarize some of these grounds and consider some ways in which democracy can begin to be reconsidered as a set of processes that escape the politics of place.

POLITICS OF SPACE: GEOGRAPHIES OF DEMOCRACY

As a result of the preoccupation with the decline of the national state in the globalization literature, most of the discussion of democracy and space has been fueled by one aspect of the politics of place, that concerning the non-congruence of scale or spatial forms between politics and economics under current conditions. This is not surprising, as the "territorial non-coincidence" problem (Murray, 1971; Picciotto, 1983, p. 11) is that aspect of the issue which seems most relevant to topics, such as the EU and the North American Free Trade Agreement (NAFTA), which tend to animate European and North American debates. The addition of culture to the list of differently scaled features of the contemporary landscape has reinforced this preoccupation, in that separatist conflicts can then be integrated into what is already a problem of unmanageable dimensions (Horsman & Marshall, 1993).

From the point of view of rethinking democracy, however, this preoccupation with scale and congruence has been less helpful than many appear to have hoped. Legitimacy problems certainly bedevil those functional, regional, and global regulatory institutions developed to cope with contemporary scale disjunctures, but there is something premature and overdirect about suggestions that any problems of legitimacy they encounter are correctable through "democratizing" them. For the most part these organizations have been insulated from popular pressures by design, and would not exist otherwise. A democratized GATT or International Monetary Fund (IMF) is almost a contradiction in terms, and the UN—for all the cosmopolitan hopes commonly placed in its being opened up to more democratically accountable procedures—would in all likelihood collapse if anything approaching a "fair" distribution of power among its members were created. Even the EU, which is a special case, given the development of the "direct" election of members of the European Parliament and thus the only real current experiment in transnational elections, is not encouraging in this regard. The European Parliament is generally acknowledged to have little power relative to the other branches of the EU's government structure, despite some enhancements to its role in shaping European policy under the Maastricht treaty.

The EU is the focus of many debates on globalization because it is seen as a test case of the idea that scale incongruities between economic and regulatory processes can be tackled through creating larger scale state structures. Nevertheless, it is hard to believe that those core functions of the EU in the economic policy field are, or will be, shaped very much by an elected body. As Gray (1996) has put it, "the idea that the 'democratic deficit' in European institutions can be filled, when the whole trend of European institutions over the past decade has been to remove economic policy from democratic accountability, is an illusion." Gray blames a revived neoliberalism, suggesting that transnational governance in Europe has deviated from some properly cosmopolitan vision of Europe's "founding fathers," but it seems clear that the democratization of European regulatory structures was deliberately put on the back burner by Monnet (a founding father of the EU) and others at a very early stage (Featherstone, 1994). Even if the European Parliament were given more power, as many argue it should be, it is not likely that the results would be any better than those attained at the national scale in relation to the global economy, or that the dominant coalitions that would result in the European party system would be any less neoliberal than the national governments currently connecting citizens to the most important aspects of EU policymaking.[5] What is clear, particularly given the already powerful tendency of the EU to promote notions of "European" belonging, community, and citizenship within EU borders, that "politics as usual" is resulting in another sense, that of an exclusionary politics of place at the European scale (Morley & Robins, 1995; Tassin, 1992). The existence of, and greater empowerment of, the European Parliament is contributing to this sort of development, not making it less likely.

Discussions of democracy in relation to European integration are more than a good example of how the dissolution of something like a politics of place is talked about only on condition that a different areal space, here something like a large national state, can be developed as a substitute for national attachments. They also point up how much discussion of democracy goes on within a framework that denigrates distanciated political relationships, often in a bizzarely imaginary way, as when, for example, Brussels is routinely described in the United Kingdom as "distant" when it is in reality not much further from many British people than London. "Brussels" here is a marker for somewhere where "we" are not, where we cannot hold decision makers accountable and where "they" are not in a position to know what "we" want. Of course, there are all sorts of specific nationally based interests, cultural prejudices, and political structures driving this sort of discourse, but it derives its power from the other important aspect of the politics of place, its promotion of metaphors of face-to-faceness and "closeness" as prerequisites of democracy.

On the whole, it is this dimension of the politics of place that has received less attention in recent years: as a policy issue it is less compelling than areal congruence, where institution-building elites and policymakers sometimes do perceive that they have an interest in tackling problems of legitimacy that institutions at new scales encounter. Yet it is this other aspect of the politics of place that seems most entrenched, and currently most amenable to academic justification, at the level of arguments about the primacy of "local" democracy or about the "self-determination" of national entities within larger national states, and at the level of quite general discussion of political theory and ethics. There has been a reassertion of closeness or face-to-face interaction in various forms as a source of morality in social life by a variety of writers, not only from those conventionally labeled as communitarians (e.g., Sandel, 1982). Bauman (1989, 1993) has, for example, developed a critique of modernity in which the distanciated chains of relationships developed by modern economic and bureaucratic organizations block presocial moral impulses grounded in direct relationships with others. Ginsburg (1994) has produced a similarly skeptical argument about the possibility of moral sentiment in relation to those distant in space, time, and social context from the self. For some writers at least, the development of cosmopolitan moral codes and impulses, where relationships with distant and unknown others are felt to be equivalent to those close to home or to the body, is a dim prospect.

Face-to-face relations are privileged in many writings on democracy. Until recently the major issue of concern in textbooks on democracy would have been the relative virtues of "direct" and "representative" forms of popular influence on the state. In debating this issue, there might be a great deal of discussion of political stability, the political competence of voters, the autonomy of politics, and feasible institutional arrangements, but for the most part not much questioning of the idea that direct relationships are generally more authentic expressions of political demands than those mediated by representatives. With a few exceptions (e.g., Birch, 1972; Pitkin, 1967) there was not much contemporary work on just what "representation" meant in democratic politics.

The situation has changed in recent years, with significant developments in theories of representation finding their way into more and more social science debates. Arguments about direct and representative democracy have tended to assume that representation was about the adequacy or accuracy of representations in relation to something else which, not being a representation itself, could be assumed to have an unproblematic identity. In more general contexts, models that set up relationships between representations and "reality" have been displaced somewhat by those that see representations as always referring to other representations in a process where reference to "reality" and questions of representational adequacy are correspondingly more complex. Every representation, on this sort of account, carries "behind" it more representations, and attempts to track back through these to some final referent or source of value are highly problematic.

In relation to democracy, this sort of account both questions the ease with which identities are commonly attributed to that to which representatives "refer," and highlights the conventional, rather than necessary, qualities of the arrangements through which representation is secured. To highlight the conventional nature of political practices is not to suggest that they can or should be disposed of. The development of conventions surrounding suffrage and the capacity to participate in elections, ballot rules and related practices, formulae for relating votes to seats, and so on are more central to what we appear to

mean by the development of democracy than general ideas about popular
representation or participation (Rosanvallon, 1992). Moreover, accepting that
there is something problematic about the idea of "direct" democracy to some
extent dampens the grounds for criticism of conventional forms of representative democracy (Derrida, 1978, 1982a). Even those criticisms of intergovernmental arrangements such as the EU, where governments are said to represent their electorates, seem on less stable ground when representation is
foregrounded as an unavoidable component of democratic practices, rather
than a regrettable or pragmatic response to problems of complexity or distance. Nevertheless, the refusal to take the identity of the represented for
granted implied by this point of view does provide opportunities for a rethinking; a rethinking, that is, as to whether or not such democratic conventions in
their present or modified forms are capable of disengagement from the particular spatial structures and associated forms of political community with
which they are usually identified.

As we have seen, a more complex attitude to representational issues is
having some influence on the way in which national states and sovereignty are
discussed, and ideas about representation have made it difficult to take the
identity of political communities for granted. This sort of argument contributes to undoing the links between democracy and the politics of place by
making it far from self-evident that democracy can and should be unproblematically referred to particular areal communities. The closure effected by
boundary-making practices in these accounts, which allows states to act as
subjects, to "speak for" the communities they embrace, makes certain forms of
democracy possible only by systematically producing nondemocracy. This is
so not only in international relations, for by limiting participation in inevitably
arbitrary ways to those living inside particular historically produced boundaries, it also reproduces exclusionary configurations of participants in the
shaping of public policy.

Discussions of "domestic" politics and "empirical" democratic theory
proceed from this starting point, arranging explanations and descriptions of
the democratic process around the relationship between individuals (voters)
and other agents (parties, classes, social movements, unions, elites, etc.) and
the state. The copresence dimension of the politics of place has strong affini-
ties with the attribution of great normative value to face-to-face and local
rather than more "stretched out" relations, especially in talk about community. In this case it is relatively easy to detect and critically discuss. As Anderson's
(1991) work on "imagined communities" has made clear, however, it equally
applies to situations in which agents are positioned as copresent at larger
scales, through membership in the same national political community. As I
suggested at the outset, it also informs discussion of entities that are imagined,
indeed often explicitly described, as though they were engaged in face-to-face
negotiation or conflict. Much writing on politics is saturated with conversa-

tional and agonistic metaphors about classes "struggling" with each other in and around state institutions, collective political actors "bargaining" and "striking compromises," interest groups "confronting" the state, citizens engaging in discussion "in the public sphere," governments "facing up to" this or that lobby, and so on.

The politics of place has, then, become ingrained in the language used to discuss democracy and domestic political processes. Talking about democracy in terms of community, togetherness, and contact is problematic. This is because this language cannot really bring out the importance of representation in democratic politics, which involves multiply mediated, indirect relationships between different sorts of actors who act through and are acted upon in various ways by other actors through networks of social and political relationships. The interest of network perspectives in examining democracy is twofold. First, they help create a situation in which economic processes and political processes can be considered in the same analytical space. This is not to say that it becomes possible for us to imagine or construct sets of democratic institutions and practices that are *geographically* congruent with the sorts of articulation of areal and network spaces forming the objects of economic geography, but that there are possibilities for developing the sorts of ideas sketched out by Castells (1989) without depending on analogies with firms or problematic conceptions of political community.

Second, they permit the analysis of how processes of representation operate in politics without restricting the relationships involved to those between "subjects," citizens, or communities on the one hand, and representatives on the other. Certainly, important aspects of what is usually meant by democracy depend on conventions to the effect that representation is "truncated" in this way. In particular, current conceptions of accountabilty are dependent on such a foreshortening of perspective. Nevertheless, as Dahl (1990) and others have pointed out, the questioning and transformation of what notions of representation and accountability mean have been part and parcel of previous spatial reorganizations of democracy.[6] If democracy is to survive in forms capable of dealing with matters that exceed areal spaces, then it seems important to develop our understanding of representation in politics beyond that embedded in current representative institutions. This does not mean that the latter should be abandoned because they do not capture "real mechanisms" of representation adequately. This would be premature (and grotesquely academic) in a context where even minimally representative institutions are far from universal and where the decline of national state capacities is a contested hypothesis rather than an established trend. It does imply, however, that if arguments about the globalization of democracy as the latest in a series of fundamental transformations in its operations forced by changes in the scale of other activities are to be sustained, they will have have to reckon with much less direct forms of representation than those which are conventionally ascribed to national arrangements. Formulae such as creating a global "state" (Chase-Dunn, 1990) or a "global forum of civil society" (Commission on Global Governance, 1995, pp. 259–260) certainly sound expansive enough, but as presently proposed they do not seem to embody the kinds of changes in our understandings of representation and accountability they otherwise imply. Thinking about democracy as involving both areal and networked forms of representation is one way of foregrounding the forms of indirect relationships that would be involved.

To criticize the dependence of conceptions of democracy on assumptions about co-presence is *not* to argue that political processes do not involve face-to-face interactions, conversations, meetings, assemblies, and so on, or that these are not important in explanatory accounts, and indeed in the negotiation of normative issues. To suggest that copresent relations are not important would, after all, be as peculiar and counterproductive as saying that areal spaces and associated metaphors are somehow unreal or not useful because they can be shown to have been invested with a significance that has led to ambiguous ethical results. Network forms of social relation are constructed, to a certain extent, through chains of situations of copresence, which nevertheless cannot provide secure vantage points from which to understand social life because every situation of copresence is simultaneously a point of mediation in a set of other exchanges and transmissions of information, resources, and representations. Furthermore, as some recent work emphasizes (White, 1992), one dimension of the processes of identity formation that it is hard to get into analytical focus unless a network perspective is adopted is the importance of disconnection, of the absence of particular ties or relations, in producing social agents and social action. By refusing to attribute a priori greater political value to unmediated social situations, then, it is possible to restore to them to their real effectiveness in relation to the other sorts of connections and gaps relevant to representation and the production of identities.

There have been some interesting attempts to think about democracy, and issues of social justice more broadly, without seeing the good life in terms of either face-to-face interaction or areal closure. Young (1990), for example, has produced a series of criticisms of liberal and communitarian theories of justice assuming autonomous, self-representing political actors, but it is clear that on her account good theories must also involve skepticism about writings privileging face-to-face relations and "closeness" in geographical or social terms. She argues for the necessity of developing our imagination of forms of political practice that involve connecting with, living with, and simply acknowledging people who are "strangers" in cultural terms, in the sense of being aware of little more than each others' existence, or unaware of each other at all. Without this, her work suggests, forms of political argument based on metaphors of community, unmediated relationships, and place can easily have exclusionary consequences, incapable as they are of coping with difference.

Deep-seated notions about political community have to be, on this sort of account, confronted with a democracy constructed around less potentially exclusive sociospatial forms, which might better facilitate coping with the sorts of indirect, mediated relationships and unknown interests and needs so characteristic of modern life. Massey (1994) similarly seeks to reconceptualize place not as an areal form but as a nexus of social, economic, and cultural networks spreading over diverse distances and embodying different intensities of interaction. Researchers like Clark (1994) have begun to explore the characteristics of network forms of urban political association and cooperation as mechanisms of developing new ideas of what political association might mean in relation to more complicated constructions of democratic space.

It is useful to counterpose this sort of work to that of Bauman (1989, 1993) and Ginsburg (1994), not to deny the difficulties involved in reorienting ethical conduct and political value away from immediate relationships and contexts, but to insist that the draining of distanciated and multiply mediated political and social relationships of the possibility of embodying democracy or social justice is a key feature of the politics of place, and perhaps the most perplexing issue raised by the question of democracy and globalization. Rather than use the globalization question, particularly the issue of the decline of the national state, to speculate about the democratization of larger scale structures or about opportunities to retrench and create more participatory local state structures, it might be better to begin to reexamine the relationships between democracy and space, be to determine whether they contain within them possibilities for overcoming the kinds of exclusions and ethical short circuits inherent in modern practices of sovereignty and the nostalgic modes of thinking about political possibilities inherent in the politics of place.

Democracy necessarily involves multiple forms of space, in the sense that the forms of representation, interest formation, and communication inherent in democracy involve processes that cannot be constrained or bounded in areal spaces or communities. In considering work in international relations theory, it was noted that a focus on political networks has been important in thinking about the spatial possibilities of democracy and representation. The focus of Wallerstein, Walker, Connolly, and others on transnational social movements is a useful starting point in thinking about network forms of political action that might articulate with areally bounded political practices in challenging ways. Nevertheless, this genre of writing has not had much to say about more inclusive mechanisms and institutional practices of democracy. These have remained the preserve, largely, of empirical democratic theory, and I now turn to these in a little more detail, not to propose any alternative institutional arrangements, but to outline some ways in which they involve networked processes that interfere with their role in the politics of place.

REPRESENTATION UNBOUND?

At the beginning of the previous section I discussed how the institutions and practices of domestic politics were commonly characterized in terms of the politics of place. "Conventional" domestic politics is, however, embodied in a variety of spatial forms. Political parties, for example, are complex organizations in spatial terms, simultaneously constituted around the areal spaces of the sovereign state and constituencies and yet articulating these with all manner of flows of information, resources, and relationships of representation that are not confined in any necessary way to the spaces imagined in the politics of place. First, and perhaps most obviously, the resources sustaining party activity are not necessarily domestic, particularly in relation to financing from corporate sources that are distributed through direct linkages, ownership structures, and relationships of alliance in all manner of transnational configurations. In terms of representation, the significance of the unboundedness of economic networks for domestic politics is not confined to their resistance to national management: "domestic" political parties act as points of articulation of the interests of "global" economic entities with national political spaces. If globalization tendencies in several important sectors of finance and industry are admitted, parties are increasingly representing such far-flung constituencies in their policymaking and coalition-building activities.[7] No doubt, interesting work could be done on the way in which the neo-liberalization of party systems has come about through their articulation with such linkages, and how these processes have become important causes of the rise of "grin and bear it" globalization rhetoric in domestic politics. In reality, parties have always been points of articulation for transnational connections: the policies and interests appealed to by Democrats and Republicans in the United States have been conditioned by shifting patterns of linkage with domestic and internationalized capital (Ferguson, 1983, 1984); work on democracy and dependency in peripheral countries has made this sort of complexity central to their accounts of domestic political development (cf. Rueschemeyer, Stephens, & Stephens, 1992, pp. 69–74, 219–221); the development of the modern British Conservative Party displays an organization and not merely an electoral appeal constituted through linkages with, and representations of, certain imperial and, particularly, Irish interests.

Parties have, at various points, been more or less successful in building transnational structures that are more about mobilizing citizens than resources or other forms of corporate or elite support. Communist and socialist internationals are perhaps the most prominent examples, and present interesting case studies of "deglobalization" in certain respects (Taylor, 1994). As a result of direct elections to the European Parliament, "European" party structures have developed, but as European elections are currently conducted largely through national party organizations and through the prism of their concerns, too much focus on weak international associations may be deflecting interest from other consequential ways in which national parties articulate transnational interests. These do not always involve business, although at present this is by far the most significant factor. To the extent that overseas voters can make meaningful differences in national elections, parties are developing overseas branches and mobilizing structures to involve (usually middle-class) voters who may not have lived and associated in their former national communities for decades (Tether, 1994). When contrasted with the exclusion of resident immigrants and migrant workers from most electorates, let alone vast numbers of other people who are affected by the externalities of particular national state policies, the energy with which this kind of mobilization can proceed is a disturbing reminder of the absurd consequences of the politics of place in terms of political justice.

To some, party structures will not seem particularly auspicious vehicles for transforming the spatial parameters of democracy. In the ways they do articulate different forms of space and exhibit capacities to act across areal boundaries, particularly in the transnational case, they seem to involve the kinds of resource flows many see as inimical to "proper" democratic practices.[8] Nevertheless, as has been recently pointed out in the globalization context (Commission on Global Governance, 1995, pp. 61–62), they are at present the only mechanisms with built-in incentives to mobilize broad-based coalitions to bring pressure to bear on governance structures at whatever scale. As such, they need to be assessed in their spatial complexity to look for characteristics that might lend themselves to less confining mechanisms of representation. Party structures are not the only elements of conventional politics through which democracy can be said to articulate network and areal spaces. In what follows, I want to suggest that voting behavior, the most ordinary form of political participation, and that which apparently constitutes the nucleus of what we consider democracy to be, is a spatially complex process that ordinarily exceeds the limits imposed on it by the politics of place.

Some of the most useful criticisms that have been made of the standard "Michigan school" of electoral studies, classically represented by Campbell, Gurin, and Miller (1954) and Campbell, Converse, Miller, and Stokes (1960), have been based on accumulating evidence that voting decisions are best seen as structured, not by autonomous decision making by voters on the basis of their social characteristics mediated by their party identification, but through networks of information flow and direct and indirect interpersonal contacts (Knoke, 1990, pp. 29–56). Thinking about voting behavior as a set of network processes has enriched a genre of academic work that has often seemed overdependent on explaining individuals making up their minds by themselves on the basis of a large number of background conditions (the economy, feelings about incumbency, socioeconomic status, party identification, and so on). Voters do not make up their minds alone, but as part of chains of discussions and flows of information connecting them directly and indirectly to individuals and groups across a variety of contexts and distances.

Although much of the research here has focused on face-to-face interactions (e.g., Finifter, 1974), the importance of indirect relationships in the study of social networks is well understood, particularly since the work of Granovetter (1973, 1974) on information in labor markets revealed the effectivity of such mediated linkages in everyday situations where face-to-face interactions had hitherto been thought crucial (see also Knoke, 1990, p. 36). Another reason for the interest of research of this kind, and why the deployment of network concepts is not a matter of saying that "everyone is linked to everyone else" or that "information is flowing everywhere," is that network analysis is explicitly concerned not only with linkages and flows, but with the absence of linkages and flows, with gaps and hiatuses in the fabric of social life that have their own effectivity, for better and worse, in shaping social change. The kinds of networks constituting voting behavior are therefore neither predictably structured along the lines of categories such as class, race, gender, and other social divisions,[9] nor socially indeterminate. The kinds of connections and transmissions of information made through them may be intentional or not. Furthermore, social accounts constructed though network analysis necessarily leave questions of the spatial constitution of processes under examination unresolved, as networks are not intrinsically "boundable"[10] in the way many other objects of social science analysis (communities, societies, groups, etc.) are imagined to be. The sets of persons and relationships producing voting decisions, like those involved in party and movement activity, do not necessarily coincide with the areal communities "authorized" to vote in particular elections and over which results are aggregated.[11]

It is important that network processes are not seen only as another set of influences on voting behavior, because the networked voting decision illustrates the extent to which voting itself is an act of representation. Voters are not only attempting to represent their own interests when choosing one candidate or program over another, but are invariably representing (or not representing, as the case may be) those of others; indeed, it would be better to say that their own interests are *formed* through relays and contestations occurring through the networks in which they are embedded. These networks are not necessarily composed purely of relations of direct and distanciated contact between persons, as technologies of various kinds clearly intervene, but interpersonal linkages have been shown to be more important than, say, media influences in many contexts (Knoke, 1990, p. 54).

To speak of voting involving the representation of (a series of) others' interests recalls theories of "virtual representation." These are usually seen as a rather dangerous set of ideas in liberal theories of politics stressing individual autonomy and in other theories where the representation of, or speaking for, other people and groups is argued to be deeply problematic in terms of the issues of power, and identity involved. Certainly, the representation of others involved in voting behavior is not exempt from any of the difficulties these arguments raise, and voting considered as an act of representation invokes many familiar problems of interest, power and representation involved in wider political contexts. Indeed, all the problems attached to representative democracy as a manner of organizing popular rule reemerge at those levels of the political process prior to those usually considered in arguments for more participatory or direct forms. Nevertheless, the question of whether or not the processes of representation involved in voting are "just" or "accurate" is not the only issue, or perhaps the main one, involved. The point is that democracy is not a process that can be seen unproblematically as involving limited and containable linkages between people represented and more or less adequate representatives; rather, it spills out in similar ways to other nonareal processes in social life, in ways that are empirically reconstructible if not ethically justifiable within the parameters of liberal political theory.[12] The problematic processes of representation going on *in* voting behavior do not disappear if we continue to write as though voting is a process involving autonomous individuals or communities making up their minds. To wheel out a perhaps overused formulation in other contexts, the electoral process unavoidably involves representation "all the way down." The fact that under modern assumptions, for democracy to work, closure is established at the level of individuals and spaces by pretending otherwise, as Ashley and Walker might put it, particularly through conventions concerning the vote, cannot erase those elements of democratic politics that embody the possibility of political representation being organized differently.

That network processes, chains of representation shaping voting decisions, do not coincide with those regions over which votes are tallied and where, formally, the results are effective is relatively easy to see in relation to subnational elections. There it is plausible that a plethora of direct and indirect relationships outside any particular jurisdiction are likely to feed into and influence voting patterns inside it. Moving toward examples more directly relevant to issues of globalization and democracy, consider the role and importance of the "ethnic vote" in U.S. politics. The Israeli–Palestinian conflict and the "troubles" in Northern Ireland are prominent recent reminders of how important dimensions of American voting behavior have always been predicated on the notion that others, not physically located within U.S. boundaries, have been represented (however problematically) by those going to polling booths, structuring the ways in which the numbers accumulate for one candidate and party or another.

Consider Rogin's (1967) classic analysis of the McCarthy vote. He argues that McCarthyism, often depicted in liberal writings of the time as a "nativist" development of American populist traditions, involved striking discontinuities with prior midwestern protest politics in terms of bases of support and ideology. One irony revealed in his analysis is the extent to which German, Eastern European, and Russian ethnic voters were crucial in the development of a political phenomenon usually seen as the epitome of a national democratic community withdrawing upon itself and opposing itself to an imaginary, conspiratorial Other invading and corrupting its communal fabric. The transnational representation occurring in this case was not "authorized" by those "Un-Americans" being represented, although in the 1940s and 1950s many direct and unmediated relationships of kin and acquaintance are likely to have been involved.[13]

In many other contexts, however, it is difficult to think of voters representing those who are excluded from their own particular electoral arrangements except by means of the portrayals and constructions of interest furnished internationally through the media. This is one reason why the exploration of the implications of globalizing tendencies for democracy is at once promising and alarming. They are promising in that they appear to produce a proliferation of opportunities for denser patterns of interaction and linkage building among people in and from different political jurisdictions, where transnational social movements would be at one extreme and talking to persons acquainted with university students who have built up sets of relatively "cosmopolitan" linkages would be another. But they are also alarming in that it is all too evident that apparently increased fluxes of people across jurisdictional boundaries, and a heightened sense of interconnectedness can just as easily promote defensive as accommodatory behavior in voters and the growth of movements and parties committed to reconstitute representational processes within the framework of the politics of place. Unfortunately, although there is a great deal of general work on cultural representation in politics that can be brought to bear on discussions of democracy, there is not enough empirical research that seeks to demonstrate how far, and through what channels, such representations are effectively embedded (Granovetter, 1985) in specific networks shaping electoral behavior and election outcomes.

It is unlikely that such work will be forthcoming unless researchers accept that the proposition that voting, indeed, so-called conventional politics in general, involves complicated, unbounded, but reconstructable processes of representation. The study of parties and elections is a sector of social science that is strongly empirical in orientation, and so it seems important to emphasize that the use of the word "representation" here is not intended to invoke a set of "flashy" theoretical arguments in opposition to empirical democratic theory. To say that representation matters is to make an empirical claim about the manner in which democracy, "representative" or not, operates. Representation, in other words, is not a matter of an ethereal realm that can best be considered by democratic theory as a supplement to empirical studies of parties and voting, but ought to be part of the essential explanatory apparatus of the latter. If we cannot understand the voting decision without empirically reconstructing flows of information and relations of representation between voters, other voters, and nonvoters, present and absent, "members" or "strangers" (Walzer, 1983), it is difficult to see how the analysis of networks of relationships and representation can be excluded from empirical studies except on what, for many purposes, may be reasonable and explicit grounds of convenience. The relative lack of the kind of empirical work on democracy and elections that might shed light on how far *existing* forms of democracy include processes which in principle and practice are resistant to areal enclosure may be one more reason why it has become so hard to imagine alternative institutional arrangements for democracy once a developing awareness of the porosity of the political geographic equivalents of "closed texts," areal spaces, gets heightened by contemporary developments. Political representation, it could be suggested, needs to be unbound not only in the sense of questioning its necessary embeddedness in areal forms of space, such as territorial states. It also could do with being released, or at least paroled under observation, from its enclosure within social, cultural, and literary theory, a place where one suspects many empirical researchers in politics would be happy to see it stay.

Much of this last section may seem far away indeed from the issues usually considered in discussions of globalization and democracy. In particular, I have moved from apparently large-scale, newsworthy issues about the decline of the national state, the development of new forms of regulation and governance, and the problematic nature of sovereignty and political community to what to some will seem like minor issues in the explanation of voting behavior. The large-scale, issues are crucial, and debate about them is enhancing our understanding of politics and social change in sometimes unexpected ways. Nevertheless, the grandiose form that much of the discussion of globalization in relation to politics takes has led to a situation in which little progress is likely to be made without a careful working-out of the spatial possibilities and limits of those democratic processes that globalization is arguably threatening. Much of the debate on globalization has exposed the extent to which our imagination of democratic possibilities is tied to (sovereign and nonsovereign) areal spaces that are invested with value as sources of political identity and held to standards of coherence as objects of study in ways that seem increasingly untenable.

None of the foregoing, of course, addresses the issue of "practical" institutional arrangements that might be developed to regulate the networked spaces of representation and influence described here, or to facilitate the sorts of contestations of the representations and linkages made through them. At least, it could be said, the literature on globalization and democracy is concerned to outline such institutional futures, providing pictures of possible future democratic political landscapes. I can only reiterate that such landscapes have a strong tendency to be informed by the politics of place, and that the aura of optimism conveyed is not borne out by what seem to be the realities behind the development of transnational forms of governance. They have a kind of misleading directness about them, fueled by narratives of democratic development in expanding spaces.

Whatever geographical forms democratic spaces take in the future, global or local, exclusionary and areal or complex and networked, they are unlikely to follow such blueprints. Transnational forms of mobilization and organizations may develop with democratization and nonareal representation both as goals and as practices internalized in the pursuit of these goals. If so, they are likely to develop around issues where exclusionary democratic practices and institutions of citizenship are central, such as labor market and immigration policy, and the growing twin crises of nationalism and refugee flows, which, currently, look as though they will only intensify rather than abate in the near future. The exclusive territoriality undergirding modern democracy is more likely to come under critical strain as a result of these sorts of issues than from the disjuncture of economic and political processes so often at the center of globalization analyses. It is unlikely, and perhaps undesirable, that areal spaces will somehow cease to be the main geographical form around which democratic politics are organized. Deeply sedimented forms of identity, conceptions of the rule of law, the numerical calculi of electoral aggregation, and, not least, modern state practices all ensure that some articulation of different geographies of representation is the most that can be expected anytime in the medium term. Perhaps it is useful to think of these issues and those affected as constituting a kind of hinterland for modern areal states, like the unincorporated countryside (or *khora*) of Periclean Athens, where many of its citizens and noncitizens lived (Sennett, 1994, pp. 52–53), a region to which in principle connections can and have to be made for democratic political justice to be possible, but which cannot be incorporated without fundamentally destabilizing those practices and institutions through which we currently imagine representation has to occur to make things happen.

But to say all this is, in a sense, to indulge in the same kinds of speculation that make the debates about globalization and democracy so unsatisfactory in the end. The national state is not in such a condition of crisis at the moment that there is not time to reflect carefully on what sorts of general possibilities are embodied in democratic practices as we currently understand them; to try and develop expanded conceptions of what representation in democratic politics might in principle mean, and only then to build on these to examine ways in which less exclusionary principles could be given effective, institutional forms. It is impossible to know what forms democracy is likely to take in its future geographical embodiments, but focusing on the truncated way in which problems of representation are considered within the framework of the politics of place at least helps underline the effects of assumptions about areal closure on the political imagination, and suggests that some of the forms it could take might well be surprising.

CONCLUSIONS

A tendency to confine political geographic analysis to areal forms of space has become more obvious in the context of debates about the political geography of globalization, where it has become deeply implicated in the way democracy is written about in relation to space. Global and local political scales are produced discursively in relation to a declining national democracy, as necessary/inevitable substitutes for an increasingly ineffective form of political arena. I have argued that this analysis reproduces a way of writing about politics centered on the copresence of agents (of various kinds) and the congruence of economics, politics, and culture. Connolly's politics of place is a convenient shorthand for this enduring set of ideas.

I have examined examples of work from two different fields in an effort to explore the resilience of the politics of place in critical analyses of globalization and to discern avenues on which future research might concentrate in order to enhance our understanding of how democracy works in relation to space. Democracy is not inherently areal in its spatial "logic." Empirically, its mechanisms are often best described in terms of networks that stretch across and interfere and articulate with areal boundaries in crucial ways. Normatively, the restriction of democratic decision-making processes to areally circumscribed communities is, to say the least, problematic, as it inhibits thinking about how we might overcome the difficulties involved in coping with distanciated relationships outside various more or less exclusionary imagined communities. Democratic theory has been much stimulated by Macpherson's (1962) notion of "possessive individualism." Our understanding of its essential historical complement, which we might term "possessive communitarianism," has a long way to go.[14]

Nonetheless, there are encouraging indications that this situation is undergoing rapid change. The influence of deconstruction, evident in some of the work on international relations discussed earlier, has led to a heightened sensitivity to assumptions about the self-sufficiency and self-identity of states and political communities. At a global level, research influenced by postcolonial theory is linking these concerns with processes of uneven development and national and racial ideologies. Network analyses in sociology and politics have, as previously outlined, begun to specify the complex chains of organizational and interpersonal interrelationships involved in electoral as well as movement activity, which exceed the areal spaces around which democratic practices are presently ordered.

The main aim of this chapter has been to attempt to undermine the entrenched link that has been established between democracy and areal spaces. In part, this has involved outlining the prevalence of the politics of place in discussions of democratic futures, and emphasizing the plural forms of space that have to come under consideration when examining democracy as it is currently practiced. There is a great deal that we do not currently understand about the practices of representation which are sustainable under the label of democracy, let alone about whether representative democracy can drive workable political arrangements in the crazy-quilt world of functional and regional institutions envisaged in some arguments in the globalization literature. The occasion offered by the current preoccupation with changing spatial forms of governance to question the necessities the politics of place imposes seems as good a "place" as any to start out from.

ACKNOWLEDGMENTS

Although I have not, for various reasons, been able to incorporate responses to all of their reactions, I would like to thank Clive Barnett, Sophie Bowlby, Kevin Cox, and Matt Sparke for their help and comments in the preparation and revision of this chapter.

NOTES

1. In essence, this picture is practically the same as that of a system of national states, internally democratic, where international relations are regulated through intergovernmentalism.

2. I discuss this work further in the next section.

3. The contrasting positions of Bennington (1994a, 1994b) and Robbins (1994) on the possibility of "cosmopolitan" politics raise many of these issues. Robbins points up the problematic nature of Bennington's arguments that, from the point of view of deconstruction, the frontier is a clearly deconstructable but thus "impassable" distinction. What may be an unavoidable stance with respect to conceptual distinctions (cf. Derrida, 1988) may be more problematic when transferred to issues of political boundaries and hierarchies.

4. Smith himself pursues such a language through a series of reflections on scale, leading him to a conception of politics similar to that expressed at times by Walker, involving the jumping between and the construction of new scales. It is difficult, in talking about politics in terms of scale, not to see emerging possibilities in areal terms. Granted, scale is not a concept that is intrinsically areal. Certainly, nonareal forms of space such as networks can be discussed in scale terms. *Generally*, however, scale does tend to be associated with "kinds of places" and to bring in its train metaphors like "sites" and "spheres" (Smith, 1993, pp. 99, 101–13). Smith (1993, p. 101) discusses a sequence of scales which, although augmented in important ways in the light of work on gender politics, is familiar from globalization discussions: the scale of the body, of home, of community, and the urban scale, the regional scale, the national, and the global.

5. Were a developed European party system to take shape around something like a European "state," which still seems unlikely, it is more probable, given the uneven development characterizing the continent, that a form of "sectional" party system, some-

thing like that which Bensel (1984) has analyzed in the U.S. context, would emerge, rather than the kinds of "cross-regional" alliances more characteristic of welfare capitalism.

6. The development of institutions involving elected representatives is one obvious example of such a change. Consider also the disappearance of earlier arrangements designed to render *citizens* "accountable" for their votes under more direct procedures (Sennett, 1994, pp. 61–67).

7. As a kind of paradigm of this, consider Tony Blair, the British Labour party leader, traveling to the South Pacific in 1995 and delivering an address apparently designed to build friendlier linkages with Rupert Murdoch's News International group, simultaneously influential in constituting British citizens as a certain kind of political community through its British newspapers and other media outlets, yet also obviously not "of" Britain or of any national space in important respects.

8. It does not seem very helpful, however, to extend a proper concern with the types of linkages political parties form with corporate entities into a position from which, because of these linkages, parties are seen as essentially "second-best" mechanisms of mobilization and representation, as though these latter processes can be unproblematically disentangled from networks of money and economic power. Movements are, after all, often dependent in myriad ways on monetary resources and even corporate support. In this sense, democracy always necessarily articulates economic and political networks, and this seems a more fruitful starting point for examining the problem of their geographical noncongruence than a problematic "separation" of private/networked economics and public/areal politics.

9. To the extent that they are, some researchers refer to them as "catnets" (cf. Tilly, 1986; White, 1992).

10. In geography, the imagery of the network as a general way of avoiding premature assumptions about boundedness and closure in talking about social change has been much stimulated by the work of Mann (1986). Unfortunately, the network as a critical metaphor for the kind of "messy" social relationships that render concepts of "society" unhelpful in examining social change is not consistently written into the explanations put forward in the body of Mann's work.

11. Unfortunately, this exaggerates the usual difficulties empirical network researchers have in obtaining relevant data, as publicly available aggregate data and electoral surveys are of limited utility in this context.

12. In a sense, all that the foregoing is intended to imply is that representation is no less problematic in "conventional" politics than it is in "texts" (although this is not to equate the two things). In an effective, practical sense, what Roland Barthes (1974, p. 9) had to say about realist readings of texts has much relevance when approaching the voting decision, where we might say that the flick of the lever or the mark in the box constituting the act of voting as an autonomous decision is, like the reference to "reality" Barthes finds problematic in realist criticism, "not the first meaning, but pretends to be so; under this illusion, it is ultimately no more than the *last* of the connotations (the one which seems both to establish and close the reading)."

13. At points like this, it would be better to have fewer studies simply of "ethnic voting patterns" in the U.S. context, and more of the mechanisms through which imaginary and real relationships with countries of origin have shaped the political process.

14. It is still common in prominent works of democratic theory to find that consideration of the justice of a particular territorial community being constituted as a decision-making "society," when a plurality of states and migration are admitted, is beyond the scope of the arguments put forward (e.g., Rawls, 1993, pp. 135–136). Possessive communitarianism has been an essential historical counterpart to possessive individualism for many of the same reasons that the development of national states has been an essential counterpart of the development of institutions of private property (cf. Giddens, 1985, pp. 190–192).

REFERENCES

Agnew, J., & Corbridge, S. (1995). *Mastering space: Hegemony, territory and international political economy.* London: Routledge.

Amin, A., & Thrift, N. (1992). Neo-Marshallian nodes in global networks. *International Journal of Urban and Regional Research, 16*(4), 571–587.

Amin, A., & Thrift, N. (1995). Institutional issues for the European regions: From markets and plans to socioeconomics and powers of association. *Economy and Society, 21*(4), 41–66.

Amin, S., Arrighi, G., Frank, A. G., & Wallerstein, I. (1990). *Transforming the revolution: Social movements and the world-system.* New York: Monthly Review Press.

Anderson, B. (1991). *Imagined communities* (rev. ed.). London: Verso.

Archibugi, D., & Held, D. (Eds.). (1995). *Cosmopolitan democracy: An agenda for a new world order.* Cambridge: Polity Press.

Arrighi, G., Hopkins, T. K., & Wallerstein, I. (1989). *Antisystemic movements.* London: Verso.

Ashley, R. K. (1987). The geopolitics of geopolitical space: Toward a critical social theory of international politics. *Alternatives, 12*, 403–434.

Ashley, R. K. (1995). The powers of anarchy: Theory, sovereignty and the domestication of global life. In J. Der Derian (Ed.), *International theory: Critical investigations* (pp. 94–128). New York: New York University Press.

Ashley, R. K., & Walker, R. B. J. (1990). Reading dissidence/writing the discipline: Crisis and the question of sovereignty in international studies. *International Studies Quarterly, 34*, 367–416.

Barthes, R. (1974). *S/Z.* New York: Farrar, Straus & Giroux.

Bauman, Z. (1989). *Modernity and the Holocaust.* Cambridge: Polity Press.

Bauman, Z. (1993). *Postmodern ethics.* Oxford: Blackwell.

Bennington, G. (1994a). The frontier: between Kant and Hegel. In *Legislations: The politics of deconstruction* (pp. 259–273). London: Verso.

Bennington, G. (1994b). La frontière infranchissable. In M. Mallet (Ed.), *Le passage des frontières* (pp. 259–273). Paris: Galilée.

Bensel, R. (1984). *Sectionalism and American political development, 1880–1980.* Madison: University of Wisconsin Press.

Birch, A. H. (1972). *Representation.* London: Pall Mall.

Brubaker, R. (1992). *Citizenship and nationhood in France and Germany.* Cambridge, MA: Harvard University Press.

Campbell, A., Converse, P. E., Miller, W. E., & Stokes, D. E. (1960). *The American voter*. New York: Wiley.

Campbell, A., Gurin, G., & Miller, W. E. (1954). *The voter decides*. Evanston, IL: Row, Peterson.

Castells, M. (1989). *The informational city: Information technology, economic restructuring and the urban-regional process*. Oxford: Blackwell.

Chase-Dunn, C. (1990). The limits of hegemony: Capitalism and global state formation. In D. P. Rapkin (Ed.), *World leadership and hegemony* (pp. 213–240). Boulder, CO: Lynne Rienner.

Clark, H. (1994). Taking up space: Redefining political legitimacy in New York City. *Environment and Planning A, 26,* 937–955.

Commission on Global Governance. (1995). *Our global neighborhood: Report of the Commission on Global Governance*. Oxford: Oxford University Press.

Connolly, W. E. (1991). Democracy and territoriality. *Millennium, 20*(3), 463–484.

Dahl, R. K. (1990). *Democracy and its critics*. New Haven: Yale University Press.

Derrida, J. (1976). *Of grammatology*. Baltimore: Johns Hopkins University Press.

Derrida, J. (1978). The theater of cruelty and the closure of representation. In *Writing and difference* (pp. 232–250). Chicago: University of Chicago Press.

Derrida, J. (1982a). Sending: On representation. *Social Research, 49*(2), 295–326.

Derrida, J. (1982b). Signature, event, context. In *Margins of philosophy* (pp. 307–330). Chicago: University of Chicago Press.

Derrida, J. (1988). Afterword. In *Limited Inc.* (pp. 111–154). Evanston: Northwestern University Press.

Dunn, J. (Ed.). (1994). *Contemporary crisis of the nation-state?* Oxford: Blackwell.

Featherstone, K. (1994). Jean Monnet and the "democratic deficit" in the European Union. *Journal of Common Market Studies, 32,* 149–170.

Ferguson, T. (1983). Party alignment and industrial structure: The investment theory of political parties in historical perspective. *Research in Political Economy, 6,* 1–82.

Ferguson, T. (1984). From Normalcy to New Deal: Industrial structure, party competition and American public policy in the Great Depression. *International Organization, 38,* 41–94.

Finifter, A. W. (1974). The friendship group as a protective environment for political deviants. *American Political Science Review, 68,* 607–625.

Gertler, M. (1988). The limits to flexibility: Comments on the post-fordist vision of production and its geography. *Transactions of the Institute of British Geographers, New Series, 13,* 419–432.

Giddens, A. (1981). *A contemporary critique of historical materialism*. London: Macmillan.

Giddens, A. (1985). *The nation-state and violence*. Cambridge: Polity Press.

Ginsburg, C. (1994). Killing a Chinese mandarin: The moral implications of distance. *Critical Inquiry, 21,* 46–60.

Gordon, D. (1988). The global economy: New edifice or crumbling foundations? *New Left Review, 168,* 24–65.

Granovetter, M. (1973). The strength of weak ties. *American Journal of Sociology, 78,* 1360–1380.

Granovetter, M. (1974). *Getting a job*. Chicago: University of Chicago Press.

Granovetter, M. (1985). Economic action and social structure: The problem of embeddedness. *American Journal of Sociology, 91,* 481–510.

Gray, J. (1996, 19 February). A union that man may put asunder. *The Guardian*, p. 13.

Guéhenno, M. (1995). *The end of the nation-state*. Minneapolis: University of Minnesota Press.

Held, D. (1991). Democracy, the nation-state and the global system. In D. Held (Ed.), *Political theory today* (pp. 169–192). Cambridge: Polity.

Held, D. (1993). Democracy: From city–states to a cosmopolitan order. In D. Held (Ed.), *Prospects for democracy: North, south, east, west* (pp. 13–52). Cambridge: Polity Press.

Held, D. (1995). *Democracy and the global order.* Cambridge: Polity Press.

Hirst, P., & Thompson, G. (1992). The problem of "globalization": International economic relations, national economic management and the formation of trading blocs. *Economy and Society, 21*, 357–396.

Hirst, P., & Thompson, G. (1995). Globalization and the future of the nation state. *Economy and Society, 24*(3), 408–442.

Horsman, M., & Marshall, A. (1993). *After the nation-state: Citizens, tribalism, and the new world disorder.* London: HarperCollins.

Katz, R. S., & Mair, P. (Eds.). (1994). *How parties organize.* Beverly Hills: Sage.

Kitschelt, H. (1990). New social movements and the decline of party organizations. In R. Dalton & M. Kuechler (Eds.), *Challenging the political order: New social and political movements in western democracies* (pp. 179–208). Oxford: Oxford University Press.

Knoke, P. (1990). *Political networks: The structural perspective.* Cambridge: Cambridge University Press.

Lawson, K. , & Merkl, P. (Eds.). (1988). *When parties fail: Emerging alternative organizations.* Princeton: Princeton University Press.

Lipietz, A. (1993). The local and the global: Regional individuality or interregionalism? *Transactions of the Institute of British Geographers, New Series, 18*, 8–18.

Lipschutz, R. D. (1992). Reconstructing world politics: The emergence of global civil society. *Millennium, 21*(3), 389–420.

MacPherson, C. B. (1962). *The political theory of possessive individualism.* Oxford: Oxford University Press.

Maisel, L. S. (Ed.). (1994). *The parties respond* (2nd ed.). Boulder: Westview.

Mann, M. (1986). *The sources of social power I: From the earliest times to 1800.* Cambridge: Cambridge University Press.

Massey, D. (1994). A global sense of place. In *Space, place and gender* (pp. 146–156). Cambridge: Polity Press.

Milward, A. (1992). *The European rescue of the nation-state.* London: Routledge.

Morley, D., & Robins, K. (1995). *Spaces of identity: Global media, electronic landscapes and cultural boundaries.* London: Routledge.

Murray, R. (1971). The internationalisation of capital and the nation-state. *New Left Review, 67*, 84–109.

Notermans, T. (1993). The abdication from national policy autonomy: Why the macroeconomic policy regime has become so unfavorable to labor. *Politics and Society, 21*(2), 133–167.

Ohmae, K. (1993). The rise of the region-state. *Foreign Affairs, 71*(2), 78–87.

Ohmae, K. (1995). *The end of the nation state.* New York: Free Press.

Painter, J., & Philo, C. (1995). Spaces of citizenship: An introduction. *Political Geography, 14*(2), 107–120.

Panitch, L. (1994). Globalization and the state. In R. Miliband & L. Panitch (Eds.), *Between globalism and nationalism (Socialist Register)* (pp. 60–93). London: Merlin.

Peterson, M. J. (1992). Transnational activity, international society and world politics. *Millennium, 21*(3), 371–388.

Picciotto, S. (1983). Jurisdictional conflicts, international law and the international state system. *International Journal of the Sociology of Law, 11,* 11–40.

Pincetl, S. (1994). Challenges to citizenship: Latino immigrants and political organizing in the Los Angeles area. *Environment and Planning A, 26,* 895–914.

Pitkin, H. F. (1967). *The concept of representation.* Berkeley: University of California Press.

Preteceille, E. (1990). Political paradoxes of urban restructuring: Globalization of the economy and localization of politics? In J. Logan & T. Swanstrom (Eds.), *Beyond the city limits* (pp. 27–57). Philadelphia: Temple University Press.

Rawls, J. (1993). *Political liberalism.* New York: Columbia University Press.

Rengger, N. J. (1992). A city which sustains all things? Communitarianism and international society. *Millennium, 21*(3), 353–369.

Robbins, B. (1994). Cosmopolitanismes. In M. Mallet (Ed.), *Le passage des frontières* (pp. 431–434). Paris: Galilée.

Rogin, M. P. (1967). *The intellectuals and McCarthy: The radical specter.* Cambridge, MA: MIT Press.

Rosanvallon, P. (1992). *Le sacre du citoyen: Histoire du suffrage universel en France.* Paris: Gallimard.

Rosenberg, J. (1994). *The empire of civil society: A critique of the realist theory of international relations.* London: Verso.

Rueschemeyer, D., Stephens, E. H., & Stephens, J. D. (1992). *Capitalist development and democracy.* Cambridge: Polity Press.

Ruggie, J. G. (1993). Territoriality and beyond: Problematizing modernity in international relations. *International Organization, 47*(1), 139–174.

Ruiz, L. E. J. (1991). After national democracy: Radical democratic politics at the edge of modernity. *Alternatives, 16,* 161–200.

Sandel, M. (1982). *Liberalism and the limits of justice.* Cambridge: Cambridge University Press.

Sennett, R. (1994). *Flesh and stone: The body and the city in western civilization.* London: Faber.

Sjoeblom, G. (1983). Political change and political accountability. In H. Daalder & P. Mair (Eds.), *Western European party systems* (pp. 369–404). Beverly Hills: Sage.

Skocpol, T. (1979). *States and social revolutions.* Cambridge: Cambridge University Press.

Smith, N. (1993). Homeless/global: Scaling places. In J. Bird, B. Curtis, T. Putnam, G. Robertson, & L. Tickner (Eds.), *Mapping the futures* (pp. 87–119). London: Routledge.

Spruyt, H. (1994a). Institutional selection in international relations: State anarchy as order. *International Organization, 48*(4), 527–558.

Spruyt, H. (1994b). *The sovereign state and its competitors: An analysis of systems change.* Princeton: Princeton University Press.

Steenbergen, B. van (Ed.). (1994). *The condition of citizenship.* London: Sage.

Storper, M. (1992). The limits to globalization: Technology districts and international trade. *Economic Geography, 68*(1), 60–93.

Streek, W. (1992). Inclusion and secession: Questions on the boundaries of associative democracy. *Politics and Society, 20*(4), 513–520.

Streek, W., & Schmitter, P. (1991). From national corporatism to transnational pluralism: Organized interests in the Single European Market. *Politics and Society, 19*(2), 133–164.

Tassin, E. (1992). Europe: A political community. In C. Mouffe (Ed.), *Dimensions of radical democracy* (pp. 169–192). London: Verso.

Taylor, P. J. (1994). The state as container: Territoriality in the modern world-system. *Progress in Human Geography, 18*(2), 151–162.

Taylor, P. J. (1995). Beyond containers: Internationality, interstateness, interterritoriality. *Progress in Human Geography, 19*(1), 1–15.

Tether, P. (1994). The overseas vote in British national elections 1982–1992. *Parliamentary Affairs, 47*(1), 73–93.

Thompson, J. E., & Krasner, S. D. (1989). Global transactions and the consolidation of sovereignty. In E. Czempiel & J. N. Rosenau (Eds.), *Global changes and theoretical challenges* (pp. 195–219). Lexington, MA: Lexington Books.

Tilly, C. (1986). *Big structures, large processes, huge comparisons.* Beverly Hills: Sage.

Tilly, C. (1992). *European revolutions.* Cambridge: Cambridge University Press.

Tilly, C. (1995). Globalization threatens labor's rights. *International Labor and Working-Class History, 47,* 1–23.

Walker, R. B. J. (1987). Realism, change and international political theory. *International Studies Quarterly, 31,* 65–86.

Walker, R. B. J. (1990). Security, sovereignty, and the challenge of world politics. *Alternatives, 15,* 3–27.

Walker, R. B. J. (1991a). On the spatiotemporal conditions of democratic practice. *Alternatives, 16,* 243–262.

Walker, R. B .J. (1991b). State sovereignty and the articulation of political space/time. *Millennium, 20*(3), 445–461.

Walker, R. B. J. (1993). *Inside/outside: International relations as political theory.* Cambridge: Cambridge University Press.

Walker, R. B. J., & Magnusson, W. (Eds.). (1990). *Contending sovereignties: Redefining political community.* London: Lynne Reiner.

Wallerstein, I. (1984). *The politics of the world-economy.* Cambridge: Cambridge University Press.

Walzer, M. (1983). *Spheres of justice: A defense of pluralism and equality.* New York: Basic Books.

White, H. (1992) *Identity and control: A structural theory of social action.* Princeton: Princeton University Press.

Young, I. M. (1990). *Justice and the politics of difference.* Princeton: Princeton University Press.

Zolberg, A. R. (1995). Working-class dissolution. *International Labor and Working-Class History, 47,* 28–38.

Author Index

Subject Index

Advanced manufacturing technologies (AMT), Canadian use of; study, 53–57
AFL-CIO, 170, 171, 173, 176, 177, 181–182, 184
anti-Soviet policy, 174
Alchian's model of economic selection, 104, 105, 108
American Federation of Labor (AFL), 170, 173–174, 175–176, 177
American Institute for Free Labor Development (AIFLD), 177, 179–180
Arthur Andersen's *Guide to Corporate Exposure Management*, 109n3
Apartheid, 184–185
Ashley, R., 252, 253
Association of Superannuation Funds of Australia (ASFA), 109n3
Austria, 203
Automobiles, 24
production, 182–183
See also Honda Motor Co.

Bank deposits, 234n11
Bank of England, 139
Bankruptcies, 137–140
Barings Bank, 137, 138–139, 159
Boundaries, national, 7
Bretton Woods agreement, 154, 155, 201, 223
Bridge building policy, 226
British Leyland. *See new name* Rover Group
Business hierarchies, global, 23–26

Callaghan, James, 234n7
Canada, 60n10
advanced manufacturing technologies; study, 53–57
macroregulatory framework, 57
Capital, 58, 125, 132
classical theory, 188
concepts of, 128–131
distributional politics and, 115
labor and, 149–150, 185–191, 212–213
mobility of, 9, 10, 46, 119–126, 201–206, 210
productive; spatial limits, 45–59

Capital Asset Pricing Model (CAPM), 91
Capital goods, 49
Capitalism, 146
global, 31–32
historical geography of, 144–145
Capital theory (classical), 188
Caribbean, 177–181
Castells, Manuel; *The Informational City*, 244–248
Center on Transnational Corporations, 169
Central Intelligence Agency (CIA), 174, 176
Chicago Board of Trade, 111n15
Christopherson, S., 57
Clark, Gordon L., 8–9, 89–108, 133–134n6
Clothing industry, 24
The Cold War, 174–177
Commodity trade, 22
Communications, 35, 54
space-transcending technologies, 47, 105, 120
See also Telecommunications media
Community, ideas of, 251, 255–256
Competition
hierarchy, regulation, and, 36–41
international, 155
product-based forms of, 122
spatial scale and, 150–151
wage regulation and, 149
weak versus strong, 129–130, 134n11
Competitive austerity, 12
Components; sourcing, localization of, 75–76
Computer industry; globalization, pattern of, 24
Confederacion Regional Obrera Mexicana (CROM), 177–178
Confederacion de Trabajadores de America Latina (CTAL), 178–179
Confederacion Interamericana de Trabajadores (CIT), 179
Congress of Industrial Organizations (CIO), 170, 175–176
Connolly, W., 241, 255
Corporations, multinational, 7, 64–67
vertically disintegrated firms, 121
See also Honda Motor Co.
Cox, Kevin R., 1–17, 115–132

The Dawes House

The Place Where You are Always Welcome

The place where you are always welcome

The Dawes House

The Place Where You are Always Welcome

A selection of letters and journals of
Rufus R. Dawes, Mary Beman Gates Dawes,
and members of their family.

Introduction and family history by
Peggy Dempsey

ISBN-13: 978-0615962771
ISBN-10: 0615962777

Cover and illustrations from the Dempsey family photo collection

Peggy Dempsey
Juliacutlerjournal@gmail.com

This book is available for sale on amazon.com

For "Sister"
Mary Frances Dawes Beach,
who saved the letters.

Acknowledgements

First and foremost I am grateful to Rufus R. Dawes and Mary Beman Gates Dawes who were prolific letter writers and who always wrote from the heart. They live on in their words.

A large measure of appreciation goes deservedly to their daughter, Mary Frances Dawes Beach, who sorted and preserved family letters, typed many of them, and distributed many to institutions where they can be properly preserved.

A huge debt of gratitude to Linda Showalter, Special Collections Librarian at Marietta College in Marietta, Ohio, for the great care she has shown to the Cutler/Dawes collection and for her generous assistance on our many trips to the Library.

Thank you also to cousin David Murray who called to ask if we were interested in some old family papers. Through David we were introduced to the large collection of Dawes/Cutler materials.

To David Vermillion, former Historian at the Dawes Arboretum for his helpful assistance in uncovering letters and documents.

To the DWDWRA (Descendants of William Dawes Who Rode Association) for their encouragement and for their enthusiasm for learning about their ancestors at Dawes Reunions.

To our friends in Marietta: cousins Barb and Jack Moberg for their enthusiasm, encouragement and hospitality; Tom Reebel and Linda Fleming for providing laughter and respite from hours in the library, and to Richard and Margit Hershey, current owners of 508 Fourth Street, for allowing us to see the house as it is now and for their interest in its history.

And especially to my husband, Rich Dempsey, great-grandson of Rufus and Mary Dawes, for his support while I so often "sink back into the nineteenth century." By marrying Rich, I was introduced to his ancestors and his cousins which propelled me "down the rabbit hole" and into a series of satisfying lifelong projects.

Contents

Introduction

Mary Frances Dawes, the fourth of six children, was born and raised in the Dawes family home at 508 Fourth Street in Marietta, Ohio. Her parents, Rufus R. Dawes and Mary Beman Gates Dawes, purchased the house in 1870 and lived there until the end of their lives. Mary Frances Dawes, who was always called Sister by the Dawes family, left home after her marriage to Arthur Granville Beach in 1896. They lived for a time in Wisconsin and Michigan but returned to Marietta in 1913 when Arthur became a professor of English at Marietta College.

The Beach family moved into the Dawes House at 508 Fourth Street after the death of Mary Gates Dawes. The home was filled with family furniture and the attic contained boxes of family letters, journals, and books. Mary Beach read and sorted through the old letters, then learned to type so that she could share some of them with her siblings and their children. She also wrote biographies based on the letters, and then distributed most of the originals to various libraries and historical institutions. A small part of this large collection of family papers and books, however, was passed down by Mary Beach to her eldest daughter Alice Beach Murray who passed it to her son David Murray. When David moved into an assisted living facility in 2008, he offered these family papers to his cousin, Rich Dempsey.

I had been aware, as Rich's wife, that Rich was descended from the Dawes family but I knew little about their family history. I had researched my own family's past, however, and was enthusiastic to learn more about Rich's family through their old books and papers. I remember our trip to David Murray's house in Syracuse, New York: we chatted with David over lunch and then he brought out boxes and plastic bags full of books and folders. The old musty books held the intoxicating appeal that all old books hold for me, but I was especially delighted to discover handwritten letters. The heavy paper covered with even script had been carefully preserved for 150 years. I was immediately drawn in, curious to know who wrote the letters and what would be revealed about their authors and the times in which they lived. David's collection also included several folders of typed manuscripts written by Rich and David's grandmother, Mary Beach. She had written biographies of her parents, Rufus R. Dawes and Mary Beman Gates Dawes, using many excerpts from their letters and journals. Old photographs were glued to the pages of her typewritten manuscripts.

That is how I began a journey back into the nineteenth century with vivid contemporary letters as my passport to the lives of the Dawes, Gates, and Cutler families. These families all lived in or near Marietta, Ohio and left behind an amazing written legacy. The letter writers speak candidly, with spirit and humor. After reading hundreds of

letters and journal entries I can almost imagine these admirable people are not really gone, just living in a far off place. My respect for the family is immense. Rich and I have since made many research trips to read additional family letters in Newark and Marietta, Ohio, and Evanston, Illinois.

My purpose in preparing this small book is to share with Dawes's descendants and those interested in the Dawes family a portion of the hundreds of letters they left behind. In this collection, the focus is on the family and home life created by Rufus and Mary Dawes at 508 Fourth Street in Marietta. I have written a brief family history to provide a context for the letters. Most of the letters that I have chosen were written by Rufus R. Dawes, with additional letters from Mary Gates Dawes and some of their children.

Among the family photos is a picture of the Dawes home labeled *The place where you are always welcome.* I think of the handwritten letters and journals, preserved by the family all these years, as an invitation into that home. Through their own words we experience the welcoming, loving home life that they created and enjoyed at 508 Fourth Street in Marietta, Ohio.

A Brief Family History

Rufus Dawes was born July 4, 1838 in Malta, Ohio. He was the fifth child of Henry Dawes and Sarah Cutler Dawes. Henry and Sarah's marriage was not a happy one, and they legally separated in 1840 with Sarah returning to her father's home, the Old Stone House in Constitution, Warren County, Ohio, six miles from Marietta. The terms of the separation agreement allowed the children to live with their mother. When the sons reached the age of ten, however, they were to live with their father.

Rufus's early childhood was filled with a loving extended family in the Old Stone House. Along with his mother and siblings, the family included his grandparents, Ephraim and Sally Cutler, his uncle, William Cutler, and

The Old Stone House, Constitution, Ohio

his aunt, Julia Cutler. Upon turning ten, Rufus stayed most of the year with his father, first in Malta, Ohio, and later in Wisconsin. There he experienced a different kind of family life. Henry Dawes was strict as a father and ambitious as a businessman.   Early on, Henry Dawes was quite parsimonious with his money.

Rufus visited Marietta when he was allowed and he began to write to his mother and sisters. In the fall of 1856, Henry Dawes had moved to Wisconsin and enrolled Rufus in Wisconsin State University at Madison. Rufus studied there for two years, spending the summers doing farm labor. In the fall of 1858, his father allowed him to transfer to Marietta College and Rufus was quite happy to be back among his friends and near his mother's side of the family.

Mary Beman Gates caught Rufus's eye in Marietta and he was immediately smitten. She was four years younger than he, lively, musical, cheerful, and pretty. He began to call on her, but she was often shy around him and did not provide much encouragement.

In the fall of 1859, Rufus left Marietta College and returned to Wisconsin to work for his father. His father had a store and had also purchased 750 acres which needed to be cleared. Rufus wrote to his sister Jane that he felt he could get ahead faster in Wisconsin than in Ohio and he was eager to help support his mother and sisters. While in Wisconsin, Rufus made stump speeches for the Republicans and was becoming well known as a promising speaker and a young man of integrity.

Rufus's plans changed in April 1861 when Fort Sumter fell to the Confederates and President Lincoln put out a call for 75,000 volunteers. Rufus organized a regiment and was elected Captain. He spent the next three years serving with the Sixth Wisconsin Volunteers as part of the Iron Brigade in the Army of the Potomac. The first part of the war he saw little action as his regiment spent most of its time drilling near Washington, D. C. In late December 1861, Rufus had ten days leave and traveled to Marietta where he visited with his family and called on Mary Gates. Soon after, in the spring of 1862, Rufus's regiment began to march south to engage in major battles: Rappahannock, Gainesville, Groveton, Second Bull Run, South Mountain, Antietam, and Fredericksburg.

Rufus next received leave on March 10, 1863 and made his way to Marietta. He again called on Mary, but she was quite shy. When Rufus returned to his regiment, he wrote to Mary asking permission to correspond with her. She wrote back declining; after all, when men and women corresponded in those days, it was assumed that they were engaged. Upon receiving Mary's letter, Rufus wrote her again, this time professing his love for her even though "I am by no means so egotistical or presumptious to assume. . . that I have inspired a like sentiment." Mary responded by giving him permission to write to her, but with the clear understanding that they were not engaged.

Shortly after their correspondence began, Rufus's regiment prepared to move out. Anticipating heavy

fighting and fearing that the few letters Mary had written to him would fall into the hands of the enemy should he be wounded, Rufus placed them in a large envelope along with a short note to Mary saying that she would be receiving these only in the event of his death. Rufus entrusted the envelope to a camp surgeon and after the battle, to his dismay, the doctor could not locate the envelope. Both the doctor and Rufus assumed that it had been lost in the confusion of the battle. It had, however, been mailed to Mary, causing her great distress as well as worry and anguish for Rufus's family. By the time word finally reached Mary that Rufus was safe, she knew that she loved him enough to become engaged.

Once they became engaged, Rufus's letters to Mary are frequent, earnest and hopeful. Rufus was involved in many more battles in 1863 including Fitzhugh's Crossing, Chancellorsville, and Gettysburg. He continued to request leave to return to Marietta to see Mary and finally was granted seven days leave beginning November 21, 1863. He traveled three days and had four days to visit and plan with Mary. Two months later, many men of the Sixth Wisconsin re-enlisted as veterans and were granted 30 days leave. His men went home to Wisconsin and Rufus travelled to Marietta where he and Mary were quietly married on January 18, 1864.

Thus far in the war, Rufus had been engaged in many battles and miraculously had not been wounded. As time passed and many others in his regiment fell, he understood

that the odds were against him surviving unscathed. As a newly married man, he very desperately wanted to survive and return to Mary. In 1864 he fought in the Wilderness, at the Bloody Angle in Spottsylvania, at Jericho Ford, North Anna, Tolopotomy, Cold Harbor, James River, and Petersburg. Family lore is that he was the only officer to participate in that many battles without being wounded. Rufus was at last discharged August 10, 1864, and arrived in Marietta in September.

Home at last, Rufus and Mary lived first with Mary's parents in her parents's house at the corner of Fourth and Putnam (now the Betsey Mills Club, named for Mary's sister). Their first child, Charles Gates Dawes, was born there in August, 1865. In the fall of 1865, Rufus, Mary and Charley moved into the "cottage" at 309 Fourth Street. They lived there for five years, and by 1870, they had added two more sons to their family: Rufus Cutler Dawes and Beman Gates Dawes. They were outgrowing the cottage so they bought a larger house, just down the street at 508 Fourth Street. They moved into the house in time for Thanksgiving 1870. A notice appeared in the *Marietta Register:*

> *Mrs. Gen. Dawes paid Mrs. A. B. Waters $15,000 for her new house on Fourth Street, and J. W. Nye paid $5,000 for the Dawes cottage on the same street near Putnam.*

After the Civil War, Rufus engaged in business, primarily selling lumber for railroad ties. Rufus and Mary were sometimes apart; Rufus occasionally travelled for his various business ventures and at least once during the summer of 1870, Mary and their three boys spent several weeks in Beverly, Massachusetts with Mary's parents and sister Bettie. Whenever Rufus and Mary were apart, they wrote frequently to one another.

After three boys, they finally had a daughter in 1872, Mary Frances Dawes. She was followed by another boy, Henry May Dawes, and a second daughter, Betsey Gates Dawes.

Rufus, who was well-liked, well-respected and had made "stump" speeches since he was 21, was elected to the 47th Congress, representing Ohio's Fifteenth District in the House of Representatives as a Republican in 1881. For the next two years, he lived in a boarding house in Washington, D.C. much of the time and resumed his practice of writing frequently to his wife. He also wrote individual letters to his children. Sometimes the children would visit their grandparents or their Aunt Bettie. During one of these visits in 1881, Mary wrote to her son Beman:

> *My dear dear Beman,*
> *. . . . . .Your father has written me at least twice every day since he went away, and sometimes three times a day--He does not write very long letters, but when ever he thinks of anything he wants to tell me he*

writes a few lines, and always writes the last
thing before he goes to bed. I enjoy getting
his letters very much. He is very homesick
for us all. You know he never likes to be
away from home and always comes back a
little sooner than we expect.

Rufus served one term in Congress and then returned to his lumber business in Marietta. He and Mary worked on a memoir of his time in the Civil War and published *Service with the Sixth Wisconsin Volunteers* in 1890.

Rufus fell ill with nervous prostration in the summer of 1889. He never fully recovered his health and had repeated illnesses throughout the remainder of his life. He retained his cheerful outlook even as he lost the use of his legs and was confined to his rolling chair. Rufus began to keep a journal again and on March 3, 1893 he wrote:

How many beautiful years have passed over
our beautiful home. The sunset years are
even brighter than the dawning.

The sunset years were bright, filled with the loving care of his family. Rufus R. Dawes died at home on August 1, 1899 at the age of 61.

Mary continued to live at 508 Fourth Street, traveling frequently to visit her six children and her many grandchildren. After her death on October 28, 1921, her daughter's family, Mary and Arthur Beach, moved into the house. Arthur Beach was an English professor at Marietta College and Mary Beach worked on her own family history writing projects. Together they raised four children.

The house continued to be a welcoming place for all of the Dawes family. In June of 1924, Charles Gates Dawes waited at 508 Fourth Street with Sister and their brothers Henry and Beman as the Republican convention decided on a nominee for Vice-President of the United States. When the decision was announced, a large crowd gathered on the lawn to celebrate the nomination of Charles Gates Dawes.

Ten years later, after a long illness, Arthur Beach died. Even with financial assistance from her brothers, Sister could not continue to maintain the house. An inventory was made of the furnishings, letters and journals were donated to various institutions, and 508 Fourth Street was sold to St. Mary's Catholic Church. One last family gathering was held at the family home, the wedding of Sister and Arthur's youngest daughter, Betsey Mills Beach to Edward Dempsey, on June 13, 1936. *The house where you are always welcome* was home to the Dawes family for 65 years.

Mary Frances Dawes,
'Sister'

Letters and Journals

A description of her father, Rufus R. Dawes, by Mary Dawes Beach, 'Sister'

Rufus's gift for making friends came into play early in life. He liked to know all about people. He was fascinated by the experiences of those he met as he was by novels and stories. He was a fine listener. He was responsive too and liked to talk. He would tell his own experiences and reactions with animation and humor, and evident enjoyment. It is odd that one who talked so freely and with such apparent openness should have been so reserved about himself. He would tell everything that happened to him with high spirit, but of his inner life, not one word. He was regarded as undemonstrative even by his mother and sisters. His feelings, his religion, his inner aspirations and his suffering were all locked in his own heart. He disliked sentimentality and one cannot escape the feeling that sometimes he feared to express himself at all lest his exceedingly sensitive and deep feeling should run away with him and he would appear to be sentimental. His emotions were profound and his loyalty unchanging. Like many people with deep feelings his humor was a pronounced characteristic, and played over the surface of his life from the beginning to the end.

Letter from Rufus R. Dawes on his 19th birthday to his sister Kate Dawes

Madison

July 4th, 1857

Dear Kate,

Your letter dated June 2nd came duly to hand and I doubt not that you will be delighted at the promptness with which it is answered. But it would have been answered four weeks sooner if it had not been for one thing and that was just this I had no money to pay postage with now this is just the reason I have not written to you before and I feel as sorry for it as you can but felt unwilling to borrow money. We went without candles for three weeks and I kept borrowing them, after we got out of money, until I was ashamed to ask and the same was the case with postage stamps. But we have got some money now and I sit down on this my 19th birthday with a much lighter heart to write you a long letter hoping to make up thereby in part for the long silence I have kept.

By the way I am going to make some money for myself this long vacation so that I will have some by me all the time for such contingencies. Father seems to think that when he has paid our board and tuition for the term that it is rather an extra expense to have to send money for anything else but I guess we can manage to get along with him by hook or crook.

Well as I said before I write on my 19th birthday. Do you know that your hopeful brother is almost a man in everything but intellect? 19 years old 5 feet 8 inches tall and weighs 160 pounds? Such is the case.

I have been led to reflect a little today. True I am almost a man and have lived 19 years but where have they all gone. I find in reflecting that there have been many weeks and even months of my life passed into eternity   a single circumstance that took place in which connected with myself I cannot call to memory, and thinking that it would have been a source of satisfaction to me if I had kept some slight record by which I might be reminded of some of the happier moments of my life and also of its darker hours, of which there have been many, I have resolved to keep a daily journal of whatever transpires which I will be glad to call to mind in future time should I be permitted to remain long in this world. But I am afraid if I keep on in this style it will be a prosy letter.

There was a great circus in town yesterday having a steam callíope (I marked the long syllable so that you won't call it calliōpe as most do) along with it. So I trudged down in the hot sun along with the rest to look at the calliope. It is a curious machine and when you stand close to it the music sounds like the noise of ten thousand pigs but at a distance of a mile you can make out that it is shrieking a tune.

I guess that we will stay at Black Earth this vacation. I can make a dollar a day any time I want it harvesting there.

I feel very proud of Uncle William's speech ever since I read it in the Independent it is a masterly thing speaking of it as a literary production. We take the Observer which was too mean to give a report of it but a student Mr. Hand who rooms in the next room takes the Independent and there was where I read it.

My marks on scholarship were 95 last term, on deportment 100. The highest ever got in the institution on scholarship is 96.

What is Henry doing now? I wish I could come to Marietta and enter the Sophomore class there next term.
10 o'clock P.M.

I have been down to see the fireworks which were a humbug. But I saw more women than I ever saw at one time before, the crowd in the park was estimated at 12 to 15 thousand and more than half were women who had come out in the cool evening to see the fireworks. Taking it all around this is the meanest 4th of July I ever saw. The crowd was the most contemptible I ever saw, gambling going on every where in every possible way, thousands of drunken men and dozens of fights and brawls and one man was shot three times and several were stabbed and there was almost a regular battle between the 2 fire companies. But I must go to bed. Write and tell me how you spent the Fourth. My love to all

Your aff Bro
Rufus

From the Journal of Rufus R. Dawes

Sunday, Nov. 28th, 1858

Went and heard two of Parson Wick's prosy sermons. Read Pickwick Papers the rest of the time.

It is utterly impossible for me to take any interest in the sermons I hear from Sabbath to Sabbath. The fact is, and perhaps it is a deplorable fact, I take no interest in religious matters. It is certainly very discreditable to me that I have lived this long without having any definite views upon such an important subject as the gospel plan of salvation. Must think of this matter.

Rufus R. Dawes

From the Journal of Rufus R. Dawes

Friday, Jan. 21st, 1859

Have today been thinking some, and the result of my cogitations was that I have concluded to try to write more, to think more, to read more, and to practice more in speaking; or in plain terms, I have determined to endeavor not to be so confoundedly lazy. I need to write more because my style is harsh and unpolished, my penmanship bad, my crythography worse, and because my command of language, already poor, is daily, from want of nourishment, becoming worse. (Of all which facts the sentence just written affords ample proof.) Horace says that the pen is the best master for acquiring a good style, and Cicero and Quintillian earnestly recommend to the orator the liberal use of it. Why should I not avail myself of the advice of these great rhetoricians? I need to think more for a variety of reasons. First, because my mind is not well disciplined as it should be. Although I have read the Latin and Greek and studied the Mathematics prescribed for the college student, yet the superficial manner in which I have done it has left me without having derived any perceptible advantage from them. I have played chess a great deal, thinking that I might acquire discipline from it, which may be possible, but while I occupy my thoughts with such things knowledge of vastly more importance than abstract discipline is fading from my memory.

A second important reason why I should think more is that there is a multitude of more important subjects upon which I have not bestowed a moment's attention.

I should read more because I am so woefully ignorant, and because reading interesting works will, I believe, strengthen my memory. I need also to acquire a taste for reading.

Was invited to a tea party at Fanny Bosworth's. Went and had a pretty fair time.

RALLY!
BOYS. RALLY!!

ENLISTMENTS WANTED FOR THE LEMONWEIR MINUTE MEN!

HEAD QUARTERS, L. M. M. CO.
Mauston, June 17, 1861.

This company is ordered by the Commander in Chief, to hold itself in readiness to be mustered into service on Monday, June 24. Men are wanted to complete the full complement of one hundred and one. Come forward boys, and place your names on the roll.

R. R. DAWES, Capt.

From the Journal of Julia P. Cutler

Thursday, July 4, 1861

I thought this morning of the living and of the dead absent from us; of Rufus who is today twenty three years old. He and his company have been received into the Sixth Wisconsin regiment under Col. Lysander Cutler. Rufus has talent and principle. He is not tall but firmly built and very athletic. He has a very bright and intelligent countenance and I think will be popular with his men. He always makes warm friends. May our fathers' God bless the lad.

Julia P. Cutler

From Rufus R. Dawes to Mary B. Gates

Hdq. 6th Wis. Vol.

Camp near Belle Plain

March 24, 1863

Miss Mary B. Gates,

The indications here are of hard work very soon. Encouraged by the sympathy and sound doctrine I met with among people at home, I shall go into the struggle cheerfully and hopefully.

I hope you will answer this note. It would give me a great deal of pleasure to correspond with you. Are you willing?

Very respectfully,

Rufus R. Dawes

From Rufus R. Dawes to Mary B. Gates

April 15, 1863
Sixth Wis. Vol.
First Division
First Corps.

Miss Mary B. Gates,

Almost a week ago I received a paper from you in acknowledgment of my note. My inference was that you wished me to understand that you politely declined to accede to my request to correspond.

Tomorrow under our present orders we are to commence our active campaign and I may not soon have another opportunity, so I have at last, at imminent peril of placing myself in a character most galling to my pride, concluded to tell you plainly why I asked you to correspond with me.

It was because I love you -- because by the strongest and holiest impulses of my nature I am drawn toward you as the only woman I ever loved, or it seems to me, I ever can love. I am by no means so egotistical or presumptuous as to assume as a reason for addressing you thus, that I have inspired a like sentiment. Indeed if I have rightly interpreted, the indications are that so great a blessing is not in store for me. If, in the face of such discouraging circumstances I am making a fool of myself by declaring a hopeless passion I can't help it. If I had not found it utterly

useless to try to help loving you I never should have written this letter. However you may regard my suit, I am sure you will find sufficient in the letter to excuse me for writing it.

Rufus R. Dawes

From Rufus R. Dawes to Mary B. Gates

6th Wis. Vol. 1st Div.
1st Corps, Army of Potomac
April 26, 1863

Mary B.,

I have received your letter and hasten to avail myself of your permission to write again. I must tell you candidly that there is but one subject upon which I find it in my heart to address you, so long as I may do so without offense. I approach it more readily because I <u>have</u> found hope in your letter, a hope which slender as it is, I would not give up for all else I hope for in this world, a hope that has almost made a coward of me for fear there will be a battle before I can know that it will be realized, or that I must give it up forever.

I am grateful to you for believing me to be sincere. I know very well that I can add nothing of force to what I have already said by argument or protestation; but I will assure you that my love is no transient or hastily conceived passion. Do you find anything inconsistent with weak human nature in my conduct toward you while in College when I tell you that it was then my constant effort to crush my love for you because I believed it a hopeless love?

Hopeless because it was unrequited, hopeless because without any fixed aim or object in life and with a doubtful future I had no right to ask you to return it.

I will tell you once when I thought of you. It would sound very silly to any one else and may to you.

Shortly after the battle opened at Antietam our colonel was shot. I succeeded to the command, becoming with my life and honor responsible for the good conduct of my regiment. You have heard the story how we were broken to pieces and driven back in confusion, more than half of our numbers bleeding or dying on the field. Orders, exhortations, entreaties were in vain to rally my men, overcome with a terrible fear of Death.

I took the Wisconsin state flag in my hand and swinging it over my head, and calling every man from Wisconsin to follow me I turned back into the open field. When I took that color in my hand I gave up all hope of life. It did not occur to me as possible that I could carry that flag into the deadly storm and live. Four men had fallen under it. I felt all the burning throng of thoughts and emotions that always come with the presence of death. I had no right to think of you then. I would have died with your name on my lips.

Notwithstanding what you have said, I shall look anxiously for an answer to this letter. God has no higher blessing for me than the realization of my hope that that day will come when you "know that the love you have for me is more than life, a love which shall last through time and eternity".

R. R. D.

P. S.   I write this on a soldier's desk, a drum head. I am on duty as field officer of the Picket. R. R. D.

From Rufus R. Dawes to Mary B. Gates

May 8, 1863

After ten days of fighting, toiling and suffering we have, north of the Rappahannock, a day of respite and comparative ease   Not a single newspaper man has been allowed to come within our lines since the movement commenced and only today have I learned that the Rebels made a raid upon the B. & O. R.R. capturing mail about the time I sent a letter in reply to yours. I am informed also by an officer of our Division staff that Army mail has been delayed until now since the fighting began.

I am much troubled lest you may not have received my letter. The thought is intolerable that by any accident you may have reason to suspect that I failed or delayed to write you. Inspired by the hope I found in your letter, I have striven to bear myself through this terrible ordeal as I thought you would be proud to have me.

R. R. D.

From Rufus R. Dawes to Mary B. Gates
(intended to be sent only in the event that Rufus was killed in battle)

April 28, 1863

We are advancing upon the enemy. I doubt not that we must have a bloody desperate battle. I leave this where I have perfect confidence it will be sent to you in case I am killed and only in that event.

I loved you dearly, sincerely and I am sure my dying prayer will be that God will bless you always and make you happy. I don't believe you will ever think lightly of the love of a man, who, if he had few other merits, gave his life freely for his country and the right.

Rufus R. Dawes

From Rufus R. Dawes to Mary B. Gates

May 8, 1863

You can scarcely imagine my embarrassment, regret and indignation at learning this afternoon that a letter I had left to be sent to you if I was killed and "only in that event" had been permitted to get into the mail. I left it with Dr. Preston, chief surgeon of our brigade, a gentleman of the strictest honor, who accepted the trust without impertinent prying and solemnly pledged himself to carry it out. And he did until our army began to retreat, when our surgeons were taken with panic.

Under the pressure of this panic the doctor put the letter in the mail or lost it. Shortly after, realizing what he had done and terribly embarrassed and chagrined, forgetting entirely the person to whom the letter was directed, he wrote to my sister Lucy, begging her not to open a letter she would receive directed in my hand writing. What an intensely annoying situation.

I can not tell you how much I have been troubled by this mistake. I said nothing I am ashamed or sorry to have you know. I did not wish to destroy your letters, and it was only under the circumstances a matter of honor to send them back to you. I shall feel very anxious to know whether you got the letter or not.

R. R. D.

From Rufus R. Dawes to Mary B. Gates

Camp near White Oak Church

May 11, 1863

I never was more shocked in my life than at receiving letters from my sisters last night written in all the anguish of believing me killed or desperately wounded. I had very little idea that you would really get my letter for I believed Dr. Preston had lost it and I was feeling very badly about that.

I shudder to think of the pain and suffering this most unfortunate mistake has caused my mother and sisters. I feel so grossly outraged now by the carelessness of Dr. Preston that I can scarcely speak to him, though he has always been one of my best and truest friends in the Army and deeply regrets his blunder, though little dreaming its consequences.

I am much distressed lest by this matter you have been placed in a position embarrassing and painful to your feelings. I am told you were affected by the letter. I cannot deny it gave me a thrill of happiness to feel that you cared something for me. But I know as a friend you would have been shocked and pained, and I would scorn to assume anything more unless from your own assurance.

I should feel very badly to think anybody would believe me capable of taking any advantage of such a thing.

It is with the greatest difficulty that I can sit up to write. I can not collect or arrange my thoughts as I would. I had

my fever broken up but it came on last night again after getting those letters.

It was impossible for me to have telegraphed to have reached Marietta as soon as several letters on their way.

I am too sick to write and must give up.

R. R. D.

From Rufus R. Dawes to Mary B. Gates

Camp near White Oak Church   May 17, 1863

My <u>dear</u> Mary,

I too am struck dumb with the greatest joy of my life. I cannot express a tithe of my feelings.

I have read your letter over and over again and great rough hardened soldier that I take pride in being I have cried over it almost like a baby . . .

I have no great confidence that my life has been so beyond reproach as that I shall profit in your esteem by its history. Quite the contrary and it would be terrible to feel that you were disappointed in me; but you have a right to know all about me and so far as I can I will tell you truly and conceal nothing.

I think you are a great deal too good for me. I wish you could know with what fear and trembling I brought myself to the desperate point of writing that first letter, or how perfectly miserable I was when I found that "terrible" letter had been sent, and all because I could not bring myself to believe you ever could love so worthless a fellow though I hoped it so earnestly.

I am poor financially. My father ceased about a year back to have any communication with me when he learned that I was determined to help my mother and sisters to be independent of him. So I have ceased to look to him for anything for I shall always help my mother when in need so

long as I have a farthing to divide. I have great confidence though that I can get rich.

I do not drink. I never did in my life. If you only knew how universal this practice is among men, how many times I have been told I was the only officer in the Army who did not drink, you would think less strange of my parading as a virtue mere freedom from this habit.

Now about a leave of absence. You may be sure I will come as soon as I can, but don't expect me at all now. No leaves are granted at present from our Corps. Col. Bragg is entitled to the next from our regiment and he wants to go. But I shall lose no opportunity, for I believe I would cheerfully walk to Marietta and back to see you one day.

You are more to me now than anything else in the world, more than life itself.

Your dear lover, Rufe

From Rufus R. Dawes to Mary B. Gates

June 2, 1863

My dear Mary,

Your letter came June 1st. How provokingly slow the "long looked for" was in travelling each way. But I was paid for waiting in the first three words "My dear Rufe".

I look forward to the joyful day when you will be my wife with the same degree of certainty that I look for Autumn to succeed Summer, for my faith in you is as strong as my love. . . . .

Bivouac on Broad Run, 10 miles from Leesburg
June 19, 1863

Eight days tonight since we have had any mail and little hope in the future. That is the greatest trial of all. We live and love in stirring times. I think my life would make a readable romance with all the standard characters and the happy finale.

I don't believe I'll ever let you out of my sight when I get home. For ten months last year I was not one night away from my regiment. That is a dismal reflection. But the happy day is coming. Wait for me.

Camp on Broad Run

June 21, 1863

. . .Got the brigade band to come over and play for us.
They played "The girl I left behind me" and it almost took
me off my feet. You know don't you that I can't sing any
more than a bear?

Line of Battle on a hill near Gettysburg

July 2, 1863 8 a.m.

God has preserved me unharmed through another
desperate bloody battle. Regiment lost 160 men killed and
wounded. I ordered a charge and we captured a regiment.
There are no communications now with the north but I
hope you will get this.

Letter from Beman Gates to Rufus R. Dawes

Marietta

August 13, 1863

Dear Sir,

Yours of the 29th of July was duly received. I am glad to be able to say that neither Mrs. Gates nor myself have any personal objections to the proposed union. I am free to say that I have confidence in your manly integrity, in the correctness of your habits and in your ability in any sphere of labor and duty to maintain a creditable position.

I hardly need say that something more than all these will be necessary to your happiness and that of a family. Unselfish affection and a determination that no body and no thing shall come between you and your wife's love will do more to make your life and hers happy than any combination of wealth, position and earthly honor.

Trusting that you have this affection and purpose and that it is reciprocated we can give you our blessing and pray for Heaven's.

Letter from Rufus Dawes to Mary Beman Gates Dawes

1864 May 14th 11. A. M.
        Saturday
        Line of battle near Spotsylvania

My dear Wife

By the blessing of God I am still alive. We have had continued fighting & hardship since I wrote two days ago beyond what I can now describe--We charged again upon the enemy's rifle pits on Thursday & were as usual driven back. Thursday night we stood in mud <u>over my boot</u> tops firing <u>all night.</u> Yesterday we were under fire all day & last night we marched all night. I am troubled very much lest I have been reported killed in the N. Y. papers. The report was extensively circulated by one of my men. I can never tell, if I live through it, the sufferings of this campaign. The army has earned the lasting gratitude of the people--

Do not give up if you see me reported killed--such things are very often mistakes. The end is not yet--tho I cannot avoid my dear wife, saying that the probabilities of coming out safely are strongly against me. If we may only finish this horrible business here, our lives are of poor moment in comparison to the blessing to humanity.

The loss of my Reg't now amounts to over one hundred & fifty, many of our best & truest. I know you are praying

for me, & suffering as only few can know, but I can't write false hopes of escaping forever--.

Good by my own dear wife. May God give you comfort & happiness if I am taken away.

Your loving husband

Letter from Rufus Dawes to Mary Beman Gates Dawes

July 10, 1864

The regiment very much regrets to have me go, not specially on account of personal popularity but because they say I am "always on hand in a pinch" and because I am the best man left, in plain words, most likely to secure favor for the regiment in consolidation because entitled to the colonelcy thus created.

I am ready to stand by the country and at the post of peril as long as any other man.   But after staying there about <u>sixteen</u> times as long as the average I believe my first duty is now at home.

Telegraph message from Rufus Dawes to Mary Dawes

August 12, 1864
Mrs. Mary B. Dawes

Honorably discharged.

R. R. Dawes

The Beman Gates home at
Fourth and Putnam

The 'Cottage' at
309 Fourth Street

The new red brick house on Fourth St.

508 Fourth Street,
Marietta, Ohio

Letter from Rufus R. Dawes to son Charles Gates Dawes

Dear Charley,

I was much rejoiced to get your good letter. That is just the way to write letters. Tell what you do and what you see and what you think. Ladies generally tell what other folks do and that is called gossiping. This is interesting but not useful.

Charles Gates Dawes

Letter from Rufus R. Dawes to Mary Beman Gates Dawes (while she was visiting family in Massachusetts)

Marietta, July 4, 1870

My dear Wife,

I am dying off for a racket in the house. It is too lonesome here. I must have you and the boys once more safe under my wing. I choose that simile as appropriate for I confess myself growing more like an old hen as I grow <u>old.</u> Thirty-two today -- young enough, but I am <u>not</u> young. Hardship, toil and anxiety have left their marks but the comforts of your love and care, and the prosperous turns in Fortune's wheel may yet obliterate them.

Rufus Cutler Dawes

Beman Gates Dawes

Letter from Rufus R. Dawes who was traveling on business to Mary Beman Gates Dawes on their wedding anniversary

Astor House, New York
January 18, 1875

One more year of our greatly blessed union has gone forever. You have been more to me than I could ask or hope. God help me to be all I ought and want to be to you. I love you, my dear wife, with all my soul and our wedding days are sad to me because they mark years gone. In each other we have had so much of joy and satisfaction that I have hardly found the room for our dear children they ought to have. But I do love them. May we all together so live that as a family our memories shall be like our memories of the past eleven years.

Mary Gates Dawes

From *Mary Beman Dawes*, a manuscript by Mary Frances Dawes Beach

The new house was red brick built in the style of the day, undistinguished for anything but simplicity. The yard that surrounded it was 180 foot square and was terraced to the street with two flights of stone steps. The wooden fence had a recessed gateway. On the gate was a chain and bell on which the children swung to the detriment of their clothes. There was a huge evergreen tree on the upper terrace and two large old sheepnose apple trees. More trees were planted and shrubs and flowers. The house gradually became covered with woodbine. The yard was decorated with acting bars, swings, sand piles and doll houses besides stone vases for flowers and an iron bird bath. Now and again there were tents, kilns, temporary gardens, tunnels, circus rings, baseball diamonds, tennis courts, dog kennels, rabbit hutches, guinea pig yards, shaky and brief chicken coops, bird houses, crow roosts, tadpole tubs, kitten boxes, fox stakes and chains, and once or twice coon shelters. About the only animals that never shared the place with the children were horses and cows. There was no barn.

Grass did not do as well as paths, worn by small shoes, that by the way had to be replaced at the rate of one pair for each boy a month. Mrs. Dawes was a lover of flowers and was successful with them but she did not care to compete with the boys and so had few until they had grown up, after

which time her yard blossomed from early spring until late fall.

The wood work in the house was soft pine and little copper-toed boots and shoes dented it. The attic was apparently arranged for children to play in and alas seemed designed, malice aforethought, to throw the noise down the long stairway. Rainy days the boys jousted with pillows in the attic or skated with roller skates and the sound as of thunder rolled down to their mother.

The place where you are always welcome

There were huge cisterns in the back yard and the boys pumped and pumped till they made skating ponds by damming up mud and snow. Really gorgeous snow forts and Esquimau houses appeared in their season and it is a debatable question whether the boys loved summer or winter more.

There were seasons of comparative quiet for their mother when the boys transferred their operations to the Beach yard across the street, or the Blauvelt's across the alley, or to the Brown's, later the Mills' on the corner below Wooster. Mrs. Dawes got used to boys. Within the distance of a block there were her own boys, three Beach boys, two Blauvelt boys, two Mills' boys, two Addy boys, George Pilsbury, three Gaitree boys, two Waters boys and some others. None of them stopped for doorbells and the hall carpet was muddy in winter and dusty in summer. The boys slid down the bannisters and Mrs. Dawes once stood in the dining room door and watched twelve boys shoot down the rail and out the front door so fast that she wasn't sure she had counted right. She said no doubt there were other times when more than that number had sailed thus through the air from the boys' room to the front yard.

From *Grandmother's Letters*, a collection of letters of Betsey Shipman Gates

March 3, 1878 to Bettie Gates

I should think the Dawes tribe now the Shedds are here might take the town. There are nine boys there, besides all the boys in the neighborhood are together all the time out of school. Mary says she does not expect to have a spear of grass left when the summer is over, much less a shrub or tree. They are a nice set of boys the whole thirteen of them.

A recollection of dinner table conversation by Mary Frances Dawes Beach

General Dawes' idea of conversation at the table was that it should not "degenerate into gossip." Rapidly and hilariously the children talked without restraint until their father felt their "conversation" was degenerating. He would then take the reins in his own hands and talk about public affairs, American history, astronomy (in which he was particularly interested) everything in fact but gossip or unkind stories. When once the plane of thought had been sufficiently raised he let the young people do the talking again and bedlam broke loose as unrestrained before him as if he were one of them, as indeed he always was in his own thought and theirs.

Letter from Rufus R. Dawes to his son, Henry May Dawes

House of Representatives
Washington, D. C. Dec 7, 1881

My dear little boy Henry

Your Papa has a great many letters to write now, and he gets very tired of writing, but has strength enough to write one more tonight, and it shall be to the little fellow that he thinks more of than all the men put together he has written to today and that would be more than twenty five. I am very homesick to have your dear Mamma and Sister and you with me to spend the evenings & keep off the Bores. Not wild Boors but men who want offices. They are as hungry and fierce as Guiteau almost. I am very tired of them. Men I never saw or heard of will waylay me to pass

Henry May Dawes

out the misery of their lives if they don't get their offices. When it is nothing at all to me. But you never saw such animals and don't know anything about them.

There is one thing you can do that none of the rest can, except maybe Sister, when you get here. You can sit in Congress

when it is in session and you shall. I saw several little boys with their fathers. I saw John H. Reagan who was Postmaster General of the Confederacy chasing his little boy all around while Congress was in session. So you can go to Congress but you must behave better than that boy. You will, I know, because you are not a rebel, you are a little Ohio man.

Son I hope you will not have the whooping cough, or, if you do, that you will have it easy and I will bid you good night.

Your Affectionate Papa

Letter from Rufus Dawes to his daughter, Mary Frances Dawes

Dec. 18, 1881

My dear little daughter,

I am alone and lonesome. I would be delighted to hear our darling Bessie screeching and you in a noisy spell and Henry on a rampage. That is just for a <u>few</u> moments until I got used to it again and that would not take long. I anticipate great delight in our winter evenings here with Mama and you. Your dear mother has had many years of care and toil and many demands upon her strength and her affection for us all. How nice it will be for awhile to have no bossing or household care and only to dress well and enjoy herself. Yes, for awhile, but for steady living, my dear child, no place on earth will ever be like the home that in these years of toil, of love, of sacrifice and of care your mother, our good angel in life, has made for us. You will always look back to it with longings whatever good comes to you in life because it has been a happy home to you, and so will every one of the boys, just as your Papa, only three weeks away, does tonight.

Henry May and Mary Frances Dawes

Letter from Rufus Dawes regarding a political maneuver in Congress to Mary Gates Dawes

April 18, 1882

Our men behaved very honorably & silently gave to <u>me</u> an emphatic endorsement. I expect to earn no name for great action but if I leave an indellible impress on our people of honest, and honorable purpose and of acting always upon principle it will be an invaluable influence on our own lives and our children's.

Tell Sister and Henry and my dear little Bessie that I am very lonely for them & wish they were here to bother me.

Your loving   R

Rufus R. Dawes

Letter from Rufus Dawes to Mary Gates Dawes

House of Representatives
Washington, D. C. April 25, 1882

My dear Wife

I am greatly troubled to see that Asthma is after you. Your letter only too plainly discloses it. It is too bad. How strange that Washington should ease you and our home bring back the awful scourge. What <u>can</u> we do for it? I shall earnestly hope that warm weather will avert it but wait with concern your next letter. Your exuberant spirits and keen enjoyment of all the good things that you found on returning home comes in part from the good health to which my dear patient, long suffering wife you have long been a stranger. From your good cheer and warm motherly heart comes Beman's increasing softening of temper. The child finds what he craves in your full and tender consideration and the reward to you & blessing to him is swift. Not that it has not always been there for him and for <u>all</u> to whom you are the most precious boon on earth, but asthma, babies, a full burden of household cares, a scanty purse, a doubtful issue to the long, long, struggle to keep things going forward have weighed on you. The burden is lighter and how manifold the blessings. But I want to say to you my dear that the strongest impulse in the heart of every child of yours is love for <u>you</u>, and it is the crown of

your life that nothing can take away -- and it is worth as much to the children as to you. It makes home sweet to them. I could see that they were hungry for you as I am now. They are all & ever good and happy in having you there which restores to them this home that I wish W. I. would pay me the salary and let me stay there with you & them in it. What is "honor," what is ambition, what is a [cause?] that men call brilliant compared to our home! I would not consider for a moment such things if they would interfere with it.

Kiss my dear little Bessie, my fine boy Henry, my loving and much loved little "Sister," and all my manly boys and my darling, although we approach the shady side, my heart is always in the sunshine in its love for you.

R.

Letter from Rufus R. Dawes to his daughter, Mary Frances Dawes

House of Representatives
Washington, D. C. April 27, 1882

My dear little Daughter

I received your letter with great pleasure. I like to think of you at home with plenty of room, fresh air and your nice little friends to play with. It is better than Grant Place for you. But it is very nice, also, for you to have been in Washington, and to have seen the Capitol of the great nation and all its places of interest, and to know for yourself its streets and parks and grand public buildings. You can tell others about these things and it will be a pleasure to you to do so. I see your little friend Gracie Humphrey every day. Her father gets off his jokes as usual, and is ever on the subject of "Price" and his "diabolical machinations"-- This joke your Mamma understands. Miss H. looks better and more cheerful.

We had a grand speech from a colored man in the House today. He stood alone of his race in Congress and lifted his voice for them before the Nation. A grand opportunity was offered. He was equal to it and his friends and his people may well be proud and again take Courage. Your Papa went over and said "I want to do myself the honor, Sir, to shake hands with you." His name is Lynch

and when you grow older you will hear of this man again, or I am no prophet.

Tell me about Bessie when you write. I can see her bright black eyes flashing as I write -- that is in my imagination. She ought to be getting old enough to spell pig pretty soon. As for Henry I shall expect that he at least can spell pig when I get home. Blakie Falty cries and bawls a great deal. I feel sorry for him. I do not believe that Henry cries now that he eats so much and is out of the hot rooms. Now my dear little girl kiss your Mother always first for me, and then Bessie and Henry and accept the best love for yourself of

Your Father

Letter from Rufus Dawes to Mary Gates Dawes

House of Representatives
Washington, D. C., April 28, 1882

My dear Wife

The enclosed is from Smith of the celebrated Sunday bill.   I think my Chinese record has <u>made</u> me and Updegraffs has <u>unmade</u> him.   That is it will defeat his <u>nomination.</u> It has made me in this way. It is accepted as showing conviction, courage and character. A true man is on trial as to these qualities. If he shows them it captures respect and confidence and the error in policy (if it is so considered) is forgiven.   Now Updegraff and his crowd stand for political cowards. I may misjudge (but I do not think I do) but my correspondence indicates my unanimous renomination and <u>election</u> too, for that matter. I think you and the children might sing "Dare to be right, dare to be true." It is with the deepest feelings of gratitude that I see these signs of approval of right action.   High and responsible public duty comes ordinarily but once in a life time to such as me.   To discharge such duty conscientiously, unselfishly, and fearlessly makes the office honorable and the record forever a crown of life. If I can only impress my boys that to do right, and let the consequences rest with the Power that overrules, is the road to true success -- that a conscience void of offense is the

real test of action on public as well as private questions, I will have left footprints in the sands -- and helped them to complete the noble characters which I believe they are forming. The highest success in this life is reached by establishing the best character as that is the only foundation upon which any substantial structure can stand.

But my dear wife, while political success is doubly acceptable when it is a reward of right action, it is worth nothing compared with the value of such a home and home life as we have established & that I feel more and more as I am kept away from it.

Your loving
R

Letter from Rufus Dawes to Mary Frances Dawes

House of Representatives,
Washington, D. C. May 10, 1882

My dear little Daughter

I think I owe you a letter. Anyhow I am thinking of you tonight and wishing I could see you and my bright eyed little Bessie. What a little delight she is to you and she always will be. You are enough older to be always a guardian over Bessie. You will every year grow wiser and stronger and able soon to help your Mother in care over Bessie and it will be a happiness for you. There is something nice for everybody to do in this world.

Your papa is looking to you, also, as a comfort and solace to him as his hair gets sprinkled more and more with gray and his whiskers with white. There is nothing pleasanter than a peaceful and happy home. I hope we are all growing to realize more and more what we have got because we are all so glad to get back to it.

Congress is going along slowly in its usual way. Talk, talk, talk is the order of the day and it is all for the country and to make sentiment and create opinion there. It is not expected to very sensibly affect votes here.

Washington is getting to be very beautiful in its coating of green. I am thinking some of going with my friend Major Hawk--the big one legged man from Ill. to the

Antietam battle field.   We may go there on Saturday and back Monday.

With my love to your mother, and to Henry, Bessie and each of the boys, I am your

Affectionate Father

Betsey Gates Dawes

Mary Frances Dawes
'Sister'

My dear little Daughter

I think I owe you a letter. Anyhow I am thinking of you tonight and wishing I could see you and my bright eyed little Bessie— What a little delight she is to you and she always will be. You are enough older to be always a guardian over Bessie. You will every year grow wiser and stronger and able more to help your Mother in care over Bessie and it will be a happiness for you — There is something nice for everybody to do in this world— Your papa is looking to you, also, as a comfort and solace to him as his hair gets sprinkled more and more with gray and his whiskers with white— There is nothing pleasanter than a peaceful and happy home— That We are all growing to realize more and

now that we have got home we are all so glad to get back to it.

Congress is going along slowly in its usual way. Talk, talk, talk is the order of the day and it is all for the country and to make sentiment and create opinion there. It is not expected to very sensibly affect votes here.

Washington is getting to be very beautiful in its coating of green. I am thinking some of going with my friend Major Hawk, — the big one legged man from Ill. to the Antietam battle field. We may go there on Saturday and back Monday.

With my love to your Mother, and to Henry, Bessie and each of the boys. I am your

Affectionate Father

Letter from Rufus R. Dawes to Mary Gates Dawes

May 13, 1882

It is a terribly cold and dreary storm. It puts me in mind of this day 18 years ago. That night of May 13th '64 through a cold pouring rain, wading swollen streams, dragging wearily through mud, in pitchy darkness, my men of the Sixth Wisconsin followed me. I was young, strong and full of nerve and held together my band and at daylight came to position with the only organization in the Brigade.

What of toil and danger we braved for our country! I look around at the selfishness, meanness, falsehood that fill every department of official life here and would feel disgusted that I fought for such a government. But it is not the office holders that are the government that we fought for. I find enough of the noble spirits of the war who are not yet dead, to know that the spirit that impelled us is not all gone. Such men as Hawk, Hepburn, Cabell (the Rebel) and Eph live to remind us that selfish meanness has not captured everything. I do not want my boys to be soldiers or heroes but I do want them to be true patriots. The first element of patriotic American citizenship is self respect, a spirit that would scorn official place at the expense of personal degradation or surrender of an iota of principle. It is not the place that gives a man either prestige or honor half so much as the independent and honorable discharge of the public duty imposed by the office. If they can only

have ingrained the idea that an office at expense of integrity, self respect or abandonment of conviction is forever a <u>mark</u> <u>of</u> <u>failure,</u> it will be so much better than to get the other idea that official distinction of itself confers honor.   It doesn't.   Our boys are on the right track in forming their political principles and establishing their moral characters and I want to keep them off this snag, struggle for place, on which so many wreck.

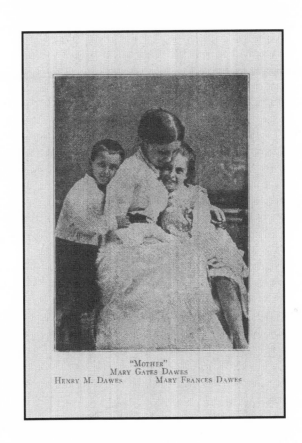

"Mother"
Mary Gates Dawes
Henry M. Dawes   Mary Frances Dawes

Letter from Rufus R. Dawes to Mary Gates Dawes

May 23, 1882

I do not think the Democrats can carry our district. But nomination or not, election or not, there is for me always peace, joy and comfort enough in your love and companionship.

You asked me about Beman acting in the opera. You did right to let him. I believe in amusement for the young, all they can get, they have only one life, let its spring time be full of flowers. The only thing is to keep their pleasures innocent and pure. There is no agency so potent to make a child good as to make him happy. Asceticism is a failure in promoting good. It is rightly directed pleasure that makes sunshine in character. Let our children have all possible fun, that is good, pure and generous. If they will only be true, sincere, honest and straight forward, life will be a comfort to them and a blessing to all about them. It is astonishing how much happiness we can confer on others if we only try. It is marvelous what pleasure it gives one to make others happy and so if the habit can be formed young it is everything.

Letter from Rufus R. Dawes to Mary Dawes

May 26, 1882

Quit reading the papers if they worry you and remember if calamity should come politically it signifies that forever after I will stay and be at home with you.

Letter from Rufus Dawes to Mary Gates Dawes just before he received the nomination for a second term in Congress

June 14, 1882

It is possible, my dear, that I am now at the culmination of my popularity as a public man. I have no ambition to go higher. It is high enough. I have now but one desire, to adjust whatever career is before me to such plans as will not separate me from you and our dear children. The happy home life we have is more in value to us and to our children than anything else this world can offer. Let us not forget that some hard struggles and adverse circumstances bravely met together and overcome have done their part in making the home we have held worth the battle made for it.

Letter from Rufus R. Dawes to Mary Gates Dawes

July 3, 1882

Tomorrow I shall be 44 years old. This is the usual occasion for moralizing. With four fine boys and two nice girls, a happy home, with the love of all in it I ought to be satisfied. I am. I only ask enough to keep you and me always in our home and that it may be kept as long as we live a home for all of our children to come to in love and joy. I do not want political promotion to interfere with this hope. I would not have it. I have had honors enough. I want to be elected this fall of course. But it won't hurt me except financially if I am not. All that I have to be thankful for and happy over is equally yours, a part of your work as much as mine. Together we have marched up and together my dear love we will go down the slope. May it be long and gentle in the decline.

Letter from Charles Gates Dawes to Mary Gates Dawes

Lincoln, Nebraska

August 12, 1889

Father's training of us children has been characterized by a generosity which showed us the spirit in which he dealt with us. And we can now thank him from the bottom of our hearts for a sternness against evil-doing which has given us strength of character, as well as for the gentleness which has so endeared him to us.

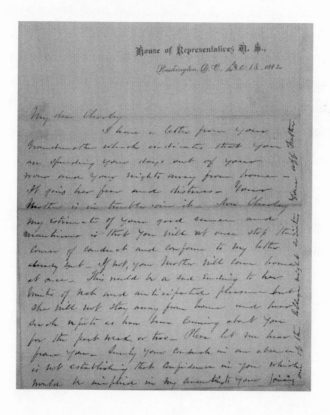

Letter from Rufus R. Dawes to Charles Gates Dawes

House of Representatives, U. S.
Washington, D. C., Dec. 13, 1882

My dear Charley

I have a letter from your Grandmother which indicates that you are spending your days out of your room and your nights away from home. It gives her fear and distress. Your Mother is in trouble over it. Now Charley my estimate of your good sense and manliness is that you will at once stop this course of conduct and conform to my letter already sent. If not, your Mother will come home at once. This would be a sad ending to her winter of rest and anticipated pleasure but she will not stay away from home and hear such reports as have been coming about you for the past week or two. Please let me hear from you. Surely your conduct in our absence is not establishing that confidence in you which would be implied in my consenting to your joining one of the College night societies.

Your aff Father

Letter from Rufus R. Dawes to his daughter, Mary Frances Dawes Beach in 1897

Dear Sister,

I had a long call from Susan Chessbro a few days ago and we indulged in much personal reminiscence. The poor old lady thanked me with tears in her eyes for bringing up so many pleasant memories of her mother and brother, who used to live near us. I brought up the old rooster fights and the rat wars and Silas' old fife and violin.

The Grand Army men came up to see me last night about returning the rebel flags. As I am one of the few living men who have a flag there (No. 40 Ordinance Museum, War Department) I have some views on the subject. I think the Confederate Army was very brave in battle, and that they had great generals and that they were heroic and faithful to their cause and that as soldiers they were all around good fellows, but nevertheless their cause was treason and their success would have ruined their country. I can't see just why we should give them these old trophies of war and much less why we should give them to a younger generation who took no part in any war but who would make a great glorification over them in honor of the Confederate soldier and in sympathy with their cause. Out of respect to the 200 of my comrades who were killed or wounded at Gettysburg capturing their old flag I object to surrendering this trophy of war service to anybody.

Battle Flag of Second Regiment Mississippi Vols

Captured together with the entire regiment by the Sixth Wisconsin Vols at Gettysburg July 1st 1863. Taken before the surrender by Corporal Asbury Waller of Co. C. Kept for two days by Sergt Wm Evans of Co. H. while wounded and a prisoner in the hands of the enemy

"The moment was a critical one involving the defeat, perhaps the utter rout, of our forces. I immediately sent for one of Meredith's regiments the Sixth Wisconsin, a gallant body of men, who, I knew could be relied upon + desired them to attack immediately. Lt Col. Dawes, their commander, ordered a charge, which was gallantly executed. The enemy made a hurried attempt to change front to meet the attack and flung his troops into a railroad cut for safety. The 95th N.Y. Vols. and the 14th Brooklyn joined in the charge; the cut was carried at the point of the bayonet. Two regiments of Davis' rebel brigade were taken prisoners"
Official Report Major Gen Doubleday Com'g 1st Army Corps

Letter from Rufus Dawes to his daughter, Mary Frances Dawes Beach, 'Sister'

Fall 1894

This paper is easier for me to write on. I am all right and feeling better than for a year. I go to the office daily and keep up my end as well as anybody. Don't fret about me.

Mother and I have pretty good times. That same old endless monotony, the letter game, goes on and it is to her pedro, six handed euchre and whist, in its excitement and interest. It is fun for me to play with <u>her.</u> I do not have the heart to cheat her so I am generally beaten.

Grandmother and Aunt Lucy keep along O.K. Grandmother is feeble but bright and always content.

Letter from Rufus Dawes to his daughter, Mary Frances Dawes Beach, 'Sister'

Marietta Oct. 28, 1894

Dear Sister,

I am alone at home this bright Sunday. Your grandfather gets no better but is going down hill and losing ground. His condition is discouraging. He wants his daughters or Grandmother all the time. He shall have everything he wants as we all feel and the doctors say he will never be much better and is not likely to outlive the winter.

All well here except Grandfather. High Jinks in the air for Hallow E'en.

Our sun has passed the zenith a little perhaps in the old home but in the softened rays there is a better light to see the true joys of home life. They are found in letting <u>good</u> children go pretty much as they please and finding no fault with them. I know that you children care as much for the good repute of home as I do or even Mother does.

Excerpt of Letter from Mary Gates Dawes to daughter Mary Frances Dawes Beach

October 9, 1896

He has been well all this summer and his helpless condition has not seemed to cause him a moment's unhappiness, company has not worried him nor made him nervous, he has been interested in politics and has followed the details of his business so that in many ways he has had no appearance of an invalid, but I have realized fully myself that he was becoming more and more helpless even before his fall which entirely disabled his left arm and prevented his walking on crutches and taking exercise of any kind except on his tricycle.

Letter from Rufus R. Dawes to daughter Mary Frances Dawes Beach

October 12, 1896

After a period of monotonous confinement I enjoy again the enlivening prospect from our bay window. The details of these experiences are not agreeable and with much to be thankful for I dismiss the subject.

Letter from Mary Gates Dawes to daughter Mary Frances Dawes Beach

November 1, 1896

The two parlors we give up entirely to your father and have made them just as bright and comfortable as possible. Rainy days he runs his tricycle in here and here his friends come to see him and he has his books and papers and easy chairs and is lifted from one to the other. He is as bright and cheery as ever. Sometimes I think he fully realizes the situation and sometimes he speaks as if he thought he would be "better."

Letter from Mary Frances Dawes Beach to her mother, Mary Gates Dawes

Ypsilanti, Mich.

June 8th 1906

My dearest Mother:

It doesn't seem as tho' it could be eleven years ago today that I left home does it? The picture that stands out clearest in my mind of that day is of Papa on the porch throwing an old shoe after us and the crowd of eight or ten went down to the carriage. I shall never forget how he made much of throwing the shoe that he might not show his feelings but I understood. I found a little poem the other day which I copied in my diary because it expresses my feelings -- not <u>perfectly</u> but well.

> Father, who left me long ago
> My soul is kin unto your own
> The dreams & strivings of my days
> Those you have known.
>
> My soul plants footsteps in your own
> And you were brave of heart & high!
> Father, is aught of worthiness?
> It is not I.

The other picture of that day is your face as you & I were up in my room & I was getting ready to go away & I

was afraid to look at you for fear I would throw myself in your arms & cry till I couldn't go.

Well they have been happy years and full of pleasure & satisfaction and I think every year will be more so. Nothing could exceed the respect & admiration I have for my husband except my love for him. There is no finer type of manhood in the world than he represents. As a home man & as a husband and father <u>he</u> <u>suits</u> <u>me</u> & the children too. Arthur claims I make him a good home & while I fall so far short of what I ought & want to do, that I hate to hear the subject mentioned, still I feel called on to say that <u>all</u> that is not bad about me & my efforts at home making, I owe to you & Papa and the perfect example of a home that you gave us.

Wedding of Mary Frances Dawes and
Arthur Granville Beach   June 8, 1896

Mary Gates Dawes with
grandchildren in the
backyard

Mary Gates Dawes

Letter from Arthur Granville Beach to his daughter, Alice Beach Murray

MARIETTA COLLEGE

FOUNDED 1835

MARIETTA, OHIO

DEPARTMENT OF ENGLISH
ARTHUR G. BEACH, PH. D.

June 15, 1924

Dear Alice :-

We have certainly had an exciting and interesting time
for the past few days. We had a radio installed in the back par
lor, thro the kindness of Ed Manley and the Union Hardware Company, and listened in to the Republican Convention at Cleveland
with the candidate for Vice President in the room with us. It
was lots of fun. Uncle Henry and Aunt Helen arrived Thursday noon,
so that we had Uncle Henry's uninterrupted flow of humorous
commentto relieve the tension. Thursday and Friday were the
interesting days, of course. Thursday evening when the roll of
st ates was called and things began to break for Uncle Charles
was quite exciting. Uncle Seman kept tab on the ballots, and he
was as excited as if he had been the candidate himself. Aunt
Caro was managing the radio, and sat close to the machine, but
we could hear distinctly anywhere in the two parlors. When the
state of Texas cast its ballot for our candidate and we knew h
he was nominated we all got up and congratulated him. Then the
fun began. The telephone began to ring, as indeed it had been and
doing for two days or more, and calls came from Marietta, New
York, Chicago, Cleveland , Columbus etc. We had to ask the
operators to shut it off finally from 12 till eight the next
morning so that we could get some sleep. The next morning it st

started again, and telegrams began to pour in as well, including
messages from President Coolidge, Hoover, Pershing etc. Newspaper
men and Marietta citizens began to pour in also. It was decided
to have a local celebration, and the Chamber of Commerce got it
up on short notice, and at one o'clock , with all the stores

offices and factories closed a long procession marched from the
court house and filled our yard and the street.Ray Sprague with a big
megaphone managed the ppogram.Uncle Charlie made a speech which
pleased the crowd immensely and started the Republican campaign off.If
everbody felt as Marietta does the election would be settled right
now.After the speech and the singing of the Star Spangled Banner
the whole crowd marfiled by and Uncle Charlie shook hands with them.
Lots of pictures were taken,both then and in the morning,which will
appear in the papers.Bwhaps the most interesting group in the procession was the D.U.Fraternity,with a big banner displayed in front
of them.Another demonstratiwn was made at the depot when Uncle Charlie
and his party,including Uncle Beman and Uncle Henry and their wives
went to the private car and started away.Our lawn,especially the
terraces,will bear the scars of thecelebration for a long time,but
we are glad to make that contribution to the cause.We have also been
running a hotel on small scale,with Anna and Mrs Shoop and another woman
woman hard at work in the kitchen and dhing room.They surely gave us
all some good food.Everybody seemed to be having a good time.I wish
ypumbght have seen it all.It seems stragely quiet now.Even the telephone
has settled down to its normal rate,and only the telegraph boy brings
a few belated messages of congratulation.I have mailed 30 or more
telegrams to Chicago.

Uncle Beman and Uncle Henry had a lot of fun pretend
ing they were Uncle Charlie.For an hour before the train left while
Uncle Charlie was taking a rest in his room Uncle Henry sat on the
porch with his pipe upside down so that the crowd that was still driving
by might think they were looking at the hero himself.

DEPARTMENT OF ENGLISH
ARTHUR G. BEACH, Ph. D.

Well,it was a very interesting experience,as I said before.You
have,of course,read it all in the papers.Our house will appear
in the papers,I presume.Mother saw the pictures Saturday and says
they are good.Uncle Charlie made her pose with him and the other
two brothers,so that she too will be gazed at far and wide,much
to her disgust.As a mere"in law" I escaped.

I hope little David appreciates the honor that has come
to the family thro his great Uncle.I hope his little"tummy"is doing
better by this time.Uncle Henry says he asked Mr Sims about Marshall
and he said he was doing splendidly.

We are hoping youcwill be able,to come down to see us befor
long.

Affectionately,

Father

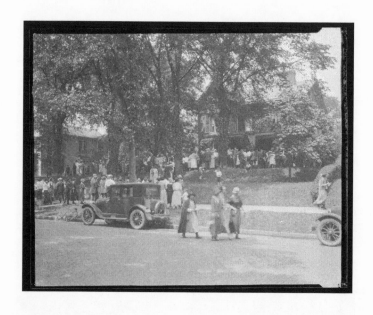

Edward Dempsey and Betsey Beach
June 1936

Addendum

The Dawes house at 508 Fourth Street remained in the family until the 1930's. Mary Frances Dawes Beach and her husband Arthur Beach lived there from about 1920 on. Arthur Beach died in January of 1934. Mary Frances "Sister" Beach remained for two more years, then moved to Evanston, Illinois, to be close to her brothers. But there was one last family gathering at the house. The occasion was the marriage of Betsey Mills Beach, granddaughter of Rufus and Mary and daughter of "Sister" and Arthur. Betsey married Edward Dempsey on June 13, 1936, and the whole clan gathered for the wedding.

Parents and siblings of Rufus R. Dawes

Henry Dawes
b. 4 May 1804, d. 4 Nov 1867

& Sarah Cutler
b. 17 Apr 1809, d. 31 Dec 1896
m. 20 Jan 1829, Old Stone House, Constitution, Washington Co., Ohio

Catherine Lucretia Dawes
b. 13 Mar 1830, d. 23 Sep 1866
& Samuel Agnew McLean
m. 16 Feb 1864, Warren Township, Ohio

Henry Manasseh Dawes
b. 11 Mar 1832, d. 13 Aug 1860

Lucy Dawes
b. 5 Dec 1833, d. 10 Dec 1898

Sarah Jane Dawes
b. 9 Jan 1836, d. 19 Mar 1921
& Rev. John Haskell Shedd
m. 28 Jul 1859

Rufus R. Dawes
b. 4 Jul 1838, d. 1 Aug 1899
& Mary Beman Gates
b. 27 Aug 1842, d. 28 Oct 1921
m. 18 Jan 1864, Marietta, OH

Ephraim Cutler Dawes
b. 27 May 1840, d. 23 Apr 1895
& Martha Frances Bosworth
b. 15 Aug 1840, d. 1925
m. 21 Jun 1866

Parents and siblings of Mary Beman Gates

Beman Gates
b. 5 Jan 1818, d. 17 Dec 1894

& Betsey Sibyl Shipman
b. 19 Nov 1816, d. 24 Jul 1895
m. 20 Oct 1841

Mary Beman Gates
b. 27 Aug 1842, d. 28 Oct 1921
& Rufus R Dawes
b. 4 Jul 1838, d. 1 Aug 1899
m. 18 Jan 1864, Marietta, OH

Charles Beman Gates
b. 3 Oct 1844
d. 31 May 1864

Betsey Shipman Gates
b. 26 Feb 1853, d. 22 Apr 1920
& William Webster Mills
b. 27 Jan 1852, d. Mar 1931
m. 12 Oct 1875, Marietta, OH

Rufus Cutler Dawes, Mary Frances Dawes Beach,
Beman Gates Dawes, Betsey Dawes Hoyt,
Charles Gates Dawes, Henry May Dawes

June 1936

Rufus R Dawes
b. 4 Jul 1838, d. 1 Aug 1899

Mary Beman Gates
b. 27 Aug 1842, d. 28 Oct 1921
m. 18 Jan 1864, Marietta, OH

Charles Gates Dawes
b. 27 Aug 1865, Marietta, d. 23 Apr 1951
& Caro Dana Blymyer
b. 6 Jan 1866, d. 3 Oct 1957
m. 24 Jan 1889

Rufus Cutler Dawes
b. 30 Jul 1867, d. 8 Jan 1940, Chicago, IL
& Helen Virginia Palmer
b. 13 Nov 1868, d. 28 Jul 1941
m. 3 Jun 1893

Beman Gates Dawes
b. 14 Jan 1870, d. 15 May 1953
& Bertie O. Burr
b. 6 Aug 1872, d. 8 Feb 1958
m. 3 Oct 1894

Mary Frances Dawes
b. 3 Mar 1872, d. 3 Jul 1956
& Rev Arthur Granville Beach
b. 29 Nov 1870, d. 27 Jan 1934
m. 8 Jun 1896, Marietta, OH

Henry May Dawes
b. 22 Apr 1877, d. 29 Sep 1952
& Helen Curtis
b. 27 Oct 1881, d. Feb 1974
m. 5 Apr 1905

Betsey Gates Dawes
b. 5 Oct 1880, d. 16 Jan 1973
& Harry Barzilla Hoyt
m. 26 Nov 1902

The Children of Rufus R. Dawes and Mary Beman Gates Dawes

Charles Gates Dawes *(1865 - 1951)*

Married Caro Blymyer, four children
- Banker and politician
- Comptroller of the Currency at the Treasury Department (1898-1901)
- Served in the First World War as Chief of Supply Procurement with the American Expeditionary Force, Seventeenth Engineers (1917-1919)
- First Director of the Bureau of the Budget (1921-1922)
- 30th Vice-President of the United States (1925–1929) under Calvin Coolidge
- Shared Nobel Peace Prize for work on Dawes Plan (reparations after WWI) (1925)
- Ambassador to the United Kingdom (1929-1931)
- Chairman of the Board of City National Bank and Trust in Evanston, Illinois (1932-1951)

Rufus Cutler Dawes *(1867 - 1940)*

Married Helen Palmer, seven children
- Businessman in oil and banking
- Delegate to the Illinois Constitutional Convention (1918)
- Served on the commission to help prepare the Dawes Plan
- President of Century of Progress, Chicago World's Fair (1927+)
- President of Museum of Science and Industry in Chicago (1927+)

Beman Gates Dawes *(1870 - 1953)*
Married Bertie Burr, five children
- Engaged in agriculture and engineering
- Member of Congress from Ohio (1905-1909)
- President of the Pure Oil Company (1914 +)
- Founded Dawes Arboretum in Newark, Ohio

Mary Frances Dawes *(1872 - 1956)*
Married Arthur Beach, four children
- Writer and family historian
- Edited and assisted with the writing of *A Pioneer College, the Story of Marietta,* by husband Arthur Beach
- Published *Grandmother's Letters (1926)* letters of Betsey Shipman Gates, and *Letters from Europe,* letters from Beman Gates written in 1868 (1927)
- Wrote several unpublished manuscripts with limited distribution to family members:
  - *Mr. And Mrs. Beman Gates of Marietta,* Ohio, unpublished manuscript
  - *The Distaff,* unpublished family letters
  - *William P. Cutler,* papers and letters
  - *Rufus R. Dawes,* biography based on letters and journals
  - *Mother's Letters,* biography of Mary Gates Dawes
  - *Rufus and Mary,* a combined biography of Rufus R. Dawes and Mary Beman Gates Dawes

Henry May Dawes *(1877 - 1952)*
Married Helen Curtis, two children
- Businessman and banker
- Comptroller of the Currency (1923-1924)
- President of Pure Oil Company (1924-1952)

Betsey Gates Dawes *(1880 - 1973)*
Married Harry Hoyt, four children
- Completed two years of college
- Raised her family in Florida

Location of Sources

The photographs are from the private collection of Richard and Peggy Dempsey.

Many of the original letters are located in the History Center of the Dawes Arboretum or the Special Collections Library, Marietta College.

Rufus Dawes's journals and the Rally Boys poster are at the Special Collections Library, Marietta College.

The quotes from Mary Frances Dawes Beach are from unpublished manuscripts and are in the family collection of Richard and Peggy Dempsey.

The letter to Alice Murray from Arthur Beach is in the family collection of Richard and Peggy Dempsey.

For Rufus Dawes's Civil War Service, see *Service with the Sixth Wisconsin Volunteers* by Rufus R. Dawes.

For additional information:
Peggy Dempsey
Juliacutlerjournal@gmail.com

Made in the USA
Lexington, KY
11 March 2014